The Plays of
Christopher Marlowe

CHRISTOPHER MARLOWE

Born Canterbury 1564
Died Deptford 1593

The Plays of
Christopher Marlowe

EDITED WITH AN INTRODUCTION BY
ROMA GILL

OXFORD UNIVERSITY PRESS
OXFORD NEW YORK TORONTO MELBOURNE

Oxford University Press, Walton Street, Oxford OX2 6DP

OXFORD LONDON GLASGOW
NEW YORK TORONTO MELBOURNE WELLINGTON
KUALA LUMPUR SINGAPORE JAKARTA HONG KONG TOKYO
DELHI BOMBAY CALCUTTA MADRAS KARACHI
NAIROBI DAR ES SALAAM CAPE TOWN

ISBN 0 19 281062 6

Introduction and notes © Oxford University Press 1971

First published as an Oxford University Press paperback
by Oxford University Press, London, 1971

Reprinted 1979

PRINTED IN GREAT BRITAIN
BY RICHARD CLAY (THE CHAUCER PRESS), LTD.,
BUNGAY, SUFFOLK

Contents

Introduction

Marlowe's reputation has altered more than that of any other writer of comparable greatness. Ideas about the man himself have changed as new information came to light: the man we now see as a secret agent, quietly and politically assassinated, is the same who was once held to have met a fitting end to his riotous life, drunk in a tavern brawl. More subtle, but hardly less extreme, have been the changes in opinion about his works. If contemporary comment and influence are any criteria, *Tamburlaine* was the play most regarded by the Elizabethans; *Doctor Faustus* quickly gained supremacy, and now, in the second half of the twentieth century, that seems to be giving pride of place to *Edward II*. Every age selects and interprets the play whose concerns are closest to its own; for this reason, although a definitive text of Marlowe's plays may one day be achieved, a definitive preference and interpretation are impossible.

During Marlowe's lifetime the necessary withholding of information led to large misunderstandings. In 1587 the University of Cambridge refused to grant him an M.A. degree. They had good reason to suppose that this son of a Canterbury shoemaker had spent much of the past six years abroad, time which, as Archbishop Parker's scholar at the College of Corpus Christi, he should have spent in studying theology. It was true that he had been away from Cambridge for long periods; true, probably, that during those absences he had been at Rheims, home of the Jesuit seminary and of those expatriate Catholics rumoured to be plotting the Queen's downfall. But Marlowe was not one of these. A letter from Her Majesty's Privy Council intervened in university affairs and hinted that Marlowe's stay in Rheims had official sanction: he 'had done Her Majestie good service, and deserved to be rewarded for his faithfull dealinge'.[1] The University took the hint and Marlowe left Cambridge a Master of Arts and, by virtue of that degree, a gentleman.

From time to time during the next six years he is heard of in London—storming the theatre with his 'high astounding terms', fighting in Hog Lane, imprisoned on a charge of manslaughter in Newgate, sharing a room with Thomas Kyd. Contemporary writers either admired or hated him. Nashe called him 'a diviner Muse' than Musaeus, Peele described him as 'the Muses' darling', and Drayton observed in him 'those brave translunary

[1] Privy Council Register, xxix° Junij 1587.

things That the first poets had'.[1] But Robert Greene, identifying Marlowe with his most flamboyant creation, resented the success of 'that atheist Tamburlaine' who could make his verses 'jet upon the stage in tragicall buskins' but who for all that was no more than 'a Coblers eldest sonne'.[2] Greene was not alone in attributing atheism to Marlowe, and grounds for this suspicion were officially presented before the Star Chamber in the spring of 1593. The room which Marlowe had shared with Thomas Kyd was searched when Kyd was arrested on a charge of inciting race riots. Papers were found there, 'vile hereticall Conceiptes Denying the Deity of Jhesus Christ our Savior',[3] and Kyd claimed that they were not his but Marlowe's.

A week before this damning evidence was brought to light an order had been made for Marlowe's arrest. He was found at the home of Sir Thomas Walsingham in Kent, where he had perhaps retreated to avoid the plague which closed the theatres. Being a gentleman he was not imprisoned, but was commanded 'to give his daily attendaunce'[4] on the Privy Council. This restricted freedom brought his death. On 30 May 1593 in the house of Eleanor Bull at Deptford he met and talked all day with three men. In the evening after supper they quarrelled, ostensibly about 'the payment of the sum of pence, that is, *le recknynge*, there'.[5] One of the three, Ingram Frizer, drew his dagger and killed the dramatist, claiming later before the coroner that Marlowe had attacked him and that his action was in self-defence. All three men, Frizer, Nicholas Skeres, and Robert Poley, had worked in some connection with Walsingham, and after his pardon for the murder, four weeks later, Frizer returned to Walsingham's service. He can have been no more than the agent of Marlowe's death, but the identity of the man ultimately responsible can only be guessed at.

The details of Marlowe's last day—the meeting in Deptford and the quarrel with Frizer—were not known until 1925 when Dr. Leslie Hotson discovered the full report of the coroner's inquest.[6] Those moralists who were Marlowe's contemporaries heard only scraps and rumours, and these they pieced together to make a story more righteous than truthful. Marlowe, said Thomas Beard, 'by profession a scholler ... but by practise a play-maker, and a Poet of scurrilitie', met his death in the London streets when 'he purposed to stab one whome hee ought a grudge unto'. He died horribly, 'for hee even cursed and blasphemed to his last gaspe, and togither with his breath an oth flew out of his mouth.' His death, said the pious summary, was

[1] *Nashe's Lenten Stuff* (1599); Prologue to *The Honours of the Garter* (1593); 'Of Poets and Poesie' (1627).
[2] *Perimedes* (1588).
[3] Harleian MS. 6848 f. 188/9.
[4] Privy Council entry dated 18 May 1593.
[5] Chancery Miscellanea, Bundle 64, File 8, No. 2416 (translated from the Latin).
[6] The full account is given in his book *The Death of Christopher Marlowe* (1925).

'a manifest signe of Gods judgement . . . in that hee compelled his owne
hand which had written those blasphemies to be the instrument to punish
him, and that in his braine, which had devised the same.'[1]

The 'blasphemies' which Beard and many other writers refer to are set out
at length in two letters written by Kyd to Sir John Puckering, Keeper of the
Great Seal, and in a formal report by one Richard Baines, a government
informer charged after Kyd's initial betrayal of his former room-mate to
investigate Marlowe's alleged atheism. The reports of Kyd and Baines are
substantially the same. Baines produced 'A note Containing the opinion of
on[e] Christopher Marly Concerning his Damnable Judgment of Religion,
and scorn of gods word' and in it he attributed to Marlowe such theories as:

. . . That the first beginning of Religion was only to keep men in awe.

. . . That Christ deserved better to Dy then Barrabas and that the
Jewes made a good Choise. . . .

. . . That if there be any god or any good Religion, then it is in the
papistes because the service of god is performed wth more Cerimonies, as
Elevation of the mass, organs, singing men, Shaven Crownes, &cta. that
all protestants are Hypocriticall asses.

. . . That St John the Evangelist was bedfellow to C[hrist] and leaned
alwaies in his bosome, that he used him as the sinners of Sodoma.

The 'note' concludes with Baines's own observation that not only did
Marlowe hold these opinions himself 'but almost into every Company he
Cometh he perswades men to Atheism willing them not to be afeard of
bugbeares and hobgoblins and utterly scorning both god and his ministers.'[2]

At least four Marlowes emerge from a study of contemporary accounts.
There is the faceless secret agent, whom the Privy Council first valued and
then feared; the blaspheming dramatist who was vilified by puritan opponents
of the stage; thirdly the poet, 'the Muses' darling'; and finally there is the
man who, as one of his detractors admitted, was 'by profession a scholler'—
the writer who began his literary career by translating Ovid's *Amores* and the
first book of Lucan's *Pharsalia* and who left unfinished at his death an epic
poem, *Hero and Leander*, based partly on the narrative of Musaeus. All four
—the spy, the blasphemer, the poet, and the scholar—have some part in the
plays of Christopher Marlowe.

The earliest of Marlowe's dramatic works is the tragedy of *Dido Queen
of Carthage*, a translation and adaptation of Virgil's story (*Æneid* Books I,
II, and IV). The first scene establishes the tone of the whole play: Jupiter,
toying with a petulant Ganymede, is nagged by Venus into disclosing his

[1] *Theatre of God's Judgements* (1597), ch. xxv.   [2] Harleian MS. 6648 f.185/6.

plans for Æneas. The action balances precariously between the high serious-
ness of Æneas' destiny and the comedy of the means used both to forward
and to delay his mission. Æneas himself appears as an obedient if rather
bewildered pawn, stupidly slow to understand Dido's declaration of love—

> *Dido.* Æneas, O Æneas, quench these flames!
> *Æneas.* What ails my Queen? Is she fall'n sick of late?   (III. iv. 23–4)

—and evincing only a remote pity at the end when the truth is revealed to
him:

> No marvel, Dido, though thou be in love,
> That daily dandlest Cupid in thy arms.   (v. i. 44–5)

However the emphasis of the play, as its title would suggest, is on Dido
not Æneas, and here Marlowe achieves remarkable success. His self-imposed
task was a difficult one: to make a tragic figure out of a puppet. Dido is
manipulated by the gods. Her love for Æneas might have grown out of her
tender hearing of his troubles—so that Æneas could have said with Othello,

> She lov'd me for the dangers I had pass'd,
> And I lov'd her that she did pity them.   (I. iii. 167–8)

Instead, Cupid is substituted for Ascanius and Dido, holding the changeling
on her lap, is surprised by the sudden swing in her affections:

> No, live, Iarbas. What hast thou deserv'd
> That I should say thou art no love of mine?
> Something thou hast deserv'd—Away, I say!
> Depart from Carthage, come not in my sight.   (III. i. 41–4)

Dido's sympathetic dignity is imperilled by this half-comic victimization,
but it is soon restored by the subsequent action. She gains stature from her
own struggles to reconcile a regal bearing with the pangs of passion, showing Æneas with a modest pride the portraits of rejected suitors, 'as fair as
fair may be' (III. i. 140) and declaring her condescension in joining the hunt:

> Æneas, think not but I honour thee
> That thus in person go with thee to hunt.   (III. iii. 1–2)

This natural reaction to a supernaturally induced emotion is paralleled by
the equally natural reactions of two other characters. Iarbas is understand-
ably angry and jealous while Anna, desperately in love with the rejected
suitor, welcomes the change in her sister that brings hope to herself:

> Alas, poor King, that labours so in vain
> For her that so delighteth in thy pain!
> Be rul'd by me, and seek some other love,
> Whose yielding heart may yield thee more relief.
>   (IV. ii. 33–6)

In the *Æneid* Anna is no more than a satellite, a confidante for her sister.
Marlowe gives her independence, so that the play's sub-plot, whose
realism is never in question, supports the main plot and helps an audience to
forget how Dido has been tricked. The comedy with the deluded Nurse also
furthers this end. The Nurse's situation caricatures Dido's; and what was,
initially, mild and pitying amusement becomes when it is transferred un-
mitigated laughter.

By the last act of the play Dido has regained her original dignity—and
more than this. In her anguish at parting from Æneas she recalls the past,
'how many neighbour kings Were up in arms, for making thee my love'
(v. i. 141–2), recklessly accepts the reputation of 'a second Helena' (l. 148)
if this could be made the price of his fidelity, and longs, with a touching
humanity, for 'a son by thee . . . That I might see Æneas in his face' (ll. 149–
50). Her grief is made the more poignant by Æneas' silent determination. He
can say little to excuse himself, and his few words carry even less conviction:

> In vain, my love, thou spend'st thy fainting breath:
> If words might move me, I were overcome.   (v. i. 153–4)

The play ends as Dido casts herself upon the sacrificial pyre; Iarbas
follows her to death, dying 'to expiate The grief that tires upon [his] inward
soul' (v. i. 316–7); and Anna imitates her sister. J. B. Steane deplores this
ending: 'The last act of *Dido* is in fact its great weakness, and the last scene
quite fatal.'[1] The suicide of Iarbas is Marlowe's own invention, but those
of Dido and Anna he had to repeat from Book IV of the *Æneid*. Here, as at
the beginning of *Doctor Faustus*, he was confronted with the problem of
converting what is acceptable only in heroic verse or in prose narrative into
stage terms. To prolong the situation would have made it ludicrous, so he
invests Dido with a business-like efficiency—

> Lay to thy hands, and help me make a fire   (v. i. 284)

—giving Steane the impression that Dido is in too much of a hurry.[2] The
deaths of Iarbas and Anna *are* too hasty; but that of Dido is slowed to a
suitably tragic pace. Her preparations are soon completed, and after an
ambiguous promise to Iarbas,

> after this is done,
> None in the world shall have my love but thou   (v. i. 289–90)

she is left alone on the stage for a final soliloquy. On to the pyre she casts
the instruments of her betrayal—Æneas' sword, his garments, and the letters
he had written her. At last she burns herself with the relics, and dies with
Virgil's resonant line,

> *Sic, sic juvat ire sub umbras.*   (v. i. 313)

---

[1] *Marlowe: A Critical Study* (1964), p. 48.   [2] ibid.

Naturally, one looks back at this first play to ask what promise it gives of the later Marlowe. Despite the uncertainty of some of its parts, and the joint attribution to Nashe, the whole is essentially Marlovian in its energy and its odd mingling of the tragic and the comic. These are seen, locally, in Æneas' description of the fall of Troy (II. i. 121 ff.) where the force and speed of the verse accumulate details into a panorama of horror:

> I rose,
> And looking from a turret might behold
> Young infants swimming in their parents' blood,
> Headless carcasses pil'd up in heaps,
> Virgins half-dead dragg'd by their golden hair
> And with main force flung on a ring of pikes,
> Old men with swords thrust through their aged sides,
> Kneeling for mercy to a Greekish lad
> Who with steel pole-axes dash'd out their brains. . . .   (191–9)

Although narrated, the episode is full of action, most of all in the vivid description of the invading Greeks swarming from the wooden horse:

> Then he unlock'd the horse; and suddenly
> From out his entrails, Neoptolemus,
> Setting his spear upon the ground, leapt forth,
> And after him a thousand Grecians more,
> In whose stern faces shin'd the quenchless fire
> That after burnt the pride of Asia.   (182–7)

These six lines immediately proclaim themselves as Marlowe's in the suddenness of the action they portray, in the imaginatively specific 'entrails'[1] and the detail of Neoptolemus' spear, the much-repeated hyperbole of 'thousand', the combination of beauty and destruction in the fire that shines and burns, and in the favourite adjectival form of 'quenchless'. The tragedy of *Dido Queen of Carthage* is the bridge between Marlowe's early poems and his great plays. Now he is no longer compelled, as he was in translating the *Amores*, to strive for an accurate word-for-word rendering of the Latin, and though Virgil's poem gives a form and discipline to his work, there is scope for invention in the greater freedom of the theatre. *Dido* is in some ways an experiment, and certainly a young man's play. Marlowe's next work for the theatre, *Tamburlaine the Great*, has all the confidence of achieved success.

Tamburlaine worries critics, and most would agree with Nathan Drake

---

[1] H. J. Oliver comments that 'only a poet of Marlowe's imagination could have described the hollow centre of the wooden horse as its "entrails".' *Dido Queen of Carthage* (Revels Plays, 1968), p. xlvi.

that 'it is impossible to speak [of this play] without a mixture of wonder and contempt.'[1] The wonder is for the play's language, the 'high astounding terms' promised by the Prologue (l. 5) in which the conqueror voices his equally high, equally astounding ambitions. These ambitions, however, and the means by which they are secured, are objects of the contempt. Tamburlaine seems to be devoid of all human emotions (except his love of beauty) and his highest goal is no more than 'The sweet fruition of an *earthly* crown' (II. vii. 29).

Part I of *Tamburlaine* is a simple exaltation of *virtus*, understood here as that soaring ambition which makes Tamburlaine 'His fortune's master' (II. i. 36) instead of Fortune's slave and which justifies the comparison of himself with Jupiter. Tamburlaine is superhuman in his relentless ambition, and this sets him beyond considerations of ordinary morality. Marlowe asks not for a close, critical examination of character and motive, but only for amazement and wonder at his hero's exploits. Certainly this is the response of most of the other characters in the play. Meeting Tamburlaine for the first time Zenocrate, perplexed by an appearance which contradicts his bearing, admits her doubt as she pleads with him:

> Ah shepherd, pity my distressed plight
> (If, as thou seem'st, thou art so mean a man)   (I. ii. 7–8)

but very soon she addresses him with the respect of 'my lord—for so you do import' (l. 33). The transformation from shepherd to warrior follows immediately as Tamburlaine throws aside his rustic cloak and invests himself with the armour and curtle-axe, 'adjuncts more beseeming Tamburlaine' (l. 43); the implications are stressed by Techelles:

> As princely lions when they rouse themselves,
> Stretching their paws, and threat'ning herds of beasts,
> So in his armour looketh Tamburlaine.   (I. ii. 52–4)

From this moment until the end of Act V the movement of Tamburlaine (and therefore of the play) is directly upwards; Helen Gardner comments that it 'could be plotted as a single rising line on a graph; there are no setbacks.'[2] The opposition Tamburlaine encounters only adds impulsion. The whining Mycetes brings scorn upon himself and ensures a favourable reception for his enemy, 'that paltry Scythian' (I. i. 53); Menaphon describes a god-like being whose appearance is

> straightly fashioned
> Like his desire, lift upwards and divine: (II. i. 7–8)

[1] *Shakespeare and His Times* (1817), ii. 245.
[2] 'The Second Part of *Tamburlaine the Great*', *Modern Language Review* xxxvii (1942), 19.

and Zenocrate is hypnotized by his looks and words:

> As looks the sun through Nilus' flowing stream,
> Or when the morning holds him in her arms,
> So looks my lordly love, fair Tamburlaine;
> His talk much sweeter than the Muses' song
> They sung for honour 'gainst Pierides.   (III. ii. 47–51)

The confrontation with Bajazeth provides the strongest opposition so far in the play, and the slanging-match between the two parties—Tamburlaine and Zenocrate on the one side, Bajazeth and Zabina on the other—reflects the later battle. Tamburlaine conquers our emotions when he speaks to Zenocrate as

> the loveliest maid alive,
> Fairer than rocks of pearl and precious stone,
>   (III. iii. 117–18)

while Bajazeth alienates them in his praise of Zabina, dwelling on her monstrous brood of sons with

> limbs more large and of a bigger size
> Than all the brats y-sprung from Typhon's loins.
>   (III. iii. 108–9)

A double crisis arises, however, in Act V when a new kind of emotion—pity—enters the play. The barbarity and viciousness of Bajazeth's imprisonment is bearable—but only just; and now the massacre of the Damascus virgins seems to defy excuse. M. C. Bradbrook tries to palliate the horror by saying

> There is no hint in the verse of the physical suffering of the virgins; they are a set of innocent white dummies, without sticky blood like Duncan's. Their death is not shocking because it is not dramatically realized. . . . Their acting was probably as formal as their speech.[1]

If the virgins' suffering can be minimized in this way, Tamburlaine's enjoyment of it cannot. A momentary pity for the 'turtles fray'd out of their nests' (v. i. 64) becomes a triumphant assertion of his mastery, his command of death:

> For there sits Death; there sits imperious Death,
> Keeping his circuit by the slicing edge.
> But I am pleas'd you shall not see him there;
> He now is seated on my horsemen's spears,
> And on their points his fleshless body feeds.   (v. i. 111–15)

When the virgins are made no more than 'dummies' the exquisite cruelty of these lines loses its effect and Tamburlaine becomes laughable, tilting at flour-sacks.

---

[1] *Themes and Conventions of Elizabethan Tragedy* (1935), p. 139.

   In this episode Marlowe seems to be playing audaciously with the affections of the audience, encouraging a clash between a normal sympathy with
the innocent victims and the admiration which his play has generated for
their oppressor. While the emotions are still shaken, he gives Tamburlaine
the longest and most humane speech of the play. Sympathies which have
dissolved on the Governor and the virgins quickly harden and re-focus
during the hymn of praise to Zenocrate and are directed wholly towards
Tamburlaine when he admits conflict within himself:

> What is beauty, saith my sufferings, then?   (v. i. 160)

The sacrifice of the virgins was necessary—if only to put the audience into a
frame of mind receptive to this meditation on the 'instinct [with which] the
soul of man is touch'd' (l. 179). The speech is also Tamburlaine's justification of the slaughter: pity, like the love of beauty, must be subordinated to a
still greater force:

> virtue solely is the sum of glory,
> And fashions men with true nobility.   (v. i. 189–90)

These two lines provide the key to understanding of the whole play, since
it is, clearly, his sense of 'virtue' that governs all Tamburlaine's actions. This
'virtue' is defined by F. P. Wilson as 'the Italian *virtù*, the power of the
human intellect and will, and the full development of that power',[1] and it is
the most difficult of all concepts to appreciate. Yet it must be accepted if
Tamburlaine is to maintain his heroic role throughout Act V.
   The slaughter of the virgins was the first part of the crisis; the second is
even greater, the deaths of Bajazeth and Zabina. The suicides themselves are
not damaging to Tamburlaine's position: Bajazeth is given lines of rhetoric
which fail to move, Zabina is not pathetic in her frenzy, and they can only
procure death by an undignified battering against the cage. The solemnity
enters with Zenocrate's lament for them and its warning, directed specifically
at Tamburlaine,

> Those that are proud of fickle empery
> And place their chiefest good in earthly pomp,
> Behold the Turk and his great emperess!   (v. i. 350–2)

Because of this the play ends on a subdued note. God-like in his conquests,
Tamburlaine can now afford the gesture of sparing Zenocrate's father as he
'takes truce with all the world' (v. i. 527), but there is the reminder of
mortality in the bodies of Bajazeth and Zabina, honoured—for the first
time—by Tamburlaine in words that echo Zenocrate's lament: 'this great
Turk and his fair emperess' (v. i. 530).
   Part I of Tamburlaine can stand alone, but it is a necessary preliminary

---

[1] *Marlowe and the Early Shakespeare* (1953), p. 51.

to Part II, where success becomes frustration. It is another Tamburlaine, or at least another aspect of Tamburlaine, that we see here. The character of Part I was professional in every action; even the hyperboles with which he wooed Zenocrate were calculated:

> Techelles, women must be flattered:
> But this is she with whom I am in love.   (I. ii. 107–8)

His subsequent coldness was no more than a strategic withdrawal, forcing Zenocrate in her distress to declare her passion and her longing to 'live and die with Tamburlaine' (III. ii. 24). The Tamburlaine of Part II is rather the private—one might almost say domestic—man, seen most frequently in the roles of husband and father. His military exploits are still successful, but he now has a wife who begs him to

> leave these arms,
> And save thy sacred person free from scathe
> And dangerous chances of the wrathful war.   (I. iii. 9–11)

The problems he encounters as a father are less straightforward than those arising on the battlefield, and he is ill equipped to deal with them. His sons worry him because they look like their mother, and he suspects they may be 'too dainty for the wars' (I. iii. 28). Two of them give him reassurance that they are as bloodthirsty as he could wish, but Calyphas remains a disappointment, preferring his mother's company and playing cards when he ought to be fighting. He is a pacifist who, when he is exhorted to please his father and join in the bloodshed, replies

> I know, sir, what it is to kill a man;
> It works remorse of conscience in me.
> I take no pleasure to be murderous,
> Nor care for blood when wine will quench my thirst.
>
> (IV. i. 27–30)

Steane finds this affirmation 'ludicrous and hypocritical' and shares Tamburlaine's opinion that the 'pacifism is only weakness';[1] but Helen Gardner, while warning against the danger of reading modern anti-war sentiments into Calyphas's speeches, finds that 'the whole treatment of Calyphas suggests something more subtle than the traditional coward; his distaste for war and his refusal to find his father impressive are positive rather than negative attitudes.'[2]

Tamburlaine can kill his son, but he cannot change him. In Part I his vaulting ambition could surmount the merely human opposition offered by Cosroe, Bajazeth, and the Governor of Damascus, but now that ambition seems itself to be human, while the forces against which it wars are eternal

[1] op. cit., p. 82.   [2] op. cit., p. 22.

and invincible. The death of Zenocrate is the first check, and during her
sickness the proud warrior is lost in the helpless husband who pitifully asks
'Physicians, will no physic do her good?' (II. iv. 38). His grief, like his love,
is extreme; but the revengeful conqueror who fires Larissa is also the husband who consciously deceives himself—'Though she be dead, yet let me
think she lives' (II. iv. 127)—and keeps his wife's body always with him. To
console himself he turns to his sons and gives them a lesson in fortification,
but even here he is disappointed by the child he cannot mould in his own
image.

The killing of Calyphas has about it an air of forced bravura, and the
barbarity is emphasized by the comments of the captive kings. When he
appears with these yoked to his chariot Tamburlaine seems demented and
his speech is not rhetoric but rant:

> Holla, ye pamper'd jades of Asia!
> What, can ye draw but twenty miles a day,
> And have so proud a chariot at your heels,
> And such a coachman as great Tamburlaine?   (IV. iii. 1–4)

His claims to be the scourge of God, of a God 'full of revenging wrath' (V. i.
181) grow more insistent as destruction rages. The first intimation of
mortality is rejected when he boasts 'Sickness or death can never conquer
me' (V. i. 220), but soon he is compelled to resign himself to the inevitable,
asking with surprise and anger

> Shall sickness prove me now to be a man,
> That have been term'd the terror of the world?   (V. iii. 44–5)

At the end of the play the man and the conqueror are reconciled, and
Tamburlaine achieves a greatness which has eluded him throughout Part II.
Dying, he calls for a map and enumerates his triumphs, counterpointing
the swell of the resounding names with the mournful lament of 'And shall I
die, and this unconquered?' (V. iii. 150).

The second part of *Tamburlaine* is a less straightforward play than the
first. Marlowe had used up much of his source material for Part I, and when
popular acclaim prompted a sequel he drew upon his general reading, and
upon his invention, to fill in the gaps with such episodes as Theridamas's
abortive seduction of Olympia. Una Ellis-Fermor compared the two and
decided that

> The first part alone reveals Marlowe's mind at work on a characteristic
> structure; much of the second, though flashes of power and passages of
> thought as clear as anything in the earlier part occur at intervals through-
> out, is, by comparison, journeyman work.[1]

[1] *Tamburlaine the Great* (1930), p. 46.

Certainly an audience is only intermittently conscious of Tamburlaine's blazing energies, but in compensation for this is the greater critical effort evident in Part II, where considerations which had been swept aside in Part I are now admitted and examined. From this beginning, the development of Marlowe can be measured by the distance he keeps from his protagonists.

It is impossible to be precise about the sequence of Marlowe's plays, but it seems reasonable to suppose that *Tamburlaine* was followed by *The Jew of Malta*, a play which defies categorization into tragedy or comedy, yet which contains elements of both. Its setting and its central figure are far removed from those of *Tamburlaine*. The wide open spaces have dwindled to the small island where a bottle-nosed Jew squats in his counting-house amassing 'Infinite riches in a little room' (I. i. 37). The Elizabethans' respect for wealth was matched by their anti-Semitism, and Marlowe could rely on a conflict of these attitudes when he created Barabas, magnificently rich and uncompromisingly Jewish. His right to be both is challenged and vindicated in the first encounter with the Maltese Christians. Although Barabas loses much of his treasure, the moral victory is his and the Christians, using conversion as a threat to defraud the Jews, stand convicted of hypocrisy. To comfort Barabas in his loss, the other Jews advise him to 'remember Job' (I. ii. 179) but he scorns their advice and rejects the heroic status that resignation might bring him. He has made provision for this event, and with such provision—

> Ten thousand portagues, besides great pearls,
> Rich costly jewels, and stones infinite,   (I. ii. 243–4)

—heroism is unnecessary.

The world of *The Jew of Malta* is wholly materialistic, dedicated to financial self-improvement. The Maltese keep a truce with the Turks 'but in hope of gold' (II. ii. 26), and they are willing to break the truce for the same reason. Where gold is the prime motive, for Christians as well as Jews, there can be little dignity of character or action; and Marlowe delights, now, in showing the meanness of humanity. The same images that he used in *Tamburlaine* to exalt are here used to diminish. Great figures from the past and from mythology are invoked: as he stirs the nuns' porridge Barabas recalls the fatal draught 'Of which great Alexander drunk and died', the Borgia's wine, Hydra's blood, 'all the poisons of the Stygian pool' (III. iv. 94 ff.); and the melodrama is comically deflated by Ithamore's comment,

> What a blessing has he given't! Was ever pot of rice-porridge so sauced?
> (III. iv. 103)

Ithamore himself addresses his prostitute mistress as Jason's golden fleece, promises that he will be Adonis, she Love's Queen—then punctures the hyperbole with his parody of Marlowe's poem:

> Thou in those groves, by Dis above,
> Shalt live with me and be my love.[1]   (IV. ii. 92–3)

Such diminution forbids greatness of character, and the characters themselves see to it that any event, however serious intrinsically, is rendered
ludicrous. The pathos of Abigail's death is turned to laughter when her plea
to the friar, 'witness that I die a Christian', is answered by him 'Ay, and a
virgin too; that grieves me most' (III. vi. 40–1). Murder becomes a joke
when crimes are accumulated, and no single death can seem tragic in a play
where a whole convent is poisoned and a whole army blown up. Even the
death of Barabas, whose cleverness has made him a sympathetic figure, is
made comic by its complicated machinery.

At the beginning of the play Barabas explains that he has

> But one sole daughter, whom I hold as dear
> As Agamemnon did his Iphigen.   (I. i. 136–7)

The interpretation of these lines is crucial to the play, and Levin seems to
miss the point when he observes that 'Agamemnon is less relevant than
Jephtha might have been.'[2] Though Iphigenia was dear to her father, he
was still prepared to sacrifice her for the sake of a greater good, a fair wind
to Troy. Gold is Barabas's greater good; for this, and for his own security,
he is prepared to sacrifice Abigail. The distance between Barabas and
Agamemnon, between money and honour, is the distance between this play
and heroic tragedy.

Like Tamburlaine, Barabas delights in ingenious cruelty, and audiences
are expected to share this delight; in *Edward II* the torture gives pleasure
only to Lightborn, and for the first time our sympathies are with the sufferer.
No play better illustrates the changes which have come about in the apprecia-
tion of Marlowe's work—changes caused not by the discovery of new information but by the differing sensibilities of society. The editor of *Edward II*
must supply, at V. v. 112, a direction for the murder of the King, since this
is absent from the early texts. Holinshed is quite explicit about the manner of
death:

> they kept him down and withall put into his fundament an horne, and
> through the same they thrust up into his bodie an hot spit . . . the which
> passing up into his intrailes, and being rolled to and fro, burnt the same,
> but so as no appearance of any wound or hurt outwardlie might be once
> perceived.[3]

---

[1] 'The Passionate Shepherd to his Love' opens with, and repeats, the line 'Come live with
me, and be my love.'
[2] *The Overreacher: A Study of Christopher Marlowe* (1954), p. 90.
[3] *Chronicles of England* (1587), p. 341.

In the play Lightborn, though he tantalizes Mortimer with the 'braver way' (v. iv. 37) which is to be kept secret, is equally unambiguous in his instructions to Matrevis and Gurney (v. v. 28 ff.). When such obscene violence could not be contemplated in the study—much less on the stage—editors muffled the horror and Edward was killed by suffocation. It was William Empson who in 1946 affirmed that the murder was a parody of the homosexual act.[1] By regarding it as a punishment barbarously fitting to the crime, attention is brought to the true nature of that crime. Edward's fault was no mere disregard of the obligations of kingship but an offence regarded as 'abhominable'—unnatural.[2] The changed attitude of the twentieth century makes it possible to present *Edward II* as Marlowe intended it—as both a homosexual play and a tragedy.

Sympathies in this play are not fixed: at different times Edward is to be loved, despised, pitied, and admired. His brother, Edmund Earl of Kent, reflects the changes of feeling and is, as F. P. Wilson noted, 'perhaps the only character in Marlowe's plays who may be regarded as a point of reference.'[3] At first Edmund speaks for the right of a king not to be abused by commoners (I. i. 106 ff.) but when Edward overreaches his royal prerogative in bestowing excessive titles on Gaveston, it is Edmund who recommends moderation:

> Brother, the least of these may well suffice
> For one of greater birth than Gaveston.   (I. i. 157–8)

Concern for the country's good drives him to forsake Edward after the barons' indictment of his extravagance, but he turns again when he realizes that 'Mortimer And Isabel do kiss while they conspire' (IV. v. 21–2). Edmund's function is to mark the changes of feeling, while Isabella does much to effect them. In the first part of the play she is largely responsible for the antipathy towards her selfish, callous husband. The barons and the bishops have right on their side, but their patriotism is flawed by their personal jealousy of Gaveston, the 'night-grown mushrump' (I. iv. 284), while Isabella seems so flawless in her injured innocence that it is difficult not to overlook the fact that she must be the originator of the plan to recall Gaveston and murder him (I. iv. 225 ff.). Hypocrisy and viciousness increase with power, and she repels the affections which now return to Edward.

The King himself is not a static figure: in the course of the play, whose five acts encompass twenty-three years of history, he grows from the petulant boy defying the advice of older and wiser men—

[1] *The Nation* clxiii (1946), 444.
[2] Cf. the Act of Henry VIII (25 Henry VIII c. 6) against 'the detestable and abhominable vice'.
[3] op. cit., p. 94.

> In spite of them
> I'll have my will, and these two Mortimers
> That cross me thus shall know I am displeas'd   (I. i. 76–8)

—to the weary king who asks forgiveness even from his tormentor: 'Forgive my thought, for having such a thought' (v. v. 82). He clings to Spencer as he had clung to Gaveston, and his love seems to ennoble its objects. In 'the men who come within the circle of his intimacy,' Una Ellis-Fermor remarked, 'Edward has the power of inspiring undying affection.'[1] Neither Gaveston nor Spencer is free from ambition; of humble birth, they both appreciate the value of a king's love. This streak of opportunism must not be denied, for although it weakens their love at the beginning it strengthens it at the end when, with nothing to gain but an ignominious death, both remain true to Edward. However offensive Edward's love might have been, both by its nature and by its excess, there was virtue in it. Comparing Edward with Doctor Faustus, Empson finds that 'The peculiarity of the mind of Marlowe [was that] it erected absolutely opposed ideals. The unmentionable thing for which the punishment was death was *the proper thing to do.*'[2]

Edward's sin, however, is venial and adequately punished under the laws of Henry VIII by death of the body. Faustus's sin is mortal, the sin against the Holy Ghost, and he himself acknowledges that 'Faustus' offence can ne'er be pardoned' (v. ii. 39). In this play Marlowe the student of theology comes to the fore. His source for *Doctor Faustus* was a 'biography' of the semi-legendary Georg or Johannes Faustus which gave sound moral lessons along with entertaining glimpses of hell. Marlowe transformed the conjurer into a scholar of distinction who disdains the devil's astronomy as 'freshmen's suppositions' (II. ii. 55) and who rejects Christian teaching about the after-life in the words of Averroës: 'His ghost be with the old philosophers' (I. iii. 60).[3] Recently the play has been called 'one of the most specious of all the false classics which clog our English Literature courses' and both its hero and its author charged with 'intellectual flaccidity', 'weakness and evasion'.[4] Yet this is the play that excited Goethe, as reported by Henry Crabb Robinson:

> I mentioned Marlowe's *Faust*. He burst out into an exclamation of praise. 'How greatly is it all planned!' He had thought of translating it. He was fully aware that Shakespeare did not stand alone.[5]

---

[1] *Christopher Marlowe* (1927), p. 113.
[2] op. cit., p. 445.
[3] '*sit anima mea cum philosophis.*' Cf. J. C. Maxwell, *Notes and Queries* cxiv (1949), 334–5.
[4] A. L. French, 'The Philosophy of *Doctor Faustus*', *Essays in Criticism* xx (April 1970), 123 and 135.
[5] *Diary, Reminiscences and Correspondence*, ed. T. Sadler (1869), ii. 434.

Goethe surrendered himself to Marlowe's magic; the modern critic is in-
hibited by those notes which tell him, for instance, that '*Bene disserere est
finis logices*' (I. i. 7) is the formulation of Ramus not of Aristotle, and that the
words Faustus quotes from 'Jerome's Bible' (I i. 38 ff.) are not in fact those
of the Vulgate. Such close reading gives no thought to the dramatic impact
of the play and, textually corrupt though it is, *Doctor Faustus* is the most
theatrically effective of Marlowe's works. The theatre is no place for close
analysis, or even plain statement: Thomas Mann in his *Doctor Faustus* can
describe a boy as 'vibrating with ability' (ch. ix) but the dramatist must *show*
this. Faustus's first speech, with its Latin quotations and its impressive roll-
call of Aristotle, Galen, Justinian, and Jerome sounds the note of authority
and characterizes a man of learning and experience.

From the point at which Faustus sells his soul the play operates on two
levels. Superficially there is the amusement of space-travel, clowns, conjuring, and Pope-baiting—though it cannot be said with certainty which of
these episodes is the work, or the design, of Marlowe himself. This runs
parallel to the real tragedy, of which Marlowe is undoubtedly author, of
the man whose aspiring mind drives him to sin against the Holy Ghost, sin
which 'shall not be forgiven him, neither in this world, neither in the world
to come' (Matthew 12: 32). No precise identification of this sin can be found
in the Bible, but Elizabethan Protestant theologians shared with their
Catholic predecessors the belief that pride and despair, seeming opposites,
were the first elements. Pride, or presumption as Donne calls it, 'takes
away the fear of God, and desperation the love of God.'[1] This is the sin of
Faustus, the man who at first, finding all human knowledge barren, aspires
to godhead through devil-worship—'A sound magician is a demi-god' (I. i.
60)—and who at the end of twenty-four years is firm only in his despair.
He commits no major crime, but the first condition of his bond with Lucifer
is damnable: 'that Faustus may be a spirit in form and substance' (II. i. 96).
A spirit or devil—in such a context the words are synonymous—is incapable
of repentance and therefore of securing God's forgiveness: the Bad Angel
tells Faustus 'Thou art a spirit; God cannot pity thee' (II. ii. 13) and an
orthodox theological mind would assent. But the play depends for its tension
on the constant availability of God's forgiveness, and almost to the end
Faustus has 'an amiable soul' (v. i. 41). His damnation is not finally sealed
until his last request for

> That heavenly Helen which I saw of late,
> Whose sweet embracings may extinguish clear
> Those thoughts that do dissuade me from my vow.   (v. i. 91–3)

The scholars witness that Helen is 'the pride of nature's works' and the 'only
paragon of excellence' (v. i. 31, 32) but the apparition who can 'make

[1] *LXXX Sermons* (1640), p. 349.

[Faustus] immortal with a kiss' is diabolic, and her embraces are as fatal as those of 'flaming Jupiter, When he appear'd to hapless Semele' (v. i. 112 ff.).

This account of the play has treated Faustus as a free agent who makes his own choice between eternal life and eternal death. The first scenes justify this treatment, especially in the presentation of the encounter between Faustus and Mephostophilis in Act I Scene iii where the devil speaks of the fall of Lucifer through 'aspiring pride and insolence' (l. 67) and identifies himself as one of the

> Unhappy spirits that fell with Lucifer,
> Conspir'd against our God with Lucifer,
> And are for ever damn'd with Lucifer.   (I. iii. 70–3)

Far more powerful than the gleeful hot-gospeller description of hell (v. ii. 111 ff.) is his account of the deprivation of the damned:

> Why, this is hell, nor am I out of it.
> Think'st thou that I who saw the face of God
> And tasted the eternal joys of heaven,
> Am not tormented with ten thousand hells
> In being depriv'd of everlasting bliss?   (I. iii. 76–80)[1]

But there is a different Mephostophilis at the end of the play who rejoices in Faustus's anguish and boasts

> 'Twas I that, when thou were't i'the way to heaven,
> Damm'd up thy passage; when thou took'st the book
> To view the scriptures, then I turn'd the leaves
> And led thine eye.   (v. ii. 86–9)

If this statement is to be accepted, then it appears that Faustus never had free will, that he was little more than a puppet manipulated by the infernal powers. It can be argued that this reversal of Mephostophilis from tormented fiend to tormentor is the final twist of the knife; very early in the action Faustus, proud of his achievement in mastering the devil, is somewhat dashed when Mephostophilis tells him blandly, 'I came now hither of my own accord' (I. iii. 44). Alternatively, it can be claimed that the Mephostophilis of Act V is not Marlowe's creation. His appearance with Lucifer and the two Angels (v. ii. 1–23 and 80–125) is to be found only in the B Text and is not even hinted in A. Whichever argument is accepted makes little difference to the last soliloquy where the great scholar pants for a hiding-place in earth, air, fire, and water, the elements whose spirits he had once so proudly thought to command.[2]

---

[1] The words are those of St. John Chrysostom: '*si decem mille gehennas quis dixerit, nihil tale est quale ab beata visione excidere*'. Cf. John Searle, *Times Literary Supplement* (15 February 1936).

[2] In his conjuration (I. iii. 16) he prays '*ignei, aerii, aquatici, terreni spiritus salvete!*'

Intense pity and fear are blended at the end of *Doctor Faustus*, and even the corruption of the text cannot obscure the greatness of Marlowe's scheme. *The Massacre at Paris* presents still more problems but the text here, an actor's garbled reminiscences, defeats any attempt to decide Marlowe's intentions or achievement. It is usually placed, as in this edition, at the end of Marlowe's dramatic works, but the only concrete evidence for a late date is Henslowe's description of the play as 'ne' [new] when he recorded a performance in January 1593; the receipts on this occasion, three pounds fourteen shillings, support his claim that the play was new to the stage at this time—but it seems to me that the tone is nearer to *The Jew of Malta* than to *Edward II*. Perhaps Marlowe wrote a rough draft, between August 1589 and August 1590,[1] and handed it over to the players two or three years later. The single surviving manuscript page of Scene xix (if this *is* accepted as holograph), with its spelling alterations and its direction 'Enter Minion' for Mugeroun at l. 12, suggests a draft rather than a finished copy. A comparison of this leaf with the printed scene (see Appendix, p. 442) gives some indication of what has been lost, especially in the Guise's speech, where the MS. version is longer and more ambitious in thought and imagery.

The Guise is the most fully characterized of all the *dramatis personae*. Like all heroes who are determined to prove villains he takes the audience into his confidence and wins a measure of respect for his honesty. The religious disputes which exercise Catholics and Protestants are for him only a means to an end:

> Religion! *O Diabole!*
> Fie, I am asham'd, however that I seem,
> To think a word of such a simple sound,
> Of so great matter should be made the ground.   (ii. 66–9)

His black ambition stretches out, with Tamburlaine's, for 'The sweet fruition of an earthly crown' (*I Tam.* II. vii. 29), but there can be no further comparison between the two. The Guise kills with a wicked humour that forbids glory or pathos—he tells the Schoolmasters, for instance, that he will 'whip [them] to death' with his poniard (ix. 81); and he indulges in a pseudo-disputation with Ramus that ends

> Your *nego argumentum*
> Cannot serve, sirrah.—Kill him.   (ix. 37–8)

His lust for power is shared by Queen Catherine who swears to 'dissolve with blood and cruelty' the peace-making marriage between her daughter

---

[1] The play shows the death of Henry III, who was murdered in August 1589. At xxii. 80 the Guise urges 'Ah Sixtus, be reveng'd upon the King', and this could indicate that Pope Sixtus V, who died in August 1590, was alive at the time of writing.

and Navarre (i. 25), arranges the murder of her elder son, and promises to disinherit Anjou 'if he grudge or cross his mother's will' (xi. 43).

The Guise and Catherine have their counterparts, respectively, in Tamburlaine and Barabas and in Isabella, although they are more exaggerated than these. Anjou, however, is unique in Marlowe's creation. There is nothing remarkable in his early scenes where he appears as an ally of the Guise, bloodthirsty and hypocritical:

> I am disguis'd, and none knows who I am,
> And therefore mean to murder all I meet.   (vi. 5–6)

It is after he has become King Henry III, suspecting and hating the Guise, that a surprising volte-face is achieved. His hatred of the Guise is historically accurate, but the accompanying care for Protestant England is Marlowe's own invention. Anjou's tirade against the domination of Rome (xxv. 56 ff.) owes much to *Edward II*,[1] but the character must have voiced similar sentiments as a prelude to his promise

> Navarre, give me thy hand: I here do swear
> To ruinate that wicked Church of Rome,
> That hatcheth up such bloody practices;
> And here protest eternal love to thee,
> And to the Queen of England specially,
> Whom God hath bless'd for hating papistry.   (xxv. 65–70)

Perhaps Marlowe imagined himself as the English Agent who attends at Henry's court and who would bring back to England the news of the King's murder. Certainly this play, unlike any other, shows its author as an orthodox, Catholic-hating, English patriot.

Critics have always disagreed—and no doubt will continue to disagree—about the thought and content of Marlowe's plays; but one opinion they almost all share. In the words of Leigh Hunt, 'If ever there was a born poet, Marlowe was one.'[2] Ben Jonson's compliment when he spoke of 'Marlowe's mighty line'[3] has, unintentionally, done something of a disservice. Marlowe is, it is true, pre-eminently the poet of power and aspiration, of infinity in verse expressed through daring hyperbole and also through his favoured forms of the present participle and the adjective ending in '-less'. But the line is made a unit in the orchestrated paragraph; each line of Tamburlaine's famous speech (Part I, II. vii. 12–29) is mighty in itself, but the accumulated force of the whole is greater than the sum of its parts. We can say with certainty that this is Marlowe; but Marlowe is not this

---

[1] I. iv. 96 ff.; the actor's memory has confused the two plays.
[2] *Imagination and Fancy* (1844, 2nd ed. 1845), p. 136.
[3] In his memorial verses to Shakespeare, prefaced to the First Folio (1623).

alone. His work shows a variety of styles, appropriate to the widely differing characters and situations, that Jonson's comment might lead us to neglect. In *The Jew of Malta* the verse glitters with a hard, epigrammatic quality— 'Look, look, master, here come two religious caterpillars' (IV. i. 21)—and in *Dido*, as in *Edward II*, he encompasses a woman's hopeless longing in lines whose second half has a dying fall, quite unlike the rising note of male aspiration:

> Had I a son by thee the grief were less,
> That I might see Æneas in his face.
> Now if thou go'st, what canst thou leave behind
> But rather will augment than ease my woe? (v. i. 149–52)

There are few lines in *Edward II* that can qualify as 'mighty'—just as the action here is the opposite of heroic. Such rhetorical speeches as there are, for instance Isabella's attempt to rally her troops on arrival in England, are instantly deflated: here, Mortimer silences the Queen with his

> Nay Madam, if you be a warrior,
> You must not grow so passionate in speeches (IV. iv. 15–16)

and then offers a workmanlike model which makes no concession to idealism (ll. 17 ff.). The pace of the play, Wolfgang Clemen has observed, permits only 'the "condensed" lament which expresses the grief in two or three lines, or translates it into a sigh or a passionate desire.'[1] The plays imposed a new discipline on Marlowe, in which he had to learn to balance the rhythms of speech against the demands of the pentameter; at first this gave rise to the much-derided pomposity of 'Gentle Achates, reach the tinder-box' (*Dido* I. i. 166) but later to the quick cut-and-thrust of the barons in *Edward II*, where a line can be divided between two or even three speakers and yet remain regular. When he began his career Marlowe was dominated by the external form he chose for his works; at the end, he is master of form and language.

ROMA GILL

Sheffield
September 1970

---

[1] *English Tragedy before Shakespeare* (1955, tr. T. S. Dorsch 1961), p. 283.

RECOMMENDED READING

Much has been written about Marlowe and the accompanying list makes no claim to be inclusive; it is personal and prejudiced.

General studies of Marlowe and his work:

J. Bakeless, *The Tragicall History of Christopher Marlowe* (1942)
T. S. Eliot, 'Christopher Marlowe' in *Selected Essays* (1927)
Una Ellis-Fermor, *Christopher Marlowe* (1927)
J. L. Hotson, *The Death of Christopher Marlowe* (1925)
P. H. Kocher, *Christopher Marlowe* (1946)
H. Levin, *The Overreacher: A Study of Christopher Marlowe* (1954)
M. M. Mahood, 'Marlowe's Heroes' in *Poetry and Humanism* (1950)
J. B. Steane, *Marlowe: A Critical Study* (1964)
F. P. Wilson, *Marlowe and the Early Shakespeare* (1953)
A. D. Wraight and V. F. Stern, *In Search of Christopher Marlowe* (1965)
C. Leech, ed., *Marlowe: A Collection of Critical Essays* (1964)
Judith O'Neill, ed., *Critics on Marlowe* (1969)

Studies of particular plays:

Tamburlaine	Ethel Seaton, 'Marlowe's Map', *Essays and Studies* x (1924), 13–35
	R. W. Battenhouse, *Marlowe's 'Tamburlaine'* (1941)
Edward II	W. D. Briggs, Introduction to his edition of *Edward II* (1914)
	C. Leech, 'Marlowe's *Edward II*: Power and Suffering', *Critical Quarterly* I. iii (1959), 181–96
Doctor Faustus	J. Jump, *Marlowe: 'Doctor Faustus'*, a selection of critical essays
	Helen Gardner, 'The Tragedy of Damnation' in *Elizabethan Drama*, ed. R. J. Kaufmann (1961)
	W. W. Greg, *Marlowe's 'Doctor Faustus' 1604–1616* (1950)

A NOTE ON
THE PRESENT EDITION

In this edition of Marlowe's dramatic works the spelling and punctuation of the early texts have been modernized, speech-headings regularized, and a few necessary stage directions have been added (in square brackets). Annotations have been kept to a minimum, and only a very small proportion of the vast textual apparatus is included. This is presented in the following form:

> oo   trench] Ed. (truce Q)

'Ed.' indicates the emendation of any editor (not necessarily the present one) and 'Q', or sometimes 'O', the reading of the original Quarto or Octavo text. This is slightly more complicated in the case of *Doctor Faustus* where there are two groups of texts (see preliminary note on that play) and where the textual notes have the form

> 25   God] A (power B)

'A' indicates the reading of the first group, 'B' that of the second.

The order of the plays attempts to be chronological—but the dates are often in doubt.

R. G.

Dido Queen of Carthage

A single Quarto published in 1594 gives the text for this play and attributes it to Marlowe and Thomas Nashe, but the style suggests that Marlowe was mainly responsible. The play was written probably before he left Cambridge in 1587, and performed not on a public stage but by the Children of the Chapel Royal.

Marlowe found the story of Dido's love for Æneas and the rivalry of Iarbas, King of Gaetulia, in Books I, II, and IV of Virgil's *Æneid*. He worked from a Latin text, translating, paraphrasing, and summarizing. Often he added to his source: the induction with Jupiter and Ganymede, the comic scene between Cupid and the Nurse, and, most important, the love of Anna for Iarbas are his inventions. Behind the tragic, romantic love story lies the account of the Trojan War, given its fullest treatment in Homer's *Iliad*. The war began when Paris, son of Priam, was invited to adjudicate among three goddesses, Venus, Juno, and Minerva. When he gave the prize to Venus, she rewarded him with the most beautiful of all women, Helen, wife of the Greek king Menelaus. Paris abducted Helen, taking her home with him to Troy. Menelaus gathered forces and attacked Troy with a siege that continued for ten years. Finally the Greeks resorted to the stratagem described in II.i.126 ff., and Troy was conquered. Protected by his mother, the goddess Venus, Æneas managed to escape and set sail for Italy but on the way his ships were driven to the coast of Africa. Here he was welcomed by Dido, herself a refugee who had begged protection and aid from Iarbas who hoped to be repaid by marriage.

THE
Tragedie of Dido
Queene of Carthage:
Played by the Children of her
Maiesties Chappell.

Written by Christopher Marlowe, and
Thomas Nash. Gent.

Actors

Iupiter.	*Ascanius.*
Ganimed,	*Dido.*
Venus.	*Anna.*
Cupid,	*Achates.*
Iuno.	*Ilioneus.*
Mercurie, or	*Iarbas.*
Hermes.	*Cloanthes.*
Æneas.	*Sergestus.*

AT LONDON,
Printed, by the Widdowe *Orwin,* for *Thomas Woodcocke,* and
are to be solde at his shop, in Paules Church-yeard, at
the signe of the blacke Beare. 1594.

[DRAMATIS PERSONAE

IMMORTALS

Jupiter
Mercury, sometimes called *Hermes*
Ganymede
Cupid
Venus
Juno

MORTALS

Æneas
Ascanius, his son
Achates ⎫
Ilioneus ⎪
Cloanthus ⎬ Trojans
Sergestus ⎭
Iarbas, King of Gaetulia
Carthaginian Lord

Dido, Queen of Carthage
Anna, her sister
Nurse

Trojans and Carthaginians attendant upon
Æneas and Dido]

[Act I Scene i]

Here the curtains draw; there is discovered Jupiter *dandling*
Ganymede *upon his knee, and* Mercury *lying asleep.*

Jupiter. Come, gentle Ganymede, and play with me;
    I love thee well, say Juno what she will.
Ganymede. I am much better for your worthless love,
    That will not shield me from her shrewish blows!
    Today, whenas I fill'd into your cups
    And held the cloth of pleasance whiles you drank,
    She reach'd me such a rap for that I spill'd,
    As made the blood run down about mine ears.
Jupiter. What? Dares she strike the darling of my thoughts?
    By Saturn's soul, and this earth-threat'ning hair,   10
    That, shaken thrice, makes nature's buildings quake,
    I vow, if she but once frown on thee more,
    To hang her meteor-like 'twixt heaven and earth,
    And bind her hand and foot with golden cords,
    As once I did for harming Hercules!
Ganymede. Might I but see that pretty sport a-foot,
    O, how would I with Helen's brother laugh,
    And bring the gods to wonder at the game!
    Sweet Jupiter, if e'er I pleas'd thine eye,
    Or seemed fair, wall'd-in with eagle's wings,   20
    Grace my immortal beauty with this boon,
    And I will spend my time in thy bright arms.
Jupiter. What is't, sweet wag, I should deny thy youth?
    Whose face reflects such pleasure to mine eyes,
    As I, exhal'd with thy fire-darting beams,
    Have oft driven back the horses of the night,
    Whenas they would have hal'd thee from my sight.
    Sit on my knee, and call for thy content,
    Control proud Fate, and cut the thread of Time.
    Why, are not all the gods at thy command,   30
    And heaven and earth the bounds of thy delight?
    Vulcan shall dance to make thee laughing sport,
    And my nine daughters sing when thou art sad;

13–15 To hang . . . Hercules] cf. *Iliad* xv.   17 Helen's brother] Helen's two brothers,
Castor and Pollux, spent alternate days on Olympus.   25 exhal'd] Perhaps a reference
to the sun's being thought to produce meteors by exhaling or drawing up vapours.
32 Vulcan] the lame blacksmith god   33 nine daughters] the Muses

From Juno's bird I'll pluck her spotted pride,
To make thee fans wherewith to cool thy face;
And Venus' swans shall shed their silver down,
To sweeten out the slumbers of thy bed;
Hermes no more shall show the world his wings,
If that thy fancy in his feathers dwell,
But as this one I'll tear them all from him,   40
                    [*Plucks a feather from* Hermes' *wings.*]
Do thou but say, 'their colour pleaseth me'.
Hold here, my little love; these linked gems   [*Gives jewels.*]
My Juno ware upon her marriage-day,
Put thou about thy neck, my own sweet heart,
And trick thy arms and shoulders with my theft.
Ganymede. I would have a jewel for mine ear,
And a fine brooch to put in my hat,
And then I'll hug with you an hundred times.
Jupiter. And shall have, Ganymede, if thou wilt be my love.

                    Enter Venus.

Venus. Ay, this is it: you can sit toying there,   50
And playing with that female wanton boy,
Whiles my Æneas wanders on the seas,
And rests a prey to every billow's pride.
Juno, false Juno, in her chariot's pomp,
Drawn through the heavens by steeds of Boreas' brood,
Made Hebe to direct her airy wheels
Into the windy country of the clouds;
Where, finding Æolus entrench'd with storms,
And guarded with a thousand grisly ghosts,
She humbly did beseech him for our bane,   60
And charg'd him drown my son with all his train.
Then gan the winds break ope their brazen doors,
And all Æolia to be up in arms.
Poor Troy must now be sack'd upon the sea,
And Neptune's waves be envious men of war;
Epeus' horse, to Ætna's hill transform'd,
Prepared stands to wrack their wooden walls;
And Æolus, like Agamemnon, sounds

---

34 Juno's bird] the peacock   38 Hermes . . . wings] The messenger of the gods was usually depicted with a winged cap and with wings on his feet.   55 Boreas] the North Wind   56 Hebe] Juno's daughter   58 Æolus] god of winds, living on the island Æolia   60 bane] destruction   66–7 Epeus' horse . . . walls] The rocks of Mt. Etna will destroy the wooden ships as the horse made by Epeus destroyed the city of Troy

The surges, his fierce soldiers, to the spoil.
See how the night, Ulysses-like, comes forth,   70
And intercepts the day, as Dolon erst.
Ay, me! the stars suppris'd, like Rhesus' steeds,
Are drawn by darkness forth Astraeus' tents.
What shall I do to save thee, my sweet boy,
Whenas the waves do threat our crystal world,
And Proteus, raising hills of floods on high,
Intends ere long to sport him in the sky?
False Jupiter, reward'st thou virtue so?
What, is not piety exempt from woe?
Then die, Æneas, in thine innocence,   80
Since that religion hath no recompense.

Jupiter. Content thee, Cytherea, in thy care,
Since thy Æneas' wandering fate is firm,
Whose weary limbs shall shortly make repose
In those fair walls I promis'd him of yore.
But first in blood must his good fortune bud,
Before he be the lord of Turnus' town,
Or force her smile that hitherto hath frown'd.
Three winters shall he with the Rutiles war,
And in the end subdue them with his sword;   90
And full three summers likewise shall he waste
In managing those fierce barbarian minds;
Which once perform'd, poor Troy, so long suppress'd,
From forth her ashes shall advance her head,
And flourish once again, that erst was dead.
But bright Ascanius, beauty's better work,
Who with the sun divides one radiant shape,
Shall build his throne amidst those starry towers
That earth-born Atlas groaning underprops:
No bounds but heaven shall bound his empery,   100
Whose azur'd gates enchased with his name,
Shall make the morning haste her grey uprise
To feed her eyes with his engraven fame.
Thus in stout Hector's race three hundred years
The Roman sceptre royal shall remain,

70-2 Ulysses-like . . . steeds] Ulysses and Diomede captured Dolon, a Trojan spy, forced
the password from him, and were thus able to enter the Trojan camp and capture the
horses of Rhesus.   73 Astraeus] husband of Aurora and father of the stars   76 Proteus]
a sea-god   82 Cytherea] Venus, here given the name of the island, Cythera, where she
is said to have landed after her birth in the sea   87 Turnus] king of the Rutuli in Italy
88 her] i.e. Fortune

Till that a princess-priest conceiv'd by Mars,
Shall yield to dignity a double birth,
Who will eternish Troy in their attempts.
Venus. How may I credit these thy flattering terms,
When yet both sea and sands beset their ships,   110
And Phoebus, as in Stygian pools, refrains
To taint his tresses in the Terrene main?
Jupiter. I will take order for that presently.
Hermes, awake! and haste to Neptune's realm,
Whereas the Wind-god, warring now with fate,
Besiege the offspring of our kingly loins,
Charge him from me to turn his stormy powers,
And fetter them in Vulcan's sturdy brass,
That durst thus proudly wrong our kinsman's peace.   [*Exit* Hermes.]
Venus farewell; thy son shall be our care.   120
Come, Ganymede, we must about this gear.
                              Exeunt Jupiter *cum* Ganymede.
Venus. Disquiet seas, lay down your swelling looks,
And court Æneas with your calmy cheer,
Whose beauteous burden well might make you proud,
Had not the heavens, conceiv'd with hell-born clouds,
Veil'd his resplendent glory from your view.
For my sake pity him, Oceanus,
That erstwhile issu'd from thy watery loins,
And had my being from thy bubbling froth.
Triton, I know, hath fill'd his trump with Troy,   130
And therefore will take pity on his toil,
And call both Thetis and Cymothoe
To succour him in this extremity.

  Enter Æneas *with* Ascanius [*and* Achates], *with one or two more.*

What, do I see my son now come on shore?
Venus, how art thou compass'd with content,
The while thine eyes attract their sought-for joys!
Great Jupiter, still honour'd may'st thou be
For this so friendly aid in time of need!
Here in this bush disguised will I stand,
Whiles my Æneas spends himself in plaints,   140
And heaven and earth with his unrest acquaints.

---

106 princess-priest] Rhea Silvia, the vestal virgin, mother of Romulus and Remus
106 conceiv'd] made pregnant   112 Terrene] Mediterranean   127 Oceanus] a powerful
sea-god   129 thy . . . froth] Venus (called also Aphrodite) rose miraculously from the
froth—*aphros*—of the ocean.   132 Thetis and Cymothoe] sea-goddesses, the former
mother of Achilles   136 attract] absorb

Æneas. You sons of care, companions of my course,
    Priam's misfortune follows us by sea,
    And Helen's rape doth haunt ye at the heels.
    How many dangers have we overpass'd!
    Both barking Scylla, and the sounding rocks,
    The Cyclops' shelves, and grim Cerania's seat
    Have you o'ergone, and yet remain alive.
    Pluck up your hearts, since Fate still rests our friend,
    And changing heavens may those good days return,   150
    Which Pergama did vaunt in all her pride.
Achates. Brave prince of Troy, thou only art our god,
    That by thy virtues free'st us from annoy,
    And makes our hopes survive to coming joys:
    Do thou but smile, and cloudy heaven will clear,
    Whose night and day descendeth from thy brows.
    Though we be now in extreme misery,
    And rest the map of weather-beaten woe,
    Yet shall the aged sun shed forth his hair,
    To make us live unto our former heat,   160
    And every beast the forest doth send forth
    Bequeath her young ones to our scanted food.
Ascanius. Father, I faint; good father, give me meat.
Æneas. Alas, sweet boy, thou must be still a while,
    Till we have fire to dress the meat we kill'd.
    Gentle Achates, reach the tinder-box,
    That we may make a fire to warm us with,
    And roast our new-found victuals on this shore.
Venus. See what strange arts necessity finds out!
    How near, my sweet Æneas, art thou driven!   170
Æneas. Hold, take this candle and go light a fire;
    You shall have leaves and windfall boughs enow,
    Near to these woods, to roast your meat withal.
    Ascanius, go and dry thy drenched limbs,
    Whiles I with my Achates rove abroad,
    To know what coast the wind hath driven us on,
    Or whether men or beasts inhabit it.   [*Exeunt* Ascanius *and others.*]
Achates. The air is pleasant, and the soil most fit
    For cities and society's supports;
    Yet much I marvel that I cannot find   180

146 barking Scylla] Scylla was transformed from the waist down into dog-like monsters,
which barked unceasingly and devoured ships in the Straits of Messina.   147 Cyclops'
shelves] the rocky coast of Sicily where the Cyclopes, one-eyed giants, lived.   147 Cerania's
seat] a promontory of Epirus   151 Pergama] Troy

No steps of men imprinted in the earth.

Venus. Now is the time for me to play my part.
    Ho, young men! Saw you, as you came,
    Any of all my sisters wand'ring here,
    Having a quiver girded to her side,
    And clothed in a spotted leopard's skin?

Æneas. I neither saw nor heard of any such.
    But what may I, fair virgin, call your name,
    Whose looks set forth no mortal form to view,
    Nor speech bewrays aught human in thy birth?   190
    Thou art a goddess that delud'st our eyes,
    And shrouds thy beauty in this borrow'd shape;
    But whether thou the Sun's bright sister be,
    Or one of chaste Diana's fellow nymphs,
    Live happy in the height of all content,
    And lighten our extremes with this one boon,
    As to instruct us under what good heaven
    We breathe as now, and what this world is call'd
    On which by tempests' fury we are cast.
    Tell us, O tell us, that are ignorant;   200
    And this right hand shall make thy altars crack
    With mountain-heaps of milk-white sacrifice.

Venus. Such honour, stranger, do I not affect.
    It is the use for Tyrian maids to wear
    Their bow and quiver in this modest sort,
    And suit themselves in purple for the nonce,
    That they may trip more lightly o'er the lawnds,
    And overtake the tusked boar in chase.
    But for the land whereof thou dost inquire,
    It is the Punic kingdom, rich and strong,   210
    Adjoining on Agenor's stately town,
    The kingly seat of southern Libya,
    Whereas Sidonian Dido rules as queen.
    But what are you that ask of me these things?
    Whence may you come, or whither will you go?

Æneas. Of Troy am I, Æneas is my name,
    Who, driven by war from forth my native world,
    Put sails to sea to seek out Italy;
    And my divine descent from sceptred Jove.
    With twice twelve Phrygian ships I plough'd the deep,   220
    And made that way my mother Venus led;

207 lawnds] open spaces   211 Agenor's . . . town] Carthage (Dido was descended from
Agenor)   213 Sidonian] from Sidon, in Phoenicia

But of them all scarce seven do anchor safe,
And they so wrack'd and welter'd by the waves,
As every tide tilts 'twixt their oaken sides,
And all of them, unburden'd of their load,
Are ballassed with billows' wat'ry weight.
But hapless I, God wot, poor and unknown,
Do trace these Libyan deserts all despis'd,
Exil'd forth Europe and wide Asia both,
And have not any coverture but heaven.   230

Venus. Fortune hath favour'd thee, whate'er thou be,
In sending thee unto this courteous coast.
A' God's name, on, and haste thee to the court,
Where Dido will receive ye with her smiles;
And for thy ships, which thou supposest lost,
Not one of them hath perish'd in the storm,
But are arrived safe not far from hence.
And so I leave thee to thy fortune's lot,
Wishing good luck unto thy wand'ring steps.   *Exit.*

Æneas. Achates, 'tis my mother that is fled;   240
I know her by the movings of her feet.
Stay, gentle Venus, fly not from thy son!
Too cruel, why wilt thou forsake me thus,
Or in these shades deceiv'st mine eye so oft?
Why talk we not together hand in hand,
And tell our griefs in more familiar terms?
But thou art gone, and leav'st me here alone
To dull the air with my discoursive moan.   *Exeunt.*

[Scene ii]

Enter Ilioneus *and* Cloanthus [*with* Iarbas *and* Sergestus].

Ilioneus. Follow, ye Trojans, follow this brave lord,
And plain to him the sum of your distress.
Iarbas. Why, what are you, or wherefore do you sue?
Ilioneus. Wretches of Troy, envied of the winds,
That crave such favour at your honour's feet,
As poor distressed misery may plead:
Save, save, O save our ships from cruel fire,
That do complain the wounds of thousand waves,
And spare our lives whom every spite pursues.
We come not, we, to wrong your Libyan gods,   10
Or steal your household Lares from their shrines;

1 brave] well-dressed   11 Lares] guardians of the home

Our hands are not prepar'd to lawless spoil,
Nor armed to offend in any kind;
Such force is far from our unweapon'd thoughts,
Whose fading weal, of victory forsook,
Forbids all hope to harbour near our hearts.

Iarbas. But tell me, Trojans—Trojans if you be—
Unto what fruitful quarters were ye bound,
Before that Boreas buckled with your sails?

Cloanthus. There is a place, Hesperia term'd by us,   20
An ancient empire, famoused for arms,
And fertile in fair Ceres' furrow'd wealth,
Which now we call Italia, of his name
That in such peace long time did rule the same.
Thither made we,
When suddenly gloomy Orion rose,
And led our ships into the shallow sands,
Whereas the southern wind with brackish breath,
Dispers'd them all amongst the wrackful rocks.
From thence a few of us escap'd to land;   30
The rest, we fear, are folded in the floods.

Iarbas. Brave men-at-arms, abandon fruitless fears,
Since Carthage knows to entertain distress.

Sergestus. Ay, but the barbarous sort do threat our ships,
And will not let us lodge upon the sands;
In multitudes they swarm unto the shore,
And from the first earth interdict our feet.

Iarbas. Myself will see they shall not trouble ye:
Your men and you shall banquet in our court,
And every Trojan be as welcome here   40
As Jupiter to silly Baucis' house.
Come in with me; I'll bring you to my Queen,
Who shall confirm my words with further deeds.

Sergestus. Thanks, gentle lord, for such unlook'd-for grace.
Might we but once more see Æneas' face,
Then would we hope to quite such friendly turns,
As shall surpass the wonder of our speech.

                                                        [*Exeunt.*]

---

15 weal] prosperity   19 buckled] grappled   23 his name] Italus, chief of the tribe
inhabiting Italy   26 gloomy Orion] The constellation was usually associated with storms.
37 first earth] beach   41 Jupiter . . . house] The simple ('silly') Baucis entertained Jupiter
in disguise.   46 quite] requite

[Act II Scene i]

Enter Æneas, Achates, and Ascanius [*and others*].

Æneas. Where am I now? These should be Carthage walls.
Achates. Why stands my sweet Æneas thus amaz'd?
Æneas. O my Achates, Theban Niobe,
    Who for her sons' death wept out life and breath,
    And, dry with grief, was turn'd into a stone,
    Had not such passions in her head as I!
    Methinks that town there should be Troy, yon Ida's hill,
    There Xanthus' stream, because here's Priamus—
    And when I know it is not, then I die.
Achates. And in this humour is Achates too;   10
    I cannot choose but fall upon my knees,
    And kiss his hand. O where is Hecuba?
    Here she was wont to sit, but, saving air,
    Is nothing here; and what is this but stone?
Æneas. O yet this stone doth make Æneas weep!
    And would my prayers (as Pygmalion's did)
    Could give it life, that under his conduct
    We might sail back to Troy, and be reveng'd
    On these hard-hearted Grecians which rejoice
    That nothing now is left of Priamus!   20
    O, Priamus is left, and this is he!
    Come, come aboard! Pursue the hateful Greeks!
Achates. What means Æneas?
Æneas. Achates, though mine eyes say this is stone,
    Yet thinks my mind that this is Priamus;
    And when my grieved heart sighs and says no,
    Then would it leap out to give Priam life.
    O, were I not at all, so thou mightst be!
    Achates, see, King Priam wags his hand!
    He is alive; Troy is not overcome!   30
Achates. Thy mind, Æneas, that would have it so,
    Deludes thy eyesight; Priamus is dead.
Æneas. Ah, Troy is sack'd, and Priamus is dead!
    And why should poor Æneas be alive?
Ascanius. Sweet father, leave to weep; this is not he,
    For were it Priam, he would smile on me.

1–38 In the *Æneid* the hero laments the fall of Troy when he sees the story of the city painted on the walls of Juno's temple in Carthage.   16 Pygmalion] the sculptor whose prayers gave life to a statue he had created

Achates. Æneas, see, here come the citizens.
Leave to lament, lest they laugh at our fears.

Enter Cloanthus, Sergestus, Ilioneus [*and others*].

Æneas. Lords of this town, or whatsoever style
Belongs unto your name, vouchsafe of ruth   40
To tell us who inhabits this fair town,
What kind of people, and who governs them;
For we are strangers driven on this shore,
And scarcely know within what clime we are.

Ilioneus. I heard Æneas' voice, but see him not,
For none of these can be our general.

Achates. Like Ilioneus speaks this noble man,
But Ilioneus goes not in such robes.

Sergestus. You are Achates, or I deceiv'd.

Achates. Æneas, see, Sergestus, or his ghost!   50

Ilioneus. He names Æneas; let us kiss his feet.

Cloanthus. It is our captain; see, Ascanius!

Sergestus. Live long Æneas and Ascanius!

Æneas. Achates, speak, for I am overjoy'd.

Achates. O Ilioneus, art thou yet alive?

Ilioneus. Blest be the time I see Achates' face!

Cloanthus. Why turns Æneas from his trusty friends?

Æneas. Sergestus, Ilioneus, and the rest,
Your sight amaz'd me. O, what destinies
Have brought my sweet companions in such plight?   60
O tell me, for I long to be resolv'd!

Ilioneus. Lovely Æneas, these are Carthage walls,
And here Queen Dido wears th' imperial crown,
Who for Troy's sake hath entertain'd us all,
And clad us in these wealthy robes we wear.
Oft hath she ask'd us under whom we serv'd;
And when we told her, she would weep for grief,
Thinking the sea had swallow'd up thy ships;
And now she sees thee, how will she rejoice!

Sergestus. See, where her servitors pass through the hall, 70
Bearing a banquet; Dido is not far.

Ilioneus. Look where she comes! Æneas, view her well.

Æneas. Well may I view her; but she sees not me.

Enter Dido [*with* Anna *and* Iarbas] *and her train.*

Dido. What stranger art thou, that dost eye me thus?

Æneas. Sometime I was a Trojan, mighty Queen,
But Troy is not: what shall I say I am?

Ilioneus. Renowmed Dido, 'tis our general,
  Warlike Æneas.
Dido. Warlike Æneas, and in these base robes!
  Go fetch the garment which Sichaeus ware.   80
               [*Exit an* Attendant.]
  Brave prince, welcome to Carthage and to me,
  Both happy that Æneas is our guest.
  Sit in this chair and banquet with a queen:
  Æneas is Æneas, were he clad
  In weeds as bad as ever Irus ware.
Æneas. This is no seat for one that's comfortless.
  May it please your grace to let Æneas wait;
  For though my birth be great, my fortune's mean,
  Too mean to be companion to a queen.
Dido. Thy fortune may be greater than thy birth.   90
  Sit down Æneas, sit in Dido's place,
  And, if this be thy son, as I suppose,
  Here let him sit. Be merry, lovely child.
Æneas. This place beseems me not; O pardon me!
Dido. I'll have it so; Æneas, be content.
Ascanius. Madam, you shall be my mother.
Dido. And so I will, sweet child. Be merry, man:
  Here's to thy better fortune and good stars.   [*Drinks.*]
Æneas. In all humility, I thank your grace.
Dido. Remember who thou art; speak like thyself: 100
  Humility belongs to common grooms.
Æneas. And who so miserable as Æneas is?
Dido. Lies it in Dido's hands to make thee blest,
  Then be assur'd thou art not miserable.
Æneas. O Priamus, O Troy, O Hecuba!
Dido. May I entreat thee to discourse at large,
  And truly too, how Troy was overcome?
  For many tales go of that city's fall,
  And scarcely do agree upon one point.
  Some say Antenor did betray the town;   110
  Others report 'twas Sinon's perjury;
  But all in this, that Troy is overcome,
  And Priam dead; yet how, we hear no news.
Æneas. A woeful tale bids Dido to unfold,
  Whose memory, like pale Death's stony mace,

77 Renowmed] a variant of 'renowned'   80 Scihaeus] Dido's late husband
85 Irus] a beggar, one of Penelope's suitors while Ulysses was away   111 Sinon's
perjury] cf. ll. 144 ff.

  Beats forth my senses from this troubled soul,
  And makes Æneas sink at Dido's feet.
Dido. What, faints Æneas to remember Troy,
  In whose defence he fought so valiantly?
  Look up, and speak.   120
Æneas. Then speak, Æneas, with Achilles' tongue;
  And, Dido, and you Carthaginian peers,
  Hear me; but yet with Myrmidons' harsh ears,
  Daily inur'd to broils and massacres,
  Lest you be mov'd too much with my sad tale.
  The Grecian soldiers, tir'd with ten years' war,
  Began to cry, 'Let us unto our ships,
  Troy is invincible, why stay we here?'
  With whose outcries Atrides being appall'd,
  Summon'd the captains to his princely tent,   130
  Who, looking on the scars we Trojans gave,
  Seeing the number of their men decreas'd,
  And the remainder weak and out of heart,
  Gave up their voices to dislodge the camp,
  And so in troops all march'd to Tenedos;
  Where when they came, Ulysses on the sand
  Assay'd with honey words to turn them back;
  And as he spoke to further his intent,
  The winds did drive huge billows to the shore,
  And heaven was darken'd with tempestuous clouds. 140
  Then he alleg'd the gods would have them stay,
  And prophesied Troy should be overcome;
  And therewithal he call'd false Sinon forth,
  A man compact of craft and perjury,
  Whose ticing tongue was made of Hermes' pipe,
  To force an hundred watchful eyes to sleep;
  And him, Epeus having made the horse,
  With sacrificing wreaths upon his head,
  Ulysses sent to our unhappy town;
  Who, grovelling in the mire of Xanthus' banks,   150
  His hands bound at his back, and both his eyes
  Turn'd up to heaven as one resolv'd to die,
  Our Phrygian shepherds hal'd within the gates,
  And brought unto the court of Priamus;
  To whom he us'd action so pitiful,

123 Myrmidons] Achilles' bodyguard, renowned for brutality   129 Atrides] Agamemnon (son of Atreus)   145 Hermes' pipe] Playing on his reed-pipe, Hermes charmed the hundred-eyed Argus to sleep and then killed him.

      Looks so remorseful, vows so forcible,
      As therewithal the old man overcome,
      Kiss'd him, embrac'd him, and unloos'd his bands:
      And then—O Dido, pardon me!
Dido. Nay, leave not here; resolve me of the rest.   160
Æneas. O, th' enchanting words of that base slave
      Made him to think Epeus' pine-tree horse
      A sacrifice t' appease Minerva's wrath!
      The rather for that one Laocoön,
      Breaking a spear upon his hollow breast,
      Was with two winged serpents stung to death.
      Whereat aghast, we were commanded straight
      With reverence to draw it into Troy,
      In which unhappy work was I employ'd.
      These hands did help to hale it to the gates,   170
      Through which it could not enter, 'twas so huge—
      O had it never enter'd, Troy had stood!
      But Priamus, impatient of delay,
      Enforc'd a wide breach in that rampir'd wall
      Which thousand battering-rams could never pierce,
      And so came in this fatal instrument,
      At whose accursed feet, as overjoy'd,
      We banqueted, till, overcome with wine,
      Some surfeited, and others soundly slept.
      Which Sinon viewing, caus'd the Greekish spies   180
      To haste to Tenedos and tell the camp.
      Then he unlock'd the horse; and suddenly
      From out his entrails, Neoptolemus,
      Setting his spear upon the ground, leapt forth,
      And after him a thousand Grecians more,
      In whose stern faces shin'd the quenchless fire
      That after burnt the pride of Asia.
      By this the camp was come unto the walls,
      And through the breach did march into the streets,
      Where, meeting with the rest, 'Kill, kill!' they cried.   190
      Frighted with this confused noise, I rose,
      And looking from a turret might behold
      Young infants swimming in their parents' blood,
      Headless carcasses pil'd up in heaps,
      Virgins half-dead dragg'd by their golden hair
      And with main force flung on a ring of pikes,
      Old men with swords thrust through their aged sides,
      Kneeling for mercy to a Greekish lad

Who with steel pole-axes dash'd out their brains.
Then buckled I mine armour, drew my sword,   200
And thinking to go down, came Hector's ghost,
With ashy visage, blueish sulphur eyes,
His arms torn from his shoulders, and his breast
Furrow'd with wounds, and, that which made me weep,
Thongs at his heels, by which Achilles' horse
Drew him in triumph through the Greekish camp,
Burst from the earth, crying 'Æneas, fly!
Troy is a-fire, the Grecians have the town!'
Dido. O Hector, who weeps not to hear thy name?
Æneas. Yet flung I forth, and, desperate of my life,   210
Ran in the thickest throngs, and with this sword
Sent many of their savage ghosts to hell.
At last came Pyrrhus, fell and full of ire,
His harness dropping blood, and on his spear
The mangled head of Priam's youngest son;
And after him his band of Myrmidons,
With balls of wild-fire in their murdering paws,
Which made the funeral flame that burnt fair Troy:
All which hemm'd me about, crying, 'This is he!'
Dido. Ah, how could poor Æneas scape their hands?   220
Æneas. My mother Venus, jealous of my health,
Convey'd me from their crooked nets and bands;
So I escap'd the furious Pyrrhus' wrath,
Who then ran to the palace of the king,
And at Jove's altar finding Priamus,
About whose wither'd neck hung Hecuba,
Folding his hand in hers, and jointly both
Beating their breasts and falling on the ground,
He with his falchion's point rais'd up at once,
And with Megaera's eyes, star'd in their face,   230
Threat'ning a thousand deaths at every glance;
To whom the aged king thus trembling spoke:
'Achilles' son, remember what I was,
Father of fifty sons, but they are slain;
Lord of my fortune, but my fortune's turn'd;
King of this city, but my Troy is fir'd;
And now am neither father, lord, nor king:

213 Pyrrhus] Neoptolemus, Achilles' son   215 Priam's youngest son] Virgil mentions
the murder of one of Priam's sons in front of his father, but the pathos of 'youngest son' is
Marlowe's, and so is the gruesome detail of the head carried on the spear.   230 Megaera]
one of the Furies

Yet who so wretched but desires to live?
O let me live, great Neoptolemus!'
Not mov'd at all, but smiling at his tears,   240
This butcher, whilst his hands were yet held up,
Treading upon his breast, struck off his hands.
Dido. O end, Æneas! I can hear no more.
Æneas. At which the frantic queen leap'd on his face,
And in his eyelids hanging by the nails,
A little while prolong'd her husband's life.
At last the soldiers pull'd her by the heels,
And swung her howling in the empty air,
Which sent an echo to the wounded king:
Whereat he lifted up his bed-rid limbs,   250
And would have grappled with Achilles' son,
Forgetting both his want of strength and hands;
Which he disdaining, whisk'd his sword about,
And with the wound thereof the king fell down.
Then from the navel to the throat at once
He ripp'd old Priam, at whose latter gasp
Jove's marble statue gan to bend the brow,
As loathing Pyrrhus for this wicked act.
Yet he, undaunted, took his father's flag,
And dipp'd it in the old king's chill-cold blood,   260
And then in triumph ran into the streets,
Through which he could not pass for slaughter'd men;
So, leaning on his sword, he stood stone still,
Viewing the fire wherewith rich Ilion burnt.
By this I got my father on my back,
This young boy in mine arms, and by the hand
Led fair Creusa, my beloved wife;
When thou, Achates, with thy sword mad'st way,
And we were round environ'd with the Greeks.
O, there I lost my wife! And had not we   270
Fought manfully, I had not told this tale.
Yet manhood would not serve; of force we fled;
And as we went unto our ships, thou know'st
We saw Cassandra sprawling in the streets,
Whom Ajax ravish'd in Diana's fane,
Her cheeks swoll'n with sighs, her hair all rent,
Whom I took up to bear unto our ships;
But suddenly the Grecians follow'd us,
And I, alas, was forc'd to let her lie!
Then got we to our ships and, being aboard,   280

Polyxena cried out, 'Æneas stay!
The Greeks pursue me; stay, and take me in!'
Mov'd with her voice, I leap'd into the sea,
Thinking to bear her on my back aboard,
For all our ships were launch'd into the deep,
And, as I swom, she, standing on the shore,
Was by the cruel Myrmidons surpris'd
And after by that Pyrrhus sacrific'd.
Dido. I die with melting ruth; Æneas, leave.
Anna. O, what became of aged Hecuba?   290
Iarbas. How got Æneas to the fleet again?
Dido. But how scap'd Helen, she that caus'd this war?
Æneas. Achates, speak; sorrow hath tir'd me quite.
Achates. What happen'd to the queen we cannot show;
We hear they led her captive into Greece.
As for Æneas, he swom quickly back;
And Helena betray'd Deiphobus,
Her lover after Alexander died,
And so was reconcil'd to Menelaus.
Dido. O, had that ticing strumpet ne'er been born!   300
Trojan, thy ruthful tale hath made me sad:
Come, let us think upon some pleasing sport,
To rid me from these melancholy thoughts.

Exeunt omnes [*except* Ascanius]. *Enter* Venus [*with* Cupid] *at another
door and takes* Ascanius *by the sleeve.*

Venus. Fair child, stay thou with Dido's waiting maid;
I'll give thee sugar-almonds, sweet conserves,
A silver girdle, and a golden purse,
And this young prince shall be thy playfellow.
Ascanius. Are you Queen Dido's son?
Cupid. Ay, and my mother gave me this fine bow.
Ascanius. Shall I have such a quiver and a bow?   310
Venus. Such bow, such quiver, and such golden shafts,
Will Dido give to sweet Ascanius.
For Dido's sake I take thee in my arms,
And stick these spangled feathers in thy hat.
Eat comfits in mine arms, and I will sing.
Now is he fast asleep, and in this grove,
Amongst green brakes, I'll lay Ascanius,
And strew him with sweet-smelling violets,
Blushing roses, purple hyacinth;

298 Alexander] Paris

These milk-white doves shall be his centronels,   320
Who, if that any seek to do him hurt,
Will quickly fly to Cytherea's fist.
Now, Cupid, turn thee to Ascanius' shape,
And go to Dido, who instead of him,
Will set thee on her lap and play with thee;
Then touch her white breast with this arrow head,
That she may dote upon Æneas' love,
And by that means repair his broken ships,
Victual his soldiers, give him wealthy gifts,
And he at last depart to Italy,   330
Or else in Carthage make his kingly throne.
Cupid. I will, fair mother; and so play my part
As every touch shall wound Queen Dido's heart.   [*Exit.*]
Venus. Sleep, my sweet nephew, in these cooling shades,
Free from the murmur of these running streams,
The cry of beasts, the rattling of the winds,
Or whisking of these leaves: all shall be still,
And nothing interrupt thy quiet sleep,
Till I return, and take thee hence again.   *Exit.*

[Act III Scene i]

Enter Cupid *solus* [*disguised as Ascanius*].

Cupid. Now Cupid, cause the Carthaginian Queen
To be enamour'd of thy brother's looks;
Convey this golden arrow in thy sleeve,
Lest she imagine thou art Venus' son;
And when she strokes thee softly on the head,
Then shall I touch her breast and conquer her.

Enter Iarbas, Anna, *and* Dido.

Iarbas. How long, fair Dido, shall I pine for thee?
'Tis not enough that thou dost grant me love,
But that I may enjoy what I desire:
That love is childish which consists in words.   10
Dido. Iarbas, know that thou, of all my wooers—
And yet have I had many mightier kings—
Hast had the greatest favours I could give.
I fear me, Dido hath been counted light
In being too familiar with Iarbas;

320 centronels] sentinels

    Albeit the gods do know no wanton thought
    Had ever residence in Dido's breast.
Iarbas. But Dido is the favour I request.
Dido. Fear not Iarbas; Dido may be thine.
Anna. Look, sister, how Æneas' little son   20
    Plays with your garments and embraceth you.
Cupid. No, Dido will not take me in her arms;
    I shall not be her son, she loves me not.
Dido. Weep not, sweet boy, thou shalt be Dido's son;
    Sit in my lap, and let me hear thee sing.

                                             [Cupid *sings.*]

    No more, my child; now talk another while,
    And tell me where learn'dst thou this pretty song.
Cupid. My cousin Helen taught it me in Troy.
Dido. How lovely is Ascanius when he smiles!
Cupid. Will Dido let me hang about her neck?
Dido. Ay, wag, and give thee leave to kiss her too.   30
Cupid. What will you give me? Now I'll have this fan.
Dido. Take it, Ascanius, for thy father's sake.
Iarbas. Come, Dido, leave Ascanius; let us walk.
Dido. Go thou away; Ascanius shall stay.
Iarbas. Ungentle Queen, is this thy love to me?
Dido. O stay, Iarbas, and I'll go with thee!
Cupid. And if my mother go, I'll follow her.
Dido. Why stay'st thou here? Thou art no love of mine.
Iarbas. Iarbas, die, seeing she abandons thee!   40
Dido. No, live, Iarbas. What hast thou deserv'd
    That I should say thou art no love of mine?
    Something thou hast deserv'd—Away, I say!
    Depart from Carthage, come not in my sight.
Iarbas. Am I not King of rich Gaetulia?
Dido. Iarbas, pardon me, and stay a while.
Cupid. Mother, look here.
Dido. What tell'st thou me of rich Gaetulia?
    Am not I Queen of Libya? Then depart.
Iarbas. I go to feed the humour of my love,   50
    Yet not from Carthage for a thousand worlds.
Dido. Iarbas!
Iarbas. Doth Dido call me back?
Dido. No; but I charge thee never look on me.
Iarbas. Then pull out both mine eyes, or let me die.   *Exit* Iarbas.
Anna. Wherefore doth Dido bid Iarbas go?
Dido. Because his loathsome sight offends mine eye,

And in my thoughts is shrin'd another love.
O Anna, didst thou know how sweet love were,
Full soon wouldst thou abjure this single life. 60
Anna. Poor soul, I know too well the sour of love:
O that Iarbas could but fancy me!
Dido. Is not Æneas fair and beautiful?
Anna. Yes, and Iarbas foul and favourless.
Dido. Is he not eloquent in all his speech?
Anna. Yes, and Iarbas rude and rustical.
Dido. Name not Iarbas: but, sweet Anna, say,
Is not Æneas worthy Dido's love?
Anna. O sister, were you empress of the world,
Æneas well deserves to be your love. 70
So lovely is he that, where'er he goes,
The people swarm to gaze him in the face.
Dido. But tell them none shall gaze on him but I,
Lest their gross eye-beams taint my lover's cheeks.
Anna, good sister Anna, go for him,
Lest with these sweet thoughts I melt clean away.
Anna. Then sister, you'll abjure Iarbas' love?
Dido. Yet must I hear that loathsome name again?
Run for Æneas, or I'll fly to him. *Exit* Anna.
Cupid. You shall not hurt my father when he comes. 80
Dido. No, for thy sake I'll love thy father well.
O dull-conceited Dido, that till now
Didst never think Æneas beautiful!
But now, for quittance of this oversight,
I'll make me bracelets of his golden hair;
His glistering eyes shall be my looking-glass;
His lips an altar, where I'll offer up
As many kisses as the sea hath sands;
Instead of music I will hear him speak;
His looks shall be my only library; 90
And thou, Æneas, Dido's treasury,
In whose fair bosom I will lock more wealth
Than twenty thousand Indias can afford.
O, here he comes! Love, love, give Dido leave
To be more modest than her thoughts admit,
Lest I be made a wonder to the world.

[*Enter* Æneas, Achates, Sergestus, Ilioneus, *and* Cloanthus.]

Achates, how doth Carthage please your lord?
Achates. That will Æneas show your majesty.

Dido. Æneas, art thou there?

Æneas. I understand your highness sent for me.   100

Dido. No; but now thou art here, tell me, in sooth,
    In what might Dido highly pleasure thee.

Æneas. So much have I receiv'd at Dido's hands
    As, without blushing, I can ask no more.
    Yet, queen of Afric, are my ships unrigg'd,
    My sails all rent in sunder with the wind,
    My oars broken, and my tackling lost,
    Yea, all my navy split with rocks and shelves;
    Nor stern nor anchor have our maimed fleet;
    Our masts the furious winds struck overboard: 110
    Which piteous wants if Dido will supply,
    We will account her author of our lives.

Dido. Æneas, I'll repair thy Trojan ships,
    Conditionally that thou wilt stay with me,
    And let Achates sail to Italy:
    I'll give thee tackling made of rivell'd gold,
    Wound on the barks of odoriferous trees;
    Oars of massy ivory, full of holes,
    Through which the water shall delight to play;
    Thy anchors shall be hew'd from crystal rocks,   120
    Which if thou lose shall shine above the waves;
    The masts, whereon thy swelling sails shall hang,
    Hollow pyramides of silver plate;
    The sails of folded lawn, where shall be wrought
    The wars of Troy, but not Troy's overthrow;
    For ballace, empty Dido's treasury:
    Take what ye will, but leave Æneas here.
    Achates, thou shalt be so meanly clad,
    As sea-born nymphs shall swarm about thy ships,
    And wanton mermaids court thee with sweet songs,   130
    Flinging in favours of more sovereign worth
    Than Thetis hangs about Apollo's neck,
    So that Æneas may but stay with me.

Æneas. Wherefore would Dido have Æneas stay?

Dido. To war against my bordering enemies.
    Æneas, think not Dido is in love;
    For if that any man could conquer me,
    I had been wedded ere Æneas came.
    See where the pictures of my suitors hang;

115 rivell'd] twisted   127 meanly] suitably   132 Than Thetis . . . neck] i.e., than the
sea about the setting sun (Apollo)

And are not these as fair as fair may be?   140
Achates. I saw this man at Troy ere Troy was sack'd.
Sergestus. I this in Greece when Paris stole fair Helen.
Ilioneus. This man and I were at Olympus' games.
Sergestus. I know this face; he is a Persian born:
    I travell'd with him to Ætolia.
Cloanthus. And I in Athens with this gentleman,
    Unless I be deceiv'd, disputed once.
Dido. But speak, Æneas; know you none of these?
Æneas. No, madam; but it seems that these are kings.
Dido. All these, and others which I never saw,   150
    Have been most urgent suitors for my love;
    Some came in person, others sent their legates,
    Yet none obtain'd me. I am free from all;
    And yet, God knows, entangled unto one.
    This was an orator, and thought by words
    To compass me, but yet he was deceiv'd;
    And this a Spartan courtier vain and wild,
    But his fantastic humours pleas'd not me;
    This was Alcion, a musician,
    But play'd he ne'er so sweet, I let him go;   160
    This was the wealthy king of Thessaly,
    But I had gold enough, and cast him off;
    This Meleager's son, a warlike prince,
    But weapons gree not with my tender years.
    The rest are such as all the world well knows:
    Yet how I swear, by heaven and him I love,
    I was as far from love as they from hate.
Æneas. O happy shall he be whom Dido loves!
Dido. Then never say that thou art miserable,
    Because it may be thou shalt be my love.   170
    Yet boast not of it, for I love thee not—
    And yet I hate thee not. O if I speak
    I shall betray myself! Æneas, speak.
    We two will go a-hunting in the woods,
    But not so much for thee—thou art but one—
    As for Achates and his followers.   *Exeunt.*

[Scene ii]

Enter Juno *to Ascanius asleep.*

Juno. Here lies my hate, Æneas' cursed brat,
    The boy wherein false Destiny delights,

The heir of Fury, the favourite of the Fates,
That ugly imp that shall outwear my wrath,
And wrong my deity with high disgrace.
But I will take another order now,
And raze th' eternal register of Time.
Troy shall no more call him her second hope,
Nor Venus triumph in his tender youth;
For here, in spite of heaven, I'll murder him,   10
And feed infection with his let-out life.
Say, Paris, now shall Venus have the ball?
Say, vengeance, now shall her Ascanius die?
O no! God wot, I cannot watch my time,
Nor quit good turns with double fee down told!
Tut, I am simple, without mind to hurt,
And have no gall at all to grieve my foes!
But lustful Jove and his adulterous child
Shall find it written on confusion's front,
That only Juno rules in Rhamnus town.   20

Enter Venus.

Venus. What should this mean? My doves are back return'd,
Who warn me of such danger prest at hand
To harm my sweet Ascanius' lovely life.
Juno, my mortal foe, what make you here?
Avaunt, old witch, and trouble not my wits.
Juno. Fie, Venus, that such causeless words of wrath
Should e'er defile so fair a mouth as thine!
Are not we both sprung of celestial race,
And banquet as two sisters with the gods?
Why is it then displeasure should disjoin   30
Whom kindred and acquaintance co-unites?
Venus. Out, hateful hag! Thou wouldst have slain my son,
Had not my doves discover'd thy intent.
But I will tear thy eyes fro forth thy head,
And feast the birds with their blood-shotten balls,
If thou but lay thy fingers on my boy.
Juno. Is this then all the thanks that I shall have
For saving him from snakes' and serpents' stings,
That would have kill'd him sleeping as he lay?
What though I was offended with thy son,   40
And wrought him mickle woe on sea and land,

20 Rhamnus town] place in Attica famed for its statue of Nemesis, goddess of revenge
22 prest] near

When, for the hate of Trojan Ganymede,
That was advanced by my Hebe's shame,
And Paris' judgement of the heavenly ball,
I muster'd all the winds unto his wrack,
And urg'd each element to his annoy?
Yet now I do repent me of his ruth,
And wish that I had never wrong'd him so.
Bootless I saw it was to war with fate,
That hath so many unresisted friends: 50
Wherefore I chang'd my counsel with the time,
And planted love where envy erst had sprung.

Venus. Sister of Jove, if that thy love be such
As these thy protestations do paint forth,
We two as friends one fortune will divide;
Cupid shall lay his arrows in thy lap,
And to a sceptre change his golden shafts;
Fancy and modesty shall live as mates,
And thy fair peacocks by my pigeons perch.
Love my Æneas, and desire is thine;   60
The day, the night, my swans, my sweets, are thine.

Juno. More than melodious are these words to me,
That overcloy my soul with their content.
Venus, sweet Venus, how may I deserve
Such amorous favours at thy beauteous hand?
But that thou mayst more easily perceive
How highly I do prize this amity,
Hark to a motion of eternal league,
Which I will make in quittance of thy love.
Thy son, thou know'st, with Dido now remains,   70
And feeds his eyes with favours of her court;
She likewise in admiring spends her time,
And cannot talk nor think of aught but him;
Why should not they, then, join in marriage,
And bring forth mighty kings to Carthage town,
Whom casualty of sea hath made such friends?
And, Venus, let there be a match confirm'd
Betwixt these two, whose loves are so alike;
And both our deities, conjoin'd in one,
Shall chain felicity unto their throne.   80

Venus. Well could I like this reconcilement's means,

---

43 Hebe's shame] Juno's daughter lost her job as cup-bearer to the gods when she 'stombled
at a starre' and spilt the wine.   44 the heavenly ball] the prize which Paris gave to Venus

But much I fear my son will ne'er consent,
Whose armed soul, already on the sea,
Darts forth her light to Lavinia's shore.
Juno. Fair Queen of love, I will divorce these doubts,
And find the way to weary such fond thoughts.
This day they both a-hunting forth will ride
Into these woods, adjoining to these walls;
When, in the midst of all their gamesome sports,
I'll make the clouds dissolve their wat'ry works,   90
And drench Silvanus' dwellings with their showers.
Then in one cave the Queen and he shall meet,
And interchangeably discourse their thoughts,
Whose short conclusion will seal up their hearts
Unto the purpose which we now propound.
Venus. Sister, I see you savour of my wiles;
Be it as you will have for this once.
Meantime, Ascanius shall be my charge,
Whom I will bear to Ida in mine arms,
And couch him in Adonis' purple down.   100

Exeunt.

[Scene iii]

Enter Dido, Æneas, Anna, Iarbas, Achates, [Cupid *as Ascanius*]
and followers.

Dido. Æneas, think not but I honour thee
That thus in person go with thee to hunt.
My princely robes thou see'st are laid aside,
Whose glittering pomp Diana's shrouds supplies;
All fellows now, dispos'd alike to sport;
The woods are wide, and we have store of game.
Fair Trojan, hold my golden bow a while,
Until I gird my quiver to my side.
Lords, go before; we two must talk alone.
Iarbas. Ungentle, can she wrong Iarbas so?   10
I'll die before a stranger have that grace.
'We two will talk alone'—what words be these?
Dido. What makes Iarbas here of all the rest?
We could have gone without your company.
Æneas. But love and duty led him on perhaps

84 Lavinia] Betrothed to Turnus at the time, she later married Æneas.   91 Silvanus'
dwellings] the woods   100 Adonis' purple down] i.e. anemones (to which Venus
metamorphosed the dead Adonis)   III. iii, 4 Diana's shrouds] robes worn by the goddess
of hunting

       To press beyond acceptance to your sight.

Iarbas. Why, man of Troy, do I offend thine eyes?
       Or art thou griev'd thy betters press so nigh?

Dido. How now, Gaetulian, are ye grown so brave,
       To challenge us with your comparisons?   20
       Peasant, go seek companions like thyself,
       And meddle not with any that I love.
       Æneas, be not mov'd at what he says,
       For otherwhile he will be out of joint.

Iarbas. Women may wrong by privilege of love;
       But should that man of men, Dido except,
       Have taunted me in these opprobrious terms,
       I would have either drunk his dying blood,
       Or else I would have given my life in gage.

Dido. Huntsmen, why pitch you not your toils apace,   30
       And rouse the light-foot deer from forth their lair?

Anna. Sister, see, see Ascanius in his pomp,
       Bearing his hunt-spear bravely in his hand!

Dido. Yea, little son, are you so forward now?

Cupid. Ay, mother; I shall one day be a man,
       And better able unto other arms;
       Meantime these wanton weapons serve my war,
       Which I will break betwixt a lion's jaws.

Dido. What, dar'st thou look a lion in the face?

Cupid. Ay, and outface him too, do what he can.   40

Anna. How like his father speaketh he in all!

Æneas. And mought I live to see him sack rich Thebes,
       And load his spear with Grecian princes' heads,
       Then would I wish me with Anchises' tomb,
       And dead to honour that hath brought me up.

Iarbas. And might I live to see thee shipp'd away,
       And hoist aloft on Neptune's hideous hills,
       Then would I wish me in fair Dido's arms,
       And dead to scorn that hath pursu'd me so.

Æneas. Stout friend Achates, dost thou know this wood?   50

Achates. As I remember, here you shot the deer
       That sav'd your famish'd soldiers' lives from death,
       When first you set your foot upon the shore;
       And here we met fair Venus, virgin-like,
       Bearing her bow and quiver at her back.

Æneas. O, how these irksome labours now delight,
       And overjoy my thoughts with their escape!
       Who would not undergo all kind of toil,

To be well stor'd with such a winter's tale?

Dido. Æneas, leave these dumps and let's away,   60
  Some to the mountains, some unto the soil,
  You to the valleys,—thou [*to* Iarbas] unto the house.

Exeunt omnes: manet Iarbas.

Iarbas. Ay, this it is which wounds me to the death,
  To see a Phrygian, far-fet o' the sea,
  Preferr'd before a man of majesty.
  O love! O hate! O cruel women's hearts,
  That imitate the moon in every change,
  And, like the planets, ever love to range!
  What shall I do, thus wronged with disdain?
  Revenge me on Æneas, or on her?   70
  On her? Fond man, that were to war 'gainst heaven,
  And with one shaft provoke ten thousand darts.
  This Trojan's end will be thy envy's aim,
  Whose blood will reconcile thee to content,
  And make love drunken with thy sweet desire.
  But Dido, that now holdeth him so dear,
  Will die with very tidings of his death;
  But time will discontinue her content,
  And mould her mind unto new fancy's shapes.
  O God of heaven, turn the hand of Fate   80
  Unto that happy day of my delight!
  And then—what then? Iarbas shall but love:
  So doth he now, though not with equal gain;
  That resteth in the rival of thy pain,
  Who ne'er will cease to soar till he be slain.   *Exit.*

[Scene iv]

The storm. Enter Æneas *and* Dido *in the cave at several times.*

Dido. Æneas!
Æneas. Dido!
Dido. Tell me, dear love, how found you out this cave?
Æneas. By chance, sweet Queen, as Mars and Venus met.
Dido. Why, that was in a net, where we are loose;
  And yet I am not free—O would I were!

60 dumps] reminiscences   61 soil] wild boar's refuge   64 far-fet o'] Some editors
emend Q's reading 'far fet to' to 'forfeit to', suggesting Iarbas means that Æneas should
have drowned. It seems to me that he is referring to Æneas' foreignness—fetched from
far across the sea.   84 That] i.e. the gain   III. iv, 4 Mars and Venus] The adulterous
deities were trapped in a net laid by Vulcan, Venus' husband.

Æneas. Why, what is it that Dido may desire
    And not obtain, be it in human power?
Dido. The thing that I will die before I ask,
    And yet desire to have before I die.   10
Æneas. It is not aught Æneas may achieve?
Dido. Æneas? No, although his eyes do pierce.
Æneas. What, hath Iarbas anger'd her in aught?
    And will she be avenged on his life?
Dido. Not anger'd me, except in ang'ring thee.
Æneas. Who, then, of all so cruel may he be
    That should detain thy eye in his defects?
Dido. The man that I do eye where'er I am,
    Whose amorous face, like Paean, sparkles fire,
    Whenas he butts his beams on Flora's bed.   20
    Prometheus hath put on Cupid's shape,
    And I must perish in his burning arms.
    Æneas, O Æneas, quench these flames!
Æneas. What ails my Queen? Is she fall'n sick of late?
Dido. Not sick, my love; but sick I must conceal
    The torment that it boots me not reveal.
    And yet I'll speak, and yet I'll hold my peace;
    Do shame her worst, I will disclose my grief.
    Æneas, thou art he—what did I say?
    Something it was that now I have forgot.   30
Æneas. What means fair Dido by this doubtful speech?
Dido. Nay, nothing; but Æneas loves me not.
Æneas. Æneas' thoughts dare not ascend so high
    As Dido's heart, which monarchs might not scale.
Dido. It was because I saw no king like thee,
    Whose golden crown might balance my content;
    But now that I have found what to affect,
    I follow one that loveth fame for me,
    And rather had seem fair to Sirens' eyes,
    Than to the Carthage Queen that dies for him.   40
Æneas. If that your majesty can look so low
    As my despised worths that shun all praise,
    With this my hand I give to you my heart,
    And vow by all the gods of hospitality,
    By heaven and earth, and my fair brother's bow,
    By Paphos, Capys, and the purple sea
    From whence my radiant mother did descend,

19 Paean] Apollo, the sun   20 Flora's bed] the earth   38 for] rather than   46 Paphos] a
city in Cyprus to which Venus came after rising from the sea   46 Capys] Æneas' grandfather

And by this sword that sav'd me from the Greeks,
Never to leave these new-upreared walls,
Whiles Dido lives and rules in Juno's town,   50
Never to like or love any but her!

Dido. What more than Delian music do I hear,
That calls my soul from forth his living seat
To move unto the measures of delight?
Kind clouds, that sent forth such a courteous storm
As made disdain to fly to fancy's lap!
Stout love, in mine arms make thy Italy,
Whose crown and kingdom rests at thy command;
Sichaeus, not Æneas, be thou call'd;
The King of Carthage, not Anchises' son.   60
Hold, take these jewels at thy lover's hand,
These golden bracelets, and this wedding-ring,
Wherewith my husband woo'd me yet a maid,
And be thou King of Libya, by my gift.   *Exeunt to the cave.*

[Act IV Scene i]

Enter Achates, [Cupid *as*] *Ascanius*, Iarbas, *and* Anna.

Achates. Did ever men see such a sudden storm,
Or day so clear so suddenly o'ercast?

Iarbas. I think some fell enchantress dwelleth here,
That can call them forth whenas she please,
And dive into black tempests' treasury,
Whenas she means to mask the world with clouds.

Anna. In all my life I never knew the like;
It hailed, it snow'd, it lighten'd, all at once.

Achates. I think it was the devils' revelling night,
There was such hurly-burly in the heavens;   10
Doubtless Apollo's axle-tree is crack'd,
Or aged Atlas' shoulder out of joint,
The motion was so over-violent.

Iarbas. In all this coil, where have ye left the Queen?

Ascanius. Nay, where's my warlike father, can you tell?

Anna. Behold where both of them come forth the cave.

Iarbas. Come forth the cave! Can heaven endure this sight?
Iarbas, curse that unrevenging Jove,

---

52 Delian music] Apollo, god of music, was born at Delos.   IV. i, 14 coil] disturbance

Whose flinty darts slept in Typhoeus' den,
Whiles these adulterers surfeited with sin.   20
Nature, why mad'st me not some poisonous beast,
That with the sharpness of my edged sting
I might have stak'd them both unto the earth,
Whilst they were sporting in this darksome cave?

          [Enter Æneas *and* Dido.]

Æneas. The air is clear, and southern winds are whist.
  Come, Dido, let us hasten to the town,
  Since gloomy Æolus doth cease to frown.
Dido. Achates and Ascanius, well met.
Æneas. Fair Anna, how escap'd you from the shower?
Anna. As others did, by running to the wood.   30
Dido. But where were you, Iarbas, all this while?
Iarbas. Not with Æneas in the ugly cave.
Dido. I see Æneas sticketh in your mind,
  But I will soon put by that stumbling-block,
  And quell those hopes that thus employ your ears.   *Exeunt.*

[Scene ii

Enter Iarbas *to sacrifice.*

Iarbas. Come, servants, come; bring forth the sacrifice,
  That I may pacify that gloomy Jove,
  Whose empty altars have enlarg'd our ills.

    [Servants *bring in the sacrifice, and then exeunt.*]

  Eternal Jove, great master of the clouds,
  Father of gladness and all frolic thoughts,
  That with thy gloomy hand corrects the heaven
  When airy creatures war amongst themselves;
  Hear, hear, O hear Iarbas' plaining prayers,
  Whose hideous echoes make the welkin howl,
  And all the woods 'Eliza' to resound!   10
  The woman that thou will'd us entertain,
  Where, straying in our borders up and down,
  She crav'd a hide of ground to build a town,
  With whom we did divide both laws and land,
  And all the fruits that plenty else sends forth,

19 Typhoeus' den] Mt. Etna, where the monster Typhoeus was imprisoned and where
Jupiter was said to make his thunderbolts   25 whist] hushed   IV. ii, 10 'Eliza'] Dido
(originally named Elissa)   13 hide of ground] Iarbas granted Dido as much land as could
be covered by an ox-hide; this she cut in strips, securing enough ground for the building
of Carthage.

Scorning our loves and royal marriage-rites,
Yields up her beauty to a stranger's bed;
Who, having wrought her shame, is straightway fled.
Now, if thou be'st a pitying god of power,
On whom ruth and compassion ever waits,   20
Redress these wrongs, and warn him to his ships,
That now afflicts me with his flattering eyes.

Enter Anna.

Anna. How now, Iarbas, at your prayers so hard?
Iarbas. Ay, Anna: is there aught you would with me?
Anna. Nay, no such weighty business of import,
But may be slack'd until another time;
Yet if you would partake with me the cause
Of this devotion that detaineth you,
I would be thankful for such courtesy.
Iarbas. Anna, against this Trojan do I pray,   30
Who seeks to rob me of thy sister's love,
And dive into her heart by colour'd looks.
Anna. Alas, poor King, that labours so in vain
For her that so delighteth in thy pain!
Be rul'd by me, and seek some other love,
Whose yielding heart may yield thee more relief.
Iarbas. Mine eye is fix'd where fancy cannot start;
O, leave me, leave me to my silent thoughts,
That register the numbers of my ruth,
And I will either move the thoughtless flint,   40
Or drop out both mine eyes in drizzling tears,
Before my sorrow's tide have any stint!
Anna. I will not leave Iarbas, whom I love,
In this delight of dying pensiveness.
Away with Dido! Anna be thy song;
Anna, that doth admire thee more than heaven.
Iarbas. I may nor will list to such loathsome change,
That intercepts the course of my desire.
Servants, come fetch these empty vessels here;
For I will fly from these alluring eyes,   50
That do pursue my peace where'er it goes.   *Exit.*
Anna. Iarbas, stay, loving Iarbas, stay,
For I have honey to present thee with.
Hard-hearted, wilt not deign to hear me speak?
I'll follow thee with outcries ne'ertheless,
And strew thy walks with my dishevell'd hair.   *Exit.*

[Scene iii]

Enter Æneas alone.

Æneas. Carthage, my friendly host, adieu,
    Since destiny doth call me from the shore:
    Hermes this night descending in a dream
    Hath summon'd me to fruitful Italy.
    Jove wills it so; my mother wills it so;
    Let my Phoenissa grant, and then I go.
    Grant she or no, Æneas must away;
    Whose golden fortunes, clogg'd with courtly ease,
    Cannot ascend to Fame's immortal house,
    Or banquet in bright Honour's burnish'd hall,   10
    Till he hath furrow'd Neptune's glassy fields,
    And cut a passage through his topless hills.
    Achates, come forth! Sergestus, Ilioneus,
    Cloanthus, haste away! Æneas calls.

Enter Achates, Cloanthus, Sergestus, *and* Ilioneus.

Achates. What wills our lord, or wherefore did he call?
Æneas. The dreams, brave mates, that did beset my bed,
    When sleep but newly had embrac'd the night,
    Commands me leave these unrenowmed realms,
    Whereas nobility abhors to stay,
    And none but base Æneas will abide.   20
    Aboard, aboard, since Fates do bid aboard,
    And slice the sea with sable-colour'd ships,
    On whom the nimble winds may all day wait,
    And follow them, as footmen, through the deep.
    Yet Dido casts her eyes like anchors out
    To stay my fleet from loosing forth the bay:
    'Come back, come back,' I hear her cry afar,
    'And let me link thy body to my lips,
    That, tied together by the striving tongues,
    We may as one sail into Italy.'   30
Achates. Banish that ticing dame from forth your mouth,
    And follow your foreseeing stars in all;
    This is no life for men-at-arms to live,
    Where dalliance doth consume a soldier's strength,
    And wanton motions of alluring eyes
    Effeminate our minds inur'd to war.

6 Phoenissa] Dido (from Phoenicia)

Ilioneus. Why, let us build a city of our own,
   And not stand lingering here for amorous looks.
   Will Dido raise old Priam forth his grave,
   And build the town again the Greeks did burn?   40
   No, no, she cares not how we sink or swim,
   So she may have Æneas in her arms.
Cloanthus. To Italy, sweet friends, to Italy!
   We will not stay a minute longer here.
Æneas. Trojans, aboard, and I will follow you.   [*Exeunt all except* Æneas.]
   I fain would go, yet beauty calls me back.
   To leave her so and not once say farewell
   Were to transgress against all laws of love:
   But if I use such ceremonious thanks
   As parting friends accustom on the shore,
   Her silver arms will coll me round about,   50
   And tears of pearl cry, 'Stay, Æneas, stay!'
   Each word she says will then contain a crown,
   And every speech be ended with a kiss.
   I may not dure this female drudgery:
   To sea, Æneas! Find out Italy!   *Exit.*

[Scene iv]

Enter Dido *and* Anna.

Dido. O Anna, run unto the water side!
   They say Æneas' men are going aboard,
   It may be he will steal away with them.
   Stay not to answer me; run, Anna, run!   [*Exit* Anna.]
   O foolish Trojans that would steal from hence,
   And not let Dido understand their drift!
   I would have given Achates store of gold,
   And Ilioneus gum and Libyan spice;
   The common soldiers rich embroider'd coats,
   And silver whistles to control the winds,   10
   Which Circes sent Sichaeus when he liv'd;
   Unworthy are they of a queen's reward.
   See where they come; how might I do to chide?

Enter Anna, *with* Æneas, Achates, Ilioneus, *and* Sergestus
[*Carthaginian* Lord *and attendants*].

Anna. 'Twas time to run; Æneas had been gone,
   The sails were hoising up, and he aboard.

51 coll] embrace

Dido. Is this thy love to me?

Æneas. O princely Dido, give me leave to speak!
    I went to take my farewell of Achates.

Dido. How haps Achates bid me not farewell?

Achates. Because I fear'd your grace would keep me here.   20

Dido. To rid thee of that doubt, aboard again:
    I charge thee put to sea and stay not here.

Achates. Then let Æneas go aboard with us.

Dido. Get you aboard; Æneas means to stay.

Æneas. The sea is rough, the winds blow to the shore.

Dido. O false Æneas! Now the sea is rough,
    But when you were aboard 'twas calm enough.
    Thou and Achates meant to sail away.

Æneas. Hath not the Carthage Queen mine only son?
    Thinks Dido I will go and leave him here?   30

Dido. Æneas, pardon me; for I forgot
    That young Ascanius lay with me this night.
    Love made me jealous, but to make amends,
    Wear the imperial crown of Libya, [*Giving him her crown and sceptre.*]
    Sway thou the Punic sceptre in my stead,
    And punish me, Æneas, for this crime.

Æneas. This kiss shall be fair Dido's punishment.

Dido. O, how a crown becomes Æneas' head!
    Stay here, Æneas, and command as King.

Æneas. How vain am I to wear this diadem,   40
    And bear this golden sceptre in my hand!
    A burgonet of steel, and not a crown,
    A sword, and not a sceptre, fits Æneas.

Dido. O keep them still, and let me gaze my fill!
    Now looks Æneas like immortal Jove:
    O where is Ganymede, to hold his cup,
    And Mercury, to fly for what he calls?
    Ten thousand Cupids hover in the air,
    And fan it in Æneas' lovely face!
    O that the clouds were here wherein thou fled'st,   50
    That thou and I unseen might sport ourselves!
    Heaven, envious of our joys, is waxen pale,
    And when we whisper, then the stars fall down,
    To be partakers of our honey talk.

Æneas. O Dido, patroness of all our lives,
    When I leave thee, death be my punishment!

42 burgonet] helmet

Swell, raging seas, frown, wayward Destinies!
Blow, winds, threaten, ye rocks and sandy shelves!
This is the harbour that Æneas seeks:
Let's see what tempests can annoy me now.   60
Dido. Not all the world can take thee from mine arms.
 Æneas may command as many Moors
 As in the sea are little water drops.
 And now, to make experience of my love,
 Fair sister Anna, lead my lover forth,
 And, seated on my jennet, let him ride
 As Dido's husband, through the Punic streets;
 And will my guard, with Mauritanian darts,
 To wait upon him as their sovereign lord.
Anna. What if the citizens repine thereat?   70
Dido. Those that dislike what Dido gives in charge
 Command my guard to slay for their offence.
 Shall vulgar peasants storm at what I do?
 The ground is mine that gives them sustenance,
 The air wherein they breathe, the water, fire,
 All that they have, their lands, their goods, their lives;
 And I, the goddess of all these, command
 Æneas ride as Carthaginian King.
Achates. Æneas for his parentage deserves
 As large a kingdom as is Libya.   80
Æneas. Ay, and unless the Destinies be false,
 I shall be planted in as rich a land.
Dido. Speak of no other land; this land is thine;
 Dido is thine, henceforth I'll call thee lord.
 Do as I bid thee, sister; lead the way,
 And from a turret I'll behold my love.
Æneas. Then here in me shall flourish Priam's race;
 And thou and I, Achates, for revenge
 For Troy, for Priam, for his fifty sons,
 Our kinsmen's lives and thousand guiltless souls,   90
 Will lead an host against the hateful Greeks,
 And fire proud Lacedaemon o'er their heads.
             Exeunt [all except Dido *and* Carthaginian Lord].
Dido. Speaks not Æneas like a conqueror?
 O blessed tempests that did drive him in!
 O happy sand that made him run aground!
 Henceforth you shall be our Carthage gods.
 Ay, but it may be he will leave my love,
 And seek a foreign land call'd Italy.

O that I had a charm to keep the winds
Within the closure of a golden ball;   100
Or that the Terrene sea were in mine arms,
That he might suffer shipwrack on my breast
As oft as he attempts to hoist up sail!
I must prevent him; wishing will not serve.
Go bid my nurse take young Ascanius,
And bear him in the country to her house;
Æneas will not go without his son.
Yet lest he should, for I am full of fear,
Bring me his oars, his tackling, and his sails.   [*Exit a* Lord.]
What if I sink his ships? O he'll frown!   110
Better he frown than I should die for grief.
I cannot see him frown; it may not be.
Armies of foes resolv'd to win this town,
Or impious traitors vow'd to have my life,
Affright me not; only Æneas' frown
Is that which terrifies poor Dido's heart;
Not bloody spears, appearing in the air,
Presage the downfall of my empery,
Nor blazing comets threatens Dido's death;
It is Æneas' frown that ends my days.   120
If he forsake me not, I never die,
For in his looks I see eternity,
And he'll make me immortal with a kiss.

Enter a Lord [*with attendants carrying tackling, etc.*]

Lord. Your nurse is gone with young Ascanius,
    And here's Æneas' tackling, oars, and sails.
Dido. Are these the sails that in despite of me
    Pack'd with the winds to bear Æneas hence?
    I'll hang ye in the chamber where I lie;
    Drive, if you can, my house to Italy!
    I'll set the casement open, that the winds   130
    May enter in, and once again conspire
    Against the life of me, poor Carthage Queen.
    But, though he go, he stays in Carthage still;
    And let rich Carthage fleet upon the seas,
    So I may have Æneas in mine arms.
    Is this the wood that grew in Carthage plains,
    And would be toiling in the wat'ry billows,
    To rob their mistress of her Trojan guest?
    O cursed tree, hadst thou but wit or sense,

To measure how I prize Æneas' love,   140
Thou wouldst have leapt from out the sailors' hands,
And told me that Æneas meant to go!
And yet I blame thee not; thou art but wood.
The water, which our poets term a nymph,
Why did it suffer thee to touch her breast,
And shrunk not back, knowing my love was there?
The water is an element, no nymph.
Why should I blame Æneas for his flight?
O Dido, blame not him, but break his oars,
These were the instruments that launch'd him forth.   150
There's not so much as this base tackling too,
But dares to heap up sorrow to my heart:
Was it not you that hoised up these sails?
Why burst you not, and they fell in the seas?
For this will Dido tie ye full of knots,
And shear ye all asunder with her hands.
Now serve to chastise shipboys for their faults;
Ye shall no more offend the Carthage Queen.
Now let him hang my favours on his masts,
And see if those will serve instead of sails;   160
For tackling, let him take the chains of gold
Which I bestow'd upon his followers;
Instead of oars, let him use his hands,
And swim to Italy; I'll keep these sure.
Come, bear them in.   *Exeunt.*

[Scene v]

Enter the Nurse, *with* Cupid *for Ascanius.*

Nurse. My lord Ascanius, ye must go with me.
Cupid. Whither must I go? I'll stay with my mother.
Nurse. No, thou shalt go with me unto my house.
        I have an orchard that hath store of plums,
        Brown almonds, services, ripe figs, and dates,
        Dewberries, apples, yellow oranges;
        A garden where are beehives full of honey,
        Musk-roses, and a thousand sort of flowers;
        And in the midst doth run a silver stream,
        Where thou shalt see the red-gill'd fishes leap,
        White swans, and many lovely water-fowls.   10
        Now speak, Ascanius, will ye go or no?

5 services] pear-trees

Cupid. Come, come, I'll go. How far hence is your house?
Nurse. But hereby, child; we shall get thither straight.
Cupid. Nurse, I am weary; will you carry me?
Nurse. Ay, so you'll dwell with me, and call me mother.
Cupid. So you'll love me, I care not if I do.
Nurse. That I might live to see this boy a man!
    How prettily he laughs! Go, ye wag,
    You'll be a twigger when you come to age.   20
    Say Dido what she will, I am not old;
    I'll be no more a widow; I am young,
    I'll have a husband, or else a lover.
Cupid. A husband, and no teeth!
Nurse. O what mean I to have such foolish thoughts!
    Foolish is love, a toy. O sacred love,
    If there be any heaven in earth, 'tis love,
    Especially in women of your years.
    Blush, blush for shame! why shouldst thou think of love?
    A grave, and not a lover, fits thy age.   30
    A grave! Why, I may live a hundred years:
    Fourscore is but a girl's age: love is sweet.
    My veins are wither'd, and my sinews dry:
    Why do I think of love, now I should die?
Cupid. Come, nurse.
Nurse. Well, if he come a-wooing, he shall speed:
    O, how unwise was I to say him nay!   *Exeunt.*

[Act V Scene i]

*Enter Æneas, with a paper in his hand, drawing the platform of the
    city; with him* Achates, [Sergestus,] Cloanthus, *and* Ilioneus.

Æneas. Triumph, my mates. Our travels are at end;
    Here will Æneas build a statelier Troy
    Than that which grim Atrides overthrew.
    Carthage shall vaunt her petty walls no more,
    For I will grace them with a fairer frame,
    And clad her in a crystal livery
    Wherein the day may evermore delight;
    From golden India Ganges will I fetch,
    Whose wealthy streams may wait upon her towers,

s.d. *platform*] ground-plan

And triple-wise entrench her round about;   10
The sun from Egypt shall rich odours bring,
Wherewith his burning beams, like labouring bees
That load their thighs with Hybla's honey's spoils,
Shall here unburden their exhaled sweets,
And plant our pleasant suburbs with her fumes.

Achates. What length or breadth shall this brave town contain?

Æneas. Not past four thousand paces at the most.

Ilioneus. But what shall it be 'call'd? Troy, as before?

Æneas. That have I not determin'd with myself.

Cloanthus. Let it be term'd Ænea, by your name.   20

Sergestus. Rather Ascania, by your little son.

Æneas. Nay, I will have it called Anchisæon,
Of my old father's name.

Enter Hermes *with* Ascanius.

Hermes. Æneas, stay; Jove's herald bids thee stay.

Æneas. Whom do I see? Jove's winged messenger!
Welcome to Carthage new-erected town.

Hermes. Why cousin, stand you building cities here,
And beautifying the empire of this Queen,
While Italy is clean out of thy mind?
Too too forgetful of thine own affairs,   30
Why wilt thou so betray thy son's good hap?
The king of gods sent me from highest heaven,
To sound this angry message in thine ears:
Vain man, what monarchy expect'st thou here?
Or with what thought sleep'st thou in Libya shore?
If that all glory hath forsaken thee,
And thou despise the praise of such attempts,
Yet think upon Ascanius' prophecy,
And young Iulus' more than thousand years,
Whom I have brought from Ida, where he slept,   40
And bore young Cupid unto Cyprus isle.

Æneas. This was my mother that beguil'd the Queen,
And made me take my brother for my son.
No marvel, Dido, though thou be in love,
That daily dandlest Cupid in thy arms.
Welcome, sweet child: where hast thou been this long?

Ascanius. Eating sweet comfits with Queen Dido's maid,
Who ever since hath lull'd me in her arms.

38-9 Ascanius' prophecy . . . years] i.e., that Ascanius (Iulus) would found an eternal
empire

Æneas. Sergestus, bear him hence unto our ships,
    Lest Dido, spying him, keep him for a pledge.   50
                        [Exit Sergestus *with* Ascanius.]
Hermes. Spend'st thou thy time about this little boy,
    And giv'st not ear unto the charge I bring?
    I tell thee, thou must straight to Italy,
    Or else abide the wrath of frowning Jove.   *[Exit.]*
Æneas. How should I put into the raging deep,
    Who have no sails nor tackling for my ships?
    What, would the gods have me, Deucalion-like,
    Float up and down where'er the billows drive?
    Though she repair'd my fleet and gave me ships,
    Yet hath she ta'en away my oars and masts,   60
    And left me neither sail nor stern aboard.
               Enter to them Iarbas.
Iarbas. How now, Æneas, sad? What means these dumps?
Æneas. Iarbas, I am clean besides myself;
    Jove hath heap'd on me such a desperate charge,
    Which neither art nor reason may achieve,
    Nor I devise by what means to contrive.
Iarbas. As how, I pray? May I entreat you tell?
Æneas. With speed he bids me sail to Italy,
    Whenas I want both rigging for my fleet,
    And also furniture for these my men.   70
Iarbas. If that be all, then cheer thy drooping looks,
    For I will furnish thee with such supplies;
    Let some of those thy followers go with me,
    And they shall have what thing soe'er thou need'st.
Æneas. Thanks, good Iarbas, for thy friendly aid.
    Achates and the rest shall wait on thee,
    Whilst I rest thankful for this courtesy.
              Exeunt Iarbas *and Æneas' train.*
    Now will I haste unto Lavinian shore,
    And raise a new foundation to old Troy.
    Witness the gods, and witness heaven and earth,   80
    How loath I am to leave these Libyan bounds,
    But that eternal Jupiter commands!
             Enter Dido *[with attendants].*
Dido [aside]. I fear I saw Æneas' little son
    Led by Achates to the Trojan fleet;
    If it be so, his father means to fly.

57 Deucalion] like Noah, saved from the flood that destroyed the rest of mankind

But here he is; now, Dido, try thy wit.
Æneas, wherefore go thy men aboard?
Why are thy ships new rigg'd? Or to what end,
Launch'd from the haven, lie they in the road?
Pardon me, though I ask; love makes me ask.   90

Æneas. O pardon me, if I resolve thee why!
Æneas will not feign with his dear love.
I must from hence: this day, swift Mercury,
When I was laying a platform for these walls,
Sent from his father Jove, appear'd to me,
And in his name rebuk'd me bitterly
For lingering here, neglecting Italy.

Dido. But yet Æneas will not leave his love.

Æneas. I am commanded by immortal Jove
To leave this town and pass to Italy;   100
And therefore must of force.

Dido. These words proceed not from Æneas' heart.

Æneas. Not from my heart, for I can hardly go;
And yet I may not stay. Dido, farewell.

Dido. Farewell! Is this the mends for Dido's love?
Do Trojans use to quit their lovers thus?
Fare well may Dido, so Æneas stay;
I die, if my Æneas say farewell.

Æneas. Then let me go, and never say farewell.

Dido. 'Let me go'; 'farewell'; 'I must from hence'.   110
These words are poison to poor Dido's soul:
O speak like my Æneas, like my love!
Why look'st thou toward the sea? The time hath been
When Dido's beauty chain'd thine eyes to her.
Am I less fair than when thou saw'st me first?
O then, Æneas, 'tis for grief of thee!
Say thou wilt stay in Carthage with thy Queen,
And Dido's beauty will return again.
Æneas, say, how canst thou take thy leave?
Wilt thou kiss Dido? O, thy lips have sworn   120
To stay with Dido! Canst thou take her hand?
Thy hand and mine have plighted mutual faith;
Therefore, unkind Æneas, must thou say,
'Then let me go, and never say farewell'?

Æneas. O Queen of Carthage, wert thou ugly-black,
Æneas could not choose but hold thee dear!
Yet must he not gainsay the gods' behest.

89 road] harbour   105 mends] reward

Dido. The gods? What gods be those that seek my death?
    Wherein have I offended Jupiter,
    That he should take Æneas from mine arms?   130
    O no! The gods weigh not what lovers do:
    It is Æenas calls Æneas hence,
    And woeful Dido, by these blubber'd cheeks,
    By this right hand, and by our spousal rites,
    Desires Æneas to remain with her.
    Si bene quid de te merui, fuit aut tibi quidquam
    Dulce meum, miserere domus labentis, et istam
    Oro, si quis adhuc precibus locus, exue mentem.

Æneas. *Desine meque tuis incendere teque querelis;*
    Italiam non sponte sequor.   140

Dido. Hast thou forgot how many neighbour kings
    Were up in arms, for making thee my love?
    How Carthage did rebel, Iarbas storm,
    And all the world calls me a second Helen
    For being entangled by a stranger's looks?
    So thou wouldst prove as true as Paris did,
    Would, as fair Troy was, Carthage might be sack'd,
    And I be call'd a second Helena!
    Had I a son by thee the grief were less,
    That I might see Æneas in his face.   150
    Now if thou go'st, what canst thou leave behind
    But rather will augment than ease my woe?

Æneas. In vain, my love, thou spend'st thy fainting breath:
    If words might move me, I were overcome.

Dido. And wilt thou not be mov'd with Dido's words?
    Thy mother was no goddess, perjur'd man,
    Nor Dardanus the author of thy stock;
    But thou art sprung from Scythian Caucasus,
    And tigers of Hyrcania gave thee suck.
    Ah foolish Dido to forbear this long!   160
    Wast thou not wrack'd upon this Libyan shore,
    And cam'st to Dido like a fisher swain?
    Repair'd not I thy ships, made thee a king,
    And all thy needy followers noblemen?
    O serpent, that came creeping from the shore,

136–8 *Si bene . . . mentem*] 'If I have ever deserved well of you, and if anything of mine has ever been sweet to you, take pity on a falling house and, I pray you—if there is still a place for prayers—give up this plan of yours' (*Æneid* IV. 317–19).   139–40 *Desine . . . sequor*] 'Cease to inflame both me and yourself with your lamentations. It is not of my own free will that I seek Italy' (*Æneid* IV. 360–1).   157 Dardanus] founder of Troy

And I for pity harbour'd in my bosom,
Wilt thou now slay me with thy venom'd sting,
And hiss at Dido for preserving thee?
Go, go and spare not; seek out Italy;
I hope that that which love forbids me do,   170
The rocks and sea-gulfs will perform at large,
And thou shalt perish in the billows' ways,
To whom poor Dido doth bequeath revenge.
Ay, traitor! And the waves shall cast thee up,
Where thou and false Achates first set foot;
Which if it chance, I'll give ye burial,
And weep upon your lifeless carcasses,
Though thou nor he will pity me a whit.
Why star'st thou in my face? If thou wilt stay,
Leap in mine arms, mine arms are open wide;   180
If not, turn from me, and I'll turn from thee;
For though thou hast the heart to say farewell,
I have not power to stay thee.   [*Exit* Æneas.]
                    Is he gone?
Ay, but he'll come-again, he cannot go;
He loves me too too well to serve me so:
Yet he that in my sight would not relent,
Will, being absent, be obdurate still.
By this is he got to the water-side;
And, see, the sailors take him by the hand,
But he shrinks back; and now, remembering me,   190
Returns amain: welcome, welcome, my love!
But where's Æneas? Ah, he's gone, he's gone!

                    [*Enter* Anna.]

Anna. What means my sister thus to rave and cry?
Dido. O Anna, my Æneas is aboard,
        And, leaving me, will sail to Italy!
        Once didst thou go, and he came back again:
        Now bring him back, and thou shalt be a queen,
        And I will live a private life with him.
Anna. Wicked Æneas!
Dido. Call him not wicked, sister; speak him fair,   200
        And look upon him with a mermaid's eye;
        Tell him, I never vow'd at Aulis' gulf
        The desolation of his native Troy,
        Nor sent a thousand ships unto the walls,

191 amain] at once   202 Aulis' gulf] where the Grecian fleet set sail for Troy

Nor ever violated faith to him.
Request him gently, Anna, to return:
I crave but this, he stay a tide or two,
That I may learn to bear it patiently;
If he depart thus suddenly, I die.
Run, Anna, run; stay not to answer me.   210
Anna. I go, fair sister: heavens grant good success!   *Exit* Anna.

Enter the Nurse

Nurse. O Dido, your little son Ascanius
Is gone! He lay with me last night,
And in the morning he was stol'n from me:
I think, some fairies have beguiled me.
Dido. O cursed hag and false dissembling wretch,
That slay'st me with thy harsh and hellish tale!
Thou for some petty gift hast let him go,
And I am thus deluded of my boy.
Away with her to prison presently,   220
Trait'ress too keen, and cursed sorceress!
Nurse. I know not what you mean by treason, I;
I am as true as any one of yours.   *Exeunt the* Nurse [*with* Attendants].
Dido. Away with her! Suffer her not to speak.
My sister comes: I like not her sad looks.

Enter Anna.

Anna. Before I came, Æneas was aboard,
And spying me, hois'd up the sails amain;
But I cried out, 'Æneas, false Æneas, stay!'
Then gan he wag his hand, which yet held up,
Made me suppose he would have heard me speak.   230
Then gan they drive into the ocean,
Which when I view'd, I cried, 'Æneas, stay!
Dido, fair Dido wills Æneas stay!'
Yet he, whose heart of adamant or flint,
My tears nor plaints could mollify a whit.
Then carelessly I rent my hair for grief,
Which seen to all, though he beheld me not,
They gan to move him to redress my ruth,
And stay a while to hear what I could say;
But he clapp'd under hatches, sail'd away.   240
Dido. O Anna, Anna, I will follow him!
Anna. How can ye go when he hath all your fleet?
Dido. I'll frame me wings of wax like Icarus,
And o'er his ships will soar unto the sun,

That they may melt and I fall in his arms;
Or else I'll make a prayer unto the waves,
That I may swim to him, like Triton's niece.
O Anna, fetch Arion's harp,
That I may tice a dolphin to the shore,
And ride upon his back unto my love!   250
Look, sister, look! Lovely Æneas' ships!
See, see, the billows heave him up to heaven,
And now down falls the keels into the deep!
O sister, sister, take away the rocks,
They'll break his ships. O Proteus, Neptune, Jove,
Save, save Æneas, Dido's liefest love!
Now is he come on shore, safe without hurt;
But see, Achates wills him put to sea,
And all the sailors merry-make for joy;
But he, remembering me, shrinks back again.   260
See, where he comes! Welcome, welcome, my love!
Anna. Ah, sister, leave these idle fantasies!
Sweet sister, cease; remember who you are.
Dido. Dido I am, unless I be deceiv'd,
And must I rave thus for a runagate?
Must I make ships for him to sail away?
Nothing can bear me to him but a ship,
And he hath all my fleet. What shall I do,
But die in fury of this oversight?
Ay, I must be the murderer of myself: 270
No, but I am not; yet I will be straight.
Anna, be glad; now have I found a mean
To rid me from these thoughts of lunacy:
Not far from hence
There is a woman famoused for arts,
Daughter unto the nymphs Hesperides,
Who will'd me sacrifice his ticing relics.
Go, Anna, bid my servants bring me fire.   *Exit* Anna.

Enter Iarbas.

Iarbas. How long will Dido mourn a stranger's flight
That hath dishonour'd her and Carthage both?   280

247 Triton's niece] The sea-monster Scylla; but it was Scylla the daughter of Nisus who
swam after her lover.   248 Arion] poet thrown overboard by sailors, rescued by a dolphin
his music had charmed   256 liefest] dearest   276 Daughter . . . Hesperides] The
Hesperides guarded the golden apples, Juno's wedding present to Jupiter. Virgil speaks
only of their having a priestess in Ethiopia.

How long shall I with grief consume my days,
And reap no guerdon for my truest love?

[*Enter attendants with wood and torches.*]

Dido. Iarbas, talk not of Æneas. Let him go!
Lay to thy hands, and help me make a fire
That shall consume all that this stranger left;
For I intend a private sacrifice,
To cure my mind, that melts for unkind love.
Iarbas. But afterwards will Dido grant me love?
Dido. Ay, ay, Iarbas; after this is done,
None in the world shall have my love but thou.   290

[*They make a fire.*]

So, leave me now; let none approach this place.

Exeunt Iarbas [*and attendants*].

Now Dido, with these relics burn thyself,
And make Æneas famous through the world
For perjury and slaughter of a queen.
Here lie the sword that in the darksome cave
He drew, and swore by to be true to me:
Thou shalt burn first; thy crime is worse than his.
Here lie the garment which I cloth'd him in
When first he came on shore: perish thou too.
These letters, lines, and perjur'd papers all   300
Shall burn to cinders in this precious flame.
And now ye gods that guide the starry frame
And order all things at your high dispose,
Grant, though the traitors land in Italy,
They may be still tormented with unrest;
And from mine ashes let a conqueror rise,
That may revenge this treason to a queen
By ploughing up his countries with the sword:
Betwixt this land and that be never league;
Litora litoribus contraria, fluctibus undas   310
Imprecor, arma armis; pugnent ipsique nepotes!
Live, false Æneas! Truest Dido dies;
Sic, sic juvat ire sub umbras.   [*Throws herself into the flames.*]

Enter Anna.

Anna. O help, Iarbas! Dido in these flames
Hath burnt herself! Ay me, unhappy me!

310–11 *Litora . . . nepotes*] 'I pray that coasts may be opposed to coasts, waves to waves, and arms to arms; may they and their descendants ever fight' (*Æneid* IV. 628–9).
313 *Sic . . . umbras*] 'Thus, thus I rejoice to enter into the shades' (*Æneid* IV. 660).

Enter Iarbas *running*.

Iarbas. Cursed Iarbas, die to expiate
    The grief that tires upon thine inward soul!
    Dido, I come to thee. Ay me, Æneas!   *[Kills himself.]*
Anna. What can my tears or cries prevail me now?
    Dido is dead! Iarbas slain, Iarbas my dear love!   320
    O sweet Iarbas, Anna's sole delight!
    What fatal Destiny envies me thus,
    To see my sweet Iarbas slay himself?
    But Anna now shall honour thee in death,
    And mix her blood with thine; this shall I do,
    That gods and men may pity this my death,
    And rue our ends, senseless of life or breath.
    Now, sweet Iarbas, stay! I come to thee.   *[Kills herself.]*

FINIS.

Tamburlaine the Great

Tamburlaine was Marlowe's first play for the public stage, where it was performed in 1587 and became an instant success. Frequent and profitable performances are recorded by Henslowe, and contemporary writers, among them Greene, Nashe, and Shakespeare, allude to its popularity with some envy. The two Parts were published together in a black-letter Octavo of 1590, whose title-page gives a full description of the action yet names no author. But Marlowe's hand is everywhere: in no other play is the 'mighty line' so evident. It seems likely that the printed text was set up from the author's own manuscript, and that the flourishes at the end of some acts— '*Finis Actus 2*'—are Marlowe's own. Something has been lost, however, as we learn from the printer's reference to the 'fond and frivolous gestures' he has 'purposely omitted'. It is impossible even to guess what these 'gestures' may have been, especially when they occurred in a play whose Prologue disdains the 'conceits [that] clownage keeps in pay'.

Much research went to the writing of *Tamburlaine*. For Part I Marlowe read the accounts of Tamburlaine's character and career written by Spanish and Italian historians; these he simplified and condensed so that Tamburlaine's swift rise to power could be seen plainly. His most important addition was the person of Zenocrate. The play was perhaps meant to end with Part I, but the public demanded a sequel. For Part II Marlowe went to more obscure and still more varied sources—to Ariosto's *Orlando Furioso* for the story of Olympia and Theridamas, for instance, and to Paul Ive's *Practise of Fortification* for Tamburlaine's lecture in III.ii. Again his major invention concerns Zenocrate; now it is her death that affects him.

For both Parts of the play Marlowe needed an atlas, and he found this in Ortelius' *Theatrum Orbis Terrarum*, which gave him not only geography but also the resonant place-names that support Tamburlaine's 'high astounding terms'.

Tamburlaine the Great.

Who, from a Scythian Shepheard
by his rare and woonderfull Conquests,
became a most puissant and migh-
tye Monarque.

And (for his tyranny, and terrour in
Warre) was tearmed,

The Scourge of God.

Deuided into two Tragicall Discourses, as they were sundrie times
shewen vpon Stages in the Citie
of London.

By the right honorable the Lord
Admyrall, his seruantes.

Now first, and newlie published.

LONDON.
Printed by Richard Ihones: at the signe
of the Rose and Crowne neere Hol-
borne Bridge. 1590.

To the Gentlemen Readers, and others

that take pleasure in reading

Histories.

Gentlemen, and courteous readers whosoever: I have here published in print for your sakes the two tragical discourses of the Scythian shepherd Tamburlaine, that became so great a conqueror and so mighty a monarch. My hope is that they will be now no less acceptable unto you to read after your serious affairs and studies than they have been lately delightful for many of you to see when the same were showed in London upon stages. I have purposely omitted and left out some fond and frivolous gestures, digressing and, in my poor opinion, far unmeet for the matter, which I thought might seem more tedious unto the wise than any way else to be regarded. Though haply they have been of some vain-conceited fondlings greatly gaped at, what times they were showed upon the stage in their graced deformities, nevertheless now, to be mixtured in print with such matter of worth, it would prove a great disgrace to so honorable and stately a history. Great folly were it in me to commend unto your wisdoms either the eloquence of the author that writ them, or the worthiness of the matter itself. I therefore leave unto your learned censures both the one and the other; and myself, the poor printer of them, unto your most courteous and favourable protection. Which if you vouchsafe to accept, you shall evermore bind me to employ what travail and service I can to the advancing and pleasuring of your excellent degree.

Yours, most humble at commandment,

R[ichard] J[ones], Printer.

10 vain-conceited] empty-headed

[DRAMATIS PERSONAE

The Prologue

Mycetes, King of Persia
Cosroe, his brother
Ceneus
Ortygius
Meander } Persian lords
Menaphon
Theridamas
Tamburlaine, the Scythian shepherd
Techelles } his followers
Usumcasane
Bajazeth, Emperor of Turkey
King of Argier
King of Fez
King of Morocco
Alcidamus, King of Arabia
Soldan of Egypt
Governor of Damascus
Agydas } Median lords
Magnetes
Capolin, an Egyptian
Philemus, a messenger
A Spy

Zenocrate, daughter of the Soldan
Anippe, her maid
Zabina, wife to Bajazeth
Ebea, her maid

Virgins of Damascus,
Messengers, Bassoes, Lords, Citizens, Moors, Soldiers,
Attendants]

The Prologue

From jigging veins of rhyming mother-wits,
And such conceits as clownage keeps in pay,
We'll lead you to the stately tent of war,
Where you shall hear the Scythian Tamburlaine
Threat'ning the world with high astounding terms,
And scourging kingdoms with his conquering sword.
View but his picture in this tragic glass,
And then applaud his fortunes as you please.

Actus I.   Scaena I.

[*Enter*] Mycetes, Cosroe, Meander, Theridamas, Ortygius, Ceneus,
[Menaphon,] *with others.*

Mycetes. Brother Cosroe, I find myself aggriev'd,
    Yet insufficient to express the same,
    For it requires a great and thund'ring speech.
    Good brother, tell the cause unto my lords;
    I know you have a better wit than I.
Cosroe. Unhappy Persia, that in former age
    Hast been the seat of mighty conquerors,
    That in their prowess and their policies
    Have triumph'd over Afric and the bounds
    Of Europe where the sun dares scarce appear   10
    For freezing meteors and congealed cold,
    Now to be rul'd and govern'd by a man
    At whose birthday Cynthia with Saturn join'd,
    And Jove, the Sun, and Mercury denied
    To shed their influence in his fickle brain!
    Now Turks and Tartars shake their swords at thee,
    Meaning to mangle all thy provinces.
Mycetes. Brother, I see your meaning well enough,
    And through your planets I perceive you think
    I am not wise enough to be a king: 20
    But I refer me to my noblemen,
    That know my wit, and can be witnesses.
    I might command you to be slain for this;
    Meander, might I not?
Meander. Not for so small a fault, my sovereign lord.
Mycetes. I mean it not, but yet I know I might.

Yet live, yea, live; Mycetes wills it so.
Meander, thou my faithful counsellor,
Declare the cause of my conceived grief,
Which is, God knows, about that Tamburlaine,   30
That like a fox in midst of harvest-time
Doth prey upon my flocks of passengers,
And, as I hear, doth mean to pull my plumes.
Therefore 'tis good and meet for to be wise.
Meander. Oft have I heard your majesty complain
Of Tamburlaine, that sturdy Scythian thief,
That robs your merchants of Persepolis
Trading by land unto the Western Isles,
And in your confines with his lawless train
Daily commits incivil outrages,   40
Hoping (misled by dreaming prophecies)
To reign in Asia, and with barbarous arms
To make himself the monarch of the East.
But ere he march in Asia, or display
His vagrant ensign in the Persian fields,
Your grace hath taken order by Theridamas,
Charg'd with a thousand horse, to apprehend
And bring him captive to your highness' throne.
Mycetes. Full true thou speak'st, and like thyself, my lord,
Whom I may term a Damon for thy love   50
Therefore 'tis best, if so it like you all,
To send my thousand horse incontinent
To apprehend that paltry Scythian.
How like you this, my honourable lords?
Is it not a kingly resolution?
Cosroe. It cannot choose, because it comes from you.
Mycetes. Then hear thy charge, valiant Theridamas,
The chiefest captain of Mycetes' host,
The hope of Persia, and the very legs
Whereon our state doth lean as on a staff   60
That holds us up and foils our neighbour foes:
Thou shalt be leader of this thousand horse,
Whose foaming gall with rage and high disdain
Have sworn the death of wicked Tamburlaine.
Go frowning forth, but come thou smiling home,
As did Sir Paris with the Grecian dame.
Return with speed, time passeth swift away,

32 passengers] travellers   50 Damon] with Pythias, a model of friendship   52 incontinent]
at once   66 Grecian dame] Helen

Our life is frail, and we may die today.
Theridamas. Before the moon renew her borrow'd light,
    Doubt not, my lord and gracious sovereign,   70
    But Tamburlaine and that Tartarian rout
    Shall either perish by our warlike hands,
    Or plead for mercy at your highness' feet.
Mycetes. Go, stout Theridamas, thy words are swords,
    And with thy looks thou conquerest all thy foes.
    I long to see thee back return from thence,
    That I may view these milk-white steeds of mine
    All loaden with the heads of killed men,
    And from their knees even to their hoofs below
    Besmear'd with blood that makes a dainty show.   80
Theridamas. Then now, my lord, I humbly take my leave.
Mycetes. Theridamas, farewell ten thousand times.   *Exit* [Theridamas].
    Ah, Menaphon, why stay'st thou thus behind,
    When other men press forward for renown?
    Go, Menaphon, go into Scythia,
    And foot by foot follow Theridamas.
Cosroe. Nay, pray you, let him stay; a greater task
    Fits Menaphon than warring with a thief.
    Create him prorex of all Africa,
    That he may win the Babylonians' hearts,   90
    Which will revolt from Persian government,
    Unless they have a wiser king than you.
Mycetes. 'Unless they have a wiser king than you!'
    These are his words; Meander, set them down.
Cosroe. And add this to them, that all Asia
    Lament to see the folly of their king.
Mycetes. Well, here I swear by this my royal seat—
Cosroe. You may do well to kiss it then.
Mycetes. Emboss'd with silk as best beseems my state,
    To be reveng'd for these contemptuous words.   100
    O where is duty and allegiance now?
    Fled to the Caspian or the Ocean main?
    What, shall I call thee brother? No, a foe,
    Monster of nature, shame unto thy stock,
    That dar'st presume thy sovereign for to mock!
    Meander, come; I am abus'd, Meander.
            Exit [*with* Meander *and others*]. *Manent* Cosroe *and* Menaphon.
Menaphon. How now my lord! What, mated and amaz'd
    To hear the King thus threaten like himself?

89 prorex] viceroy   107 mated] daunted

Cosroe. Ah Menaphon, I pass not for his threats.
    The plot is laid by Persian noblemen   110
    And captains of the Median garrisons
    To crown me emperor of Asia.
    But this it is that doth excruciate
    The very substance of my vexed soul:
    To see our neighbours that were wont to quake
    And tremble at the Persian monarch's name,
    Now sits and laughs our regiment to scorn;
    And that which might resolve me into tears,
    Men from the farthest equinoctial line
    Have swarm'd in troops into the Eastern India,   120
    Lading their ships with gold and precious stones,
    And made their spoils from all our provinces.
Menaphon. This should entreat your highness to rejoice,
    Since fortune gives you opportunity
    To gain the title of a conqueror
    By curing of this maimed empery.
    Afric and Europe bordering on your land,
    And continent to your dominions,
    How easily may you with a mighty host
    Pass into Graecia, as did Cyrus once,   130
    And cause them to withdraw their forces home,
    Lest you subdue the pride of Christendom!   [*Trumpets within.*]
Cosroe. But Menaphon, what means this trumpet's sound?
Menaphon. Behold, my lord, Ortygius and the rest
    Bringing the crown to make you emperor!
          Enter Ortygius *and* Ceneus *bearing a crown, with others.*
Ortygius. Magnificent and mighty prince Cosroe,
    We in the name of other Persian states
    And commons of this mighty monarchy,
    Present thee with th' imperial diadem.
Ceneus. The warlike soldiers and the gentlemen,   140
    That heretofore have fill'd Persepolis
    With Afric captains taken in the field,
    Whose ransom made them march in coats of gold,
    With costly jewels hanging at their ears,
    And shining stones upon their lofty crests,
    Now living idle in the walled towns,
    Wanting both pay and martial discipline,
    Begin in troops to threaten civil war,
    And openly exclaim against the king.

117 regiment] government   119 equinoctial line] the equator

Therefore, to stay all sudden mutinies, 150
We will invest your highness emperor;
Whereat the soldiers will conceive more joy
Than did the Macedonians at the spoil
Of great Darius and his wealthy host.

Cosroe. Well, since I see the state of Persia droop
And languish in my brother's government,
I willingly receive th' imperial crown,
And vow to wear it for my country's good,
In spite of them shall malice my estate.

Ortygius. And, in assurance of desir'd success, 160
We here do crown thee monarch of the East,
Emperor of Asia and of Persia,
Great lord of Media and Armenia,
Duke of Africa and Albania,
Mesopotamia and of Parthia,
East India and the late-discover'd isles,
Chief lord of all the wide vast Euxine Sea,
And of the ever-raging Caspian Lake.

All. Long live Cosroe, mighty emperor!

Cosroe. And Jove may never let me longer live 170
Than I may seek to gratify your love,
And cause the soldiers that thus honour me
To triumph over many provinces;
By whose desires of discipline in arms
I doubt not shortly but to reign sole king,
And with the army of Theridamas,
Whither we presently will fly, my lords,
To rest secure against my brother's force.

Ortygius. We knew, my lord, before we brought the crown,
Intending your investion so near 180
The residence of your despised brother,
The lords would not be too exasperate
To injury or suppress your worthy title;
Or, if they would, there are in readiness
Ten thousand horse to carry you from hence,
In spite of all suspected enemies.

Cosroe. I know it well, my lord, and thank you all.

Ortygius. Sound up the trumpets, then. [*Trumpets sounded.*]
All. God save the king! *Exeunt.*

153–4 the Macedonians . . . host] Alexander the Great, King of Macedon, defeated Darius III, King of Persia, at the battle of Issus in 333 B.C. 177 presently] immediately 180 investion] investiture

Actus I.   Scaena 2.

[*Enter*] Tamburlaine *leading* Zenocrate, Techelles, Usumcasane,
[Agydas, Magnetes,] *other* Lords, *and* Soldiers *loaden with treasure.*

Tamburlaine. Come lady, let not this appall your thoughts;
    The jewels and the treasure we have ta'en
    Shall be reserv'd, and you in better state
    Than if you were arriv'd in Syria,
    Even in the circle of your father's arms,
    The mighty Soldan of Egyptia.

Zenocrate. Ah shepherd, pity my distressed plight
    (If, as thou seem'st, thou art so mean a man)
    And seek not to enrich thy followers
    By lawless rapine from a silly maid,   10
    Who, travelling with these Median lords
    To Memphis, from my uncle's country of Media,
    Where all my youth I have been governed,
    Have pass'd the army of the mighty Turk,
    Bearing his privy signet and his hand
    To safe conduct us thorough Africa.

Magnetes. And, since we have arrived in Scythia,
    Besides rich presents from the puissant Cham,
    We have his highness' letters to command
    Aid and assistance, if we stand in need.   20

Tamburlaine. But now you see these letters and commands
    Are countermanded by a greater man,
    And through my provinces you must expect
    Letters of conduct from my mightiness,
    If you intend to keep your treasure safe.
    But, since I love to live at liberty,
    As easily may you get the Soldan's crown
    As any prizes out of my precinct,
    For they are friends that help to wean my state,
    Till men and kingdoms help to strengthen it,   30
    And must maintain my life exempt from servitude.
    But tell me, madam, is your grace betroth'd?

Zenocrate. I am, my lord—for so you do import.

Tamburlaine. I am a lord, for so my deeds shall prove,
    And yet a shepherd by my parentage.
    But lady, this fair face and heavenly hue
    Must grace his bed that conquers Asia,

10 silly] simple   29 they are friends . . . state] these prizes help my state to grow

And means to be a terror to the world,
Measuring the limits of his empery
By east and west, as Phoebus doth his course.   40
Lie here, ye weeds that I disdain to wear!
This complete armour and this curtle-axe
Are adjuncts more beseeming Tamburlaine.
And, madam, whatsoever you esteem
Of this success, and loss unvalued,
Both may invest you empress of the East;
And these, that seem but silly country swains,
May have the leading of so great an host
As with their weight shall make the mountains quake,
Even as when windy exhalations,   50
Fighting for passage, tilt within the earth.

Techelles. As princely lions when they rouse themselves,
Stretching their paws, and threat'ning herds of beasts,
So in his armour looketh Tamburlaine.
Methinks I see kings kneeling at his feet,
And he with frowning brows and fiery looks
Spurning their crowns from off their captive heads.

Usumcasane. And making thee and me, Techelles, kings,
That even to death will follow Tamburlaine.

Tamburlaine. Nobly resolv'd, sweet friends and followers!   60
These lords, perhaps, do scorn our estimates,
And think we prattle with distemper'd spirits;
But, since they measure our deserts so mean,
That in conceit bear empires on our spears,
Affecting thoughts co-equal with the clouds,
They shall be kept our forced followers
Till with their eyes they view us emperors.

Zenocrates. The gods, defenders of the innocent,
Will never prosper your intended drifts
That thus oppress poor friendless passengers.   70
Therefore at least admit us liberty,
Even as thou hop'st to be eternized
By living Asia's mighty emperor.

Agydas. I hope our lady's treasure and our own
May serve for ransom to our liberties.
Return our mules and empty camels back,
That we may travel into Syria,
Where her betrothed lord, Alcidamus,
Expects th' arrival of her highness' person.

42 curtle-axe] cutlass   45 unvalued] invaluable   64 conceit] imagination   69 drifts] plans

Magnetes. And wheresoever we repose ourselves,   80
    We will report but well of Tamburlaine.
Tamburlaine. Disdains Zenocrate to live with me?
    Or you, my lords, to be my followers?
    Think you I weigh this treasure more than you?
    Not all the gold in India's wealthy arms
    Shall buy the meanest soldier in my train.
    Zenocrate, lovelier than the love of Jove,
    Brighter than is the silver Rhodope,
    Fairer than whitest snow on Scythian hills,
    Thy person is more worth to Tamburlaine   90
    Than the possession of the Persian crown,
    Which gracious stars have promis'd at my birth.
    A hundred Tartars shall attend on thee,
    Mounted on steeds swifter than Pegasus;
    Thy garments shall be made of Median silk,
    Enchas'd with precious jewels of mine own,
    More rich and valurous than Zenocrate's;
    With milk-white harts upon an ivory sled
    Thou shalt be drawn amidst the frozen pools,
    And scale the icy mountains' lofty tops,   100
    Which with thy beauty will be soon resolv'd.
    My martial prizes with five hundred men
    Won on the fifty-headed Volga's waves,
    Shall all we offer to Zenocrate,
    And then myself to fair Zenocrate.
Techelles. What now! In love?
Tamburlaine. Techelles, women must be flattered:
    But this is she with whom I am in love.

Enter a Soldier.

Soldier. News, news!
Tamburlaine. How now, what's the matter?   110
Soldier. A thousand Persian horsemen are at hand,
    Sent from the King to overcome us all.
Tamburlaine. How now, my lords of Egypt and Zenocrate!
    Now must your jewels be restor'd again,
    And I that triumph'd so be overcome?
    How say you, lordings, is not this your hope?
Agydas. We hope yourself will willingly restore them.
Tamburlaine. Such hope, such fortune, have the thousand horse.

---

88 silver Rhodope] Thracian mountain range, famous for its silver mines   97 valurous]
valuable

    Soft ye, my lords and sweet Zenocrate!
    You must be forced from me ere you go.   120
    A thousand horsemen? We five hundred foot?
    An odds too great for us to stand against?
    But are they rich? And is their armour good?
Soldier. Their plumed helms are wrought with beaten gold,
    Their swords enamell'd, and about their necks
    Hangs massy chains of gold down to the waist;
    In every part exceeding brave and rich.
Tamburlaine. Then shall we fight courageously with them?
    Or look you I should play the orator?
Techelles. No, cowards and faint-hearted runaways   130
    Look for orations when the foe is near:
    Our swords shall play the orators for us.
Usumcasane. Come, let us meet them at the mountain-foot,
    And with a sudden and an hot alarm
    Drive all their horses headlong down the hill.
Techelles. Come, let us march.
Tamburlaine. Stay, Techelles; ask a parley first.

               The Soldiers *enter.*

    Open the mails, yet guard the treasure sure.
    Lay out our golden wedges to the view,
    That their reflections may amaze the Persians;   140
    And look we friendly on them when they come.
    But if they offer word or violence,
    We'll fight, five hundred men-at-arms to one,
    Before we part with our possession;
    And 'gainst the general we will lift our swords,
    And either lanch his greedy thirsting throat,
    Or take him prisoner, and his chain shall serve
    For manacles till he be ransom'd home.
Techelles. I hear them come. Shall we encounter them?
Tamburlaine. Keep all your standings, and not stir a foot: 150
    Myself will bide the danger of the brunt.

          Enter Theridamas, *with others.*

Theridamas. Where is this Scythian Tamburlaine?
Tamburlaine. Whom seek'st thou, Persian? I am Tamburlaine.
Theridamas. Tamburlaine!
    A Scythian shepherd so embellished
    With nature's pride and richest furniture!
    His looks do menace heaven and dare the gods;

138 mails] baggage   146 lanch] pierce

His fiery eyes are fix'd upon the earth,
As if he now devis'd some stratagem,
Or meant to pierce Avernus' darksome vaults   160
To pull the triple-headed dog from hell.
Tamburlaine. Noble and mild this Persian seems to be,
If outward habit judge the inward man.
Techelles. His deep affections make him passionate.
Tamburlaine. With what a majesty he rears his looks.
In thee, thou valiant man of Persia,
I see the folly of thy emperor.
Art thou but captain of a thousand horse,
That by characters graven in thy brows,
And by thy martial face and stout aspect,   170
Deserv'st to have the leading of an host?
Forsake thy king, and do but join with me,
And we will triumph over all the world.
I hold the Fates bound fast in iron chains,
And with my hand turn Fortune's wheel about;
And sooner shall the sun fall from his sphere
Than Tamburlaine be slain or overcome.
Draw forth thy sword, thou mighty man-at-arms,
Intending but to raze my charmed skin,
And Jove himself will stretch his hand from heaven   180
To ward the blow, and shield me safe from harm.
See how he rains down heaps of gold in showers,
As if he meant to give my soldiers pay;
And, as a sure and grounded argument
That I shall be the monarch of the East,
He sends this Soldan's daughter rich and brave,
To be my queen and portly emperess.
If thou wilt stay with me, renowmed man,
And lead thy thousand horse with my conduct,
Besides thy share of this Egyptian prize,   190
Those thousand horse shall sweat with martial spoil
Of conquer'd kingdoms and of cities sack'd.
Both we will walk upon the lofty cliffs;
And Christian merchants, that with Russian stems
Plough up huge furrows in the Caspian Sea,
Shall vail to us as lords of all the lake.
Both we will reign as consuls of the earth,
And mighty kings shall be our senators.

161 triple-headed dog] Cerberus   187 portly] stately   188 renowmed] a variant form
of renowned   194 stems] ships   196 vail] lower sails   196 lake] ocean

Jove sometime masked in a shepherd's weed,
And by those steps that he hath scal'd the heavens   200
May we become immortal like the gods.
Join with me now in this my mean estate
(I call it mean because, being yet obscure,
The nations far-remov'd admire me not)
And when my name and honour shall be spread
As far as Boreas claps his brazen wings,
Or fair Boötes sends his cheerful light,
Then shalt thou be competitor with me,
And sit with Tamburlaine in all his majesty.

Theridamas. Not Hermes, prolocutor to the gods,   210
    Could use persuasions more pathetical.
Tamburlaine. Nor are Apollo's oracles more true
    Than thou shalt find my vaunts substantial.
Techelles. We are his friends, and if the Persian king
    Should offer present dukedoms to our state,
    We think it loss to make exchange for that
    We are assur'd of by our friend's success.
Usumcasane. And kingdoms at the least we all expect,
    Besides the honour in assured conquests,
    Where kings shall crouch unto our conquering swords,   220
    And hosts of soldiers stand amaz'd at us,
    When with their fearful tongues they shall confess,
    These are the men that all the world admires.
Theridamas. What strong enchantments tice my yielding soul!
    Ah, these resolved, noble Scythians!
    But shall I prove a traitor to my king?
Tamburlaine. No, but the trusty friend of Tamburlaine.
Theridamas. Won with thy words and conquer'd with thy looks,
    I yield myself, my men and horse to thee,
    To be partaker of thy good or ill,   230
    As long as life maintains Theridamas.
Tamburlaine. Theridamas my friend, take here my hand,
    Which is as much as if I swore by heaven,
    And call'd the gods to witness of my vow.
    Thus shall my heart be still combin'd with thine,
    Until our bodies turn to elements,
    And both our souls aspire celestial thrones.
    Techelles and Casane, welcome him.
Techelles. Welcome, renowmed Persian, to us all.
Usumcasane. Long may Theridamas remain with us.   240

208 competitor] partner   210 prolocutor to] spokesman for   211 pathetical] moving

Tamburlaine. These are my friends, in whom I more rejoice
    Than doth the King of Persia in his crown;
    And, by the love of Pylades and Orestes,
    Whose statues we adore in Scythia,
    Thyself and them shall never part from me
    Before I crown you kings in Asia.
    Make much of them, gentle Theridamas,
    And they will never leave thee till the death.
Theridamas. Nor thee nor them, thrice-noble Tamburlaine,
    Shall want my heart to be with gladness pierc'd   250
    To do you honour and security.
Tamburlaine. A thousand thanks, worthy Theridamas.
    And now, fair madam and my noble lords,
    If you will willingly remain with me,
    You shall have honours as your merits be;
    Or else you shall be forc'd with slavery.
Agydas. We yield unto thee, happy Tamburlaine.
Tamburlaine. For you then, madam, I am out of doubt.
Zenocrate. I must be pleas'd perforce, wretched Zenocrate!   *Exeunt.*

Actus 2.   Scaena *1*.

[*Enter*] Cosroe, Menaphon, Ortygius, Ceneus, *with other* Soldiers.

Cosroe. Thus far are we towards Theridamas,
    And valiant Tamburlaine, the man of fame,
    The man that in the forehead of his fortune
    Bears figures of renown and miracle.
    But tell me, that hast seen him, Menaphon,
    What stature wields he, and what personage?
Menaphon. Of stature tall, and straightly fashioned
    Like his desire, lift upwards and divine;
    So large of limbs, his joints so strongly knit,
    Such breadth of shoulders as might mainly bear   10
    Old Atlas' burden; 'twixt his manly pitch
    A pearl more worth than all the world is plac'd,
    Wherein by curious sovereignty of art
    Are fix'd his piercing instruments of sight,
    Whose fiery circles bear encompassed
    A heaven of heavenly bodies in their spheres,

243 Pylades] who assisted Orestes in the murder of his mother   II. i, 8 lift] lifted
10 mainly] strongly   11 pitch] shoulders

That guides his steps and actions to the throne
Where honour sits invested royally;
Pale of complexion, wrought in him with passion,
Thirsting with sovereignty, with love of arms;   20
His lofty brows in folds do figure death,
And in their smoothness amity and life;
About them hangs a knot of amber hair,
Wrapped in curls, as fierce Achilles' was,
On which the breath of heaven delights to play,
Making it dance with wanton majesty.
His arms and fingers long and sinewy,
Betokening valour and excess of strength.
In every part proportion'd like the man
Should make the world subdu'd to Tamburlaine.   30

Cosroe. Well hast thou portray'd in thy terms of life
The face and personage of a wondrous man.
Nature doth strive with Fortune and his stars
To make him famous in accomplish'd worth;
And well his merits show him to be made
His fortune's master and the king of men,
That could persuade, at such a sudden pinch,
With reasons of his valour and his life,
A thousand sworn and overmatching foes.
Then when our powers in points of swords are join'd   40
And clos'd in compass of the killing bullet,
Though strait the passage and the port be made
That leads to palace of my brother's life,
Proud is his fortune if we pierce it not.
And when the princely Persian diadem
Shall overweigh his weary witless head,
And fall like mellow'd fruit, with shakes of death,
In fair Persia noble Tamburlaine
Shall be my regent, and remain as King.

Ortygius. In happy hour we have set the crown   50
Upon your kingly head, that seeks our honour
In joining with the man ordain'd by heaven
To further every action to the best.

Ceneus. He that with shepherds and a little spoil
Durst, in disdain of wrong and tyranny,
Defend his freedom 'gainst a monarchy,
What will he do supported by a king,
Leading a troop of gentlemen and lords,

37 pinch] exigency   42 port] gateway

And stuff'd with treasure for his highest thoughts!

Cosroe. And such shall wait on worthy Tamburlaine.   60
    Our army will be forty thousand strong,
    When Tamburlaine and brave Theridamas
    Have met us by the river Araris,
    And all conjoin'd to meet the witless King,
    That now is marching near to Parthia,
    And with unwilling soldiers faintly arm'd,
    To seek revenge on me and Tamburlaine.
    To whom, sweet Menaphon, direct me straight.

Menaphon. I will, my lord.   *Exeunt.*

Act. 2.   Scaena 2.

[*Enter*] Mycetes, Meander, *with other* Lords *and* Soldiers.

Mycetes. Come my Meander, let us to this gear.
    I tell you true, my heart is swoll'n with wrath
    On this same thievish villain Tamburlaine,
    And of that false Cosroe, my traitorous brother.
    Would it not grieve a king to be so abus'd,
    And have a thousand horsemen ta'en away?
    And, which is worst, to have his diadem
    Sought for by such scald knaves as love him not?
    I think it would. Well then, by heavens I swear,   10
    Aurora shall not peep out of her doors,
    But I will have Cosroe by the head,
    And kill proud Tamburlaine with point of sword.
    Tell you the rest, Meander: I have said.

Meander. Then having pass'd Armenian deserts now,
    And pitch'd our tents under the Georgian hills,
    Whose tops are cover'd with Tartarian thieves
    That lie in ambush, waiting for a prey,
    What should we do but bid them battle straight,
    And rid the world of those detested troops?
    Lest, if we let them linger here a while,   20
    They gather strength by power of fresh supplies.
    This country swarms with vile outrageous men
    That live by rapine and by lawless spoil,
    Fit soldiers for the wicked Tamburlaine;
    And he that could with gifts and promises

63 Araris] the Araxes, flowing through Armenia into the Caspian   II. ii, 1 gear] business
8 scald] contemptible

Inveigle him that led a thousand horse,
And make him false his faith unto his king,
Will quickly win such as are like himself.
Therefore cheer up your minds; prepare to fight.
He that can take or slaughter Tamburlaine,   30
Shall rule the province of Albania.
Who brings that traitor's head, Theridamas,
Shall have a government in Media,
Beside the spoil of him and all his train.
But, if Cosroe (as our spials say,
And as we know) remains with Tamburlaine,
His highness' pleasure is that he should live,
And be reclaim'd with princely lenity.

                    [*Enter a* Spy.]

Spy. An hundred horsemen of my company,
      Scouting abroad upon these champion plains,   40
      Have view'd the army of the Scythians,
      Which make report it far exceeds the King's.
Meander. Suppose they be in number infinite,
      Yet being void of martial discipline,
      All running headlong after greedy spoils,
      And more regarding gain than victory,
      Like to the cruel brothers of the earth,
      Sprung of the teeth of dragons venomous,
      Their careless swords shall lanch their fellows' throats
      And make us triumph in their overthrow.   50
Mycetes. Was there such brethren, sweet Meander, say,
      That sprung of teeth of dragons venomous?
Meander. So poets say, my lord.
Mycetes. And 'tis a pretty toy to be a poet.
      Well, well, Meander, thou art deeply read,
      And having thee, I have a jewel sure.
      Go on, my lord, and give your charge, I say;
      Thy wit will make us conquerors today.
Meander. Then, noble soldiers, to entrap these thieves
      That live confounded in disorder'd troops,   60
      If wealth or riches may prevail with them,
      We have our camels laden all with gold,
      Which you that be but common soldiers

35 spials] spies   40 champion plains] open country   47-9 Like ... throats] Armed
men sprang from the dragon's teeth sowed by Cadmus and, fighting among themselves,
destroyed one another.

Shall fling in every corner of the field;
And while the base-born Tartars take it up,
You, fighting more for honour than for gold,
Shall massacre those greedy-minded slaves;
And when their scatter'd army is subdu'd,
And you march on their slaughter'd carcasses,
Share equally the gold that bought their lives,   70
And live like gentlemen in Persia.
Strike up the drum, and march courageously:
Fortune herself doth sit upon our crests.
Mycetes. He tells you true, my masters, so he does.
Drums, why sound ye not when Meander speaks?   [*Drums sound.*]
                                                                Exeunt.

Actus 2.   Scaena 3.

[*Enter*] Cosroe, Tamburlaine, Theridamas, Techelles, Usumcasane,
                    Ortygius, *with others.*

Cosroe. Now worthy Tamburlaine, have I repos'd
In thy approved fortunes all my hope.
What think'st thou, man, shall come of our attempts?
For even as from assured oracle,
I take thy doom for satisfaction.
Tamburlaine. And so mistake you not a whit, my lord,
For fates and oracles of heaven have sworn
To royalize the deeds of Tamburlaine,
And make them blest that share in his attempts.
And doubt you not but, if you favour me,   10
And let my fortunes and my valour sway
To some direction in your martial deeds,
The world will strive with hosts of men-at-arms
To swarm unto the ensign I support.
The host of Xerxes, which by fame is said
To drink the mighty Parthian Araris,
Was but a handful to that we will have.
Our quivering lances, shaking in the air,
And bullets like Jove's dreadful thunderbolts
Enroll'd in flames and fiery smouldering mists,   20

2 approved] tested   5 I take . . . satisfaction] I take your opinion (doom) for the truth
16 To drink . . . Araris] The army of Xerxes was said to be so great that they drank the
river dry.

    Shall threat the gods more than Cyclopian wars;
    And with our sun-bright armour, as we march,
    We'll chase the stars from heaven, and dim their eyes
    That stand and muse at our admired arms.
Theridamas. You see, my lord, what working words he hath;
    But, when you see his actions top his speech,
    Your speech will stay, or so extol his worth
    As I shall be commended and excus'd
    For turning my poor charge to his direction
    And these his two renowmed friends, my lord,   30
    Would make one thrust and strive to be retain'd
    In such a great degree of amity.
Techelles. With duty and with amity we yield
    Our utmost service to the fair Cosroe.
Cosroe. Which I esteem as portion of my crown.
    Usumcasane and Techelles both,
    When She that rules in Rhamnus' golden gates,
    And makes a passage for all prosperous arms,
    Shall make me solely emperor of Asia,
    Then shall your meeds and valours be advanc'd   40
    To rooms of honour and nobility.
Tamburlaine. Then haste, Cosroe, to be king alone,
    That I with these my friends and all my men
    May triumph in our long-expected fate.
    The King your brother is now hard at hand:
    Meet with the fool, and rid your royal shoulders
    Of such a burden as outweighs the sands
    And all the craggy rocks of Caspia.

                [*Enter a* Messenger.]

Messenger. My lord, we have discovered the enemy
    Ready to charge you with a mighty army.   50
Cosroe. Come, Tamburlaine, now whet thy winged sword,
    And lift thy lofty arm into the clouds,
    That it may reach the King of Persia's crown,
    And set it safe on my victorious head.
Tamburlaine. See where it is, the keenest curtle-axe
    That e'er made passage thorough Persian arms!
    These are the wings shall make it fly as swift
    As doth the lightning or the breath of heaven,

21 Cyclopian wars] The Cyclopes, children of Cronus, armed Zeus (Jove) with thunderbolts
to make war on their brothers the Titans.   37 She . . . gates] Nemesis, goddess of vengeance, who had a shrine at Rhamnus

And kill as sure as it swiftly flies.

Cosroe. Thy words assure me of kind success.   60
    Go valiant soldier, go before and charge
    The fainting army of that foolish king.

Tamburlaine. Usumcasane and Techelles, come;
    We are enough to scare the enemy,
    And more than needs to make an emperor.   [*Exeunt.*]

[*Actus 2.   Scaena 4.*]

To the battle, and Mycetes *comes out alone with his crown in his
hand, offering to hide it.*

Mycetes. Accurs'd be he that first invented war!
    They knew not, ah, they knew not, simple men,
    How those were hit by pelting cannon-shot
    Stand staggering like a quivering aspen-leaf
    Fearing the force of Boreas' boist'rous blasts.
    In what a lamentable case were I,
    If nature had not given me wisdom's lore!
    For kings are clouts that every man shoots at,
    Our crown the pin that thousands seek to cleave.
    Therefore in policy I think it good   10
    To hide it close; a goodly stratagem,
    And far from any man that is a fool.
    So shall not I be known; or if I be,
    They cannot take away my crown from me.
    Here will I hide it in this simple hole.

Enter Tamburlaine.

Tamburlaine. What, fearful coward, straggling from the camp
    When kings themselves are present in the field?

Mycetes. Thou liest.

Tamburlaine.   Base villain, dar'st thou give the lie?

Mycetes. Away, I am the King! Go, touch me not.
    Thou break'st the law of arms unless thou kneel,   20
    And cry me 'Mercy, noble King!'

Tamburlaine. Are you the witty King of Persia?

Mycetes. Ay, marry am I: have you any suit to me?

Tamburlaine. I would entreat you to speak but three wise words.

Mycetes. So I can when I see my time.

Tamburlaine. Is this your crown?

8 clouts] archery targets   9 pin] centre of the target

Mycetes. Ay: didst thou ever see a fairer?

Tamburlaine. You will not sell it, will ye?

Mycetes. Such another word, and I will have thee executed.
  Come, give it me.

Tamburlaine.   No, I took it prisoner.   30

Mycetes. You lie, I gave it you.

Tamburlaine.   Then 'tis mine.

Mycetes. No, I mean I let you keep it.

Tamburlaine. Well, I mean you shall have it again.
  Here, take it for a while; I lend it thee
  Till I may see thee hemm'd with armed men;
  Then shalt thou see me pull it from thy head.
  Thou art no match for mighty Tamburlaine.   [*Exit.*]

Mycetes. O gods, is this Tamburlaine the thief?
  I marvel much he stole it not away.

         Sound trumpets to the battle, and he runs in.

      [*Actus 2.   Scaena 5.*]

[*Enter*] Cosroe, Tamburlaine, Theridamas, Menaphon, Meander,
    Ortygius, Techelles, Usumcasane, *with others.*

Tamburlaine. Hold thee, Cosroe; wear two imperial crowns.
  Think thee invested now as royally,
  Even by the mighty hand of Tamburlaine,
  As if as many kings as could encompass thee
  With greatest pomp had crown'd thee emperor.

Cosroe. So do I, thrice-renowmed man-at-arms;
  And none shall keep the crown but Tamburlaine.
  Thee do I make my regent of Persia,
  And general lieutenant of my armies.
  Meander, you that were our brother's guide,   10
  And chiefest counsellor in all his acts,
  Since he is yielded to the stroke of war,
  On your submission we with thanks excuse,
  And give you equal place in our affairs.

Meander. Most happy Emperor, in humblest terms
  I vow my service to your majesty,
  With utmost virtue of my faith and duty.

Cosroe. Thanks good Meander. Then, Cosroe, reign,
  And govern Persia in her former pomp.
  Now send embassage to thy neighbour kings,   20

And let them know the Persian king is chang'd
From one that knew not what a king should do
To one that can command what 'longs thereto.
And now we will to fair Persepolis
With twenty thousand expert soldiers.
The lords and captains of my brother's camp
With little slaughter take Meander's course,
And gladly yield them to my gracious rule.
Ortygius and Menaphon, my trusty friends,
Now will I gratify your former good,   30
And grace your calling with a greater sway.

Ortygius. And as we ever aim'd at your behoof,
And sought your state all honour it deserv'd,
So will we with our powers and our lives
Endeavour to preserve and prosper it.

Cosroe. I will not thank thee, sweet Ortygius;
Better replies shall prove my purposes.
And now, Lord Tamburlaine, my brother's camp
I leave to thee and to Theridamas,
To follow me to fair Persepolis.   40
Then will we march to all those Indian mines
My witless brother to the Christians lost,
And ransom them with fame and usury.
And, till thou overtake me, Tamburlaine,
Staying to order all the scatter'd troops,
Farewell, lord regent and his happy friends.
I long to sit upon my brother's throne.

Meander. Your majesty shall shortly have your wish,
And ride in triumph through Persepolis.   *Exeunt.*

        Manent Tamburlaine, Techelles, Theridamas, Usumcasane.

Tamburlaine. And ride in triumph through Persepolis!   50
Is it not brave to be a king, Techelles,
Usumcasane and Theridamas?
Is it not passing brave to be a king,
And ride in triumph through Persepolis?

Techelles. O my lord, 'tis sweet and full of pomp.

Usumcasane. To be a king, is half to be a god.

Theridamas. A god is not so glorious as a king:
I think the pleasure they enjoy in heaven,
Cannot compare with kingly joys in earth;
To wear a crown enchas'd with pearl and gold,   60

43 with fame and usury] to our renown and profit   53 passing] exceedingly

    Whose virtues carry with it life and death;
    To ask and have, command and be obey'd;
    When looks breed love, with looks to gain the prize,
    Such power attractive shines in princes' eyes.
Tamburlaine. Why say, Theridamas, wilt thou be a king?
Theridamas. Nay, though I praise it, I can live without it.
Tamburlaine. What say my other friends, will you be kings?
Techelles. Ay, if I could, with all my heart, my lord.
Tamburlaine. Why, that's well said, Techelles; so would I
    And so would you my masters, would you not?   70
Usumcasane. What then, my lord?
Tamburlaine. Why then, Casane, shall we wish for aught
    The world affords in greatest novelty,
    And rest attemptless, faint, and destitute?
    Methinks we should not. I am strongly mov'd,
    That if I should desire the Persian crown,
    I could attain it with a wondrous ease;
    And would not all our soldiers soon consent,
    If we should aim at such a dignity?
Theridamas. I know they would with our persuasions.   80
Tamburlaine. Why then, Theridamas, I'll first assay
    To get the Persian kingdom to myself;
    Then thou for Parthia; they for Scythia and Media;
    And if I prosper, all shall be as sure
    As if the Turk, the Pope, Afric, and Greece,
    Came creeping to us with their crowns apiece.
Techelles. Then shall we send to this triumphing king,
    And bid him battle for his novel crown?
Usumcasane. Nay, quickly then, before his room be hot.
Tamburlaine. 'Twill prove a pretty jest, in faith, my friends.   90
Theridamas. A jest to charge on twenty thousand men!
    I judge the purchase more important far.
Tamburlaine. Judge by thyself, Theridamas, not me;
    For presently Techelles here shall haste
    To bid him battle ere he pass too far,
    And lose more labour than the gain will quite.
    Then shalt thou see the Scythian Tamburlaine
    Make but a jest to win the Persian crown.
    Techelles, take a thousand horse with thee,
    And bid him turn him back to war with us,   100
    That only made him king to make us sport.
    We will not steal upon him cowardly,

74 attemptless] without trying   92 purchase] undertaking   96 quite] pay for

But give him warning and more warriors.
Haste thee, Techelles; we will follow thee.   [*Exit* Techelles.]
What saith Theridamas?
Theridamas.   Go on, for me.   *Exeunt.*

Actus 2.   Scaena 6.

[*Enter*] Cosroe, Meander, Ortygius, Menaphon, *with other* Soldiers.

Cosroe. What means this devilish shepherd to aspire
        With such a giantly presumption,
        To cast up hills against the face of heaven,
        And dare the force of angry Jupiter?
        But, as he thrust them underneath the hills,
        And press'd out fire from their burning jaws,
        So will I send this monstrous slave to hell,
        Where flames shall ever feed upon his soul.
Meander. Some powers divine, or else infernal, mix'd
        Their angry seeds at his conception;   10
        For he was never sprung of human race,
        Since with the spirit of his fearful pride,
        He dares so doubtlessly resolve of rule,
        And by profession be ambitious.
Ortygius. What god, or fiend, or spirit of the earth,
        Or monster turned to a manly shape,
        Or of what mould or mettle he be made,
        What star or state soever govern him,
        Let us put on our meet encountering minds;
        And in detesting such a devilish thief,   20
        In love of honour and defence of right,
        Be arm'd against the hate of such a foe,
        Whether from earth, or hell, or heaven he grow.
Cosroe. Nobly resolv'd, my good Ortygius;
        And since we all have suck'd one wholesome air,
        And with the same proportion of elements
        Resolve, I hope we are resembled,
        Vowing our loves to equal death and life;
        Let's cheer our soldiers to encounter him,
        That grievous image of ingratitude,   30
        That fiery thirster after sovereignty,
        And burn him in the fury of that flame

2-6 giantly . . . jaws] Rebelling against Jupiter, the Giants piled Mt. Pelion on Mt. Ossa,
but were conquered and thrown under Mt. Etna.   14 by profession] openly   26-7 same
. . . Resolve] dissolve into the same elements when we die

That none can quench but blood and empery.
Resolve, my lords and loving soldiers, now
To save your king and country from decay.
Then strike up, drum; and all the stars that make
The loathsome circle of my dated life,
Direct my weapon to his barbarous heart,
That thus opposeth him against the gods,
And scorns the powers that govern Persia!   40

                                                        [*Exeunt.*]

[*Actus 2.   Scaena 7.*]

Enter to the battle; and after the battle, enter Cosroe *wounded,*
Theridamas, Tamburlaine, Techelles, Usumcasane, *with others.*

Cosroe. Barbarous and bloody Tamburlaine,
Thus to deprive me of my crown and life!
Treacherous and false Theridamas,
Even at the morning of my happy state,
Scarce being seated in my royal throne,
To work my downfall and untimely end!
An uncouth pain torments my grieved soul
And death arrests the organ of my voice,
Who, ent'ring at the breach thy sword hath made,
Sacks every vein and artier of my heart.   10
Bloody and insatiate Tamburlaine!
Tamburlaine. The thirst of reign and sweetness of a crown,
That caus'd the eldest son of heavenly Ops
To thrust his doting father from his chair,
And place himself in the imperial heaven,
Mov'd me to manage arms against thy state.
What better precedent than mighty Jove?
Nature, that fram'd us of four elements
Warring within our breasts for regiment,
Doth teach us all to have aspiring minds.   20
Our souls, whose faculties can comprehend
The wondrous architecture of the world,
And measure every wand'ring planet's course,
Still climbing after knowledge infinite,
And always moving as the restless spheres,
Wills us to wear ourselves and never rest
Until we reach the ripest fruit of all,

13 eldest . . . Ops] Jupiter, son of Saturn and Ops

That perfect bliss and sole felicity,
The sweet fruition of an earthly crown.

Theridamas. And that made me to join with Tamburlaine; 30
For he is gross and like the massy earth
That moves not upwards, nor by princely deeds
Doth mean to soar above the highest sort.

Techelles. And that made us, the friends of Tamburlaine,
To lift our swords against the Persian king.

Usumcasane. For as when Jove did thrust old Saturn down,
Neptune and Dis gain'd each of them a crown,
So do we hope to reign in Asia,
If Tamburlaine be plac'd in Persia.

Cosroe. The strangest men that ever nature made! 40
I know not how to take their tyrannies.
My bloodless body waxeth chill and cold,
And with my blood my life slides through my wound;
My soul begins to take her flight to hell,
And summons all my senses to depart.
The heat and moisture, which did feed each other,
For want of nourishment to feed them both,
Is dry and cold; and now doth ghastly Death
With greedy talents gripe my bleeding heart,
And like a harpy tires on my life. 50
Theridamas and Tamburlaine, I die:
And fearful vengeance light upon you both!

                        [Dies. Tamburlaine] *takes the crown and puts it on.*

Tamburlaine. Not all the curses which the Furies breathe
Shall make me leave so rich a prize as this.
Theridamas, Techelles, and the rest,
Who think you now is King of Persia?

All. Tamburlaine! Tamburlaine!

Tamburlaine. Though Mars himself, the angry god of arms,
And all the earthly potentates conspire
To dispossess me of this diadem, 60
Yet will I wear it in despite of them,
As great commander of this eastern world,
If you but say that Tamburlaine shall reign.

All. Long live Tamburlaine, and reign in Asia!

Tamburlaine. So; now it is more surer on my head
Than if the gods had held a parliament,
And all pronounc'd me King of Persia. *[Exeunt.]*

                             Finis Actus 2.

50 tires] preys

Actus 3.   Scaena 1.

[*Enter*] Bajazeth, *the* Kings of Fez, Morocco, *and* Argier, [Bassoes,]
with others, in great pomp.

Bajazeth. Great kings of Barbary, and my portly bassoes,
    We hear the Tartars and the eastern thieves,
    Under the conduct of one Tamburlaine,
    Presume a bickering with your emperor,
    And think to rouse us from our dreadful siege
    Of the famous Grecian Constantinople.
    You know our army is invincible:
    As many circumcised Turks we have,
    And warlike bands of Christians renied
    As hath the Ocean or the Terrene sea   10
    Small drops of water when the moon begins
    To join in one her semicircled horns.
    Yet would we not be brav'd with foreign power,
    Nor raise our siege before the Grecians yield,
    Or breathless lie before the city walls.
Fez. Renowmed emperor and mighty general,
    What if you sent the bassoes of your guard
    To charge him to remain in Asia,
    Or else to threaten death and deadly arms
    As from the mouth of mighty Bajazeth?   20
Bajazeth. Hie thee, my basso, fast to Persia.
    Tell him thy lord, the Turkish emperor,
    Dread lord of Afric, Europe and Asia,
    Great king and conqueror of Graecia,
    The Ocean, Terrene, and the coal-black Sea,
    The high and highest monarch of the world,
    Wills and commands (for say not I entreat)
    Not once to set his foot in Africa,
    Or spread his colours in Graecia,
    Lest he incur the fury of my wrath.   30
    Tell him I am content to take a truce,
    Because I hear he bears a valiant mind;
    But if, presuming on his silly power,
    He be so mad to manage arms with me,
    Then stay thou with him; say, I bid thee so.
    And if before the sun have measur'd heaven

s.d. Bassoes] high-ranking Turkish officers   9 renied] renegade   10 Terrene sea]
Mediterranean

With triple circuit, thou re-greet us not,
We mean to take his morning's next arise
For messenger he will not be reclaim'd,
And mean to fetch thee in despite of him.   40
Basso. Most great and puissant monarch of the earth,
    Your basso will accomplish your behest,
    And show your pleasure to the Persian,
    As fits the legate of the stately Turk.   *Exit* Basso.
Argier. They say he is the King of Persia;
    But if he dare attempt to stir your siege,
    'Twere requisite he should be ten times more,
    For all flesh quakes at your magnificence.
Bajazeth. True, Argier, and tremble at my looks.
Morocco. The spring is hinder'd by your smothering host,   50
    For neither ran can fall upon the earth,
    Nor sun reflex his virtuous beams thereon,
    The ground is mantled with such multitudes.
Bajazeth. All this is true as holy Mahomet,
    And all the trees are blasted with our breaths.
Fez. What thinks your greatness best to be achiev'd
    In pursuit of the city's overthrow?
Bajazeth. I will the captive pioners of Argier
    Cut off the water that by leaden pipes
    Runs to the city from the mountain Carnon;   60
    Two thousand horse shall forage up and down,
    That no relief or succour come by land;
    And all the sea my galleys countermand.
    Then shall our footmen lie within the trench,
    And with their cannons, mouth'd like Orcus' gulf,
    Batter the walls, and we will enter in;
    And thus the Grecians shall be conquered.   *Exeunt.*

Actus 3.   Scaena 2.

[*Enter*] Agydas, Zenocrate, Anippe, *with others.*
Agydas. Madam Zenocrate, may I presume
    To know the cause of these unquiet fits
    That work such trouble to your wonted rest?
    'Tis more than pity such a heavenly face
    Should by heart's sorrow wax so wan and pale,
    When your offensive rape by Tamburlaine

39 reclaim'd] restrained   58 pioners] sappers   65 Orcus' gulf] hell's mouth

(Which of your whole displeasures should be most)
Hath seem'd to be digested long ago.

Zenocrate. Although it be digested long ago,
    As his exceeding favours have deserv'd,   10
    And might content the queen of heaven as well
    As it hath chang'd my first-conceiv'd disdain,
    Yet since a farther passion feeds my thoughts
    With ceaseless and disconsolate conceits,
    Which dyes my looks so lifeless as they are,
    And might, if my extremes had full events,
    Make me the ghastly counterfeit of death.

Agydas. Eternal heaven sooner be dissolv'd,
    And all that pierceth Phoebe's silver eye,
    Before such hap fall to Zenocrate!   20

Zenocrate. Ah, life and soul, still hover in his breast,
    And leave my body senseless as the earth,
    Or else unite you to his life and soul,
    That I may live and die with Tamburlaine!

       Enter [behind] Tamburlaine with Techelles and others.

Agydas. With Tamburlaine! Ah fair Zenocrate,
    Let not a man so vile and barbarous,
    That holds you from your father in despite,
    And keeps you from the honours of a queen,
    Being suppos'd his worthless concubine,
    Be honour'd with your love but for necessity!   30
    So now the mighty Soldan hears of you,
    Your highness needs not doubt but in short time
    He will with Tamburlaine's destruction
    Redeem you from this deadly servitude.

Zenocrate. Leave to wound me with these words,
    And speak of Tamburlaine as he deserves.
    The entertainment we have had of him
    Is far from villainy or servitude,
    And might in noble minds be counted princely.

Agydas. How can you fancy one that looks so fierce,   40
    Only dispos'd to martial stratagems?
    Who, when he shall embrace you in his arms,
    Will tell how many thousand men he slew;
    And when you look for amorous discourse,
    Will rattle forth his facts of war and blood,
    Too harsh a subject for your dainty ears.

11 queen of heaven] Juno   16 if . . . events] if my passions had their full consequences
45 facts] deeds

Zenocrate. As looks the sun through Nilus' flowing stream,
    Or when the morning holds him in her arms,
    So looks my lordly love, fair Tamburlaine;
    His talk much sweeter than the Muses' song   50
    They sung for honour 'gainst Pierides,
    Or when Minerva did with Neptune strive;
    And higher would I rear my estimate
    Than Juno, sister to the highest god,
    If I were match'd with mighty Tamburlaine.

Agydas. Yet be not so inconstant in your love,
    But let the young Arabian live in hope
    After your rescue to enjoy his choice.
    You see, though first the King of Persia,
    Being a shepherd, seem'd to love you much,   60
    Now in his majesty he leaves those looks,
    Those words of favour, and those comfortings,
    And gives no more than common courtesies.

Zenocrate. Thence rise the tears that so distain my cheeks,
    Fearing his love through my unworthiness.

               Tamburlaine *goes to her, and takes her away lovingly by*
              the hand, looking wrathfully on Agydas, *and says nothing.*
                                [*Exeunt all except* Agydas.]

Agydas. Betray'd by fortune and suspicious love,
    Threaten'd with frowning wrath and jealousy,
    Surpris'd with fear of hideous revenge,
    I stand aghast; but most astonied
    To see his choler shut in secret thoughts,   70
    And wrapt in silence of his angry soul.
    Upon his brows was portray'd ugly death,
    And in his eyes the fury of his heart,
    That shine as comets, menacing revenge,
    And casts a pale complexion on his cheeks:
    As when the seaman sees the Hyades
    Gather an army of Cimmerian clouds
    (Auster and Aquilon with winged steeds,
    All sweating, tilt about the watery heavens,
    With shivering spears enforcing thunder-claps,   80
    And from their shields strike flames of lightening),
    All fearful folds his sails, and sounds the main,

---

51 Pierides] the daughters of Pierus, who competed with the Muses   52 Minerva . . .
strive] Minerva (Athena) fought Neptune for possession of Athens.   57 the young
Arabian] cf. I. ii, 78.   77 Cimmerian] dark   78 Auster and Aquilon] south and north
winds

Lifting his prayers to the heavens for aid
Against the terror of the winds and waves:
So fares Agydas for the late-felt frowns,
That sent a tempest to my daunted thoughts,
And makes my soul divine her overthrow.

Enter Techelles *with a naked dagger* [*and* Usumcasane].

Techelles. See you, Agydas, how the King salutes you!
 He bids you prophesy what it imports.
Agydas. I prophesied before, and now I prove   90
 The killing frowns of jealousy and love.
 He needed not with words confirm my fear,
 For words are vain where working tools present
 The naked action of my threaten'd end.
 It says, 'Agydas, thou shalt surely die,
 And of extremities elect the least;
 More honour and less pain it may procure,
 To die by this resolved hand of thine
 Than stay the torments he and heaven have sworn.'
 Then haste, Agydas, and prevent the plagues   100
 Which thy prolonged fates may draw on thee.
 Go wander free from fear of tyrant's rage,
 Removed from the torments and the hell
 Wherewith he may excruciate thy soul;
 And let Agydas by Agydas die,
 And with this stab slumber eternally.   [*Stabs himself.*]
Techelles. Usumcasane, see how right the man
 Hath hit the meaning of my lord the King.
Usumcasane. Faith, and Techelles, it was manly done;
 And since he was so wise and honourable,   110
 Let us afford him now the bearing hence,
 And crave his triple-worthy burial.
Techelles. Agreed, Casane; we will honour him.
          [*Exeunt, bearing out the body.*]

Actus 3. Scaena 3.

[*Enter*] Tamburlaine, Techelles, Usumcasane, Theridamas, Basso,
    Zenocrate, [Anippe,] *with others.*

Tamburlaine. Basso, by this thy lord and master knows
 I mean to meet him in Bithynia.

    See how he comes! Tush, Turks are full of brags,
    And menace more than they can well perform.
    He meet me in the field and fetch thee hence!
    Alas, poor Turk, his fortune is too weak
    T' encounter with the strength of Tamburlaine.
    View well my camp, and speak indifferently:
    Do not my captains and my soldiers look
    As if they meant to conquer Africa?   10
Basso. Your men are valiant, but their number few,
    And cannot terrify his mighty host.
    My lord, the great commander of the world,
    Besides fifteen contributory kings,
    Hath now in arms ten thousand janizaries,
    Mounted on lusty Mauritanian steeds,
    Brought to the war by men of Tripoli;
    Two hundred thousand footmen that have serv'd
    In two set battles fought in Graecia;
    And for the expedition of this war,   20
    If he think good, can from his garrisons
    Withdraw as many more to follow him.
Techelles. The more he brings, the greater is the spoil;
    For, when they perish by our warlike hands,
    We mean to seat our footmen on their steeds,
    And rifle all those stately janizars.
Tamburlaine. But will those kings accompany your lord?
Basso. Such as his highness please; but some must stay
    To rule the provinces he late subdu'd.
Tamburlaine. Then fight courageously: their crowns are yours;   30
    This hand shall set them on your conquering heads
    That made me emperor of Asia.
Usumcasane. Let him bring millions infinite of men,
    Unpeopling western Africa and Greece,
    Yet we assure us of the victory.
Theridamas. Even he, that in a trice vanquish'd two kings
    More mighty than the Turkish emperor,
    Shall rouse him out of Europe, and pursue
    His scatter'd army till they yield or die.
Tamburlaine. Well said, Theridamas! Speak in that mood,   40
    For *will* and *shall* best fitteth Tamburlaine,
    Whose smiling stars gives him assured hope
    Of martial triumph ere he meet his foes.
    I that am term'd the scourge and wrath of god,

15 janizaries] guardsmen   19 set] pitched (i.e. not casual encounters)

The only fear and terror of the world,
Will first subdue the Turk, and then enlarge
Those Christian captives which you keep as slaves,
Burdening their bodies with your heavy chains,
And feeding them with thin and slender fare,
That naked row about the Terrene sea,   50
And when they chance to breathe and rest a space,
Are punish'd with bastones so grievously
That they lie panting on the galley's side,
And strive for life at every stroke they give.
These are the cruel pirates of Argier,
That damned train, the scum of Africa,
Inhabited with straggling runagates,
That make quick havoc of the Christian blood.
But, as I live, that town shall curse the time
That Tamburlaine set foot in Africa.   60

   Enter Bajazeth *with his* Bassoes *and contributory Kings* [*of* Fez,
      Morocco, *and* Argier; Zabina *and* Ebea].

Bajazeth. Bassoes and janizaries of my guard,
      Attend upon the person of your lord,
      The greatest potentate of Africa.
Tamburlaine. Techelles and the rest, prepare your swords;
      I mean t' encounter with that Bajazeth.
Bajazeth. Kings of Fez, Moroccus, and Argier,
      He calls me Bajazeth, whom you call lord!
      Note the presumption of this Scythian slave!
      I tell thee, villain, those that lead my horse
      Have to their names titles of dignity;   70
      And dar'st thou bluntly call me Bajazeth?
Tamburlaine. And know thou, Turk, that those which lead my horse
      Shall lead thee captive thorough Africa;
      And dar'st thou bluntly call me Tamburlaine?
Bajazeth. By Mahomet my kinsman's sepulchre,
      And by the holy Alcoran I swear,
      He shall be made a chaste and lustless eunuch,
      And in my sarell tend my concubines;
      And all his captains, that thus stoutly stand,
      Shall draw the chariot of my emperess,   80
      Whom I have brought to see their overthrow!
Tamburlaine. By this my sword that conquer'd Persia,
      Thy fall shall make me famous through the world!

52 bastones] cudgels   78 sarell] seraglio

I will not tell thee how I'll handle thee,
But every common soldier of my camp
Shall smile to see thy miserable state.

Fez. What means the mighty Turkish emperor,
To talk with one so base as Tamburlaine?

Morocco. Ye Moors and valiant men of Barbary,
How can ye suffer these indignities?   90

Argier. Leave words, and let them feel your lances' points,
Which glided through the bowels of the Greeks.

Bajazeth. Well said, my stout contributory kings!
Your threefold army and my hugy host
Shall swallow up these base-born Persians.

Techelles. Puissant, renowm'd, and mighty Tamburlaine,
Why stay we thus prolonging all their lives?

Theridamas. I long to see those crowns won by our swords,
That we may reign as kings of Africa.

Usumcasane. What coward would not fight for such a prize?   100

Tamburlaine. Fight all courageously, and be you kings:
I speak it, and my words are oracles.

Bajazeth. Zabina, mother of three braver boys
Than Hercules, that in his infancy
Did pash the jaws of serpents venomous,
Whose hands are made to gripe a warlike lance,
Their shoulders broad, for complete armour fit,
Their limbs more large and of a bigger size
Than all the brats y-sprung from Typhon's loins,
Who, when they come unto their father's age,   110
Will batter turrets with their manly fists—
Sit here upon this royal chair of state,
And on thy head wear my imperial crown,
Until I bring this sturdy Tamburlaine
And all his captains bound in captive chains.

Zabina. Such good success happen to Bajazeth!

Tamburlaine. Zenocrate, the loveliest maid alive,
Fairer than rocks of pearl and precious stone,
The only paragon of Tamburlaine;
Whose eyes are brighter than the lamps of heaven,   120
And speech more pleasant than sweet harmony;
That with thy looks canst clear the darken'd sky,
And calm the rage of thund'ring Jupiter—

104-5 Hercules . . . venomous] In his cradle Hercules strangled two snakes.   109 Typhon]
Typhon, or Typhoeus, a hundred-headed giant, father of many monsters, among them
Cerberus   119 paragon] consort

Sit down by her, adorned with my crown,
As if thou wert the empress of the world.
Stir not, Zenocrate, until thou see
Me march victoriously with all my men,
Triumphing over him and these his kings,
Which I will bring as vassals to thy feet.
Till then, take thou my crown, vaunt of my worth,   130
And manage words with her, as we will arms.

Zenocrate. And may my love, the King of Persia,
Return with victory and free from wound!

Bajazeth. Now shalt thou feel the force of Turkish arms,
Which lately made all Europe quake for fear.
I have of Turks, Arabians, Moors, and Jews,
Enough to cover all Bithynia.
Let thousands die: their slaughter'd carcasses
Shall serve for walls and bulwarks to the rest;
And as the heads of Hydra, so my power,   140
Subdu'd, shall stand as mighty as before.
If they should yield their necks unto the sword,
Thy soldiers' arms could not endure to strike
So many blows as I have heads for thee.
Thou know'st not, foolish-hardy Tamburlaine,
What 'tis to meet me in the open field,
That leave no ground for thee to march upon.

Tamburlaine. Our conquering swords shall marshal us the way
We use to march upon the slaughter'd foe,
Trampling their bowels with our horses' hoofs,   150
Brave horses bred on the white Tartarian hills.
My camp is like to Julius Caesar's host,
That never fought but had the victory;
Nor in Pharsalia was there such hot war
As these my followers willingly would have.
Legions of spirits fleeting in the air
Direct our bullets and our weapons' points,
And make your strokes to wound the senseless air;
And when she sees our bloody colours spread,
Then Victory begins to take her flight,   160
Resting herself upon my milk-white tent.
But come, my lords, to weapons let us fall;
The field is ours, the Turk, his wife, and all.

Exit with his followers.

140 heads of Hydra] As one head was cut off, two others grew in its place.   154 Pharsalia]
where Julius Caesar defeated Pompey in 48 B.C.

Bajazeth. Come, kings and bassoes, let us glut our swords,
    That thirst to drink the feeble Persians' blood.   *Exit with his followers.*
Zabina. Base concubine, must thou be plac'd by me
    That am the empress of the mighty Turk?
Zenocrate. Disdainful Turkess and unreverend boss,
    Call'st thou me concubine that am betroth'd
    Unto the great and mighty Tamburlaine?   170
Zabina. To Tamburlaine, the great Tartarian thief!
Zenocrate. Thou wilt repent these lavish words of thine
    When thy great basso-master and thyself
    Must plead for mercy at his kingly feet,
    And sue to me to be your advocate.
Zabina. And sue to thee! I tell thee, shameless girl,
    Thou shalt be laundress to my waiting-maid.
    How lik'st thou her, Ebea? Will she serve?
Ebea. Madam, she thinks perhaps she is too fine;
    But I shall turn her into other weeds,   180
    And make her dainty fingers fall to work.
Zenocrate. Hear'st thou, Anippe, how thy drudge doth talk?
    And how my slave, her mistress, menaceth?
    Both for their sauciness shall be employ'd
    To dress the common soldiers' meat and drink;
    For we will scorn they should come near ourselves.
Anippe. Yet sometimes let your highness send for them
    To do the work my chambermaid disdains.
              They sound the battle within, and stay.
Zenocrate. Ye gods and powers that govern Persia,
    And made my lordly love her worthy king,   190
    Now strengthen him against the Turkish Bajazeth,
    And let his foes, like flocks of fearful roes
    Pursu'd by hunters, fly his angry looks,
    That I may see him issue conqueror!
Zabina. Now, Mahomet, solicit God himself,
    And make him rain down murdering shot from heaven,
    To dash the Scythians' brains, and strike them dead,
    That dare to manage arms with him
    That offer'd jewels to thy sacred shrine
    When first he warr'd against the Christians!   200
                  To the battle again.
Zenocrate. By this the Turks lie weltering in their blood,
    And Tamburlaine is lord of Africa.
Zabina. Thou art deceiv'd. I heard the trumpets sound
168 boss] fat woman

As when my emperor overthrew the Greeks,
And led them captive into Africa.
Straight will I use thee as thy pride deserves;
Prepare thyself to live and die my slave.
Zenocrate. If Mahomet should come from heaven and swear
 My royal lord is slain or conquered,
 Yet should he not persuade me otherwise   210
 But that he lives and will be conqueror.

  Bajazeth *flies and he* [Tamburlaine] *pursues him. The battle short and*
      they enter. Bajazeth *is overcome.*

Tamburlaine. Now, king of bassoes, who is conqueror?
Bajazeth. Thou, by the fortune of this damned foil.
Tamburlaine. Where are your stout contributory kings?

    Enter Techelles, Theridamas, *and* Usumcasane.

Techelles. We have their crowns; their bodies strow the field.
Tamburlaine. Each man a crown! Why, kingly fought, i'faith!
 Deliver them into my treasury.
Zenocrate. Now let me offer to my gracious lord
 His royal crown again so highly won.
Tamburlaine. Nay, take the Turkish crown from her, Zenocrate, 220
 And crown me Emperor of Africa.
Zabina. No, Tamburlaine; though now thou gat the best,
 Thou shalt not yet be lord of Africa.
Theridamas. Give her the crown, Turkess, you were best.
      He takes it from her, and gives it Zenocrate.
Zabina. Injurious villains, thieves, runagates,
 How dare you thus abuse my majesty?
Theridamas. Here, madam, you are empress; she is none.
Tamburlaine. Not now, Theridamas; her time is past:
 The pillars, that have bolster'd up those terms,
 Are fall'n in clusters at my conquering feet.   230
Zabina. Though he be prisoner, he may be ransomed.
Tamburlaine. Not all the world shall ransom Bajazeth.
Bajazeth. Ah, fair Zabina, we have lost the field;
 And never had the Turkish emperor
 So great a foil by any foreign foe.
 Now will the Christian miscreants be glad,
 Ringing with joy their superstitious bells,
 And making bonfires for my overthrow.
 But ere I die, those foul idolaters
 Shall make me bonfires with their filthy bones;   240

213 foil] defeat 229 terms] statuary busts

For though the glory of this day be lost,
Afric and Greece have garrisons enough
To make me sovereign of the earth again.
Tamburlaine. Those walled garrisons will I subdue,
And write myself great lord of Africa.
So from the East unto the furthest West
Shall Tamburlaine extend his puissant arm.
The galleys and those pilling brigandines,
That yearly sail to the Venetian gulf,
And hover in the Straits for Christians' wrack,   250
Shall lie at anchor in the Isle Asant,
Until the Persian fleet and men-of-war,
Sailing along the oriental sea,
Have fetch'd about the Indian continent,
Even from Persepolis to Mexico,
And thence unto the Straits of Jubalter,
Where they shall meet and join their force in one,
Keeping in awe the Bay of Portingale,
And all the ocean by the British shore;
And by this means I'll win the world at last.   260
Bajazeth. Yet set a ransom on me, Tamburlaine.
Tamburlaine. What, think'st thou Tamburlaine esteems thy gold?
I'll make the kings of India, ere I die,
Offer their mines to sue for peace to me,
And dig for treasure to appease my wrath.
Come, bind them both, and one lead in the Turk;
The Turkess let my love's maid lead away.   *They bind them.*
Bajazeth. Ah, villains, dare ye touch my sacred arms?
O Mahomet! O sleepy Mahomet!
Zabina. O cursed Mahomet, that mak'st us thus   270
The slaves to Scythians rude and barbarous!
Tamburlaine. Come, bring them in; and for this happy conquest
Triumph, and solemnize a martial feast.   *Exeunt.*

Finis Actus tertii.

248 pilling] pillaging   250 Straits] of Otranto   251 Isle Asant] Zante, off the west
coast of Greece   256 Jubalter] Gibraltar   258 Portingale] Portugal (the Bay of Biscay)

Actus 4.   Scaena 1.

[*Enter*] Soldan *of Egypt with three or four* Lords, Capolin [*and a* Messenger].

Soldan. Awake, ye men of Memphis! Hear the clang
    Of Scythian trumpets; hear the basilisks,
    That, roaring, shake Damascus' turrets down!
    The rogue of Volga holds Zenocrate,
    The Soldan's daughter, for his concubine,
    And with a troop of thieves and vagabonds
    Hath spread his colours to our high disgrace,
    While you faint-hearted base Egyptians
    Lie slumbering on the flow'ry banks of Nile,
    As crocodiles that unaffrighted rest   10
    While thund'ring cannons rattle on their skins.
Messenger. Nay, mighty Soldan, did your greatness see
    The frowning looks of fiery Tamburlaine,
    That with his terror and imperious eyes
    Commands the hearts of his associates,
    It might amaze your royal majesty.
Soldan. Villain, I tell thee, were that Tamburlaine
    As monstrous as Gorgon, prince of hell,
    The Soldan would not start a foot from him.
    But speak, what power hath he?
Messenger.   Mighty lord,   20
    Three hundred thousand men in armour clad,
    Upon their prancing steeds, disdainfully
    With wanton paces trampling on the ground;
    Five hundred thousand footmen threat'ning shot,
    Shaking their swords, their spears, and iron bills,
    Environing their standard round, that stood
    As bristle-pointed as a thorny wood;
    Their warlike engines and munition
    Exceed the forces of their martial men.
Soldan. Nay, could their numbers countervail the stars,   30
    Or ever-drizzling drops of April showers,
    Or wither'd leaves that autumn shaketh down,
    Yet would the Soldan by his conquering power
    So scatter and consume them in his rage,
    That not a man should live to rue their fall.
Capolin. So might your highness, had you time to sort

2 basilisks] cannon   30 countervail] equal

Your fighting men, and raise your royal host.
But Tamburlaine by expedition
Advantage takes of your unreadiness.
Soldan. Let him take all th' advantages he can.   40
Were all the world conspir'd to fight for him,
Nay, were he devil, as he is no man,
Yet in revenge of fair Zenocrate,
Whom he detaineth in despite of us,
This arm should send him down to Erebus
To shroud his shame in darkness of the night.
Messenger. Pleaseth your mightiness to understand,
His resolution far exceedeth all.
The first day when he pitcheth down his tents,
White is their hue, and on his silver crest   50
A snowy feather spangled white he bears,
To signify the mildness of his mind,
That satiate with spoil refuseth blood.
But when Aurora mounts the second time,
As red as scarlet is his furniture;
Then must his kindled wrath be quench'd with blood,
Not sparing any that can manage arms.
But if these threats move not submission,
Black are his colours, black pavilion;
His spear, his shield, his horse, his armour, plumes,   60
And jetty feathers menace death and hell;
Without respect of sex, degree, or age,
He razeth all his foes with fire and sword.
Soldan. Merciless villain, peasant ignorant
Of lawful arms or martial discipline!
Pillage and murder are his usual trades.
The slave usurps the glorious name of war.
See, Capolin, the fair Arabian king,
That hath been disappointed by this slave
Of my fair daughter and his princely love,   70
May have fresh warning to go war with us,
And be reveng'd for her disparagement.   [*Exeunt*]

45 Erebus] Hades

Actus 4.   Scaena 2.

[*Enter*] Tamburlaine, Techelles, Theridamas, Usumcasane, Zenocrate,
Anippe, *two* Moors *drawing* Bajazeth *in his cage, and his wife*
[Zabina] *following him.*

Tamburlaine. Bring out my footstool.   *They take him out of the cage.*
Bajazeth. Ye holy priests of heavenly Mahomet,
    That, sacrificing, slice and cut your flesh,
    Staining his altars with your purple blood,
    Make heaven to frown, and every fixed star
    To suck up poison from the moorish fens,
    And pour it in this glorious tyrant's throat!
Tamburlaine. The chiefest God, first mover of that sphere
    Enchas'd with thousands ever-shining lamps,
    Will sooner burn the glorious frame of heaven   10
    Than it should so conspire my overthrow.
    But villain, thou that wishest this to me,
    Fall prostrate on the low disdainful earth,
    And be the footstool of great Tamburlaine,
    That I may rise into my royal throne.
Bajazeth. First shalt thou rip my bowels with thy sword,
    And sacrifice my heart to death and hell,
    Before I yield to such a slavery.
Tamburlaine. Base villain, vassal, slave to Tamburlaine,
    Unworthy to embrace or touch the ground   20
    That bears the honour of my royal weight.
    Stoop, villain, stoop! Stoop, for so he bids
    That may command thee piecemeal to be torn,
    Or scatter'd like the lofty cedar-trees
    Struck with the voice of thund'ring Jupiter.
Bajazeth. Then as I look down to the damned fiends,
    Fiends, look on me! And thou, dread god of hell,
    With ebon sceptre strike this hateful earth,
    And make it swallow both of us at once!
                                                He gets up upon him to his chair.
Tamburlaine. Now clear the triple region of the air,   30
    And let the majesty of heaven behold
    Their scourge and terror tread on emperors.
    Smile, stars that reign'd at my nativity,

5 fixed star] i.e. one attached to the firmament, unlike the wandering stars (planets)
7 glorious] vainglorious   30 triple region] The atmosphere was thought to have three
zones, the highest and lowest being warm and the middle one cold.

And dim the brightness of their neighbour lamps;
Disdain to borrow light of Cynthia!
For I, the chiefest lamp of all the earth,
First rising in the east with mild aspect,
But fixed now in the meridian line,
Will send up fire to your turning spheres,
And cause the sun to borrow light of you.   40
My sword struck fire from his coat of steel
Even in Bithynia, when I took this Turk:
As when a fiery exhalation,
Wrapt in the bowels of a freezing cloud,
Fighting for passage, makes the welkin crack,
And casts a flash of lightning to the earth.
But ere I march to wealthy Persia,
Or leave Damascus and th' Egyptian fields,
As was the fame of Clymene's brain-sick son
That almost brent the axle-tree of heaven,   50
So shall our swords, our lances, and our shot
Fill all the air with fiery meteors.
Then when the sky shall wax as red as blood,
It shall be said I made it red myself,
To make me think of naught but blood and war.

Zabina. Unworthy king, that by thy cruelty
Unlawfully usurp'st the Persian seat,
Dar'st thou, that never saw an emperor
Before thou met my husband in the field,
Being thy captive, thus abuse his state,   60
Keeping his kingly body in a cage,
That roofs of gold and sun-bright palaces
Should have prepar'd to entertain his grace?
And treading him beneath thy loathsome feet,
Whose feet the kings of Africa have kiss'd?

Techelles. You must devise some torment worse, my lord,
To make these captives rein their lavish tongues.

Tamburlaine. Zenocrate, look better to your slave.

Zenocrate. She is my handmaid's slave, and she shall look
That these abuses flow not from her tongue.   70
Chide her, Anippe.

Anippe. Let these be warnings for you then, my slave,
How you abuse the person of the King;

35 Cynthia] the moon   38 fixed . . . line] i.e. fixed at the height of his glory, unlike other
suns, which must decline   49 Clymene's . . . son] Phaeton, who tried to drive the sun's
chariot   50 brent] burnt

    Or else I swear to have you whipp'd stark nak'd.

Bajazeth. Great Tamburlaine, great in my overthrow,
    Ambitious pride shall make thee fall as low,
    For treading on the back of Bajazeth,
    That should be horsed on four mighty kings.

Tamburlaine. Thy names and titles and thy dignities
    Are fled from Bajazeth and remain with me,   80
    That will maintain it against a world of kings.
    Put him in again.   *[They put him into the cage.]*

Bajazeth. Is this a place for mighty Bajazeth?
    Confusion light on him that helps thee thus.

Tamburlaine. There whiles he lives shall Bajazeth be kept,
    And where I go be thus in triumph drawn;
    And thou, his wife, shall feed him with the scraps
    My servitors shall bring thee from my board,
    For he that gives him other food than this,
    Shall sit by him and starve to death himself: 90
    This is my mind, and I will have it so.
    Not all the kings and emperors of the earth,
    If they would lay their crowns before my feet,
    Shall ransom him, or take him from his cage.
    The ages that shall talk of Tamburlaine,
    Even from this day to Plato's wondrous year,
    Shall talk how I have handled Bajazeth.
    These Moors, that drew him from Bithynia
    To fair Damascus, where we now remain,
    Shall lead him with us whereso'er we go.   100
    Techelles, and my loving followers,
    Now may we see Damascus' lofty towers,
    Like to the shadows of Pyramides
    That with their beauties grac'd the Memphian fields.
    The golden stature of their feather'd bird,
    That spreads her wings upon the city walls,
    Shall not defend it from our battering shot.
    The townsmen mask in silk and cloth of gold,
    And every house is as a treasury;
    The men, the treasure, and the town is ours.   110

Theridamas. Your tents of white now pitch'd before the gates,
    And gentle flags of amity display'd,
    I doubt not but the Governor will yield,
    Offering Damascus to your majesty.

---

96 Plato's . . . year] Plato had estimated that in 36,000 years all the planets would return
simultaneously to their original starting-points.

Tamburlaine. So shall he have his life, and all the rest.
    But if he stay until the bloody flag
    Be once advanc'd on my vermilion tent,
    He dies, and those that kept us out so long;
    And when they see me march in black array,
    With mournful streamers hanging down their heads,   120
    Were in that city all the world contain'd,
    Not one should scape, but perish by our swords.
Zenocrate. Yet would you have some pity for my sake,
    Because it is my country's and my father's.
Tamburlaine. Not for the world, Zenocrate, if I have sworn.
    Come, bring in the Turk.   *Exeunt.*

Act. 4.   Scaena 3.

[*Enter*] Soldan, [*Alcidamus King of*] Arabia, Capolin, *with streaming*
colours, and Soldiers.

Soldan. Methinks we march as Meleager did,
    Environed with brave Argolian knights,
    To chase the savage Calydonian boar;
    Or Cephalus with lusty Theban youths
    Against the wolf that angry Themis sent
    To waste and spoil the sweet Aonian fields.
    A monster of five hundred thousand heads,
    Compact of rapine, piracy, and spoil,
    The scum of men, the hate and scourge of god,
    Raves in Egypta, and annoyeth us.   10
    My lord, it is the bloody Tamburlaine,
    A sturdy felon and a base-bred thief,
    By murder raised to the Persian crown,
    That dares control us in our territories.
    To tame the pride of this presumptuous beast,
    Join your Arabians with the Soldan's power;
    Let us unite our royal bands in one,
    And hasten to remove Damascus' siege.
    It is a blemish to the majesty
    And high estate of mighty emperors,   20
    That such a base usurping vagabond
    Should brave a king, or wear a princely crown.

1 Meleager] who led the hunt for the boar ravaging the fields of Calydon
4–7 Cephalus . . . fields] Ovid (but not the Greek poets) tells this story of the hunting of
the boar (*Metamorphoses* VII).

Arabia. Renowmed Soldan, have ye lately heard
    The overthrow of mighty Bajazeth
    About the confines of Bithynia?
    The slavery wherewith he persecutes
    The noble Turk and his great emperess?
Soldan. I have, and sorrow for his bad success.
    But noble lord of great Arabia,
    Be so persuaded that the Soldan is   30
    No more dismay'd with tidings of his fall,
    Than in the haven when the pilot stands,
    And views a stranger's ship rent in the winds,
    And shivered against a craggy rock:
    Yet in compassion of his wretched state,
    A sacred vow to heaven and him I make,
    Confirming it with Ibis' holy name,
    That Tamburlaine shall rue the day, the hour,
    Wherein he wrought such ignominious wrong
    Unto the hallow'd person of a prince,   40
    Or kept the fair Zenocrate so long,
    As concubine, I fear, to feed his lust.
Arabia. Let grief and fury hasten on revenge;
    Let Tamburlaine for his offences feel
    Such plagues as heaven and we can pour on him.
    I long to break my spear upon his crest,
    And prove the weight of his victorious arm;
    For fame, I fear, hath been too prodigal
    In sounding through the world his partial praise.
Soldan. Capolin, hast thou survey'd our powers?   50
Capolin. Great emperors of Egypt and Arabia,
    The number of your hosts united is:
    A hundred and fifty thousand horse,
    Two hundred thousand foot, brave men-at-arms,
    Courageous and full of hardiness,
    As frolic as the hunters in the chase
    Of savage beasts amid the desert woods.
Arabia. My mind presageth fortunate success;
    And, Tamburlaine, my spirit doth foresee
    The utter ruin of thy men and thee.   60
Soldan. Then rear your standards; let your sounding drums
    Direct our soldiers to Damascus' walls.
    Now Tamburlaine, the mighty Soldan comes,
    And leads with him the great Arabian king,

37 Ibis] the sacred Egyptian bird   49 partial] prejudiced

To dim thy baseness and obscurity,
Famous for nothing but for theft and spoil;
To raze and scatter thy inglorious crew
Of Scythians and slavish Persians.   *Exeunt.*

Actus 4.   Scaena 4.

The banquet, and to it cometh Tamburlaine *all in scarlet,* Theridamas,
Techelles, Usumcasane, [Zenocrate, Zabina,] *the Turk* [Bajazeth
in his cage], *with others.*

Tamburlaine. Now hang our bloody colours by Damascus,
Reflexing hues of blood upon their heads
While they walk quivering on their city walls,
Half-dead for fear before they feel my wrath.
Then let us freely banquet and carouse
Full bowls of wine unto the god of war,
That means to fill your helmets full of gold,
And make Damascus' spoils as rich to you
As was to Jason Colchos' golden fleece.
And now Bajazeth, hast thou any stomach?   10
Bajazeth. Ay, such a stomach, cruel Tamburlaine, as I could willingly feed
upon thy blood-raw heart.
Tamburlaine. Nay, thine own is easier to come by, pluck out that, and 'twill
serve thee and thy wife. Well Zenocrate, Techelles and the rest, fall to
your victuals.
Bajazeth. Fall to, and never may your meat digest!
Ye Furies, that can mask invisible,
Dive to the bottom of Avernus' pool
And in your hands bring hellish poison up
And squeeze it in the cup of Tamburlaine;   20
Or winged snakes of Lerna, cast your stings
And leave your venom in this tyrant's dish.
Zabina. And may this banquet prove as ominous
As Progne's to th' adulterous Thracian king
That fed upon the substance of his child!
Zenocrate. My lord, how can you suffer these
Outrageous curses by these slaves of yours?
Tamburlaine. To let them see, divine Zenocrate,

9 Jason] He led the Argonauts to Colchis in search of the Golden Fleece.   21 snakes of
Lerna] Poison from the hydra of Lerna made Hercules' arrows deadly.   24–5 Progne's
. . . child] Tereus, King of Thrace, raped his wife's sister, Philomela; in revenge his wife
Progne murdered their son Itys, and cooked him as a banquet for his father.

I glory in the curses of my foes,
Having the power from the empyreal heaven   30
To turn them all upon their proper heads.

Techelles. I pray you give them leave, madam; this speech is a goodly
refreshing to them.

Theridamas. But if his highness would let them be fed, it would do them
more good.

Tamburlaine. Sirrah, why fall you not to? Are you so daintily brought up,
you cannot eat your own flesh?

Bajazeth. First, legions of devils shall tear thee in pieces.

Usumcasane. Villain, knowest thou to whom thou speakest?

Tamburlaine. O let him alone. Here, eat, sir; take it from my sword's point,
or I'll thrust it to thy heart.   *He takes it and stamps upon it.*

Theridamas. He stamps it under his feet, my lord.   42

Tamburlaine. Take it up, villain, and eat it; or I will make thee slice the
brawns of thy arms into carbonadoes and eat them.

Usumcasane. Nay, 'twere better he killed his wife, and then she shall be sure
not to be starved, and he be provided for a month's victual beforehand.

Tamburlaine. Here is my dagger. Dispatch her while she is fat, for if she
live but a while longer she will fall into a consumption with fretting, and
then she will not be worth the eating.

Theridamas. Dost thou think that Mahomet will suffer this?   50

Techelles. 'Tis like he will, when he cannot let it.

Tamburlaine. Go to, fall to your meat. What, not a bit? Belike he hath not
been watered today; give him some drink.
          They give him water to drink, and he flings it on the ground.
Fast, and welcome, sir, while hunger make you eat. How now, Zenocrate,
doth not the Turk and his wife make a goodly show at a banquet?

Zenocrate. Yes, my lord.

Theridamas. Methinks 'tis a great deal better than a consort of music.

Tamburlaine. Yet music would do well to cheer up Zenocrate. Pray thee, tell
why art thou so sad? If thou wilt have a song, the Turk shall strain his
voice. But why is it?   60

Zenocrate. My lord, to see my father's town besieg'd,
    The country wasted where myself was born,
    How can it but afflict my very soul?
    If any love remain in you, my lord,
    Or if my love unto your majesty
    May merit favour at your highness' hands,
    Then raise your siege from fair Damascus' walls,
    And with my father take a friendly truce.

Tamburlaine. Zenocrate, were Egypt Jove's own land,

31 proper] own   44 carbonadoes] steaks for broiling   51 let] prevent

Yet would I with my sword make Jove to stoop.   70
I will confute those blind geographers
That make a triple region in the world,
Excluding regions which I mean to trace,
And with this pen reduce them to a map,
Calling the provinces, cities, and towns,
After my name and thine, Zenocrate.
Here at Damascus will I make the point
That shall begin the perpendicular.
And wouldst thou have me buy thy father's love
With such a loss? Tell me, Zenocrate.   80
Zenocrate. Honour still wait on happy Tamburlaine;
     Yet give me leave to plead for him, my lord.
Tamburlaine. Content thyself; his person shall be safe,
     And all the friends of fair Zenocrate,
     If with their lives they will be pleas'd to yield,
     Or may be forc'd to make me emperor;
     For Egypt and Arabia must be mine.
     —Feed, you slave; thou mayst think thyself happy to be fed from my
trencher.
Bajazeth. My empty stomach, full of idle heat,   90
     Draws bloody humours from my feeble parts,
     Preserving life by hasting cruel death.
     My veins are pale, my sinews hard and dry,
     My joints benumb'd; unless I eat, I die.
Zabina. Eat, Bajazeth. Let us live in spite of them, looking some happy power
     will pity and enlarge us.
Tamburlaine. Here, Turk, wilt thou have a clean trencher?
Bajazeth. Ay tyrant, and more meat.
Tamburlaine. Soft, sir, you must be dieted; too much eating will make you
surfeit.   100
Theridamas. So it would, my lord, specially having so small a walk and so
little exercise.

Enter a second course of crowns.

Tamburlaine. Theridamas, Techelles, and Casane, here are the cates you
     desire to finger, are they not?
Theridamas. Ay, my lord, but none save kings must feed with these.
Techelles. 'Tis enough for us to see them, and for Tamburlaine only to enjoy
     them.
Tamburlaine. Well, here is now to the Soldan of Egypt, the King of Arabia,
     and the Governor of Damascus. Now take these three crowns, and pledge

71-2 geographers . . . triple region] dividing it into Europe, Asia, and Africa

me, my contributory kings. I crown you here, Theridamas, King of
Argier; Techelles, King of Fez; and Usumcasane, King of Moroccus.
How say you to this, Turk? These are not your contributory kings.   112

Bajazeth. Nor shall they long be thine, I warrant them.

Tamburlaine. Kings of Argier, Moroccus, and of Fez,
    You that have marched with happy Tamburlaine
    As far as from the frozen place of heaven
    Unto the wat'ry morning's ruddy bower,
    And thence by land unto the torrid zone,
    Deserve these titles I endow you with
    By valour and by magnanimity.   120
    Your births shall be no blemish to your fame,
    For virtue is the fount whence honour springs,
    And they are worthy she investeth kings.

Theridamas. And since your highness hath so well vouchsaf'd,
    If we deserve them not with higher meeds
    Than erst our states and actions have retain'd,
    Take them away again, and make us slaves.

Tamburlaine. Well said, Theridamas. When holy Fates
    Shall stablish me in strong Egyptia,
    We mean to travel to th' antarctic pole,   130
    Conquering the people underneath our feet,
    And be renowm'd as never emperors were.
    Zenocrate, I will not crown thee yet,
    Until with greater honours I be grac'd.   [*Exeunt.*]

Finis Actus Quarti.

Actus 5.   Scaena 1.

[*Enter*] the Governor of *Damascus with three or four* Citizens, *and
    four* Virgins *with branches of laurel in their hands.*

Governor. Still doth this man, or rather god of war,
    Batter our walls and beat our turrets down;
    And to resist with longer stubbornness,
    Or hope of rescue from the Soldan's power,
    Were but to bring our wilful overthrow,
    And make us desperate of our threatn'd lives.
    We see his tents have now been altered
    With terrors to the last and cruel'st hue.
    His coal-black colours, everywhere advanc'd,
    Threaten our city with a general spoil;   10

22 virtue] virtùs, strength

And if we should with common rites of arms
Offer our safeties to his clemency,
I fear the custom proper to his sword,
Which he observes as parcel of his fame,
Intending so to terrify the world,
By any innovation or remorse
Will never be dispens'd with till our deaths.
Therefore, for these our harmless virgins' sakes,
Whose honours and whose lives rely on him,
Let us have hope that their unspotted prayers,   20
Their blubber'd cheeks, and hearty humble moans
Will melt his fury into some remorse,
And use us like a loving conqueror.
1 Virgin. If humble suits or imprecations
(Utter'd with tears of wretchedness and blood
Shed from the heads and hearts of all our sex,
Some made your wives, and some your children)
Might have entreated your obdurate breasts
To entertain some care of our securities
Whiles only danger beat upon our walls,   30
These more than dangerous warrants of our death
Had never been erected as they be,
Nor you depend on such weak helps as we.
Governor. Well, lovely virgins, think our country's care,
Our love of honour, loath to be enthrall'd
To foreign powers and rough imperious yokes,
Would not with too much cowardice or fear,
Before all hope of rescue were denied,
Submit yourselves and us to servitude.
Therefore, in that your safeties and our own,   40
Your honours, liberties, and lives were weigh'd
In equal care and balance with our own,
Endure as we the malice of our stars,
The wrath of Tamburlaine and power of wars;
Or be the means the overweighing heavens
Have kept to qualify these hot extremes,
And bring us pardon in your cheerful looks.
2 Virgin. Then here, before the majesty of heaven
And holy patrons of Egyptia,
With knees and hearts submissive we entreat   50
Grace to our words and pity to our looks,
That this device may prove propitious,

14 parcel] essential part

And through the eyes and ears of Tamburlaine
Convey events of mercy to his heart;
Grant that these signs of victory we yield
May bind the temples of his conquering head,
To hide the folded furrows of his brows,
And shadow his displeased countenance
With happy looks of ruth and lenity.
Leave us, my lord, and loving countrymen: 60
What simple virgins may persuade, we will.

Governor. Farewell, sweet virgins, on whose safe return
Depends our city, liberty, and lives.   *Exeunt [all except the* Virgins].

[*Enter*] Tamburlaine, Techelles, Theridamas, Usumcasane, *with
others*; Tamburlaine *all in black and very melancholy.*

Tamburlaine. What, are the turtles fray'd out of their nests?
Alas, poor fools, must you be first shall feel
The sworn destruction of Damascus?
They know my custom; could they not as well
Have sent ye out when first my milk-white flags,
Through which sweet mercy threw her gentle beams,
Reflexing them on your disdainful eyes,   70
As now when fury and incensed hate
Flings slaughtering terror from my coal-black tents,
And tells for truth, submissions comes too late?

1 Virgin. Most happy King and emperor of the earth,
Image of honour and nobility,
For whom the powers divine have made the world,
And on whose throne the holy Graces sit;
In whose sweet person is compris'd the sum
Of nature's skill and heavenly majesty;
Pity our plights! O, pity poor Damascus!   80
Pity old age, within whose silver hairs
Honour and reverence evermore have reign'd!
Pity the marriage-bed, where many a lord,
In prime and glory of his loving joy,
Embraceth now with tears of ruth and blood
The jealous body of his fearful wife,
Whose cheeks and hearts, so punish'd with conceit,
To think thy puissant never-stayed arm
Will part their bodies, and prevent their souls
From heavens of comfort yet their age might bear,   90
Now wax all pale and wither'd to the death,

64 turtles] turtle-doves   64 fray'd] frightened   86 jealous] apprehensive

As well for grief our ruthless Governor
Have thus refus'd the mercy of thy hand
(Whose sceptre angels kiss and Furies dread)
As for their liberties, their loves, or lives:
O then for these, and such as we ourselves,
For us, for infants, and for all our bloods,
That never nourish'd thought against thy rule,
Pity, O pity, sacred emperor,
The prostrate service of this wretched town;   100
And take in sign thereof this gilded wreath,
Whereto each man of rule hath given his hand,
And wish'd, as worthy subjects, happy means
To be investers of thy royal brows
Even with the true Egyptian diadem.
Tamburlaine. Virgins, in vain ye labour to prevent
    That which mine honour swears shall be perform'd.
    Behold my sword; what see you at the point?
1 Virgin. Nothing but fear and fatal steel, my lord.
Tamburlaine. Your fearful minds are thick and misty, then,   110
    For there sits Death; there sits imperious Death,
    Keeping his circuit by the slicing edge.
    But I am pleas'd you shall not see him there;
    He now is seated on my horsemen's spears,
    And on their points his fleshless body feeds.
    Techelles, straight go charge a few of them
    To charge these dames, and shew my servant Death,
    Sitting in scarlet on their armed spears.
Virgins. O, pity us!
Tamburlaine. Away with them, I say, and shew them Death!   120
                                               They take them away.

    I will not spare these proud Egyptians,
    Nor change my martial observations
    For all the wealth of Gihon's golden waves,
    Or for the love of Venus, would she leave
    The angry god of arms and lie with me.
    They have refus'd the offer of their lives,
    And know my customs are as peremptory
    As wrathful planets, death, or destiny.
                        Enter Techelles.
    What, have your horsemen shown the virgins Death?
Techelles. They have, my lord, and on Damascus' walls   130

123 Gihon] a river in Eden (Genesis 2: 13)

Have hoisted up their slaughtered carcasses.
Tamburlaine. A sight as baneful to their souls, I think,
    As are Thessalian drugs or mithridate.
    But go, my lords, put the rest to the sword.

                  Exeunt [all except Tamburlaine].

    Ah, fair Zenocrate, divine Zenocrate!
    Fair is too foul an epithet for thee,
    That in thy passion for thy country's love,
    And fear to see thy kingly father's harm,
    With hair dishevell'd wip'st thy watery cheeks,
    And like to Flora in her morning's pride,   140
    Shaking her silver tresses in the air,
    Rain'st on the earth resolved pearl in showers,
    And sprinklest sapphires on thy shining face,
    Where Beauty, mother to the Muses, sits,
    And comments volumes with her ivory pen,
    Taking instructions from thy flowing eyes;
    Eyes, when that Ebena steps to heaven,
    In silence of thy solemn evening's walk,
    Making the mantle of the richest night,
    The moon, the planets, and the meteors, light;   150
    There angels in their crystal armours fight
    A doubtful battle with my tempted thoughts
    For Egypt's freedom and the Soldan's life,
    His life that so consumes Zenocrate,
    Whose sorrows lay more siege unto my soul
    Than all my army to Damascus' walls;
    And neither Persian's sovereign nor the Turk
    Troubled my senses with conceit of foil
    So much by much as doth Zenocrate.
    What is beauty, saith my sufferings, then?   160
    If all the pens that ever poets held
    Had fed the feeling of their masters' thoughts,
    And every sweetness that inspir'd their hearts,
    Their minds, and muses on admired themes;
    If all the heavenly quintessence they still
    From their immortal flowers of poesy,
    Wherein as in a mirror we perceive
    The highest reaches of a human wit;
    If these had made one poem's period,
    And all combin'd in beauty's worthiness,   170

147 Ebena] There is no goddess of this name; perhaps Marlowe is personifying night (from
ebenus, ebony).   158 conceit of foil] thought of defeat

Yet should there hover in their restless heads
One thought, one grace, one wonder, at the least,
Which into words no virtue can digest.
But how unseemly is it for my sex,
My discipline of arms and chivalry,
My nature, and the terror of my name,
To harbour thoughts effeminate and faint!
Save only that in beauty's just applause,
With whose instinct the soul of man is touch'd,
And every warrior that is rapt with love   180
Of fame, of valour, and of victory,
Must needs have beauty beat on his conceits:
I thus conceiving and subduing both,
That which hath stopp'd the tempest of the gods,
Even from the fiery-spangled veil of heaven,
To feel the lovely warmth of shepherd's flames,
And march in cottages of strowed reeds,
Shall give the world to note, for all my birth,
That virtue solely is the sum of glory,
And fashions men with true nobility.   190
Who's within there?

     Enter two or three [Attendants].

Hath Bajazeth been fed today?
Attendant. Ay, my lord.
Tamburlaine. Bring him forth; and let us know if the town be ransacked.
         [*Exeunt* Attendants.]

    Enter Techelles, Theridamas, Usumcasane, *and others.*

Techelles. The town is ours, my lord, and fresh supply
Of conquest and of spoil is offer'd us.
Tamburlaine. That's well, Techelles. What's the news?
Techelles. The Soldan and the Arabian king together
March on us with such eager violence
As if there were no way but one with us.   200
Tamburlaine. No more there is not, I warrant thee, Techelles.
   They bring in the Turk [Bajazeth *in his cage, and* Zabina].
Theridamas. We know the victory is ours, my lord,
But let us save the reverend Soldan's life
For fair Zenocrate that so laments his state.
Tamburlaine. That will we chiefly see unto, Theridamas,
For sweet Zenocrate, whose worthiness
Deserves a conquest over every heart.
And now, my footstool, if I lose the field,

You hope of liberty and restitution?
Here let him stay, my masters, from the tents, 210
Till we have made us ready for the field.
Pray for us, Bajazeth; we are going.

Exeunt [all except Bajazeth *and* Zabina].

Bajazeth. Go, never to return with victory!
Millions of men encompass thee about,
And gore thy body with as many wounds!
Sharp forked arrows light upon thy horse!
Furies from the black Cocytus' lake
Break up the earth, and with their firebrands
Enforce thee run upon the baneful pikes!
Volleys of shot pierce through thy charmed skin, 220
And every bullet dipp'd in poison'd drugs!
Or roaring cannons sever all thy joints,
Making thee mount as high as eagles soar!

Zabina. Let all the swords and lances in the field
Stick in his breast as in their proper rooms!
At every pore let blood come dropping forth,
That ling'ring pains may massacre his heart,
And madness send his damned soul to hell!

Bajazeth. Ah fair Zabina, we may curse his power,
The heavens may frown, the earth for anger quake; 230
But such a star hath influence in his sword
As rules the skies and countermands the gods
More than Cimmerian Styx or Destiny.
And then shall we in this detested guise,
With shame, with hunger, and with horror aye
Griping our bowels with retorqued thoughts,
And have no hope to end our ecstasies.

Zabina. Then is there left no Mahomet, no God,
No fiend, no fortune, nor no hope of end
To our infamous, monstrous slaveries? 240
Gape earth, and let the fiends infernal view
A hell as hopeless and as full of fear
As are the blasted banks of Erebus,
Where shaking ghosts with ever-howling groans
Hover about the ugly ferryman
To get a passage to Elysium!
Why should we live? O wretches, beggars, slaves!
Why live we, Bajazeth, and build up nests

217 Cocytus] a river in Hades   233 Styx] the chief river in Hades, which the gods swore
by   236 retorqued] turned back upon themselves   237 ecstasies] passions

So high within the region of the air,
By living long in this oppression,   250
That all the world will see and laugh to scorn
The former triumphs of our mightiness
In this obscure infernal servitude?
Bajazeth. O life more loathsome to my vexed thoughts
    Than noisome parbreak of the Stygian snakes,
    Which fills the nooks of hell with standing air,
    Infecting all the ghosts with cureless griefs!
    O dreary engines of my loathed sight,
    That sees my crown, my honour, and my name
    Thrust under yoke and thraldom of a thief,   260
    Why feed ye still on day's accursed beams,
    And sink not quite into my tortur'd soul?
    You see my wife, my queen, and emperess,
    Brought up and propped by the hand of Fame,
    Queen of fifteen contributory queens,
    Now thrown to rooms of black abjection,
    Smear'd with blots of basest drudgery,
    And villeiness to shame, disdain, and misery.
    Accursed Bajazeth, whose words of ruth,
    That would with pity cheer Zabina's heart,   270
    And make our souls resolve in ceaseless tears,
    Sharp hunger bites upon and gripes the root
    From whence the issues of my thoughts do break!
    O poor Zabina! O my queen, my queen,
    Fetch me some water for my burning breast,
    To cool and comfort me with longer date,
    That in the shorten'd sequel of my life,
    I may pour forth my soul into thine arms
    With words of love, whose moaning intercourse
    Hath hitherto been stay'd with wrath and hate   280
    Of our expressless bann'd inflictions.
Zabina. Sweet Bajazeth, I will prolong thy life
    As long as any blood or spark of breath
    Can quench or cool the torments of my grief.   *She goes out.*
Bajazeth. Now Bajazeth, abridge thy baneful days,
    And beat thy brains out of thy conquer'd head,
    Since other means are all forbidden me
    That may be ministers of my decay.
    O highest lamp of ever-living Jove,

255 parbreak] vomit   256 standing] stagnant   268 villeiness] slave   281 bann'd]
cursed

Accursed day, infected with my griefs,   290
Hide now thy stained face in endless night,
And shut the windows of the lightsome heavens!
Let ugly darkness with her rusty coach,
Engirt with tempests wrapt in pitchy clouds,
Smother the earth with never-fading mists,
And let her horses from their nostrils breathe
Rebellious winds and dreadful thunder-claps,
That in this terror Tamburlaine may live,
And my pin'd soul, resolv'd in liquid air,
May still excruciate his tormented thoughts.   300
Then let the stony dart of senseless cold
Pierce through the centre of my wither'd heart,
And make a passage for my loathed life!

He brains himself against the cage.

Enter Zabina.

Zabina. What do mine eyes behold? My husband dead!
His skull all riven in twain, his brains dash'd out,
The brains of Bajazeth, my lord and sovereign!
O Bajazeth, my husband and my lord!
O Bajazeth! O Turk! O Emperor!   308
Give him his liquor? Not I. Bring milk and fire, and my blood I bring
him again. Tear me in pieces. Give me the sword with a ball of wild-fire
upon it. Down with him! Down with him! Go to my child; away, away,
away! Ah, save that infant, save him, save him! I, even I, speak to her.
The sun was down—streamers white, red, black, here, here, here! Fling
the meat in his face. Tamburlaine, Tamburlaine! Let the soldiers be
buried. Hell, death, Tamburlaine, hell! Make ready my coach, my chair,
my jewels. I come, I come, I come, I come!

She runs against the cage, and brains herself.

[*Enter*] Zenocrate *with* Anippe.

Zenocrate. Wretched Zenocrate, that liv'st to see
Damascus' walls dy'd with Egyptian blood,
Thy father's subjects and thy countrymen;
The streets strow'd with dissever'd joints of men,   320
And wounded bodies gasping yet for life;
But most accurs'd, to see the sun-bright troop
Of heavenly virgins and unspotted maids,
Whose looks might make the angry god of arms
To break his sword and mildly treat of love,
On horsemen's lances to be hoisted up,

And guiltlessly endure a cruel death.
For every fell and stout Tartarian steed,
That stamp'd on others with their thund'ring hoofs,
When all their riders charg'd their quiv'ring spears,   330
Began to check the ground and rein themselves,
Gazing upon the beauty of their looks.
Ah Tamburlaine, wert thou the cause of this,
That term'st Zenocrate thy dearest love?
Whose lives were dearer to Zenocrate
Than her own life, or aught save thine own love.
But see, another bloody spectacle!
Ah, wretched eyes, the enemies of my heart,
How are ye glutted with these grievous objects,
And tell my soul more tales of bleeding ruth!   340
See, see, Anippe, if they breathe or no.
Anippe. No breath, nor sense, nor motion in them both.
Ah madam, this their slavery hath enforc'd,
And ruthless cruelty of Tamburlaine!
Zenocrate. Earth cast up fountains from thy entrails,
And wet thy cheeks for their untimely deaths;
Shake with their weight in sign of fear and grief.
Blush heaven, that gave them honour at their birth
And let them die a death so barbarous.
Those that are proud of fickle empery   350
And place their chiefest good in earthly pomp,
Behold the Turk and his great emperess!
Ah Tamburlaine my love, sweet Tamburlaine,
That fights for sceptres and for slippery crowns,
Behold the Turk and his great emperess!
Thou that in conduct of thy happy stars,
Sleep'st every night with conquest on thy brows,
And yet wouldst shun the wavering turns of war,
In fear and feeling of the like distress,
Behold the Turk and his great emperess!   360
Ah mighty Jove and holy Mahomet,
Pardon my love, O pardon his contempt
Of earthly fortune and respect of pity;
And let not conquest ruthlessly pursu'd
Be equally against his life incens'd
In this great Turk and hapless emperess!
And pardon me that was not mov'd with ruth
To see them live so long in misery!
Ah, what may chance to thee, Zenocrate?

Anippe. Madam, content yourself, and be resolv'd,   370
    Your love hath Fortune so at his command,
    That she shall stay and turn her wheel no more,
    As long as life maintains his mighty arm
    That fights for honour to adorn your head.

                Enter [Philemus] *a messenger.*

Zenocrate. What other heavy news now brings Philemus?
Philemus. Madam, your father and the Arabian king,
    The first affecter of your excellence,
    Comes now as Turnus 'gainst Æneas did,
    Armed with lance into the Egyptian fields,
    Ready for battle 'gainst my lord the King.   380
Zenocrate. Now shame and duty, love and fear presents
    A thousand sorrows to my martyr'd soul.
    Whom should I wish the fatal victory,
    When my poor pleasures are divided thus,
    And rack'd by duty from my cursed heart?
    My father and my first-betrothed love
    Must fight against my life and present love;
    Wherein the change I use condemns my faith,
    And makes my deeds infamous through the world.
    But as the gods to end the Trojans' toil,   390
    Prevented Turnus of Lavinia,
    And fatally enrich'd Æneas' love,
    So for a final issue to my griefs,
    To pacify my country and my love,
    Must Tamburlaine by their resistless powers,
    With virtue of a gentle victory,
    Conclude a league of honour to my hope;
    Then as the powers divine have pre-ordain'd,
    With happy safety of my father's life
    Send like defence of fair Arabia.   400

    They sound to the battle. And Tamburlaine *enjoys the victory: after,*
                    Arabia *enters wounded.*

Arabia. What cursed power guides the murdering hands
    Of this infamous tyrant's soldiers,
    That no escape may save their enemies,
    Nor fortune keep themselves from victory?
    Lie down Arabia, wounded to the death,

377 affecter] lover   378 Turnus 'gainst Æneas] Æneas won Lavinia (cf. ll. 31–2) despite
her previous betrothal to his rival Turnus.   388 use] have made   392 fatally] Turnus
was killed in the battle.

       And let Zenocrate's fair eyes behold
       That, as for her thou bear'st these wretched arms,
       Even so for her thou diest in these arms,
       Leaving thy blood for witness of thy love.
Zenocrate. Too dear a witness for such love, my lord!   410
       Behold Zenocrate, the cursed object
       Whose fortunes never mastered her griefs;
       Behold her wounded in conceit for thee,
       As much as thy fair body is for me.
Arabia. Then shall I die with full contented heart,
       Having beheld divine Zenocrate,
       Whose sight with joy would take away my life
       As now it bringeth sweetness to my wound,
       If I had not been wounded as I am.
       Ah, that the deadly pangs I suffer now   420
       Would lend an hour's licence to my tongue,
       To make discourse of some sweet accidents
       Have chanc'd thy merits in this worthless bondage,
       And that I might be privy to the state
       Of thy deserv'd contentment and thy love.
       But making now a virtue of thy sight,
       To drive all sorrow from my fainting soul,
       Since death denies me further cause of joy,
       Depriv'd of care, my heart with comfort dies,
       Since thy desired hand shall close mine eyes.   430
                                                   [Dies.]

     Enter Tamburlaine, *leading the* Soldan; Techelles, Theridamas,
               Usumcasane, *with others.*

Tamburlaine. Come, happy father of Zenocrate,
       A title higher than thy Soldan's name.
       Though my right hand have thus enthralled thee,
       Thy princely daughter here shall set thee free;
       She that hath calm'd the fury of my sword,
       Which had ere this been bath'd in streams of blood
       As vast and deep as Euphrates or Nile.
Zenocrate. O sight thrice-welcome to my joyful soul,
       To see the king my father issue safe
       From dangerous battle of my conquering love!   440
Soldan. Well met, my only dear Zenocrate,
       Though with the loss of Egypt and my crown.
Tamburlaine. 'Twas I, my lord, that gat the victory;
       And therefore grieve not at your overthrow.

    Since I shall render all into your hands,
    And add more strength to your dominions
    Than ever yet confirm'd th' Egyptian crown.
    The god of war resigns his room to me,
    Meaning to make me general of the world.
    Jove, viewing me in arms, looks pale and wan,   450
    Fearing my power should pull him from his throne.
    Where'er I come the Fatal Sisters sweat,
    And grisly Death, by running to and fro,
    To do their ceaseless homage to my sword;
    And here in Afric, where it seldom rains,
    Since I arriv'd with my triumphant host,
    Have swelling clouds, drawn from wide-gasping wounds,
    Been oft resolv'd in bloody purple showers,
    A meteor that might terrify the earth,
    And make it quake at every drop it drinks.   460
    Millions of souls sit on the banks of Styx,
    Waiting the back return of Charon's boat;
    Hell and Elysium swarm with ghosts of men
    That I have sent from sundry foughten fields
    To spread my fame through hell and up to heaven.
    And see, my lord, a sight of strange import,
    Emperors and kings lie breathless at my feet;
    The Turk and his great empress, as it seems,
    Left to themselves while we were at the fight,
    Have desperately despatch'd their slavish lives;   47c
    With them Arabia, too, hath left his life:
    All sights of power to grace my victory.
    And such are objects fit for Tamburlaine,
    Wherein as in a mirror may be seen
    His honour, that consists in shedding blood
    When men presume to manage arms with him.
Soldan. Mighty hath God and Mahomet made thy hand
    Renowmed Tamburlaine, to whom all kings
    Of force must yield their crowns and emperies;
    And I am pleas'd with this my overthrow,   480
    If, as beseems a person of thy state,
    Thou hast with honour us'd Zenocrate.
Tamburlaine. Her state and person wants no pomp, you see;
    And for all blot of foul inchastity,
    I record heaven, her heavenly self is clear.

452 the Fatal Sisters] the goddesses Clotho, Lachesis, and Atropos, who governed the lives
and deaths of men

Then let me find no further time to grace
Her princely temples with the Persian crown;
But here these kings that on my fortunes wait,
And have been crown'd for proved worthiness
Even by this hand that shall establish them,   490
Shall now, adjoining all their hands with mine,
Invest her here my Queen of Persia.
What saith the noble Soldan, and Zenocrate?
Soldan. I yield with thanks and protestations
Of endless honour to thee for her love.
Tamburlaine. Then doubt I not but fair Zenocrate
Will soon consent to satisfy us both.
Zenocrate. Else should I much forget myself, my lord.
Theridamas. Then let us set the crown upon her head,
That long hath linger'd for so high a seat.   500
Techelles. My hand is ready to perform the deed,
For now her marriage-time shall work us rest.
Usumcasane. And here's the crown, my lord; help set it on.
Tamburlaine. Then sit thou down, divine Zenocrate,
And here we crown thee Queen of Persia
And all the kingdoms and dominions
That late the power of Tamburlaine subdu'd:
As Juno, when the giants were suppress'd,
That darted mountains at her brother Jove,
So looks my love, shadowing in her brows   510
Triumphs and trophies for my victories;
Or as Latona's daughter bent to arms,
Adding more courage to my conquering mind.
To gratify the sweet Zenocrate,
Egyptians, Moors, and men of Asia,
From Barbary unto the Western Indie,
Shall pay a yearly tribute to thy sire;
And from the bounds of Afric to the banks
Of Ganges shall his mighty arm extend.
And now, my lords and loving followers,   520
That purchas'd kingdoms by your martial deeds,
Cast off your armour, put on scarlet robes,
Mount up your royal places of estate,
Environed with troops of noblemen,
And there make laws to rule your provinces.
Hang up your weapons on Alcides' post,

508-9 As Juno . . . Jove] Cf. II. vi. 3 and note.   512 Latona's daughter] Diana, the
huntress   526 Alcides' post] doorpost of the temple of Hercules

For Tamburlaine takes truce with all the world.
Thy first-betrothed love, Arabia,
Shall we with honour, as beseems, entomb
With this great Turk and his fair emperess.   530
Then, after all these solemn exequies,
We will our rites of marriage solemnize.   [*Exeunt.*]

Finis Actus Quinti et
Ultimi huius
Primae Partis.

Tamburlaine the Greate.

*VVith his impaßionate furie, for the
death of his Lady and Loue faire Zenocrate: his forme of exhortation and discipline
to his three Sonnes, and the manner of
his owne death.*

The second part.

LONDON

Printed by E.A, for Ed. White, and are to be solde
at his Shop neere the little North doore of Saint Paules
Church at the Signe of the Gun.

1 6 0 6.

[DRAMATIS PERSONAE

The Prologue

Tamburlaine, King of Persia
Calyphas
Amyras } his sons
Celebinus
Theridamas, King of Argier
Techelles, King of Fez
Usumcasane, King of Morocco
Orcanes, King of Natolia
King of Trebizon
King of Soria
King of Jerusalem
King of Amasia
Gazellus, Viceroy of Byron
Uribassa
Sigismund, King of Hungary
Frederick
Baldwin } lords of Hungary
Callapine, son to Bajazeth and prisoner to Tamburlaine
Almeda, his keeper
The Captain of Balsera
His Son
Governor of Babylon
Maximus
Perdicas
A Captain
A Messenger

Zenocrate, wife to Tamburlaine
Olympia, wife to the Captain of Balsera

Lords, Citizens, Physicians, Soldiers, Pioners, Turkish Concubines,
Attendants]

The Prologue

The general welcomes Tamburlaine receiv'd,
When he arrived last upon our stage,
Hath made our poet pen his second part,
Where death cuts off the progress of his pomp,
And murd'rous Fates throws all his triumphs down.
But what became of fair Zenocrate,
And with how many cities' sacrifice
He celebrated her sad funeral,
Himself in presence shall unfold at large.

Actus 1.   Scaena 1.

[*Enter*] Orcanes *King of Natolia*, Gazellus *Viceroy of Byron*, Uribassa,
and their train, with drums and trumpets.

Orcanes. Egregious viceroys of these eastern parts,
    Plac'd by the issue of great Bajazeth,
    And sacred lord, the mighty Callapine,
    Who lives in Egypt prisoner to that slave
    Which kept his father in an iron cage,
    Now have we march'd from fair Natolia
    Two hundred leagues, and on Danubius' banks
    Our warlike host in complete armour rest,
    Where Sigismund, the king of Hungary,
    Should meet our person to conclude a truce.   10
    What, shall we parle with the Christian?
    Or cross the stream, and meet him in the field?
Gazellus. King of Natolia, let us treat of peace:
    We all are glutted with the Christians' blood,
    And have a greater foe to fight against,
    Proud Tamburlaine, that now in Asia
    Near Guyron's head doth set his conquering feet,
    And means to fire Turkey as he goes:
    'Gainst him, my lord, must you address your power.
Uribassa. Besides, King Sigismund hath brought from Christendom   20
    More than his camp of stout Hungarians:

s.d. Orcanes] In subsequent directions Orcanes is usually referred to as Natolia.   4 kept
 . . . cage] Cf. Part I, IV. ii.   17 Guyron] near the borders of Natolia (Asia Minor)

> Slavonians, Almain rutters, Muffs, and Danes,
> That with the halberd, lance, and murdering axe,
> Will hazard that we might with surety hold.
>
> *Orcanes.* Though from the shortest northern parallel,
> Vast Gruntland, compass'd with the frozen sea,
> Inhabited with tall and sturdy men,
> Giants as big as hugy Polypheme,
> Millions of soldiers cut the arctic line,
> Bringing the strength of Europe to these arms,   30
> Our Turkey blades shall glide through all their throats,
> And make this champion mead a bloody fen;
> Danubius' stream, that runs to Trebizon,
> Shall carry wrapp'd within his scarlet waves,
> As martial presents to our friends at home,
> The slaughter'd bodies of these Christians;
> The Terrene main wherein Danubius falls,
> Shall by this battle be the Bloody Sea;
> The wand'ring sailors of proud Italy
> Shall meet those Christians fleeting with the tide,   40
> Beating in heaps against their argosies,
> And make fair Europe, mounted on her bull,
> Trapp'd with the wealth and riches of the world,
> Alight, and wear a woeful mourning weed.
>
> *Gazellus.* Yet stout Orcanes, Pro-rex of the world,
> Since Tamburlaine hath muster'd all his men,
> Marching from Cairo northward with his camp,
> To Alexandria and the frontier towns,
> Meaning to make a conquest of our land,
> 'Tis requisite to parle for a peace   50
> With Sigismund, the king of Hungary,
> And save our forces for the hot assaults
> Proud Tamburlaine intends Natolia.
>
> *Orcanes.* Viceroy of Byron, wisely hast thou said.
> My realm, the centre of our empery,
> Once lost, all Turkey would be overthrown;
> And for that cause the Christians shall have peace.
> Slavonians, Almain rutters, Muffs, and Danes
> Fear not Orcanes, but great Tamburlaine—

---

22 Almain rutters] German cavalry   22 Muffs] Swiss   26 Gruntland] Greenland
28 Polypheme] the one-eyed giant killed by Ulysses   33–7 Danubius . . . falls] Orcanes
envisages two currents from the Danube delta, one crossing the Black Sea to Trebizond,
the other rushing through the Aegean to the Mediterranean (Terrene).   42 Europe . . .
bull] Jupiter assumed the shape of a bull when he carried off Europa.

Nor he, but Fortune that hath made him great.   60
We have revolted Grecians, Albanese,
Sicilians, Jews, Arabians, Turks, and Moors,
Natolians, Sorians, black Egyptians,
Illyrians, Thracians, and Bithynians,
Enough to swallow forceless Sigismund,
Yet scarce enough t' encounter Tamburlaine.
He brings a world of people to the field:
From Scythia to the oriental plage
Of India, where raging Lantchidol
Beats on the regions with his boisterous blows,   70
That never seaman yet discovered,
All Asia is in arms with Tamburlaine;
Even from the midst of fiery Cancer's tropic
To Amazonia under Capricorn,
And thence, as far as Archipelago,
All Afric is in arms with Tamburlaine:
Therefore, viceroys, the Christians must have peace.

[*Enter*] Sigismund, Frederick, Baldwin, *and their train, with drums
and trumpets.*

Sigismund. Orcanes, as our legates promis'd thee,
We with our peers have cross'd Danubius' stream
To treat of friendly peace or deadly war.   80
Take which thou wilt; for as the Romans us'd,
I here present thee with a naked sword.
Wilt thou have war, then shake this blade at me;
If peace, restore it to my hands again,
And I will sheathe it to confirm the same.

Orcanes. Stay Sigismund. Forgett'st thou I am he
That with the cannon shook Vienna walls,
And made it dance upon the continent,
As when the massy substance of the earth
Quiver about the axle-tree of heaven?   90
Forgett'st thou that I sent a shower of darts,
Mingled with powder'd shot and feather'd steel,
So thick upon the blink-ey'd burghers' heads,
That thou thyself, then County Palatine,
The King of Boheme, and the Austric Duke,
Sent heralds out, which basely on their knees,

68 oriental plage] eastern shore   69 Lantchidol] the part of the Indian Ocean touching
Australia, which Ortelius describes as '*terra . . . nondum cognita*'   73–5 Even . . .
Archipelago] from the Canary Isles (where the meridian intersects the Tropic of Cancer)
southwards to Amazonia, below Capricorn; and northwards again to the Aegean islands

In all your names desir'd a truce of me?
Forgett'st thou, that to have me raise my siege,
Waggons of gold were set before my tent,
Stamp'd with the princely fowl that in her wings   100
Carries the fearful thunderbolts of Jove?
How canst thou think of this, and offer war?
Sigismund. Vienna was besieg'd, and I was there,
Then County Palatine, but now a king;
And what we did was in extremity.
But now Orcanes, view my royal host,
That hides these plains, and seems as vast and wide
As doth the desert of Arabia
To those that stand on Badgeth's lofty tower,
Or as the ocean to the traveller   110
That rests upon the snowy Appenines;
And tell me whether I should stoop so low,
Or treat of peace with the Natolian king.
Gazellus. Kings of Natolia and of Hungary,
We came from Turkey to confirm a league,
And not to dare each other to the field.
A friendly parle might become ye both.
Frederick. And we from Europe to the same intent;
Which if your general refuse or scorn,
Our tents are pitch'd, our men stand in array,   120
Ready to charge you ere you stir your feet.
Orcanes. So prest are we: but yet if Sigismund
Speak as a friend, and stand not upon terms,
Here is his sword; let peace be ratified
On these conditions specified before,
Drawn with advice of our ambassadors.
Sigismund. Then here I sheathe it, and give thee my hand,
Never to draw it out, or manage arms,
Against thyself or thy confederates;
But whilst I live will be at truce with thee.   130
Orcanes. But Sigismund, confirm it with an oath,
And swear in sight of heaven and by thy Christ.
Sigismund. By Him that made the world and sav'd my soul,
The Son of God and issue of a maid,
Sweet Jesus Christ, I solemnly protest
And vow to keep this peace inviolable.
Orcanes. By sacred Mahomet, the friend of God,
Whose holy Alcoran remains with us,

109 Badgeth] Baghdad   122 prest] prepared

Whose glorious body, when he left the world,
Clos'd in a coffin mounted up the air,   140
And hung on stately Mecca's temple roof,
I swear to keep this truce inviolable.
Of whose conditions and our solemn oaths,
Sign'd with our hands, each shall retain a scroll,
As memorable witness of our league.
Now Sigismund, if any Christian king
Encroach upon the confines of thy realm,
Send word, Orcanes of Natolia
Confirm'd this league beyond Danubius' stream,
And they will, trembling, sound a quick retreat;   150
So am I fear'd among all nations.
Sigismund. If any heathen potentate or king
Invade Natolia, Sigismund will send
A hundred thousand horse train'd to the war,
And back'd by stout lanciers of Germany,
The strength and sinews of the imperial seat.
Orcanes. I thank thee, Sigismund; but when I war,
All Asia Minor, Africa and Greece
Follow my standard and my thund'ring drums.
Come, let us go and banquet in our tents.   160
I will despatch chief of my army hence
To fair Natolia and to Trebizon,
To stay my coming 'gainst proud Tamburlaine.
Friend Sigismund, and peers of Hungary,
Come banquet and carouse with us a while,
And then depart we to our territories.   *Exeunt.*

Actus 1.   Scaena 2.

[*Enter*] Callapine *with* Almeda *his keeper.*

Callapine. Sweet Almeda, pity the ruthful plight
Of Callapine, the son of Bajazeth,
Born to be monarch of the western world,
Yet here detain'd by cruel Tamburlaine.
Almeda. My lord I pity it, and with my heart
Wish your release; but he whose wrath is death,
My sovereign lord, renowmed Tamburlaine,
Forbids you further liberty than this.
Callapine. Ah, were I now but half so eloquent
To paint in words what I'll perform in deeds,   10

I know thou wouldst depart from hence with me.
Almeda. Not for all Afric; therefore move me not.
Callapine. Yet hear me speak, my gentle Almeda.
Almeda. No speech to that end, by your favour sir.
Callapine. By Cairo runs—
Almeda. No talk of running, I tell you sir.
Callapine. A little further, gentle Almeda.
Almeda. Well sir, what of this?
Callapine. By Cairo runs to Alexandria bay
    Darotes' stream, wherein at anchor lies   20
    A Turkish galley of my royal fleet,
    Waiting my coming to the river-side,
    Hoping by some means I shall be releas'd;
    Which, when I come aboard, will hoist up sail,
    And soon put forth into the Terrene sea,
    Where 'twixt the isles of Cyprus and of Crete,
    We quickly may in Turkish seas arrive.
    Then shalt thou see a hundred kings and more,
    Upon their knees, all bid me welcome home.
    Amongst so many crowns of burnish'd gold,   30
    Choose which thou wilt, all are at thy command.
    A thousand galleys mann'd with Christian slaves
    I freely give thee, which shall cut the Straits,
    And bring armadoes from the coasts of Spain,
    Fraughted with gold of rich America.
    The Grecian virgins shall attend on thee,
    Skilful in music and in amorous lays,
    As fair as was Pygmalion's ivory girl,
    Or lovely Iö metamorphosed.
    With naked negroes shall thy coach be drawn,   40
    And as thou rid'st in triumph through the streets,
    The pavement underneath thy chariot wheels
    With Turkey carpets shall be covered,
    And cloth of arras hung about the walls,
    Fit objects for thy princely eye to pierce.
    A hundred bassoes cloth'd in crimson silk
    Shall ride before thee on Barbarian steeds;
    And when thou go'st, a golden canopy
    Enchas'd with precious stones, which shine as bright

---

20 Darotes] a town on the river between Cairo and Alexandria   38 Pygmalion's ivory
girl] a statue he had created, given life by Venus   39 Iö metamorphosed] Iö, loved by
Jupiter, was turned into a heifer by the god's jealous wife.   46 bassoes] high-ranking
officers   48 go'st] walk

As that fair veil that covers all the world   50
When Phoebus, leaping from his hemisphere,
Descendeth downward to th' Antipodes:
And more than this, for all I cannot tell.
Almeda. How far hence lies the galley, say you?
Callapine. Sweet Almeda, scarce half a league from hence.
Almeda. But need we not be spied going aboard?
Callapine. Betwixt the hollow hanging of a hill
  And crooked bending of a craggy rock,
  The sails wrapp'd up, the mast and tacklings down,
  She lies so close that none can find her out.   60
Almeda. I like that well. But tell me, my lord, if I should let you go, would
  you be as good as your word? Shall I be made a king for my labour?
Callapine. As I am Callapine the emperor,
  And by the hand of Mahomet I swear,
  Thou shalt be crown'd a king, and be my mate.
Almeda. Then here I swear, as I am Almeda,
  Your keeper under Tamburlaine the Great
  (For that's the style and title I have yet)
  Although he sent a thousand armed men
  To intercept this haughty enterprise,   70
  Yet would I venture to conduct your grace,
  And die before I brought you back again!
Callapine. Thanks, gentle Almeda. Then let us haste,
  Lest time be past, and lingering let us both.
Almeda. When you will, my lord; I am ready.
Callapine. Even straight. And farewell, cursed Tamburlaine!
  Now go I to revenge my father's death.   *Exeunt.*

Actus 1. Scaena 3.

[*Enter*] Tamburlaine *with* Zenocrate, *and his three sons*, Calyphas,
    Amyras, *and* Celebinus, *with drums and trumpets.*

Tamburlaine. Now, bright Zenocrate, the world's fair eye,
  Whose beams illuminate the lamps of heaven,
  Whose cheerful looks do clear the cloudy air
  And clothe it in a crystal livery,
  Now rest thee here on fair Larissa plains,
  Where Egypt and the Turkish empire parts,
  Between thy sons, that shall be emperors,

5 Larissa] between Cairo and Damascus

And every one commander of a world.

Zenocrate. Sweet Tamburlaine, when wilt thou leave these arms,
    And save thy sacred person free from scathe   10
    And dangerous chances of the wrathful war?

Tamburlaine. When heaven shall cease to move on both the poles,
    And when the ground whereon my soldiers march
    Shall rise aloft and touch the horned moon,
    And not before, my sweet Zenocrate.
    Sit up, and rest thee like a lovely queen.
    So; now she sits in pomp and majesty,
    When these my sons more precious in mine eyes
    Than all the wealthy kingdoms I subdu'd,
    Plac'd by her side, look on their mother's face.   20
    But yet methinks their looks are amorous,
    Not martial as the sons of Tamburlaine.
    Water and air, being symboliz'd in one,
    Argue their want of courage and of wit;
    Their hair as white as milk and soft as down,
    Which should be like the quills of porcupines,
    As black as jet, and hard as iron or steel,
    Bewrays they are too dainty for the wars.
    Their fingers made to quaver on a lute,
    Their arms to hang about a lady's neck,   30
    Their legs to dance and caper in the air,
    Would make me think them bastards, not my sons,
    But that I know they issu'd from thy womb,
    That never look'd on man but Tamburlaine.

Zenocrate. My gracious lord, they have their mother's looks,
    But, when they list, their conquering father's heart.
    This lovely boy, the youngest of the three,
    Not long ago bestrid a Scythian steed,
    Trotting the ring, and tilting at a glove,
    Which when he tainted with his slender rod,   40
    He rein'd him straight, and made him so curvet
    As I cried out for fear he should have fall'n.

Tamburlaine. Well done, my boy! Thou shalt have shield and lance,
    Armour of proof, horse, helm, and curtle-axe,
    And I will teach thee how to charge thy foe,
    And harmless run among the deadly pikes.
    If thou wilt love the wars and follow me,
    Thou shalt be made a king and reign with me,
    Keeping in iron cages emperors.

23 in one] in one humour, the phlegmatic   40 tainted] touched

If thou exceed thy elder brothers' worth,   50
And shine in complete virtue more than they,
Thou shalt be king before them, and thy seed
Shall issue crowned from their mother's womb.
Celebinus. Yes father, you shall see me, if I live,
Have under me as many kings as you,
And march with such a multitude of men
As all the world shall tremble at their view.
Tamburlaine. These words assure me, boy, thou art my son.
When I am old and cannot manage arms,
Be thou the scourge and terror of the world.   60
Amyras. Why may not I, my lord, as well as he,
Be term'd the scourge and terror of the world?
Tamburlaine. Be all a scourge and terror to the world,
Or else you are not sons of Tamburlaine.
Calyphas. But while my brothers follow arms, my lord,
Let me accompany my gracious mother.
They are enough to conquer all the world,
And you have won enough for me to keep.
Tamburlaine. Bastardly boy, sprung from some coward's loins,
And not the issue of great Tamburlaine!   70
Of all the provinces I have subdu'd
Thou shalt not have a foot, unless thou bear
A mind courageous and invincible.
For he shall wear the crown of Persia
Whose head hath deepest scars, whose breast most wounds,
Which being wroth sends lightning from his eyes,
And in the furrows of his frowning brows
Harbours revenge, war, death, and cruelty;
For in a field, whose superficies
Is cover'd with a liquid purple veil,   80
And sprinkled with the brains of slaughter'd men,
My royal chair of state shall be advanc'd;
And he that means to place himself therein,
Must armed wade up to the chin in blood.
Zenocrate. My lord, such speeches to our princely sons
Dismays their minds before they come to prove
The wounding troubles angry war affords.
Celebinus. No madam, these are speeches fit for us;
For if his chair were in a sea of blood
I would prepare a ship and sail to it,   90
Ere I would lose the title of a king.
Amyras. And I would strive to swim through pools of blood,

      Or make a bridge of murder'd carcasses,
      Whose arches should be fram'd with bones of Turks,
      Ere I would lose the title of a king.
Tamburlaine. Well lovely boys, you shall be emperors both,
      Stretching your conquering arms from east to west.
      And sirrah, if you mean to wear a crown,
      When we shall meet the Turkish deputy
      And all his viceroys, snatch it from his head,   100
      And cleave his pericranion with thy sword.
Calyphas. If any man will hold him, I will strike,
      And cleave him to the channel with my sword.
Tamburlaine. Hold him, and cleave him too, or I'll cleave thee!
      For we will march against them presently.
      Theridamas, Techelles, and Casane
      Promis'd to meet me on Larissa plains,
      With hosts apiece against this Turkish crew;
      For I have sworn by sacred Mahomet
      To make it parcel of my empery.   110
      The trumpets sound; Zenocrate, they come.
          Enter Theridamas, *and his train, with drums and trumpets.*
      Welcome Theridamas, King of Argier.
Theridamas. My lord, the great and mighty Tamburlaine,
      Arch-monarch of the world, I offer here
      My crown, myself, and all the power I have,
      In all affection at thy kingly feet.
Tamburlaine. Thanks, good Theridamas.
Theridamas. Under my colours march ten thousand Greeks,
      And of Argier and Afric's frontier towns
      Twice twenty thousand valiant men-at-arms,   120
      All which have sworn to sack Natolia;
      Five hundred brigandines are under sail,
      Meet for your service on the sea, my lord,
      That launching from Argier to Tripoli,
      Will quickly ride before Natolia,
      And batter down the castles on the shore.
Tamburlaine. Well said, Argier. Receive thy crown again.
          Enter Techelles *and* Usumcasane *together.*
      Kings of Moroccus and of Fez, welcome.
Usumcasane. Magnificent and peerless Tamburlaine,
      I and my neighbour King of Fez have brought   130
      To aid thee in this Turkish expedition,

101 pericranion] skull   103 channel] throat

A hundred thousand expert soldiers.
From Azamor to Tunis near the sea
Is Barbary unpeopled for thy sake,
And all the men in armour under me,
Which with my crown I gladly offer thee.
Tamburlaine. Thanks King of Moroccus; take your crown again.
Techelles. And, mighty Tamburlaine, our earthly god,
Whose looks make this inferior world to quake,
I here present thee with the crown of Fez,   140
And with an host of Moors train'd to the war,
Whose coal-black faces make their foes retire
And quake for fear, as if infernal Jove,
Meaning to aid thee in these Turkish arms,
Should pierce the black circumference of hell,
With ugly Furies bearing fiery flags,
And millions of his strong tormenting spirits:
From strong Tesella unto Biledull
All Barbary is unpeopled for thy sake.
Tamburlaine. Thanks King of Fez; take here thy crown again.   150
Your presence, loving friends and fellow kings,
Makes me to surfeit in conceiving joy.
If all the crystal gates of Jove's high court
Were open'd wide, and I might enter in
To see the state and majesty of heaven,
It could not more delight me than your sight.
Now will we banquet on these plains a while,
And after march to Turkey with our camp,
In number more than are the drops that fall
When Boreas rents a thousand swelling clouds;   160
And proud Orcanes of Natolia
With all his viceroys shall be so afraid,
That, though the stones, as at Deucalion's flood,
Were turn'd to men, he should be overcome.
Such lavish will I make of Turkish blood,
That Jove shall send his winged messenger
To bid me sheathe my sword and leave the field;
The sun, unable to sustain the sight,
Shall hide his head in Thetis' watery lap,
And leave his steeds to fair Boötes' charge;   170
For half the world shall perish in this fight.

148 Tesella . . . Biledull] a town and a province in the very north of Africa   163 Deucalion's
flood] Deucalion and his wife, the only mortals left alive after the flood that destroyed
Hellas, re-peopled the world by throwing stones over their shoulders.

But now, my friends, let me examine ye;
How have ye spent your absent time from me?
Usumcasane. My lord, our men of Barbary have march'd
　　Four hundred miles with armour on their backs,
　　And lain in leaguer fifteen months and more;
　　For since we left you at the Soldan's court,
　　We have subdu'd the southern Guallatia,
　　And all the land unto the coast of Spain.
　　We kept the narrow Strait of Gibraltar,   180
　　And made Canaria call us kings and lords.
　　Yet never did they recreate themselves,
　　Or cease one day from war and hot alarms;
　　And therefore let them rest a while, my lord.
Tamburlaine. They shall, Casane, and 'tis time, i'faith.
Techelles. And I have march'd along the river Nile
　　To Machda, where the mighty Christian priest,
　　Call'd John the Great, sits in a milk-white robe,
　　Whose triple mitre I did take by force,
　　And made him swear obedience to my crown.   190
　　From thence unto Cazates did I march,
　　Where Amazonians met me in the field,
　　With whom, being women, I vouchsaf'd a league,
　　And with my power did march to Zanzibar,
　　The western part of Afric, where I view'd
　　The Ethiopian sea, rivers and lakes,
　　But neither man nor child in all the land.
　　Therefore I took my course to Manico,
　　Where, unresisted, I remov'd my camp;
　　And by the coast of Byather at last   200
　　I came to Cubar, where the negroes dwell,
　　And conquering that, made haste to Nubia;
　　There, having sack'd Borno, the kingly seat,
　　I took the king and led him bound in chains
　　Unto Damasco, where I stay'd before.
Tamburlaine. Well done, Techelles! What saith Theridamas?
Theridamas. I left the confines and the bounds of Afric,
　　And made a voyage into Europe,

176 in leaguer] besieging   178 Guallatia] a region in the western Sahara   188 John
the Great] Prester John   194 Zanzibar] the name Ortelius gives to a vast, unpopulated
area in south-west Africa bordering on the Atlantic (his Oceanus Aethiopicus)
198–205 Therefore . . . Damasco] Techelles marched north from Zanzibar, through Biafra
to modern Nigeria; then eastwards to Nubia with its capital Borno (near modern Lake
Chad) and up to Damascus.

Where by the river Tyros I subdu'd
Stoka, Padalia, and Codemia;   210
Then cross'd the sea and came to Oblia,
And Nigra Silva, where the devils dance,
Which in despite of them I set on fire.
From thence I cross'd the gulf call'd by the name
Mare Majore of the inhabitants.
Yet shall my soldiers make no period
Until Natolia kneel before your feet.

Tamburlaine. Then will we triumph, banquet, and carouse;
Cooks shall have pensions to provide us cates,
And glut us with the dainties of the world;   220
Lachryma Christi and Calabrian wines
Shall common soldiers drink in quaffing bowls,
Ay, liquid gold, when we have conquer'd him,
Mingled with coral and with orient pearl.
Come, let us banquet and carouse the whiles.   *Exeunt.*

Finis Actus primi.

Actus 2. Scaena 1.

[*Enter*] Sigismund, Frederick, Baldwin, *with their train.*

Sigismund. Now say, my lords of Buda and Bohemia,
What motion is it that inflames your thoughts,
And stirs your valours to such sudden arms?
Frederick. Your majesty remembers, I am sure,
What cruel slaughter of our Christian bloods
These heath'nish Turks and pagans lately made
Betwixt the city Zula and Danubius;
How through the midst of Varna and Bulgaria,
And almost to the very walls of Rome,
They have, not long since, massacr'd our camp.   10
It resteth now, then, that your majesty
Take all advantages of time and power,
And work revenge upon these infidels.
Your highness knows, for Tamburlaine's repair,
That strikes a terror to all Turkish hearts,

209-15 Where . . . Majore] After his forays by the Tyros (modern Dniester) Theridamas
concentrated on the area northwest of the Black Sea (Mare Majore). Ortelius marks a Black
Forest (Nigra Silva) just north of Odessa.   221 Lachryma Christi] a sweet Italian wine
II. i, 2 motion] idea   6-9 Betwixt . . . Rome] Zula and Varna appear as cities on the
Danube; to the south of the river Ortelius marks a province 'Romania', just north of Con-
stantinople. Marlowe misread this as 'Roma'—the 'nia' appears much lower on the map.

Natolia hath dismiss'd the greatest part
Of all his army, pitch'd against our power
Betwixt Cutheia and Orminius' mount,
And sent them marching up to Belgasar,
Acantha, Antioch, and Caesarea,   20
To aid the kings of Soria and Jerusalem.
Now then, my lord, advantage take hereof,
And issue suddenly upon the rest,
That in the fortune of their overthrow,
We may discourage all the pagan troop
That dare attempt to war with Christians.

Sigismund. But calls not then your grace to memory
The league we lately made with King Orcanes,
Confirm'd by oath and articles of peace,
And calling Christ for record of our truths?   30
This should be treachery and violence
Against the grace of our profession.

Baldwin. No whit, my lord; for with such infidels,
In whom no faith nor true religion rests,
We are not bound to those accomplishments
The holy laws of Christendom enjoin;
But, as the faith which they profanely plight
Is not by necessary policy
To be esteem'd assurance for ourselves,
So what we vow to them should not infringe   40
Our liberty of arms and victory.

Sigismund. Though I confess the oaths they undertake
Breed little strength to our security,
Yet those infirmities that thus defame
Their faiths, their honours, and their religion,
Should not give us presumption to the like.
Our faiths are sound, and must be consummate,
Religious, righteous, and inviolate.

Frederick. Assure your grace, 'tis superstition
To stand so strictly on dispensive faith;   50
And, should we lose the opportunity
That God hath given to venge our Christians' death,
And scourge their foul blasphemous paganism,
As fell to Saul, to Balaam, and the rest

18-20 Betwixt . . . Caesarea] Orcanes' army is marching southwards from Natolia to meet
Tamburlaine approaching through Egypt and Syria.   47 consummate] fulfilled   54-5 to
Saul, to Balaam . . . command] Saul failed to kill Agag (I Samuel 15) and Balaam to curse the
children of Israel (Numbers 22–4), but only Saul suffered God's anger; Balaam was obedient.

That would not kill and curse at God's command
So surely will the vengeance of the Highest,
And jealous anger of His fearful arm,
Be pour'd with rigour on our sinful heads,
If we neglect this offer'd victory.

Sigismund. Then arm, my lords, and issue suddenly,   60
    Giving commandment to our general host
    With expedition to assail the pagan,
    And take the victory our God hath given.   *Exeunt.*

Actus 2.   Scaena 2.

[*Enter*] Orcanes, Gazellus, Uribassa, *with their train.*

Orcanes. Gazellus, Uribassa and the rest,
    Now will we march from proud Orminius' mount
    To fair Natolia, where our neighbour kings
    Expect our power and our royal presence,
    T' encounter with the cruel Tamburlaine,
    That nigh Larissa sways a mighty host,
    And with the thunder of his martial tools
    Makes earthquakes in the hearts of men and heaven.

Gazellus. And now come we to make his sinews shake
    With greater power than erst his pride hath felt.   10
    An hundred kings by scores will bid him arms,
    And hundred thousands subjects to each score:
    Which, if a shower of wounding thunderbolts
    Should break out of the bowels of the clouds,
    And fall as thick as hail upon our heads,
    In partial aid of that proud Scythian,
    Yet should our courages and steeled crests,
    And numbers more than infinite of men,
    Be able to withstand and conquer him.

Uribassa. Methinks I see how glad the Christian king   20
    Is made for joy of your admitted truce,
    That could not but before be terrified
    With unacquainted power of our host.
                Enter a Messenger.

Messenger. Arm, dread sovereign, and my noble lords!
    The treacherous army of the Christians,
    Taking advantage of your slender power,

16 partial] prejudiced

    Comes marching on us, and determines straight
    To bid us battle for our dearest lives.
Orcanes. Traitors, villains, damned Christians!
    Have I not here the articles of peace   30
    And solemn covenants we have both confirm'd,
    He by his Christ, and I by Mahomet?
Gazellus. Hell and confusion light upon their heads
    That with such treason seek our overthrow,
    And cares so little for their prophet Christ!
Orcanes. Can there be such deceit in Christians,
    Or treason in the fleshly heart of man,
    Whose shape is figure of the highest God?
    Then if there be a Christ, as Christians say,
    But in their deeds deny him for their Christ;   40
    If he be son to everliving Jove,
    And hath the power of his outstretched arm;
    If he be jealous of his name and honour
    As is our holy prophet Mahomet,
    Take here these papers as our sacrifice
    And witness of thy servant's perjury!
    Open, thou shining veil of Cynthia,
    And make a passage from th' empyreal heaven,
    That he that sits on high and never sleeps,
    Nor in one place is circumscriptible,   50
    But everywhere fills every continent
    With strange infusion of his sacred vigour,
    May in his endless power and purity
    Behold and venge this traitor's perjury!
    Thou Christ that art esteem'd omnipotent,
    If thou wilt prove thyself a perfect God,
    Worthy the worship of all faithful hearts,
    Be now reveng'd upon this traitor's soul,
    And make the power I have left behind
    (Too little to defend our guiltless lives)   60
    Sufficient to discomfort and confound
    The trustless force of those false Christians!
    To arms my lords! On Christ still let us cry:
    If there be Christ, we shall have victory.   [*Exeunt.*]

[*Actus 2.   Scaena 3.*]

Sound to the battle; and Sigismund *comes out wounded.*

Sigismund. Discomfited is all the Christian host,
    And God hath thunder'd vengeance from on high
    For my accurs'd and hateful perjury.
    O just and dreadful punisher of sin,
    Let the dishonour of the pains I feel
    In this my mortal well-deserved wound
    End all my penance in my sudden death!
    And let this death, wherein to sin I die,
    Conceive a second life in endless mercy.   [*Dies.*]

Enter Orcanes, Gazellus, Uribassa, *with others.*

Orcanes. Now lie the Christians bathing in their bloods,   10
    And Christ or Mahomet hath been my friend.
Gazellus. See here the perjur'd traitor Hungary,
    Bloody and breathless for his villainy!
Orcanes. Now shall his barbarous body be a prey
    To beasts and fowls, and all the winds shall breathe
    Through shady leaves of every senseless tree
    Murmurs and hisses for his heinous sin.
    Now scalds his soul in the Tartarian streams,
    And feeds upon the baneful tree of hell,
    That Zoacum, that fruit of bitterness,   20
    That in the midst of fire is engraff'd,
    Yet flourisheth as Flora in her pride,
    With apples like the heads of damned fiends.
    The devils there in chains of quenchless flame
    Shall lead his soul through Orcus' burning gulf
    From pain to pain, whose change shall never end.
    What say'st thou yet, Gazellus, to his foil,
    Which we referr'd to justice of his Christ
    And to his power, which here appears as full
    As rays of Cynthia to the clearest sight?   30
Gazellus. 'Tis but the fortune of the wars, my lord,
    Whose power is often prov'd a miracle.
Orcanes. Yet in my thoughts shall Christ be honoured,
    Not doing Mahomet an injury,
    Whose power had share in this our victory;
    And since this miscreant hath disgrac'd his faith,

20 Zoacum] a tree in hell described in the Koran   21 engraff'd] rooted   25 Orcus
. . . gulf] hell-mouth   27 foil] defeat

    And died a traitor both to heaven and earth,
    We will both watch and ward shall keep his trunk
    Amidst these plains for fowls to prey upon.
    Go, Uribassa, give it straight in charge.   40
Uribassa. I will, my lord.   *Exit* Uribassa.
Orcanes. And now Gazellus, let us haste and meet
    Our army, and our brother of Jerusalem,
    Of Soria, Trebizon, and Amasia;
    And happily, with full Natolian bowls
    Of Greekish wine, now let us celebrate
    Our happy conquest and his angry fate.   *Exeunt.*

Actus 2.   Scaena ultima [4].

The arras is drawn, and Zenocrate *lies in her bed of state;* Tamburlaine
sitting by her; three Physicians *about her bed, tempering potions;*
   Theridamas, Techelles, Usumcasane, *and the three sons* [Calyphas,
            Amyras, *and* Celebinus].

Tamburlaine. Black is the beauty of the brightest day;
    The golden ball of heaven's eternal fire
    That danc'd with glory on the silver waves,
    Now wants the fuel that inflam'd his beams,
    And all with faintness and for foul disgrace,
    He binds his temples with a frowning cloud,
    Ready to darken earth with endless night.
    Zenocrate, that gave him light and life,
    Whose eyes shot fire from their ivory bowers,
    And temper'd every soul with lively heat,   10
    Now by the malice of the angry skies,
    Whose jealousy admits no second mate,
    Draws in the comfort of her latest breath,
    All dazzled with the hellish mists of death.
    Now walk the angels on the walls of heaven,
    As sentinels to warn th' immortal souls
    To entertain divine Zenocrate.
    Apollo, Cynthia, and the ceaseless lamps
    That gently look'd upon this loathsome earth,
    Shine downwards now no more, but deck the heavens   20
    To entertain divine Zenocrate.
    The crystal springs, whose taste illuminates
    Refined eyes with an eternal sight,
    Like tried silver runs through Paradise

    To entertain divine Zenocrate.
    The cherubins and holy seraphins,
    That sing and play before the King of Kings,
    Use all their voices and their instruments
    To entertain divine Zenocrate.
    And in this sweet and curious harmony,   30
    The god that tunes this music to our souls
    Holds out his hand in highest majesty
    To entertain divine Zenocrate.
    Then let some holy trance convey my thoughts
    Up to the palace of th' empyreal heaven,
    That this my life may be as short to me
    As are the days of sweet Zenocrate.
    Physicians, will no physic do her good?
Physician. My lord, your majesty shall soon perceive;
    And if she pass this fit, the worst is past.   40
Tamburlaine. Tell me, how fares my fair Zenocrate?
Zenocrates. I fare, my lord, as other empresses,
    That, when this frail and transitory flesh
    Hath suck'd the measure of that vital air
    That feeds the body with his dated health,
    Wanes with enforc'd and necessary change.
Tamburlaine. May never such a change transform my love,
    In whose sweet being I repose my life;
    Whose heavenly presence beautified with health,
    Gives light to Phoebus and the fixed stars;   50
    Whose absence makes the sun and moon as dark
    As when, oppos'd in one diameter,
    Their spheres are mounted on the serpent's head,
    Or else descended to his winding train.
    Live still, my love, and so conserve my life,
    Or, dying, be the author of my death.
Zenocrate. Live still, my lord! O let my sovereign live!
    And sooner let the fiery element
    Dissolve, and make your kingdom in the sky,
    Than this base earth should shroud your majesty;   60
    For should I but suspect your death by mine,
    The comfort of my future happiness,
    And hope to meet your highness in the heavens,
    Turn'd to despair, would break my wretched breast,
    And fury would confound my present rest.

52-4 oppos'd . . . train] When Scorpio is in line with the earth, the sun and moon are in
eclipse.   58 fiery element] the sphere of fire believed to surround the globe

But let me die, my love; yet, let me die;
With love and patience let your true love die:
Your grief and fury hurts my second life.
Yet let me kiss my lord before I die,
And let me die with kissing of my lord.   70
But since my life is lengthen'd yet a while,
Let me take leave of these my loving sons,
And of my lords, whose true nobility
Have merited my latest memory.
Sweet sons, farewell! In death resemble me,
And in your lives your father's excellency.
Some music, and my fit will cease, my lord.   *They call music.*
Tamburlaine. Proud fury and intolerable fit
That dares torment the body of my love,
And scourge the scourge of the immortal God!   80
Now are those spheres where Cupid us'd to sit,
Wounding the world with wonder and with love,
Sadly supplied with pale and ghastly death,
Whose darts do pierce the centre of my soul.
Her sacred beauty hath enchanted heaven,
And had she liv'd before the siege of Troy,
Helen, whose beauty summon'd Greece to arms,
And drew a thousand ships to Tenedos,
Had not been nam'd in Homer's Iliads:
Her name had been in every line he wrote.   90
Or had those wanton poets, for whose birth
Old Rome was proud, but gaz'd a while on her,
Nor Lesbia nor Corinna had been nam'd:
Zenocrate had been the argument
Of every epigram or elegy.   *The music sounds and she dies.*
What, is she dead? Techelles, draw thy sword,
And wound the earth, that it may cleave in twain,
And we descend into th' infernal vaults,
To hale the Fatal Sisters by the hair,
And throw them in the triple moat of hell,   100
For taking hence my fair Zenocrate.
Casane and Theridamas, to arms!
Raise cavalieros higher than the clouds,
And with the cannon break the frame of heaven;

88 Tenedos] the island near Troy where the Greeks lurked during the siege   93 Lesbia
. . . Corinna] the lovers of Catullus and Ovid   99 the Fatal Sisters] the goddesses Clotho,
Lachesis, and Atropos, who governed the lives and deaths of men   103 cavalieros]
mounds to support heavy guns

Batter the shining palace of the sun,
And shiver all the starry firmament,
For amorous Jove hath snatch'd my love from hence,
Meaning to make her stately queen of heaven.
What god soever holds thee in his arms,
Giving thee nectar and ambrosia,   110
Behold me here, divine Zenocrate,
Raving, impatient, desperate and mad,
Breaking my steeled lance, with which I burst
The rusty beams of Janus' temple doors,
Letting out death and tyrannizing war,
To march with me under this bloody flag!
And if thou pitiest Tamburlaine the Great,
Come down from heaven and live with me again!
Theridamas. Ah, good my lord, be patient! She is dead,
And all this raging cannot make her live.   120
If words might serve, our voice hath rent the air;
If tears, our eyes have water'd all the earth;
If grief, our murder'd hearts have strained forth blood.
Nothing prevails, for she is dead, my lord.
Tamburlaine. For she is dead! Thy words do pierce my soul.
Ah, sweet Theridamas, say so no more!
Though she be dead, yet let me think she lives,
And feed my mind that dies for want of her.
Where'er her soul be, thou shalt stay with me,
Embalm'd with cassia, ambergris, and myrrh,   130
Not lapp'd in lead, but in a sheet of gold,
And till I die thou shalt not be interr'd.
Then in as rich a tomb as Mausolus'
We both will rest, and have one epitaph
Writ in as many several languages
As I have conquer'd kingdoms with my sword.
This cursed town will I consume with fire,
Because this place bereft me of my love.
The houses, burnt, will look as if they mourn'd;
And here will I set up her stature,   140
And march about it with my mourning camp,
Drooping and pining for Zenocrate.   *The arras is drawn.*

114 Janus ... doors] The doors of Janus' temple in Rome were opened when a war was
started.   133 Mausolus] His widow erected an expensive memorial, the Mausoleum.
140 stature] statue

Actus 3.   Scaena 1.

Enter the Kings of Trebizon *and* Soria, *one bringing a sword and
another a sceptre; next Natolia* [Orcanes] *and* Jerusalem *with
the imperial crown; after* Callapine, *and after him* [Almeda
and] *other lords.* Orcanes *and* Jerusalem *crown him and
the other give him the sceptre.*

Orcanes. Callapinus Cyricelibes, otherwise Cybelius, son and successive heir
to the late mighty emperor Bajazeth, by the aid of God and his friend
Mahomet, Emperor of Natolia, Jerusalem, Trebizon, Soria, Amasia,
Thracia, Illyria, Carmonia, and all the hundred and thirty kingdoms late
contributory to his mighty father. Long live Callapinus, Emperor of
Turkey!

Callapine. Thrice-worthy kings of Natolia and the rest,
 I will requite your royal gratitudes
 With all the benefits my empire yields;
 And, were the sinews of th' imperial seat   10
 So knit and strengthen'd as when Bajazeth
 My royal lord and father fill'd the throne,
 Whose cursed fate hath so dismember'd it,
 Then should you see this thief of Scythia,
 This proud usurping king of Persia,
 Do us such honour and supremacy,
 Bearing the vengeance of our father's wrongs,
 As all the world should blot our dignities
 Out of the book of base-born infamies.
 And now I doubt not but your royal cares   20
 Hath so provided for this cursed foe,
 That since the heir of mighty Bajazeth,
 An emperor so honour'd for his virtues,
 Revives the spirits of true Turkish hearts,
 In grievous memory of his father's shame,
 We shall not need to nourish any doubt,
 But that proud Fortune, who hath follow'd long
 The martial sword of mighty Tamburlaine,
 Will now retain her old inconstancy,
 And raise our honour to as high a pitch   30
 In this our strong and fortunate encounter;
 For so hath heaven provided my escape
 From all the cruelty my soul sustain'd,
 By this my friendly keeper's happy means,

That Jove, surcharg'd with pity of our wrongs,
Will pour it down in showers on our heads,
Scourging the pride of cursed Tamburlaine.
Orcanes. I have a hundred thousand men in arms,
　　Some that in conquest of the perjur'd Christian,
　　Being a handful to a mighty host,   40
　　Think them in number yet sufficient
　　To drink the river Nile or Euphrates,
　　And for their power enow to win the world.
Jerusalem. And I as many from Jerusalem,
　　Judaea, Gaza, and Scalonia's bounds,
　　That on Mount Sinai, with their ensigns spread,
　　Look like the parti-colour'd clouds of heaven
　　That show fair weather to the neighbour morn.
Trebizon. And I as many bring from Trebizon,
　　Chio, Famastro, and Amasia,   50
　　All bordering on the Mare Major sea,
　　Riso, Sancina, and the bordering towns
　　That touch the end of famous Euphrates,
　　Whose courages are kindled with the flames
　　The cursed Scythian sets on all their towns,
　　And vow to burn the villain's cruel heart.
Soria. From Soria with seventy thousand strong,
　　Ta'en from Aleppo, Soldino, Tripoli,
　　And so unto my city of Damasco,
　　I march to meet and aid my neighbour kings,   60
　　All which will join against this Tamburlaine,
　　And bring him captive to your highness' feet.
Orcanes. Our battle then in martial manner pitch'd,
　　According to our ancient use, shall bear
　　The figure of the semi-circled moon,
　　Whose horns shall sprinkle through the tainted air
　　The poison'd brains of this proud Scythian.
Callapine. Well then my noble lords, for this my friend
　　That freed me from the bondage of my foe,
　　I think it requisite and honourable   70
　　To keep my promise and to make him king,
　　That is a gentleman, I know, at least.
Almeda. That's no matter, sir, for being a king; for Tamburlaine came up of
　　nothing.
Jerusalem. Your majesty may choose some 'pointed time,
　　Performing all your promise to the full;

45 Scalonia] Ascalon

'Tis naught for your majesty to give a kingdom.
Callapine. Then will I shortly keep my promise, Almeda.
Almeda. Why, I thank your majesty.   *Exeunt.*

Actus 3.   Scaena 2.

[*Enter*] Tamburlaine *with* Usumcasane, *and his three sons* [Calyphas,
    Amyras, *and* Celebinus]; *four bearing the hearse of* Zenocrate;
        and the drums sounding a doleful march; the town burning.

Tamburlaine. So burn the turrets of this cursed town,
    Flame to the highest region of the air,
    And kindle heaps of exhalations,
    That being fiery meteors, may presage
    Death and destruction to th' inhabitants!
    Over my zenith hang a blazing star,
    That may endure till heaven be dissolv'd,
    Fed with the fresh supply of earthly dregs,
    Threat'ning a death and famine to this land!
    Flying dragons, lightning, fearful thunder-claps,   10
    Singe these fair plains, and make them seem as black
    As is the island where the Furies mask,
    Compass'd with Lethe, Styx, and Phlegethon,
    Because my dear Zenocrate is dead!
Calyphas. This pillar plac'd in memory of her,
    Where in Arabian, Hebrew, Greek, is writ,
    This town being burnt by Tamburlaine the Great
    Forbids the world to build it up again.
Amyras. And here this mournful streamer shall be plac'd,
    Wrought with the Persian and Egyptian arms,   20
    To signify she was a princess born,
    And wife unto the monarch of the East.
Celebinus. And here this table as a register
    Of all her virtues and perfections.
Tamburlaine. And here the picture of Zenocrate,
    To show her beauty which the world admir'd;
    Sweet picture of divine Zenocrate,
    That hanging here will draw the gods from heaven,
    And cause the stars fix'd in the southern arc,
    Whose lovely faces never any view'd   30
    That have not pass'd the centre's latitude,
    As pilgrims travel to our hemisphere,

12 the island] Hades   12 mask] lurk   31 centre's latitude] equator

Only to gaze upon Zenocrate.
Thou shalt not beautify Larissa plains,
But keep within the circle of mine arms.
At every town and castle I besiege,
Thou shalt be set upon my royal tent;
And when I meet an army in the field,
Those looks will shed such influence in my camp
As if Bellona, goddess of the war,   40
Threw naked swords and sulphur-balls of fire
Upon the heads of all our enemies.
And now my lords, advance your spears again.
Sorrow no more, my sweet Casane, now.
Boys, leave to mourn; this town shall ever mourn,
Being burnt to cinders for your mother's death.
Calyphas. If I had wept a sea of tears for her,
It would not ease the sorrow I sustain.
Amyras. As is that town, so is my heart consum'd
With grief and sorrow for my mother's death.   50
Celebinus. My mother's death hath mortified my mind,
And sorrow stops the passage of my speech.
Tamburlaine. But now, my boys, leave off, and list to me,
That mean to teach you rudiments of war.
I'll have you learn to sleep upon the ground,
March in your armour thorough watery fens,
Sustain the scorching heat and freezing cold,
Hunger and thirst, right adjuncts of the war,
And after this to scale a castle wall,
Besiege a fort, to undermine a town,   60
And make whole cities caper in the air.
Then next, the way to fortify your men;
In champion grounds what figure serves you best,
For which the quinque-angle form is meet,
Because the corners there may fall more flat
Whereas the fort may fittest be assail'd,
And sharpest where th' assault is desperate:
The ditches must be deep, the counterscarps
Narrow and steep, the walls made high and broad,
The bulwarks and the rampires large and strong,   70
With cavalieros and thick counterforts,
And room within to lodge six thousand men.
It must have privy ditches, countermines,
And secret issuings to defend the ditch;

63 champion] open

It must have high argins and cover'd ways
To keep the bulwark fronts from battery,
And parapets to hide the musketeers,
Casemates to place the great artillery,
And store of ordnance, that from every flank
May scour the outward curtains of the fort,   80
Dismount the cannon of the adverse part,
Murder the foe, and save the walls from breach.
When this is learn'd for service on the land,
By plain and easy demonstration
I'll teach you how to make the water mount,
That you may dry-foot march through lakes and pools,
Deep rivers, havens, creeks, and little seas,
And make a fortress in the raging waves,
Fenc'd with the concave of a monstrous rock,
Invincible by nature of the place.   90
When this is done, then are ye soldiers,
And worthy sons of Tamburlaine the Great.
Calyphas. My lord, but this is dangerous to be done;
We may be slain or wounded ere we learn.
Tamburlaine. Villain, art thou the son of Tamburlaine,
And fear'st to die, or with a curtle-axe
To hew thy flesh and make a gaping wound?
Hast thou beheld a peal of ordnance strike
A ring of pikes, mingled with shot and horse,
Whose shatter'd limbs, being toss'd as high as heaven,   100
Hang in the air as thick as sunny motes,
And canst thou, coward, stand in fear of death?
Hast thou not seen my horsemen charge the foe,
Shot through the arms, cut overthwart the hands,
Dyeing their lances with their streaming blood,
And yet at night carouse within my tent,
Filling their empty veins with airy wine,
That being concocted, turns to crimson blood,
And wilt thou shun the field for fear of wounds?
View me, thy father, that hath conquer'd kings,   110
And with his host march'd round about the earth,
Quite void of scars and clear from any wound,
That by the wars lost not a dram of blood,
And see him lance his flesh to teach you all.   *He cuts his arm.*
A wound is nothing, be it ne'er so deep;
Blood is the god of war's rich livery.

75 argins] ramparts   96 curtle-axe] cutlass   108 concocted] digested

Now look I like a soldier, and this wound
As great a grace and majesty to me,
As if a chair of gold enamelled,
Enchas'd with diamonds, sapphires, rubies,   120
And fairest pearl of wealthy India,
Were mounted here under a canopy,
And I sat down, cloth'd with the massy robe
That late adorn'd the Afric potentate,
Whom I brought bound unto Damascus' walls.
Come boys, and with your fingers search my wound,
And in my blood wash all your hands at once,
While I sit smiling to behold the sight.
Now, my boys, what think you of a wound?

Calyphas. I know not what I should think of it; methinks 'tis a pitiful
  sight.   131

Celebinus. 'Tis nothing. Give me a wound, father.

Amyras. And me another, my lord.

Tamburlaine. Come, sirrah, give me your arm.

Celebinus. Here father, cut it bravely as you did your own.

Tamburlaine. It shall suffice thou dar'st abide a wound.

My boy, thou shalt not lose a drop of blood
Before we meet the army of the Turk;
But then run desperate through the thickest throngs,
Dreadless of blows, of bloody wounds, and death;   140
And let the burning of Larissa walls,
My speech of war, and this my wound you see,
Teach you, my boys, to bear courageous minds,
Fit for the followers of great Tamburlaine.
Usumcasane now come, let us march
Towards Techelles and Theridamas
That we have sent before to fire the towns,
The towers and cities of these hateful Turks,
And hunt that coward faint-heart runaway,
With that accursed traitor Almeda,   150
Till fire and sword have found them at a bay.

Usumcasane. I long to pierce his bowels with my sword,
That hath betray'd my gracious sovereign,
That curs'd and damned traitor Almeda.

Tamburlaine. Then let us see if coward Callapine
Dare levy arms against our puissance,
That we may tread upon his captive neck,
And treble all his father's slaveries.   *Exeunt.*

Actus 3.   Scaena 3.

[*Enter*] Techelles, Theridamas, [Soldiers, Pioners] *and their train.*

Theridamas. Thus have we march'd northward from Tamburlaine,
  Unto the frontier point of Soria;
  And this is Balsera, their chiefest hold,
  Wherein is all the treasure of the land.
Techelles. Then let us bring our light artillery,
  Minions, falc'nets, and sakers, to the trench,
  Filling the ditches with the walls' wide breach,
  And enter in to seize upon the gold.
  How say ye, soldiers, shall we not?
Soldiers. Yes, my lord, yes. Come, let's about it.   10
Theridamas. But stay a while; summon a parle, drum.
  It may be they will yield it quietly,
  Knowing two kings, the friends to Tamburlaine,
  Stand at the walls with such a mighty power.
   Summon the battle. [*Enter above*] Captain *with* [Olympia] *his wife*
            and Son.
Captain. What require you, my masters?
Theridamas. Captain, that thou yield up thy hold to us.
Captain. To you! Why, do you think me weary of it?
Techelles. Nay, captain, thou art weary of thy life,
  If thou withstand the friends of Tamburlaine.
Theridamas. These pioners of Argier in Africa,   20
  Even in the cannon's face, shall raise a hill
  Of earth and faggots higher than thy fort,
  And over thy argins and cover'd ways
  Shall play upon the bulwarks of thy hold
  Volleys of ordnance, till the breach be made
  That with his ruin fills up all the trench;
  And when we enter in, not heaven itself
  Shall ransom thee, thy wife, and family.
Techelles. Captain, these Moors shall cut the leaden pipes
  That bring fresh water to thy men and thee.   30
  And lie in trench before thy castle walls,
  That no supply of victual shall come in,
  Nor any issue forth but they shall die;
  And, therefore, captain, yield it quietly.
Captain. Were you that are the friends of Tamburlaine,
  Brothers to holy Mahomet himself,
  I would not yield it. Therefore do your worst:

6 Minions . . . sakers] small pieces of ordnance

      Raise mounts, batter, intrench, and undermine,
      Cut off the water, all convoys that can,   40
      Yet I am resolute: and so farewell.   *[Exeunt above.]*
Theridamas. Pioners, away, and where I stuck the stake,
      Intrench with those dimensions I prescrib'd.
      Cast up the earth towards the castle wall,
      Which, till it may defend you, labour low,
      And few or none shall perish by their shot.
Pioners. We will, my lord.   *Exeunt* [Pioners].
Techelles. A hundred horse shall scout about the plains
      To spy what force comes to relieve the hold.
      Both we, Theridamas, will intrench our men,
      And with the Jacob's staff measure the height   50
      And distance of the castle from the trench,
      That we may know if our artillery
      Will carry full point-blank unto their walls.
Theridamas. Then see the bringing of our ordnance
      Along the trench into the battery,
      Where we will have gabions of six foot broad,
      To save our cannoneers from musket-shot;
      Betwixt which shall our ordnance thunder forth,
      And with the breach's fall, smoke, fire and dust,
      The crack, the echo, and the soldiers' cry,   60
      Make deaf the air and dim the crystal sky.
Techelles. Trumpets and drums, alarum presently!
      And, soldiers, play the men! The hold is yours!   *[Exeunt.]*

               [Actus 3.   Scaena 4.]

    Enter the Captain *with* [Olympia] *his wife and* Son.

Olympia. Come good my lord, and let us haste from hence
      Along the cave that leads beyond the foe;
      No hope is left to save this conquer'd hold.
Captain. A deadly bullet gliding through my side
      Lies heavy on my heart. I cannot live.
      I feel my liver pierc'd and all my veins,
      That there begin and nourish every part,
      Mangled and torn, and all my entrails bath'd
      In blood that straineth from their orifex.
      Farewell, sweet wife! Sweet son, farewell! I die.   10
                                  [Dies.]

56 gabions] barricades

Olympia. Death, whither art thou gone, that both we live?
    Come back again, sweet Death, and strike us both!
    One minute end our days, and one sepulchre
    Contain our bodies! Death, why com'st thou not?
    Well, this must be the messenger for thee:
    Now ugly Death, stretch out thy sable wings,
    And carry both our souls where his remains.
    Tell me sweet boy, art thou content to die?
    These barbarous Scythians, full of cruelty,
    And Moors, in whom was never pity found,   20
    Will hew us piecemeal, put us to the wheel,
    Or else invent some torture worse than that;
    Therefore die by thy loving mother's hand,
    Who gently now will lance thy ivory throat,
    And quickly rid thee both of pain and life.
Son. Mother, dispatch me, or I'll kill myself,
    For think ye I can live and see him dead?
    Give me your knife, good mother, or strike home:
    The Scythians shall not tyrannize on me.
    Sweet mother strike, that I may meet my father.   30
                                                    She stabs him.

Olympia. Ah sacred Mahomet, if this be sin,
    Entreat a pardon of the God of heaven,
    And purge my soul before it come to thee!
                Enter Theridamas, Techelles, *and all their train.*
Theridamas. How now, madam, what are you doing?
Olympia. Killing myself, as I have done my son,
    Whose body with his father's I have burnt,
    Lest cruel Scythians should dismember him.
Techelles. 'Twas bravely done, and like a soldier's wife.
    Thou shalt with us to Tamburlaine the Great,
    Who when he hears how resolute thou wert,   40
    Will match thee with a viceroy or a king.
Olympia. My lord deceas'd was dearer unto me
    Than any viceroy, king, or emperor,
    And for his sake here will I end my days.
Theridamas. But lady, go with us to Tamburlaine,
    And thou shalt see a man greater than Mahomet,
    In whose high looks is much more majesty,
    Than from the concave superficies
    Of Jove's vast palace, the empyreal orb,
    Unto the shining bower where Cynthia sits,   50
    Like lovely Thetis, in a crystal robe;

That treadeth fortune underneath his feet,
And makes the mighty god of arms his slave;
On whom Death and the Fatal Sisters wait
With naked swords and scarlet liveries;
Before whom, mounted on a lion's back,
Rhamnusia bears a helmet full of blood,
And strows the way with brains of slaughter'd men;
By whose proud side the ugly Furies run,
Hearkening when he shall bid them plague the world;   60
Over whose zenith, cloth'd in windy air,
And eagle's wings join'd to her feather'd breast,
Fame hovereth, sounding of her golden trump,
That to the adverse poles of that straight line
Which measureth the glorious frame of heaven
The name of mighty Tamburlaine is spread;
And him, fair lady, shall thy eyes behold.
Come.

Olympia. Take pity of a lady's ruthful tears,
That humbly craves upon her knees to stay   70
And cast her body in the burning flame
That feeds upon her son's and husband's flesh.

Techelles. Madam, sooner shall fire consume us both
Than scorch a face so beautiful as this,
In frame of which Nature hath show'd more skill
Than when she gave eternal chaos form,
Drawing from it the shining lamps of heaven.

Theridamas. Madam, I am so far in love with you,
That you must go with us: no remedy.

Olympia. Then carry me, I care not, where you will,   80
And let the end of this my fatal journey
Be likewise end to my accursed life.

Techelles. No, madam, but the beginning of your joy:
Come willingly therefore.

Theridamas. Soldiers, now let us meet the general,
Who by this time is at Natolia,
Ready to charge the army of the Turk.
The gold, the silver, and the pearl ye got
Rifling this fort, divide in equal shares.
This lady shall have twice so much again   90
Out of the coffers of our treasury.   *Exeunt.*

57 Rhamnusia] Nemesis   64 straight line] the axletree of heaven, on which all the spheres
were thought to revolve

Actus 3.   Scaena 5.

[*Enter*] Callapine, Orcanes, Jerusalem, Trebizon, Soria, Almeda,
                    with their train [*and* Messenger].

Messenger. Renowmed emperor, mighty Callapine,
    God's great lieutenant over all the world!
    Here at Aleppo, with an host of men,
    Lies Tamburlaine, this king of Persia;
    In number more than are the quivering leaves
    Of Ida's forest, where your highness' hounds
    With open cry pursues the wounded stag;
    Who means to girt Natolia's walls with siege,
    Fire the town, and over-run the land.
Callapine. My royal army is as great as his,   10
    That from the bounds of Phrygia to the sea
    Which washeth Cyprus with his brinish waves,
    Covers the hills, the valleys, and the plains.
    Viceroys and peers of Turkey, play the men!
    Whet all your swords to mangle Tamburlaine,
    His sons, his captains, and his followers:
    By Mahomet, not one of them shall live!
    The field wherein this battle shall be fought
    For ever term the Persians' sepulchre,
    In memory of this our victory.   20
Orcanes. Now he that calls himself the scourge of Jove,
    The emperor of the world, and earthly god,
    Shall end the warlike progress he intends,
    And travel headlong to the lake of hell,
    Where legions of devils (knowing he must die
    Here in Natolia by your highness' hands)
    All brandishing their brands of quenchless fire,
    Stretching their monstrous paws, grin with their teeth,
    And guard the gates to entertain his soul.
Callapine. Tell me, viceroys, the number of your men,   30
    And what our army royal is esteem'd.
Jerusalem. From Palestina and Jerusalem,
    Of Hebrews three score thousand fighting men
    Are come, since last we show'd your majesty.
Orcanes. So from Arabia Desert, and the bounds
    Of that sweet land whose brave metropolis
    Re-edified the fair Semiramis,

36–7 metropolis . . . Semiramis] Babylon, which Semiramis rebuilt

Came forty thousand warlike foot and horse,
Since last we number'd to your majesty.
Trebizon. From Trebizon in Asia the Less,   40
Naturaliz'd Turks and stout Bithynians
Came to my bands full fifty thousand more,
That fighting, know not what retreat doth mean,
Nor e'er return but with the victory,
Since last we number'd to your majesty.
Soria. Of Sorians from Halla is repair'd,
And neighbour cities of your highness' land,
Ten thousand horse, and thirty thousand foot,
Since last we number'd to your majesty;
So that the army royal is esteem'd   50
Six hundred thousand valiant fighting men.
Callapine. Then welcome, Tamburlaine, unto thy death!
Come puissant viceroys, let us to the field,
The Persians' sepulchre, and sacrifice
Mountains of breathless men to Mahomet,
Who now with Jove opens the firmament
To see the slaughter of our enemies.

[*Enter*] Tamburlaine *with his three sons* [Calyphas, Amyras, Celebinus],
Usumcasane, *with other.*

Tamburlaine. How now, Casane! See, a knot of kings,
Sitting as if they were a-telling riddles!
Usumcasane. My lord, your presence makes them pale and wan: 60
Poor souls, they look as if their deaths were near.
Tamburlaine. Why so he is, Casane: I am here.
But yet I'll save their lives, and make them slaves.
Ye petty kings of Turkey, I am come,
As Hector did into the Grecian camp,
To overdare the pride of Graecia,
And set his warlike person to the view
Of fierce Achilles, rival of his fame.
I do you honour in the simile,
For if I should, as Hector did Achilles   70
(The worthiest knight that ever brandish'd sword),
Challenge in combat any of you all,
I see how fearfully ye would refuse,
And fly my glove as from a scorpion.
Orcanes. Now thou art fearful of thy army's strength,
Thou wouldst with overmatch of person fight.
But shepherd's issue, base-born Tamburlaine,

Think of thy end; this sword shall lance thy throat.

Tamburlaine. Villain, the shepherd's issue, at whose birth
    Heaven did afford a gracious aspect,   80
    And join'd those stars that shall be opposite
    Even till the dissolution of the world,
    And never meant to make a conqueror
    So famous as is mighty Tamburlaine,
    Shall so torment thee, and that Callapine,
    That like a roguish runaway, suborn'd
    That villain there, that slave, that Turkish dog,
    To false his service to his sovereign,
    As ye shall curse the birth of Tamburlaine.

Callapine. Rail not, proud Scythian: I shall now revenge   90
    My father's vile abuses and mine own.

Jerusalem. By Mahomet, he shall be tied in chains,
    Rowing with Christians in a brigandine
    About the Grecian isles to rob and spoil,
    And turn him to his ancient trade again.
    Methinks the slave should make a lusty thief.

Callapine. Nay, when the battle ends, all we will meet,
    And sit in council to invent some pain
    That most may vex his body and his soul.

Tamburlaine. Sirrah Callapine, I'll hang a clog about your neck for running
away again: you shall not trouble me thus to come and fetch you.   101
    But as for you, viceroy, you shall have bits,
    And harness'd like my horses, draw my coach,
    And when ye stay, be lash'd with whips of wire.
    I'll have you learn to feed on provender,
    And in a stable lie upon the planks.

Orcanes. But Tamburlaine, first thou shalt kneel to us,
    And humbly crave a pardon for thy life.

Trebizon. The common soldiers of our mighty host
    Shall bring thee bound unto the general's tent.   110

Soria. And all have jointly sworn thy cruel death,
    Or bind thee in eternal torments' wrath.

Tamburlaine. Well, sirs, diet yourselves; you know I shall have occasion
shortly to journey you.

Celebinus. See, father, how Almeda the jailor looks upon us!

Tamburlaine. Villain, traitor, damned fugitive,
    I'll make thee wish the earth had swallow'd thee!
    Seest thou not death within my wrathful looks?
    Go villain, cast thee headlong from a rock,
    Or rip thy bowels and rend out thy heart,   120

      T' appease my wrath; or else I'll torture thee,
      Searing thy hateful flesh with burning irons
      And drops of scalding lead, while all thy joints
      Be rack'd and beat asunder with the wheel;
      For if thou liv'st, not any element
      Shall shroud thee from the wrath of Tamburlaine.

Callapine. Well in despite of thee, he shall be king.
      Come Almeda; receive this crown of me.
      I here invest thee King of Ariadan,
      Bordering on Mare Rosso, near to Mecca.   130

Orcanes. What! Take it, man.

Almeda. Good my lord, let me take it.

Callapine. Dost thou ask him leave? Here, take it.

Tamburlaine. Go to, sirrah! Take your crown, and make up the half dozen.
      So sirrah, now you are a king, you must give arms.

Orcanes. So he shall, and wear thy head in his scutcheon.

Tamburlaine. No, let him hang a bunch of keys on his standard, to put him
      in remembrance he was a jailor; that when I take him, I may knock out his
      brains with them, and lock you in the stable, when you shall come sweating
      from my chariot.   140

Trebizon. Away! Let us to the field, that the villain may be slain.

Tamburlaine. Sirrah, prepare whips, and bring my chariot to my tent; for
      as soon as the battle is done, I'll ride in triumph through the camp.

          Enter Theridamas, Techelles, *and their train.*

      How now, ye petty kings? Lo, here are bugs
      Will make the hair stand upright on your heads,
      And cast your crowns in slavery at their feet!
      Welcome, Theridamas and Techelles both.
      See ye this rout, and know ye this same king?

Theridamas. Ay, my lord; he was Callapine's keeper.   149

Tamburlaine. Well now you see he is a king. Look to him, Theridamas, when
      we are fighting, lest he hide his crown as the foolish king of Persia did.

Soria. No, Tamburlaine; he shall not be put to that exigent, I warrant thee.

Tamburlaine. You know not, sir.
      But now, my followers and my loving friends,
      Fight as you ever did, like conquerors,
      The glory of this happy day is yours.
      My stern aspect shall make fair Victory,
      Hovering betwixt our armies, light on me,
      Loaden with laurel-wreaths to crown us all.

Techelles. I smile to think how, when this field is fought   160

130 Mare Rosso] the Red Sea

> And rich Natolia ours, our men shall sweat
> With carrying pearl and treasure on their backs.
> *Tamburlaine.* You shall be princes all immediately.
> Come fight, ye Turks, or yield us victory.
> *Orcanes.* No, we will meet thee, slavish Tamburlaine.   *Exeunt.*

Actus 4.   Scaena 1.

Alarm. Amyras *and* Celebinus *issue from the tent where* Calyphas
sits asleep.

Amyras. Now in their glories shine the golden crowns
   Of these proud Turks, much like so many suns
   That half dismay the majesty of heaven.
   Now brother, follow we our father's sword,
   That flies with fury swifter than our thoughts,
   And cuts down armies with his conquering wings.
Celebinus. Call forth our lazy brother from the tent,
   For if my father miss him in the field,
   Wrath, kindled in the furnace of his breast,
   Will send a deadly lightning to his heart.   10
Amyras. Brother, ho! What, given so much to sleep
   You cannot leave it, when our enemies' drums
   And rattling cannons thunder in our ears
   Our proper ruin and our father's foil?
Calyphas. Away, ye fools! My father needs not me,
   Nor you, in faith, but that you will be thought
   More childish-valorous than manly-wise.
   If half our camp should sit and sleep with me,
   My father were enough to scare the foe.
   You do dishonour to his majesty,   20
   To think our helps will do him any good.
Amyras. What, dar'st thou then be absent from the fight,
   Knowing my father hates thy cowardice,
   And oft hath warn'd thee to be still in field,
   When he himself amidst the thickest troops
   Beats down our foes, to flesh our taintless swords?
Calyphas. I know, sir, what it is to kill a man;
   It works remorse of conscience in me.
   I take no pleasure to be murderous,
   Nor care for blood when wine will quench my thirst.   30

26 taintless] unstained

Celebinus. O cowardly boy! Fie, for shame, come forth!
    Thou dost dishonour manhood and thy house.
Calyphas. Go, go, tall stripling, fight you for us both,
    And take my other toward brother here,
    For person like to prove a second Mars.
    'Twill please my mind as well to hear both you
    Have won a heap of honour in the field,
    And left your slender carcasses behind,
    As if I lay with you for company.
Amyras. You will not go then?   40
Calyphas. You say true.
Amyras. Were all the lofty mounts of Zona Mundi
    That fill the midst of farthest Tartary
    Turn'd into pearl and proffer'd for my stay,
    I would not bide the fury of my father
    When, made a victor in these haughty arms,
    He comes and finds his sons have had no shares
    In all the honours he propos'd for us.
Calyphas. Take you the honour, I will take my ease;
    My wisdom shall excuse my cowardice.   50
    I go into the field before I need?

                Alarm; and Amyras *and* Celebinus *run in.*
    The bullets fly at random where they list;
    And, should I go and kill a thousand men,
    I were as soon rewarded with a shot,
    And sooner far than he that never fights;
    And should I go and do nor harm nor good,
    I might have harm, which all the good I have,
    Join'd with my father's crown, would never cure.
    I'll to cards. Perdicas!

                [*Enter* Perdicas.]

Perdicas. Here my lord.   60
Calyphas. Come, thou and I will go to cards to drive away the time.
Perdicas. Content, my lord; but what shall we play for?
Calyphas. Who shall kiss the fairest of the Turks' concubines first, when
    my father hath conquered them.
Perdicas. Agreed, i'faith.   *They play.*
Calyphas. They say I am a coward, Perdicas, and I fear as little their taratan-
    taras, their swords, or their cannons as I do a naked lady in a net of gold,
    and, for fear I should be afraid, would put it off and come to bed with me.
Perdicas. Such a fear, my lord, would never make ye retire.   69

34 toward] promising   42 Zona Mundi] the Urals

Calyphas. I would my father would let me be put in the front of such a
   battle once, to try my valour!   *Alarm.*
   What a coil they keep! I believe there will be some hurt done anon
   amongst them.   [Calyphas *and* Perdicas *retire to back of stage.*]
      Enter Tamburlaine, Theridamas, Techelles, Usumcasane, Amyras,
         Celebinus, *leading the Turkish Kings* [*of Natolia* (Orcanes),
               Jerusalem, Trebizon, *and* Soria; *and* Soldiers].
Tamburlaine. See now ye slaves, my children stoops your pride,
      And leads your glories sheep-like to the sword!
      Bring them, my boys, and tell me if the wars
      Be not a life that may illustrate gods,
      And tickle not your spirits with desire
      Still to be train'd in arms and chivalry?
Amyras. Shall we let go these kings again, my lord,   80
      To gather greater numbers 'gainst our power,
      That they may say, it is not chance doth this,
      But matchless strength and magnanimity?
Tamburlaine. No, no, Amyras; tempt not fortune so;
      Cherish thy valour still with fresh supplies,
      And glut it not with stale and daunted foes.
      But where's this coward villain, not my son,
      But traitor to my name and majesty?   *He goes in and brings him out.*
      Image of sloth, and picture of a slave,
      The obloquy and scorn of my renown!   90
      How may my heart, thus fired with mine eyes,
      Wounded with shame and kill'd with discontent,
      Shroud any thought may hold my striving hands
      From martial justice on thy wretched soul?
Theridamas. Yet pardon him, I pray your majesty.
Techelles and *Usumcasane.* Let all of us entreat your highness' pardon.
Tamburlaine. Stand up, ye base, unworthy soldiers!
      Know ye not yet the argument of arms?
Amyras. Good my lord, let him be forgiven for once,
      And we will force him to the field hereafter.   100
Tamburlaine. Stand up my boys, and I will teach ye arms,
      And what the jealousy of wars must do.
      O Samarcanda, where I breathed first,
      And joy'd the fire of this martial flesh,
      Blush, blush fair city, at thine honour's foil,
      And shame of nature, which Jaertis' stream

---

72 coil] commotion   73 s.d. Calyphas and Perdicas presumably return to the 'tent' in
which Calyphas was sleeping at the beginning of the scene.   77 illustrate] add lustre to
98 argument of arms] meaning of military life   106 Jaertis' stream] the river Jaxartes

Embracing thee with deepest of his love,
Can never wash from thy distained brows!
Here Jove, receive his fainting soul again,
A form not meet to give that subject essence   110
Whose matter is the flesh of Tamburlaine,
Wherein an incorporeal spirit moves,
Made of the mould whereof thyself consists,
Which makes me valiant, proud, ambitious,
Ready to levy power against thy throne,
That I might move the turning spheres of heaven;
For earth and all this airy region
Cannot contain the state of Tamburlaine.   [*Stabs* Calyphas.]
By Mahomet, thy mighty friend I swear,
In sending to my issue such a soul,   120
Created of the massy dregs of earth,
The scum and tartar of the elements,
Wherein was neither courage, strength or wit,
But folly, sloth, and damned idleness,
Thou hast procur'd a greater enemy
Than he that darted mountains at thy head,
Shaking the burden mighty Atlas bears,
Whereat thou trembling hidd'st thee in the air,
Cloth'd with a pitchy cloud for being seen.
And now, ye canker'd curs of Asia,   130
That will not see the strength of Tamburlaine
Although it shine as brightly as the sun,
Now you shall feel the strength of Tamburlaine,
And by the state of his supremacy,
Approve the difference 'twixt himself and you.
Orcanes. Thou show'st the difference 'twixt ourselves and thee,
In this thy barbarous damned tyranny.
Jerusalem. Thy victories are grown so violent
That shortly heaven, fill'd with the meteors
Of blood and fire thy tyrannies have made,   140
Will pour down blood and fire on thy head,
Whose scalding drops will pierce thy seething brains,
And with our bloods, revenge our bloods on thee.
Tamburlaine. Villains, these terrors and these tyrannies
(If tyrannies war's justice ye repute)
I execute, enjoin'd me from above,
To scourge the pride of such as Heaven abhors;

126 Than he . . . head] Cf. Part I, II. vi. 1–6 and note.

Nor am I made arch-monarch of the world,
Crown'd and invested by the hand of Jove,
For deeds of bounty or nobility;   150
But, since I exercise a greater name,
The scourge of God and terror of the world,
I must apply myself to fit those terms,
In war, in blood, in death, in cruelty,
And plague such peasants as resist in me
The power of heaven's eternal majesty.
Theridamas, Techelles, and Casane,
Ransack the tents and the pavilions
Of these proud Turks, and take their concubines,
Making them bury this effeminate brat;   160
For not a common soldier shall defile
His manly fingers with so faint a boy.
Then bring those Turkish harlots to my tent,
And I'll dispose them as it likes me best.
Meanwhile, take him in.

Soldiers. We will, my lord.   [*Exeunt with the body of* Calyphas.]
Jerusalem. O damned monster, nay, a fiend of hell,
Whose cruelties are not so harsh as thine,
Nor yet impos'd with such a bitter hate!
Orcanes. Revenge it, Rhadamanth and Æacus,   170
And let your hates, extended in his pains,
Expel the hate wherewith he pains our souls!
Trebizon. May never day give virtue to his eyes,
Whose sight, compos'd of fury and of fire,
Doth send such stern affections to his heart!
Soria. May never spirit, vein or artier feed
The cursed substance of that cruel heart;
But, wanting moisture and remorseful blood,
Dry up with anger, and consume with heat!
Tamburlaine. Well bark, ye dogs! I'll bridle all your tongues, 180
And bind them close with bits of burnish'd steel,
Down to the channels of your hateful throats,
And with the pains my rigour shall inflict,
I'll make ye roar, that earth may echo forth
The far-resounding torments ye sustain:
As when an herd of lusty Cimbrian bulls
Run mourning round about the females' miss,
And stung with fury of their following,

170 Rhadamanth and Æacus] two of the three judges in Hades   187-8 females' miss ...
following] lamenting the loss of their females and furious at following them

Fill all the air with troublous bellowing.
I will, with engines never exercis'd, 190
Conquer, sack, and utterly consume
Your cities and your golden palaces,
And with the flames that beat against the clouds
Incense the heavens and make the stars to melt,
As if they were the tears of Mahomet
For hot consumption of his country's pride.
And till by vision or by speech I hear
Immortal Jove say 'Cease, my Tamburlaine',
I will persist a terror to the world,
Making the meteors that like armed men, 200
Are seen to march upon the towers of heaven,
Run tilting round about the firmament,
And break their burning lances in the air,
For honour of my wondrous victories.
Come, bring them in to our pavilion. *Exeunt.*

Actus 4. Scaena 2.

[*Enter*] Olympia *alone.*

Olympia. Distress'd Olympia, whose weeping eyes
Since thy arrival here beheld no sun,
But, clos'd within the compass of a tent,
Hath stain'd thy cheeks and made thee look like death,
Devise some means to rid thee of thy life,
Rather than yield to his detested suit
Whose drift is only to dishonour thee;
And since this earth, dew'd with thy brinish tears,
Affords no herbs whose taste may poison thee,
Nor yet this air, beat often with thy sighs, 10
Contagious smells and vapours to infect thee,
Nor thy close cave a sword to murder thee,
Let this invention be the instrument.

Enter Theridamas.

Theridamas. Well met, Olympia. I sought thee in my tent,
But when I saw the place obscure and dark,
Which with thy beauty thou wast wont to light,
Enrag'd, I ran about the fields for thee,
Supposing amorous Jove had sent his son,
The winged Hermes, to convey thee hence.
But now I find thee, and that fear is past, 20

Tell me Olympia, wilt thou grant my suit?
Olympia. My lord and husband's death, with my sweet son's,
    With whom I buried all affections
    Save grief and sorrow which torment my heart,
    Forbids my mind to entertain a thought
    That tends to love, but meditate on death,
    A fitter subject for a pensive soul.
Theridamas. Olympia, pity him in whom thy looks
    Have greater operation and more force
    Than Cynthia's in the watery wilderness,   30
    For with thy view my joys are at the full,
    And ebb again as thou depart'st from me.
Olympia. Ah, pity me, my lord, and draw your sword,
    Making a passage for my troubled soul,
    Which beats against this prison to get out,
    And meet my husband and my loving son!
Theridamas. Nothing but still thy husband and thy son?
    Leave this, my love, and listen more to me:
    Thou shalt be stately Queen of fair Argier,
    And, cloth'd in costly cloth of massy gold,   40
    Upon the marble turrets of my court
    Sit like to Venus in her chair of state,
    Commanding all thy princely eye desires;
    And I will cast off arms and sit with thee,
    Spending my life in sweet discourse of love.
Olympia. No such discourse is pleasant in mine ears,
    But that where every period ends with death,
    And every line begins with death again.
    I cannot love, to be an emperess.
Theridamas. Nay, lady, then if nothing will prevail,   50
    I'll use some other means to make you yield.
    Such is the sudden fury of my love,
    I must and will be pleas'd, and you shall yield:
    Come to the tent again.
Olympia. Stay, good my lord; and, will you save my honour,
    I'll give your grace a present of such price
    As all the world cannot afford the like.
Theridamas. What is it?
Olympia. An ointment which a cunning alchemist
    Distilled from the purest balsamum   60
    And simplest extracts of all minerals,
    In which the essential form of marble stone,

61 simplest extracts] essences

Temper'd by science metaphysical,
And spells of magic from the mouths of spirits,
With which if you but 'noint your tender skin,
Nor pistol, sword, nor lance, can pierce your flesh.

Theridamas. Why madam, think ye to mock me thus palpably?

Olympia. To prove it, I will 'noint my naked throat,
Which when you stab, look on your weapon's point,
And you shall see't rebated with the blow.   70

Theridamas. Why gave you not your husband some of it,
If you lov'd him, and it so precious?

Olympia. My purpose was, my lord, to spend it so,
But was prevented by his sudden end;
And for a present easy proof hereof,
That I dissemble not, try it on me.

Theridamas. I will, Olympia, and will keep it for
The richest present of this eastern world.   *She 'noints her throat.*

Olympia. Now stab, my lord, and mark your weapon's point,
That will be blunted if the blow be great.   80

Theridamas. Here, then, Olympia.   [*Stabs her.*]
What, have I slain her? Villain, stab thyself!
Cut off this arm that murdered my love,
In whom the learned rabbis of this age
Might find as many wondrous miracles
As in the theoria of the world!
Now hell is fairer than Elysium;
A greater lamp than that bright eye of heaven,
From whence the stars do borrow all their light,
Wanders about the black circumference;   90
And now the damned souls are free from pain,
For every Fury gazeth on her looks.
Infernal Dis is courting of my love,
Inventing masques and stately shows for her,
Opening the doors of his rich treasury
To entertain this queen of chastity,
Whose body shall be tomb'd with all the pomp
The treasure of my kingdom may afford.   *Exit, taking her away.*

70 rebated] blunted   86 theoria] contemplation   93 Dis] ruler of the underworld

Actus 4.   Scaena 3.

[*Enter*] Tamburlaine *drawn in his chariot by* Trebizon *and* Soria
*with bits in their mouths, reins in his left hand, in his right hand a
whip, with which he scourgeth them.* Techelles, Theridamas,
Usumcasane, Amyras, Celebinus: [Orcanes *King of*] Natolia
and Jerusalem *led by with five or six common* Soldiers.

Tamburlaine. Holla, ye pamper'd jades of Asia!
    What, can ye draw but twenty miles a day,
    And have so proud a chariot at your heels,
    And such a coachman as great Tamburlaine?
    But from Asphaltis, where I conquer'd you,
    To Byron here, where thus I honour you?
    The horse that guide the golden eye of heaven,
    And blow the morning from their nostrils,
    Making their fiery gait above the clouds,
    Are not so honour'd in their governor   10
    As you, ye slaves, in mighty Tamburlaine.
    The headstrong jades of Thrace Alcides tam'd,
    That King Ægeus fed with human flesh,
    And made so wanton that they knew their strengths,
    Were not subdu'd with valour more divine
    Than you by this unconquer'd arm of mine.
    To make you fierce, and fit my appetite,
    You shall be fed with flesh as raw as blood,
    And drink in pails the strongest muscadel.
    If you can live with it, then live, and draw   20
    My chariot swifter than the racking clouds;
    If not, then die like beasts, and fit for naught
    But perches for the black and fatal ravens.
    Thus am I right the scourge of highest Jove;
    And see the figure of my dignity,
    By which I hold my name and majesty.
Amyras. Let me have coach, my lord, that I may ride,
    And thus be drawn by these two idle kings.
Tamburlaine. Thy youth forbids such ease, my kingly boy;
    They shall tomorrow draw my chariot,   30
    While these their fellow-kings may be refresh'd.
Orcanes. O thou that sway'st the region under earth,

12–14 headstrong jades . . . strengths] Hercules (Alcides) as one of his labours captured the
man-eating horses of Diomedes (Aegeus), a Thracian king.   21 racking] driving before
the wind

And art a king as absolute as Jove,
Come as thou didst in fruitful Sicily,
Surveying all the glories of the land,
And as thou took'st the fair Proserpina,
Joying the fruit of Ceres' garden-plot,
For love, for honour, and to make her queen,
So for just hate, for shame, and to subdue
This proud contemner of thy dreadful power,   40
Come once in fury and survey his pride,
Haling him headlong to the lowest hell!

Theridamas. Your majesty must get some bits for these,
To bridle their contemptuous cursing tongues,
That like unruly never-broken jades,
Break through the hedges of their hateful mouths,
And pass their fixed bounds exceedingly.

Techelles. Nay, we will break the hedges of their mouths,
And pull their kicking colts out of their pastures.

Usumcasane. Your majesty already hath devis'd   50
A mean, as fit as may be, to restrain
These coltish coach-horse tongues from blasphemy.

Celebinus. How like you that, sir king? Why speak you not?

Jerusalem. Ah cruel brat, sprung from a tyrant's loins!
How like his cursed father he begins
To practise taunts and bitter tyrannies!

Tamburlaine. Ay Turk, I tell thee, this same boy is he
That must, advanc'd in higher pomp than this,
Rifle the kingdoms I shall leave unsack'd,
If Jove esteeming me too good for earth,   60
Raise me to match the fair Aldebaran,
Above the threefold astracism of heaven,
Before I conquer all the triple world.
Now fetch me out the Turkish concubines;
I will prefer them for the funeral
They have bestow'd on my abortive son.

                    The Concubines *are brought in.*

Where are my common soldiers now, that fought
So lion-like upon Asphaltis' plains?

Soldiers. Here, my lord.

Tamburlaine. Hold ye, tall soldiers, take ye queens apiece—   70
I mean such queens as were kings' concubines.
Take them; divide them, and their jewels too,

61 Aldebaran] the 'eye' of Taurus   62 threefold astracism] Taurus   63 triple world]
i.e., Europe, Asia, and Africa   65 prefer] promote

And let them equally serve all your turns.

Soldiers. We thank your majesty.

Tamburlaine. Brawl not, I warn you, for your lechery,
    For every man that so offends shall die.

Orcanes. Injurious tyrant, wilt thou so defame
    The hateful fortunes of thy victory,
    To exercise upon such guiltless dames
    The violence of thy common soldiers' lust?   80

Tamburlaine. Live continent then ye slaves, and meet not me
    With troops of harlots at your slothful heels.

Concubines. O pity us, my lord, and save our honours!

Tamburlaine. Are ye not gone, ye villains, with your spoils?

                                They run away with the Ladies.

Jerusalem. O merciless, infernal cruelty!

Tamburlaine. Save your honours! 'Twere but time indeed,
    Lost long before you knew what honour meant.

Theridamas. It seems they meant to conquer us, my lord,
    And make us jesting pageants for their trulls.

Tamburlaine. And now themselves shall make our pageant,   90
    And common soldiers jest with all their trulls.
    Let them take pleasure soundly in their spoils,
    Till we prepare our march to Babylon,
    Whither we next make expedition.

Techelles. Let us not be idle then, my lord,
    But presently be prest to conquer it.

Tamburlaine. We will, Techelles. Forward then, ye jades!
    Now crouch, ye kings of greatest Asia,
    And tremble when ye hear this scourge will come
    That whips down cities and controlleth crowns,   100
    Adding their wealth and treasure to my store.
    The Euxine Sea, north to Natolia;
    The Terrene, west; the Caspian, north-north-east;
    And on the south, Sinus Arabicus
    Shall all be loaded with the martial spoils
    We will convey with us to Persia.
    Then shall my native city Samarcanda,
    And crystal waves of fresh Jaertis' stream,
    The pride and beauty of her princely seat,
    Be famous through the furthest continents;   110
    For there my palace royal shall be plac'd,
    Whose shining turrets shall dismay the heavens,
    And cast the fame of Ilion's tower to hell.

102 Euxine Sea] Black Sea   104 Sinus Arabicus] Red Sea

Thorough the streets, with troops of conquer'd kings,
I'll ride in golden armour like the sun,
And in my helm a triple plume shall spring,
Spangled with diamonds, dancing in the air,
To note me emperor of the three-fold world:
Like to an almond tree y-mounted high
Upon the lofty and celestial mount   120
Of ever-green Selinus, quaintly deck'd
With blooms more white than Erycina's brows,
Whose tender blossoms tremble every one
At every little breath that thorough heaven is blown.
Then in my coach, like Saturn's royal son
Mounted his shining chariot gilt with fire,
And drawn with princely eagles through the path
Pav'd with bright crystal and enchas'd with stars
When all the gods stand gazing at his pomp,
So will I ride through Samarcanda streets,   130
Until my soul, dissever'd from this flesh
Shall mount the milk-white way, and meet him there.
To Babylon, my lords, to Babylon!   *Exeunt.*

Finis Actus Quarti.

Actus 5.   Scaena 1.

Enter the Governor *of Babylon upon the walls with* [Maximus *and*]
others.

Governor. What saith Maximus?
Maximus. My lord, the breach the enemy hath made
       Gives such assurance of our overthrow
       That little hope is left to save our lives,
       Or hold our city from the conqueror's hands.
       Then hang out flags, my lord, of humble truce,
       And satisfy the people's general prayers,
       That Tamburlaine's intolerable wrath
       May be suppress'd by our submission.
Governor. Villain, respects thou more thy slavish life   10
       Than honour of thy country or thy name?
       Is not my life and state as dear to me,
       The city and my native country's weal,

122 Erycina] Venus (who had a temple on Mt. Eryx)

As any thing of price with thy conceit?
Have we not hope, for all our batter'd walls,
To live secure and keep his forces out,
When this our famous lake of Limnasphaltis
Makes walls afresh with every thing that falls
Into the liquid substance of his stream,
More strong than are the gates of death or hell?   20
What faintness should dismay our courages,
When we are thus defenc'd against our foe,
And have no terror but his threat'ning looks?

     Enter another [Citizen], *kneeling to the* Governor.

Citizen. My lord, if ever you did deed of ruth,
And now will work a refuge to our lives,
Offer submission, hang up flags of truce,
That Tamburlaine may pity our distress
And use us like a loving conqueror
Though this be held his last day's dreadful siege,
Wherein he spareth neither man nor child,   30
Yet are there Christians of Georgia here,
Whose state he ever pitied and reliev'd,
Will get his pardon, if your grace would send.

Governor. How is my soul environed,
And this eterniz'd city Babylon
Fill'd with a pack of faint-heart fugitives
That thus entreat their shame and servitude!

     [*Enter a second* Citizen.]

2 Citizen. My lord, if ever you will win our hearts,
Yield up the town, save our wives and children;
For I will cast myself from off these walls,   40
Or die some death of quickest violence,
Before I bide the wrath of Tamburlaine.

Governor. Villains, cowards, traitors to our state,
Fall to the earth, and pierce the pit of hell,
That legions of tormenting spirits may vex
Your slavish bosoms with continual pains!
I care not, nor the town will never yield
As long as any life is in my breast.

     Enter Theridamas *and* Techelles, *with other* Soldiers.

Theridamas. Thou desperate governor of Babylon,
To save thy life, and us a little labour,   50
Yield speedily the city to our hands,

14 As . . . conceit] As anything that you hold valuable

Or else be sure thou shalt be forc'd with pains
More exquisite than ever traitor felt.

Governor. Tyrant, I turn the traitor in thy throat,
And will defend it in despite of thee.
Call up the soldiers to defend these walls.

Techelles. Yield, foolish governor; we offer more
Than ever yet we did to such proud slaves
As durst resist us till our third day's siege.
Thou seest us prest to give the last assault,   60
And that shall bide no more regard of parley.

Governor. Assault and spare not; we will never yield.

Alarm, and they scale the walls. [*Exeunt above.*]

Enter Tamburlaine [*drawn in his chariot by the Kings of* Trebizon
and Soria] *with* Usumcasane, Amyras, *and* Celebinus, *with*
[Attendants *and*] *others; the two spare Kings* [Orcanes *of*
Natolia *and* Jerusalem].

Tamburlaine. The stately buildings of fair Babylon,
Whose lofty pillars, higher than the clouds,
Were wont to guide the seaman in the deep,
Being carried thither by the cannon's force
Now fill the mouth of Limnasphaltis' lake,
And make a bridge unto the batter'd walls.
Where Belus, Ninus, and great Alexander
Have rode in triumph, triumphs Tamburlaine,   70
Whose chariot wheels have burst th' Assyrians' bones,
Drawn with these kings on heaps of carcasses.
Now in the place where fair Semiramis,
Courted by kings and peers of Asia,
Hath trod the measures, do my soldiers march;
And in the streets, where brave Assyrian dames
Have rid in pomp like rich Saturnia,
With furious words and frowning visages
My horsemen brandish their unruly blades.

Enter Theridamas *and* Techelles, *bringing the* Governor *of Babylon.*

Who have ye there, my lord?   80

Theridamas. The sturdy governor of Babylon,
That made us all the labour for the town,
And us'd such slender reckoning of your majesty.

Tamburlaine. Go bind the villain. He shall hang in chains
Upon the ruins of this conquer'd town.

69 Belus, Ninus, and great Alexander] Belus was reputed to have founded Babylon, and
Ninus, Nineveh; Alexander the Great conquered Babylon.   77 Saturnia] Juno

Sirrah, the view of our vermilion tents
Which threaten'd more than if the region
Next underneath the element of fire
Were full of comets and of blazing stars,
Whose flaming trains should reach down to the earth,   90
Could not affright you; no, nor I myself,
The wrathful messenger of mighty Jove,
That with his sword hath quail'd all earthly kings,
Could not persuade you to submission,
But still the ports were shut. Villain, I say,
Should I but touch the rusty gates of hell,
The triple-headed Cerberus would howl,
And wake black Jove to crouch and kneel to me;
But I have sent volleys of shot to you,
Yet could not enter till the breach was made.   100

Governor. Nor, if my body could have stopp'd the breach,
Shouldst thou have enter'd, cruel Tamburlaine.
'Tis not thy bloody tents can make me yield,
Nor yet thyself, the anger of the Highest;
For though thy cannon shook the city-walls,
My heart did never quake, or courage faint.

Tamburlaine. Well, now I'll make it quake. Go draw him up,
Hang him up in chains upon the city-walls,
And let my soldiers shoot the slave to death.

Governor. Vile monster, born of some infernal hag,   110
And sent from hell to tyrannize on earth,
Do all thy worst; nor death, nor Tamburlaine,
Torture, or pain, can daunt my dreadless mind.

Tamburlaine. Up with him, then! His body shall be scarr'd.

Governor. But, Tamburlaine, in Limnasphaltis' lake
There lies more gold than Babylon is worth,
Which when the city was besieg'd, I hid:
Save but my life, and I will give it thee.

Tamburlaine. Then, for all your valour, you would save your life?
Whereabout lies it?   120

Governor. Under a hollow bank, right opposite
Against the western gate of Babylon.

Tamburlaine. Go thither some of you, and take his gold;

                                   [*Exeunt some* Attendants.]

The rest forward with execution.
Away with him hence, let him speak no more.
I think I make your courage something quail.

               [*Exeunt* Attendants *with the* Governor *of Babylon.*]

When this is done, we'll march from Babylon,
And make our greatest haste to Persia.
These jades are broken winded and half-tir'd;
Unharness them, and let me have fresh horse.   130
So, now their best is done to honour me,
Take them and hang them both up presently.

Trebizon. Vile tyrant! Barbarous bloody Tamburlaine!

Tamburlaine. Take them away Theridamas; see them despatch'd.

Theridamas. I will, my lord.   [*Exit with the Kings of* Trebizon *and* Soria.]

Tamburlaine. Come Asian viceroys, to your tasks a while,
And take such fortune as your fellows felt.

Orcanes. First let thy Scythian horse tear both our limbs,
Rather than we should draw thy chariot,
And like base slaves abject our princely minds   140
To vile and ignominious servitude.

Jerusalem. Rather lend me thy weapon, Tamburlaine,
That I may sheathe it in this breast of mine.
A thousand deaths could not torment our hearts
More than the thought of this doth vex our souls.

Amyras. They will talk still, my lord, if you do not bridle them.

Tamburlaine. Bridle them, and let me to my coach.   *They bridle them.*

[*The* Governor *of Babylon appears hanging in chains on the walls.*
        Enter Theridamas.]

Amyras. See now my lord, how brave the captain hangs!

Tamburlaine. 'Tis brave indeed, my boy: well done!
Shoot first my lord, and then the rest shall follow.   150

Theridamas. Then have at him to begin withal.   *Theridamas shoots.*

Governor. Yet save my life, and let this wound appease
The mortal fury of great Tamburlaine!

Tamburlaine. No, though Asphaltis' lake were liquid gold,
And offer'd me as ransom for thy life,
Yet shouldst thou die. Shoot at him all at once.   *They shoot.*
So, now he hangs like Bagdet's governor,
Having as many bullets in his flesh
As there be breaches in her batter'd wall.
Go now and bind the burghers hand and foot,   160
And cast them headlong in the city's lake.
Tartars and Persians shall inhabit there;
And to command the city, I will build
A citadel that all Africa,
Which hath been subject to the Persian king,
Shall pay me tribute for in Babylon.

Techelles. What shall be done with their wives and children, my lord?
Tamburlaine. Techelles, drown them all, man, woman, and child;
     Leave not a Babylonian in the town.
Techelles. I will about it straight. Come soldiers.   170
                                 Exit.

Tamburlaine. Now Casane, where's the Turkish Alcoran,
     And all the heaps of superstitious books
     Found in the temples of that Mahomet
     Whom I have thought a god? They shall be burnt.
Usumcasane. Here they are, my lord.
Tamburlaine. Well said! Let there be a fire presently.   *[They light a fire.]*
     In vain, I see, men worship Mahomet.
     My sword hath sent millions of Turks to hell,
     Slew all his priests, his kinsmen, and his friends,
     And yet I live untouch'd by Mahomet.   180
     There is a God, full of revenging wrath,
     From whom the thunder and the lightning breaks,
     Whose scourge I am, and him will I obey.
     So, Casane, fling them in the fire.   *[They burn the books.]*
     Now Mahomet, if thou have any power,
     Come down thyself and work a miracle.
     Thou art not worthy to be worshipped
     That suffers flames of fire to burn the writ
     Wherein the sum of thy religion rests.
     Why send'st thou not a furious whirlwind down,   190
     To blow thy Alcoran up to thy throne,
     Where men report thou sitt'st by God himself?
     Or vengeance on the head of Tamburlaine
     That shakes his sword against thy majesty,
     And spurns the abstracts of thy foolish laws?
     Well soldiers, Mahomet remains in hell;
     He cannot hear the voice of Tamburlaine.
     Seek out another godhead to adore:
     The God that sits in heaven, if any god,
     For he is God alone, and none but he.   200

                [Enter Techelles.]

Techelles. I have fulfill'd your highness' will, my lord.
     Thousands of men drown'd in Asphaltis' lake,
     Have made the water swell above the banks,
     And fishes, fed by human carcasses,
     Amaz'd, swim up and down upon the waves,
     As when they swallow asafoetida,

  Which makes them fleet aloft and gasp for air.
Tamburlaine. Well then my friendly lords, what now remains,
  But that we leave sufficient garrison,
  And presently depart to Persia,   210
  To triumph after all our victories?
Theridamas. Ay good my lord, let us in haste to Persia;
  And let this captain be remov'd the walls
  To some high hill about the city here.
Tamburlaine. Let it be so; about it, soldiers.
  But stay—I feel myself distemper'd suddenly.
Techelles. What is it dares distemper Tamburlaine?
Tamburlaine. Something, Techelles, but I know not what.
  But forth ye vassals! Whatsoe'er it be,
  Sickness or death can never conquer me.   220
                Exeunt.

Actus 5. Scaena 2.

 Enter Callapine, Amasia, [*a* Captain] *with drums and trumpets.*

Callapine. King of Amasia, now our mighty host
  Marcheth in Asia Major, where the streams
  Of Euphrates and Tigris swiftly runs;
  And here may we behold great Babylon,
  Circled about with Limnasphaltis' lake,
  Where Tamburlaine with all his army lies,
  Which being faint and weary with the siege,
  We may lie ready to encounter him
  Before his host be full from Babylon,
  And so revenge our latest grievous loss,   10
  If God or Mahomet send any aid.
Amasia. Doubt not my lord, but we shall conquer him.
  The monster that hath drunk a sea of blood,
  And yet gapes still for more to quench his thirst,
  Our Turkish swords shall headlong send to hell;
  And that vile carcass, drawn by warlike kings,
  The fowls shall eat; for never sepulchre
  Shall grace that base-born tyrant Tamburlaine.
Callapine. When I record my parents' slavish life,
  Their cruel death, mine own captivity,   20
  My viceroys' bondage under Tamburlaine,
  Methinks I could sustain a thousand deaths
  To be reveng'd of all his villainy.
  Ah sacred Mahomet, thou that hast seen

Millions of Turks perish by Tamburlaine,
Kingdoms made waste, brave cities sack'd and burnt,
And but one host is left to honour thee;
Aid thy obedient servant Callapine,
And make him after all these overthrows
To triumph over cursed Tamburlaine!   30
Amasia. Fear not my lord; I see great Mahomet,
Clothed in purple clouds and on his head
A chaplet brighter than Apollo's crown,
Marching about the air with armed men,
To join with you against this Tamburlaine.
Captain. Renowmed general, mighty Callapine,
Though God himself and holy Mahomet
Should come in person to resist your power,
Yet might your mighty host encounter all,
And pull proud Tamburlaine upon his knees   40
To sue for mercy at your highness' feet.
Callapine. Captain, the force of Tamburlaine is great,
His fortune greater, and the victories
Wherewith he hath so sore dismay'd the world
Are greatest to discourage all our drifts.
Yet, when the pride of Cynthia is at full,
She wanes again; and so shall his, I hope;
For we have here the chief selected men
Of twenty several kingdoms at the least.
Nor ploughman, priest, nor merchant, stays at home;   50
All Turkey is in arms with Callapine;
And never will we sunder camps and arms
Before himself or his be conquered.
This is the time that must eternize me
For conquering the tyrant of the world.
Come soldiers, let us lie in wait for him,
And if we find him absent from his camp,
Or that it be rejoin'd again at full,
Assail it, and be sure of victory.   *Exeunt.*

Actus 5.   Scaena 3.

[*Enter*] Theridamas, Techelles, Usumcasane.
Theridamas. Weep heavens, and vanish into liquid tears!
Fall, stars that govern his nativity,

And summon all the shining lamps of heaven
To cast their bootless fires to the earth,
And shed their feeble influence in the air;
Muffle your beauties with eternal clouds,
For Hell and Darkness pitch their pitchy tents,
And Death, with armies of Cimmerian spirits,
Gives battle 'gainst the heart of Tamburlaine.
Now in defiance of that wonted love   10
Your sacred virtues pour'd upon his throne,
And made his state an honour to the heavens,
These cowards invisibly assail his soul,
And threaten conquest on our sovereign;
But if he die, your glories are disgrac'd,
Earth droops, and says that hell in heaven is plac'd.

Techelles. O then, ye powers that sway eternal seats,
And guide this massy substance of the earth,
If you retain desert of holiness,
As your supreme estates instruct our thoughts,   20
Be not inconstant, careless of your fame,
Bear not the burden of your enemies' joys,
Triumphing in his fall whom you advanc'd;
But as his birth, life, health, and majesty
Were strangely blest and governed by heaven,
So honour, heaven, till heaven dissolved be,
His birth, his life, his health, and majesty!

Usumcasane. Blush heaven, to lose the honour of thy name,
To see thy footstool set upon thy head;
And let no baseness in thy haughty breast   30
Sustain a shame of such inexcellence,
To see the devils mount in angels' thrones,
And angels dive into the pools of hell.
And though they think their painful date is out,
And that their power is puissant as Jove's,
Which makes them manage arms against thy state,
Yet make them feel the strength of Tamburlaine,
Thy instrument and note of majesty,
Is greater far than they can thus subdue;
For if he die, thy glory is disgrac'd,   40
Earth droops, and says that hell in heaven is plac'd.

[*Enter* Tamburlaine *drawn by captive kings* (Orcanes *of Natolia,*
and Jerusalem), Amyras, Celebinus, Physicians.]

Tamburlaine. What daring god torments my body thus,

And seeks to conquer mighty Tamburlaine?
Shall sickness prove me now to be a man,
That have been term'd the terror of the world?
Techelles and the rest, come, take your swords,
And threaten him whose hand afflicts my soul.
Come, let us march against the powers of heaven,
And set black streamers in the firmament,
To signify the slaughter of the gods.   50
Ah, friends, what shall I do? I cannot stand.
Come, carry me to war against the gods,
That thus envy the health of Tamburlaine.
Theridamas. Ah good my lord, leave these impatient words,
Which add much danger to your malady!
Tamburlaine. Why, shall I sit and languish in this pain?
No, strike the drums, and, in revenge of this,
Come, let us charge our spears, and pierce his breast
Whose shoulders bear the axis of the world,
That if I perish, heaven and earth may fade.   60
Theridamas, haste to the court of Jove;
Will him to send Apollo hither straight
To cure me, or I'll fetch him down myself.
Techelles. Sit still, my gracious lord; this grief will cease,
And cannot last, it is so violent.
Tamburlaine. Not last, Techelles? No, for I shall die.
See where my slave, the ugly monster Death,
Shaking and quivering, pale and wan for fear,
Stands aiming at me with his murdering dart,
Who flies away at every glance I give,   70
And when I look away, comes stealing on.
Villain, away, and hie thee to the field!
I and mine army come to load thy bark
With souls of thousand mangled carcasses.
Look where he goes! But see, he comes again,
Because I stay! Techelles, let us march,
And weary Death with bearing souls to hell.
Physician. Pleaseth your majesty to drink this potion,
Which will abate the fury of your fit
And cause some milder spirits govern you.   80
Tamburlaine. Tell me, what think you of my sickness now?
Physician. I view'd your urine, and the hypostasis,
Thick and obscure, doth make your danger great.

82 hypostasis] sediment

Your veins are full of accidental heat,
Whereby the moisture of your blood is dried.
The humidum and calor, which some hold
Is not a parcel of the elements,
But of a substance more divine and pure,
Is almost clean extinguished and spent;
Which being the cause of life, imports your death.　　90
Besides my lord, this day is critical,
Dangerous to those whose crisis is as yours.
Your artiers, which alongst the veins convey
The lively spirits which the heart engenders,
Are parch'd and void of spirit, that the soul,
Wanting those organons by which it moves,
Cannot endure, by argument of art.
Yet if your majesty may escape this day,
No doubt but you shall soon recover all.

Tamburlaine. Then will I comfort all my vital parts,　　100
　　And live, in spite of death, above a day.　　*Alarm within.*

[*Enter a* Messenger.]

Messenger. My lord, young Callapine, that lately fled from your majesty,
hath now gathered a fresh army, and, hearing your absence in the field,
offers to set upon us presently.

Tamburlaine. See, my physicians, now, how Jove hath sent
　　A present medicine to recure my pain!
　　My looks shall make them fly; and might I follow,
　　There should not one of all the villain's power
　　Live to give offer of another fight.

Usumcasane. I joy, my lord, your highness is so strong,　　110
　　That can endure so well your royal presence,
　　Which only will dismay the enemy.

Tamburlaine. I know it will, Casane. Draw, you slaves!
　　In spite of death, I will go show my face.

　　Alarm. Tamburlaine *goes in, and comes out again with all the rest.*

　　Thus are the villains, cowards, fled for fear,
　　Like summer's vapours vanish'd by the sun;
　　And could I but a while pursue the field,
　　That Callapine should be my slave again.

84–97 Your . . . endure] Tamburlaine has a high fever, dehydrating his body; the lack of
moisture ('humidum') deprives him of natural warmth ('calor') and since these two are the
cause of life, his death is imminent. Moreover, the stars are against him (Renaissance
physicians still believed in the influence of the planets on man's body). His arteries are
dried up, and no longer able to convey the 'spirits' from the heart which are the instruments
('organons') giving life to the soul; this, therefore, must die.

But I perceive my martial strength is spent;
In vain I strive and rail against those powers   120
That mean t'invest me in a higher throne,
As much too high for this disdainful earth.
Give me a map; then let me see how much
Is left for me to conquer all the world,
That these my boys may finish all my wants.   *One brings a map.*
Here I began to march towards Persia,
Along Armenia and the Caspian Sea,
And thence unto Bithynia, where I took
The Turk and his great empress prisoners;
Then march'd I into Egypt and Arabia;   130
And here, not far from Alexandria,
Whereas the Terrene and the Red Sea meet,
Being distant less than full a hundred leagues,
I meant to cut a channel to them both,
That men might quickly sail to India.
From thence to Nubia near Borno lake,
And so along the Æthiopian sea,
Cutting the tropic line of Capricorn,
I conquer'd all as far as Zanzibar.
Then by the northern part of Africa,   140
I came at last to Graecia, and from thence
To Asia, where I stay against my will;
Which is from Scythia, where I first began,
Backward and forwards near five thousand leagues.
Look here, my boys; see, what a world of ground
Lies westward from the midst of Cancer's line
Unto the rising of this earthly globe,
Whereas the sun, declining from our sight,
Begins the day with our Antipodes!
And shall I die, and this unconquered?   150
Lo, here, my sons, are all the golden mines,
Inestimable drugs and precious stones,
More worth than Asia and the world beside;
And from th'Antarctic Pole eastward behold
As much more land, which never was descried,
Wherein are rocks of pearl that shine as bright
As all the lamps that beautify the sky!
And shall I die, and this unconquered?
Here, lovely boys; what death forbids my life,
That let your lives command in spite of death.   160

134 cut a channel] Tamburlaine, it seems, planned a Suez Canal.

Amyras. Alas, my lord, how should our bleeding hearts,
    Wounded and broken with your highness' grief,
    Retain a thought of joy or spark of life?
    Your soul gives essence to our wretched subjects,
    Whose matter is incorporate in your flesh.
Celebinus. Your pains do pierce our souls; no hope survives,
    For by your life we entertain our lives.
Tamburlaine. But sons, this subject, not of force enough
    To hold the fiery spirit it contains,
    Must part, imparting his impressions   170
    By equal portions into both your breasts;
    My flesh, divided in your precious shapes,
    Shall still retain my spirit, though I die,
    And live in all your seeds immortally.
    Then now remove me, that I may resign
    My place and proper title to my son.
    First, take my scourge and my imperial crown,
    And mount my royal chariot of estate,
    That I may see thee crown'd before I die.
    Help me, my lords, to make my last remove.   180
Theridamas. A woeful change, my lord, that daunts our thoughts
    More than the ruin of our proper souls.
Tamburlaine. Sit up, my son, let me see how well
    Thou wilt become thy father's majesty.   *They crown him.*
Amyras. With what a flinty bosom should I joy
    The breath of life and burden of my soul!
    If not resolv'd into resolved pains,
    My body's mortified lineaments
    Should exercise the motions of my heart,
    Pierc'd with the joy of any dignity!   190
    O father, if the unrelenting ears
    Of death and hell be shut against my prayers,
    And that the spiteful influence of heaven
    Deny my soul fruition of her joy,
    How should I step or stir my hateful feet
    Against the inward powers of my heart,
    Leading a life that only strives to die,
    And plead in vain unpleasing sovereignty?
Tamburlaine. Let not thy love exceed thine honour, son,
    Nor bar thy mind that magnanimity   200
    That nobly must admit necessity.
    Sit up my boy, and with those silken reins
    Bridle the steeled stomachs of those jades.

Theridamas. My lord, you must obey his majesty,
    Since fate commands and proud necessity.
Amyras. Heavens witness me with what a broken heart
    And damned spirit I ascend this seat,
    And send my soul, before my father die,
    His anguish and his burning agony!
Tamburlaine. Now fetch the hearse of fair Zenocrate;   210
    Let it be plac'd by this my fatal chair,
    And serve as parcel of my funeral.
Usumcasane. Then feels your majesty no sovereign ease,
    Nor may our hearts, all drown'd in tears of blood,
    Joy any hope of your recovery?
Tamburlaine. Casane, no; the monarch of the earth,
    And eyeless monster that torments my soul,
    Cannot behold the tears ye shed for me,
    And therefore still augments his cruelty.
Techelles. Then let some god oppose his holy power   220
    Against the wrath and tyranny of Death,
    That his tear-thirsty and unquenched hate
    May be upon himself reverberate!   *They bring in the hearse.*
Tamburlaine. Now eyes, enjoy your latest benefit,
    And when my soul hath virtue of your sight,
    Pierce through the coffin and the sheet of gold,
    And glut your longings with a heaven of joy.
    So, reign my son; scourge and control those slaves,
    Guiding thy chariot with thy father's hand.
    As precious is the charge thou undertak'st   230
    As that which Clymene's brain-sick son did guide,
    When wandering Phœbe's ivory cheeks were scorch'd,
    And all the earth, like Ætna, breathing fire.
    Be warn'd by him, then; learn with awful eye
    To sway a throne as dangerous as his;
    For if thy body thrive not full of thoughts
    As pure and fiery as Phyteus' beams,
    The nature of these proud rebelling jades
    Will take occasion by the slenderest hair,
    And draw thee piecemeal like Hippolytus   240
    Through rocks more steep and sharp than Caspian cliffs.
    The nature of thy chariot will not bear

212 parcel] part   231 Clymene's . . . son] Phaeton, who presumed to drive the sun's chariot and would have destroyed the earth if Jupiter had not killed him with a flash of lightning   237 Phyteus] Apollo   240 Hippolytus] whose chariot horses bolted when a bull rose from the sea

A guide of baser temper than myself,
More than heaven's coach the pride of Phaëton.
Farewell, my boys! my dearest friends, farewell!
My body feels, my soul doth weep to see
Your sweet desires depriv'd my company,
For Tamburlaine, the scourge of God, must die.   [*Dies.*]
Amyras. Meet heaven and earth, and here let all things end,
For earth hath spent the pride of all her fruit,   250
And heaven consum'd his choicest living fire!
Let earth and heaven his timeless death deplore,
For both their worths will equal him no more!   [*Exeunt.*]

FINIS.

The Jew of Malta

Although 'The famouse tragedie of the Riche Jew of Malta' was entered in the Stationers' Register in 1594, no text survives earlier than the Quarto of 1633. This was printed, as Heywood's Dedicatory Epistle tells us, following revivals of the play at Court and at a public theatre, the Cockpit. For these revivals Heywood wrote new prologues and epilogues, but there is no reason to suppose that he made any alterations to the text of the play. This has survived in a rather corrupt form: it is often difficult to sort out verse from prose.

The Jew of Malta must have been written after the assassination of the Duke of Guise in December 1588, but the reference to this in Machiavel's Prologue (line 3) suggests that the event was a recent one, thus giving the play a date of 1589 or 1590. No single source has yet been traced, so while Marlowe's wide reading could have supplied some of the details it seems that the violent, farcical action came from his own imagination.

The Famous

TRAGEDY

OF

THE RICH IEVV

OF *MALTA.*

AS IT VVAS PLAYD
BEFORE THE KING AND
QVEENE, IN HIS MAJESTIES
Theatre at *White-Hall,* by her Majesties
Servants at the *Cock-pit.*

Written by CHRISTOPHER MARLO.

LONDON;
Printed by *I. B.* for *Nicholas Vavasour,* and are to be sold
at his Shop in the Inner-Temple, neere the
Church. 1633.

THE EPISTLE DEDICATORY

TO MY WORTHY FRIEND, MR THOMAS
HAMMON, OF GRAYS INN, &c.

This play, composed by so worthy an author as Mr Marlowe, and the part of the Jew presented by so unimitable an actor as Mr Alleyn, being in this later age commended to the stage; as I ushered it unto the Court, and presented it to the Cock-pit, with these Prologues and Epilogues here inserted, so now being newly brought to the press, I was loath it should be published without the ornament of an Epistle; making choice of you unto whom to devote it; than whom (of all those gentlemen and acquaintance within the compass of my long knowledge) there is none more able to tax ignorance, or attribute right to merit. Sir, you have been pleased to grace some of mine own works with your courteous patronage: I hope this will not be the worse accepted, because commended by me; over whom none can claim more power or privilege than yourself. I had no better a New Year's gift to present you with; receive it therefore as a continuance of the inviolable obligement, by which he rests still engaged; who, as he ever hath, shall always remain,

Tuissimus,

THO. HEYWOOD

Gracious and great, that we so boldly dare
('Mongst other plays that now in fashion are)
To present this, writ many years agone,
And in that age thought second unto none,
We humbly crave your pardon. We pursue
The story of a rich and famous Jew
Who liv'd in Malta: you shall find him still,
In all his projects, a sound Machevill;
And that's his character. He that hath passed
So many censures, is now come at last   10
To have your princely ears: grace you him; then
You crown the action, and renown the pen.

EPILOGUE

It is our fear (dread Sovereign) we have bin
Too tedious; neither can't be less than sin
To wrong your princely patience. If we have,
(Thus low dejected) we your pardon crave;
And if aught here offend your ear or sight,
We only act and speak what others write.

THE PROLOGUE TO THE STAGE
AT THE COCK-PIT

We know not how our play may pass this stage,
But by the best of *poets in that age   *Marlo.
The Malta Jew had being and was made;
And he then by the best of †actors play'd: †Allin.
In *Hero and Leander* one did gain
A lasting memory; in Tamburlaine,
This Jew, with others many, th' other wan
The attribute of peerless, being a man
Whom we may rank with (doing no one wrong)
Proteus for shapes, and Roscius for a tongue,   10
So could he speak, so vary; nor is't hate
To merit in *him who doth personate   *Perkins.
Our Jew this day; nor is it his ambition
To exceed or equal, being of condition
More modest: this is all that he intends
(And that too, at the urgence of some friends)
To prove his best, and, if none here gainsay it,
The part he hath studied, and intends to play it.

EPILOGUE

In graving with Pygmalion to contend,
Or painting with Apelles, doubtless the end
Must be disgrace; our actor did not so:
He only aim'd to go, but not out-go.
Nor think that this day any prize was play'd;
Here were no bets at all, no wagers laid;
All the ambition that his mind doth swell,
Is but to hear from you (by me) 'twas well.

4 † Allin] Edward Alleyn, 1566–1626   10 Roscius] Alleyn was frequently compared with
this most famous of Roman actors (died *c.* 60 B.C.).   12 Perkins] Richard Perkins, acting
c. 1602–38   Ep. 1 Pygmalion] celebrated sculptor of Cyprus   2 Apelles] Greek painter
at the time of Alexander the Great

[DRAMATIS PERSONAE

Machevill, the Prologue

Barabas, the Jew
Ferneze, Governor of Malta
Calymath, son to the Emperor of Turkey
Don Mathias
Don Lodowick, the Governor's son
Martin del Bosco, the Spanish Vice-Admiral
Ithamore, a Turkish slave
Jacomo
Barnardine } friars
Pilia-Borza
Two Merchants
Three Jews

Abigail, daughter to Barabas
Katharine, mother to Mathias
Bellamira, a courtesan
Abbess

Nuns, Knights, Officers, Bassoes, Turks, Guard, Slaves,
Messenger, Carpenters, Attendants]

[THE PROLOGUE]
Machevill

Albeit the world think Machevill is dead,
Yet was his soul but flown beyond the Alps,
And now the Guise is dead, is come from France
To view this land, and frolic with his friends.
To some perhaps my name is odious;
But such as love me, guard me from their tongues,
And let them know that I am Machevill,
And weigh not men, and therefore not men's words.
Admir'd I am of those that hate me most.
Though some speak openly against my books,   10
Yet will they read me, and thereby attain
To Peter's chair; and when they cast me off,
Are poison'd by my climbing followers.
I count religion but a childish toy,
And hold there is no sin but ignorance.
Birds of the air will tell of murders past.
I am asham'd to hear such fooleries!
Many will talk of title to a crown:
What right had Caesar to the empery?
Might first made kings, and laws were then most sure   20
When like the Draco's, they were writ in blood.
Hence comes it, that a strong built citadel
Commands much more than letters can import:
Which maxim had Phalaris observ'd,
H'ad never bellow'd in a brazen bull
Of great ones' envy; o' the poor petty wits,
Let me be envied and not pitied.
But whither am I bound? I come not, I,
To read a lecture here in Britanie,
But to present the tragedy of a Jew,   30
Who smiles to see how full his bags are cramm'd;
Which money was not got without my means.
I crave but this: grace him as he deserves,
And let him not be entertain'd the worse
Because he favours me.   [*Exit.*]

3 the Guise] The Duke of Guise, assassinated December 1588, was responsible for
the St. Bartholomew massacre in 1572; he is the central figure of *The Massacre at Paris*.
21 Draco] Athenian author of laws (623 B.C.) so severe they were said to be written in blood
24 Phalaris] Sicilian tyrant (*c.* 579–544 B.C.) roasted in the bull he used for torturing his
enemies

Enter Barabas *in his Counting-house, with heaps of gold before him.*

Barabas. So that of thus much that return was made;
            And of the third part of the Persian ships
            There was the venture summ'd and satisfied.
            As for those Samnites, and the men of Uz,
            That bought my Spanish oils and wines of Greece,
            Here have I purs'd their paltry silverlings.
            Fie, what a trouble 'tis to count this trash!
            Well fare the Arabians, who so richly pay
            The things they traffic for with wedge of gold,
            Whereof a man may easily in a day   10
            Tell that which may maintain him all his life.
            The needy groom that never finger'd groat,
            Would make a miracle of thus much coin;
            But he whose steel-barr'd coffers are cramm'd full,
            And all his life-time hath been tired,
            Wearying his fingers' ends with telling it,
            Would in his age be loath to labour so,
            And for a pound to sweat himself to death.
            Give me the merchants of the Indian mines,
            That trade in metal of the purest mould;   20
            The wealthy Moor, that in the eastern rocks
            Without control can pick his riches up,
            And in his house heap pearl like pebble stones,
            Receive them free, and sell them by the weight;
            Bags of fiery opals, sapphires, amethysts,
            Jacinths, hard topaz, grass-green emeralds,
            Beauteous rubies, sparkling diamonds,
            And seld-seen costly stones of so great price,
            As one of them indifferently rated,
            And of a carat of this quantity,   30
            May serve in peril of calamity,
            To ransom great kings from captivity.
            This is the ware wherein consists my wealth;
            And thus methinks should men of judgement frame
            Their means of traffic from the vulgar trade,
            And as their wealth increaseth, so inclose
            Infinite riches in a little room.
            But now how stands the wind?

Into what corner peers my halcyon's bill?
Ha! to the east? Yes. See how stands the vanes?   40
East and by south: why then I hope my ships
I sent for Egypt and the bordering isles
Are gotten up by Nilus' winding banks;
Mine argosy from Alexandria,
Loaden with spice and silks, now under sail,
Are smoothly gliding down by Candy shore
To Malta, through our Mediterranean sea.
But who comes here?

Enter a Merchant.

How now?
Merchant. Barabas, thy ships are safe,
    Riding in Malta road; and all the merchants   50
    With other merchandise are safe arriv'd,
    And have sent me to know whether yourself
    Will come and custom them.
Barabas. The ships are safe thou say'st, and richly fraught?
Merchant. They are.
Barabas. Why then, go bid them come ashore,
    And bring with them their bills of entry:
    I hope our credit in the custom-house
    Will serve as well as I were present there.
    Go send 'em three-score camels, thirty mules,   60
    And twenty waggons to bring up the ware.
    But art thou master in a ship of mine,
    And is thy credit not enough for that?
Merchant. The very custom barely comes to more
    Than many merchants of the town are worth,
    And therefore far exceeds my credit, sir.
Barabas. Go tell 'em the Jew of Malta sent thee, man:
    Tush, who amongst 'em knows not Barabas?
Merchant. I go.
Barabas.   So then, there's somewhat come.
    Sirrah, which of my ships art thou master of?   70
Merchant. Of the Speranza, sir.
Barabas.   And saw'st thou not
    Mine argosy at Alexandria?
    Thou couldst not come from Egypt, or by Caire,
    But at the entry there into the sea,
    Where Nilus pays his tribute to the main,

---

39 halcyon] kingfisher   46 Candy] Crete   52 custom them] see them through the customs

        Thou needs must sail by Alexandria.
Merchant. I neither saw them, nor inquir'd of them;
        But this we heard some of our seamen say,
        They wonder'd how you durst with so much wealth
        Trust such a crazed vessel, and so far   80
Barabas. Tush, they are wise! I know her and her strength.
        But go, go thou thy ways, discharge thy ship,
        And bid my factor bring his loading in.   [*Exit* Merchant.]
        And yet I wonder at this argosy.

                Enter a second Merchant.

2 Merchant. Thine argosy from Alexandria,
        Know, Barabas, doth ride in Malta road,
        Laden with riches, and exceeding store
        Of Persian silks, of gold, and orient pearl.
Barabas. How chance you came not with those other ships
        That sail'd by Egypt?
2 Merchant.   Sir, we saw 'em not.   90
Barabas. Belike they coasted round by Candy shore
        About their oils or other businesses.
        But 'twas ill done of you to come so far
        Without the aid or conduct of their ships.
2 Merchant. Sir, we were wafted by a Spanish fleet
        That never left us till within a league,
        That had the galleys of the Turk in chase.
Barabas. O, they were going up to Sicily. Well, go
        And bid the merchants and my men dispatch,
        And come ashore, and see the fraught discharg'd.   100
2 Merchant. I go.   *Exit.*
Barabas. Thus trolls our fortune in by land and sea,
        And thus are we on every side enrich'd.
        These are the blessings promis'd to the Jews,
        And herein was old Abram's happiness:
        What more may heaven do for earthly man
        Than thus to pour out plenty in their laps,
        Ripping the bowels of the earth for them,
        Making the sea their servant, and the winds
        To drive their substance with successful blasts?   110
        Who hateth me but for my happiness?
        Or who is honour'd now but for his wealth?
        Rather had I, a Jew, be hated thus,
        Than pitied in a Christian poverty;

80 crazed] rotten   95 wafted] convoyed   102 trolls] flows

For I can see no fruits in all their faith,
But malice, falsehood, and excessive pride,
Which methinks fits not their profession.
Haply some hapless man hath conscience,
And for his conscience lives in beggary.
They say we are a scatter'd nation: 120
I cannot tell; but we have scambled up
More wealth by far than those that brag of faith.
There's Kirriah Jairim, the great Jew of Greece,
Obed in Bairseth, Nones in Portugal,
Myself in Malta, some in Italy,
Many in France, and wealthy every one;
Ay, wealthier far than any Christian.
I must confess we come not to be kings:
That's not our fault: alas, our number's few,
And crowns come either by succession,   130
Or urg'd by force; and nothing violent,
Oft have I heard tell, can be permanent.
Give us a peaceful rule; make Christians kings,
That thirst so much for principality.
I have no charge, nor many children,
But one sole daughter, whom I hold as dear
As Agamemnon did his Iphigen;
And all I have is hers. But who comes here?

Enter three Jews.

1 Jew. Tush, tell not me! 'Twas done of policy.
2 Jew. Come therefore, let us go to Barabas,   140
For he can counsel best in these affairs.
And here he comes.
Barabas.   Why, how now, countrymen?
Why flock you thus to me in multitudes?
What accident's betided to the Jews?
1 Jew. A fleet of warlike galleys, Barabas,
Are come from Turkey, and lie in our road:
And they this day sit in the council-house
To entertain them and their embassy.
Barabas. Why, let 'em come, so they come not to war;
Or let 'em war, so we be conquerors.   150
(*Aside.*) Nay, let 'em combat, conquer, and kill all.
So they spare me, my daughter, and my wealth.

121 scambled up] scraped together   137 Agamemnon . . . Iphigen] But Agamemnon
sacrificed his daughter Iphigenia to obtain a fair wind to Troy.   139 of policy] craftily

1 Jew. Were it for confirmation of a league,
    They would not come in warlike manner thus.
2 Jew. I fear their coming will afflict us all.
Barabas. Fond men, what dream you of their multitudes?
    What need they treat of peace that are in league?
    The Turks and those of Malta are in league:
    Tut, tut, there is some other matter in't.
1 Jew. Why, Barabas, they come for peace or war.   160
Barabas. Haply for neither, but to pass along
    Towards Venice by the Adriatic sea,
    With whom they have attempted many times,
    But never could effect their stratagem.
3 Jew. And very wisely said; it may be so.
2 Jew. But there's a meeting in the senate-house,
    And all the Jews in Malta must be there.
Barabas. Umh; all the Jews in Malta must be there?
    Ay, like enough; why then, let every man
    Provide him, and be there for fashion-sake.   170
    If anything shall there concern our state,
    Assure yourselves I'll look unto (*Aside.*) myself.
1 Jew. I know you will. Well brethren, let us go.
2 Jew. Let's take our leaves. Farewell, good Barabas.
Barabas. Do so. Farewell, Zaareth; farewell, Temainte.   [*Exeunt* Jews.]
    And Barabas, now search this secret out.
    Summon thy senses, call thy wits together:
    These silly men mistake the matter clean.
    Long to the Turk did Malta contribute;
    Which tribute all in policy, I fear,   180
    The Turks have let increase to such a sum
    As all the wealth of Malta cannot pay;
    And now by that advantage thinks, belike,
    To seize upon the town. Ay, that he seeks.
    Howe'er the world go, I'll make sure for one,
    And seek in time to intercept the worst,
    Warily guarding that which I ha' got.
    Ego mihimet sum semper proximus.
    Why, let 'em enter. Let 'em take the town.   [*Exit.*]

163 With . . . attempted] whom they have attacked   188 *Ego . . . proximus*] 'I am always the closest to myself'

[*Scaena 2*]

Enter [Ferneze, *the*] *Governor of Malta*, Knights [*and* Officers], *met by*
Bassoes *of the Turk* [*and*] Calymath.

Ferneze. Now bassoes, what demand you at our hands?
Basso. Know knights of Malta, that we came from Rhodes,
  From Cyprus, Candy, and those other isles
  That lie betwixt the Mediterranean seas.
Ferneze. What's Cyprus, Candy, and those other isles
  To us or Malta? What at our hands demand ye?
Calymath. The ten years' tribute that remains unpaid.
Ferneze. Alas, my lord, the sum is over-great!
  I hope your highness will consider us.
Calymath. I wish, grave Governor, 'twere in my power 10
  To favour you; but 'tis my father's cause,
  Wherein I may not, nay, I dare not dally.
Ferneze. Then give us leave, great Selim-Calymath.
Calymath. Stand all aside, and let the knights determine,
  And send to keep our galleys under sail,
  For happily we shall not tarry here.
  Now Governor, how are you resolv'd?
Ferneze. Thus: since your hard conditions are such
  That you will needs have ten years' tribute past,
  We may have time to make collection 20
  Amongst the inhabitants of Malta for't.
Basso. That's more than is in our commission.
Calymath. What Callapine, a little courtesy!
  Let's know their time, perhaps it is not long;
  And 'tis more kingly to obtain by peace
  Than to enforce conditions by constraint.
  What respite ask you, Governor?
Ferneze. But a month.
Calymath. We grant a month, but see you keep your promise.
  Now launch our galleys back again to sea, 30
  Where we'll attend the respite you have ta'en,
  And for the money send our messenger.
  Farewell, great Governor and brave knights of Malta.
          Exeunt [Calymath *and* Bassoes].
Ferneze. And all good fortune wait on Calymath.
  Go one and call those Jews of Malta hither:
  Were they not summon'd to appear today?

Officer. They were, my lord; and here they come.

Enter Barabas *and three* Jews.

1 Knight. Have you determin'd what to say to them?

Ferneze. Yes, give me leave; and, Hebrews, now come near.
    From the Emperor of Turkey is arriv'd   40
    Great Selim-Calymath, his highness' son,
    To levy of us ten years' tribute past:
    Now then, here know that it concerneth us.

Barabas. Then, good my lord, to keep your quiet still,
    Your lordship shall do well to let them have it.

Ferneze. Soft Barabas, there's more 'longs to't than so.
    To what this ten years' tribute will amount,
    That we have cast, but cannot compass it
    By reason of the wars, that robb'd our store;
    And therefore are we to request your aid.   50

Barabas. Alas, my lord, we are no soldiers!
    And what's our aid against so great a prince?

1 Knight. Tut, Jew, we know thou art no soldier:
    Thou art a merchant and a money'd man,
    And 'tis thy money, Barabas, we seek.

Barabas. How, my lord, my money!

Ferneze.   Thine and the rest.
    For, to be short, amongst you 't must be had.

1 Jew. Alas, my lord, the most of us are poor!

Ferneze. Then let the rich increase your portions.

Barabas. Are strangers with your tribute to be tax'd?   60

2 Knight. Have strangers leave with us to get their wealth?
    Then let them with us contribute.

Barabas. How, equally?

Ferneze.   No, Jew, like infidels;
    For through our sufferance of your hateful lives,
    Who stand accursed in the sight of heaven,
    These taxes and afflictions are befall'n,
    And therefore thus we are determined.
    Read there the articles of our decrees.

Officer. 'First, the tribute-money of the Turks shall all be levied amongst the
    Jews, and each of them to pay one half of his estate.'   70

Barabas. How! Half his estate? I hope you mean not mine.

Ferneze. Read on.

Officer. 'Secondly, he that denies to pay, shall straight become a Christian.

Barabas. How, a Christian! Hum, what's here to do?

---

48 cast] calculated   65 stand accursed] because of the Crucifixion

Officer. 'Lastly, he that denies this, shall absolutely lose all he has.'
All 3 Jews. O my lord, we will give half!
Barabas. O earth-metalled villains, and no Hebrews born!
  And will you basely thus submit yourselves
  To leave your goods to their arbitrement?
Ferneze. Why Barabas, wilt thou be christened?   80
Barabas. No, Governor, I will be no convertite.
Ferneze. Then pay thy half.
Barabas. Why, know you what you did by this device?
  Half of my substance is a city's wealth.
  Governor, it was not got so easily;
  Nor will I part so slightly therewithal.
Ferneze. Sir, half is the penalty of our decree.
  Either pay that, or we will seize on all.
Barabas. Corpo di Dio, Stay, you shall have half;
  Let me be us'd but as my brethren are.   90
Ferneze. No, Jew, thou hast denied the articles,
  And now it cannot be recall'd.

       [*Exeunt* Officers, *on a sign from* Ferneze.]

Barabas. Will you then steal my goods?
  Is theft the ground of your religion?
Ferneze. No, Jew, we take particularly thine
  To save the ruin of a multitude.
  And better one want for a common good,
  Than many perish for a private man.
  Yet Barabas, we will not banish thee,
  But here in Malta, where thou got'st thy wealth,   100
  Live still; and if thou canst, get more.
Barabas. Christians, what or how can I multiply?
  Of naught is nothing made.
1 Knight. From naught at first thou cam'st to little wealth,
  From little unto more, from more to most.
  If your first curse fall heavy on thy head,
  And make thee poor and scorn'd of all the world,
  'Tis not our fault, but thy inherent sin.
Barabas. What, bring you Scripture to confirm your wrongs?
  Preach me not out of my possessions.   110
  Some Jews are wicked, as all Christians are;
  But say the tribe that I descended of
  Were all in general cast away for sin,
  Shall I be tried by their transgression?
  The man that dealeth righteously shall live;

89 *Corpo di Dio*] 'God's body' 106 your first curse] see above l. 65

And which of you can charge me otherwise?
Ferneze. Out, wretched Barabas!
    Sham'st thou not thus to justify thyself,
    As if we knew not thy profession? (*religion*)
    If thou rely upon thy righteousness,   120
    Be patient, and thy riches will increase.
    Excess of wealth is cause of covetousness;
    And covetousness, O, 'tis a monstrous sin!
Barabas. Ay, but theft is worse. Tush! Take not from me then,
    For that is theft; and, if you rob me thus,
    I must be forc'd to steal, and compass more.
1 Knight. Grave Governor, list not to his exclaims.
    Convert his mansion to a nunnery;
    His house will harbour many holy nuns.
Ferneze. It shall be so.

                    Enter Officers.

                    Now, officers, have you done?   130
1 Officer. Ay, my lord. We have seiz'd upon the goods
    And wares of Barabas, which being valu'd,
    Amount to more than all the wealth in Malta;
    And of the other we have seized half.
Ferneze. Then we'll take order for the residue.
Barabas. Well then, my lord, say, are you satisfied?
    You have my goods, my money, and my wealth,
    My ships, my store, and all that I enjoy'd;
    And having all, you can request no more,
    Unless your unrelenting flinty hearts   140
    Suppress all pity in your stony breasts,
    And now shall move you to bereave my life.
Ferneze. No, Barabas, to stain our hands with blood
    Is far from us and our profession.
Barabas. Why, I esteem the injury far less,
    To take the lives of miserable men
    Than be the causers of their misery.
    You have my wealth, the labour of my life,
    The comfort of mine age, my children's hope;
    And therefore ne'er distinguish of the wrong.   150
Ferneze. Content thee, Barabas; thou hast naught but right.
Barabas. Your extreme right does me exceeding wrong:
    But take it to you i' the devil's name!
Ferneze. Come, let us in, and gather of these goods

135 we'll . . . residue] we'll look after the rest of the business

    The money for this tribute of the Turk.

1 Knight. 'Tis necessary that be look'd unto;
    For if we break our day, we break the league,
    And that will prove but simple policy.

                           Exeunt [*all except* Barabas *and the three* Jews].

Barabas. Ay, policy! That's their profession,
    And not simplicity, as they suggest.   160
    The plagues of Egypt, and the curse of heaven,
    Earth's barrenness, and all men's hatred,
    Inflict upon them, thou great *Primus Motor*!
    And here upon my knees, striking the earth,
    I ban their souls to everlasting pains,
    And extreme tortures of the fiery deep,
    That thus have dealt with me in my distress!

1 Jew. O yet be patient, gentle Barabas.

Barabas. O silly brethren, born to see this day!
    Why stand you thus unmov'd with my laments?   170
    Why weep you not to think upon my wrongs?
    Why pine not I, and die in this distress?

1 Jew. Why, Barabas, as hardly can we brook
    The cruel handling of ourselves in this:
    Thou seest they have taken half our goods.

Barabas. Why did you yield to their extortion?
    You were a multitude, and I but one;
    And of me only have they taken all.

1 Jew. Yet brother Barabas, remember Job.

Barabas. What tell you me of Job? I wot his wealth   180
    Was written thus: he had seven thousand sheep,
    Three thousand camels, and two hundred yoke
    Of labouring oxen, and five hundred
    She-asses; but for every one of those,
    Had they been valu'd at indifferent rate,
    I had at home, and in mine argosy,
    And other ships that came from Egypt last,
    As much as would have bought his beasts and him,
    And yet have kept enough to live upon
    So that not he but I may curse the day,   190
    Thy fatal birthday, forlorn Barabas;
    And henceforth wish for an eternal night,
    That clouds of darkness may enclose my flesh,
    And hide these extreme sorrows from mine eyes.

158 simple policy] bad management   163 *Primus Motor*] 'First Mover' (God)   165 ban] curse

   For only I have toil'd to inherit here
   The months of vanity, and loss of time,
   And painful nights have been appointed me.
2 Jew. Good Barabas, be patient.
Barabas. Ay, I pray leave me in my patience. You, that were ne'er possess'd
 of wealth, are pleas'd with want.   200
   But give him liberty at least to mourn,
   That in a field amidst his enemies,
   Doth see his soldiers slain, himself disarm'd,
   And knows no means of his recovery.
   Ay, let me sorrow for this sudden chance;
   'Tis in the trouble of my spirit I speak:
   Great injuries are not so soon forgot.
1 Jew. Come, let us leave him in his ireful mood,
   Our words will but increase his ecstasy.
2 Jew. On, then: but, trust me, 'tis a misery   210
   To see a man in such affliction.
   Farewell Barabas.   *Exeunt* [Jews].
Barabas.   Ay, fare you well.
   See the simplicity of these base slaves,
   Who, for the villains have no wit themselves,
   Think me to be a senseless lump of clay,
   That will with every water wash to dirt!
   No, Barabas is born to better chance,
   And fram'd of finer mould than common men,
   That measure naught but by the present time.
   A reaching thought will search his deepest wits, 220
   And cast with cunning for the time to come;
   For evils are apt to happen every day.
   But whither wends my beauteous Abigail?

     Enter Abigail, *the Jew's daughter.*

   O, what has made my lovely daughter sad?
   What woman! Moan not for a little loss;
   Thy father has enough in store for thee.
Abigail. Not for myself, but aged Barabas,
   Father, for thee lamenteth Abigail.
   But I will learn to leave these fruitless tears,
   And urg'd thereto with my afflictions,   230
   With fierce exclaims run to the senate-house,
   And in the senate reprehend them all,
   And rent their hearts with tearing of my hair,
   Till they reduce the wrongs done to my father.

Barabas. No, Abigail, things past recovery
    Are hardly cur'd with exclamations.
    Be silent, daughter; sufferance breeds ease,
    And time may yield us an occasion,
    Which on the sudden cannot serve the turn.
    Besides, my girl, think me not all so fond   240
    As negligently to forgo so much
    Without provision for thyself and me.
    Ten thousand portagues, besides great pearls,
    Rich costly jewels, and stones infinite,
    Fearing the worst of this before it fell,
    I closely hid.
Abigail.   Where, father?
Barabas.   In my house, my girl.
Abigail. Then shall they ne'er be seen of Barabas;
    For they have seiz'd upon thy house and wares.
Barabas. But they will give me leave once more, I trow,
    To go into my house.
Abigail.   That may they not,   250
    For there I left the Governor placing nuns,
    Displacing me; and of thy house they mean
    To make a nunnery, where none but their own sect
    Must enter in, men generally barr'd.
Barabas. My gold, my gold, and all my wealth is gone!
    You partial heavens, have I deserv'd this plague?
    What, will you thus oppose me, luckless stars,
    To make me desperate in my poverty?
    And knowing me impatient in distress,
    Think me so mad as I will hang myself,   260
    That I may vanish o'er the earth in air,
    And leave no memory that e'er I was?
    No, I will live; nor loathe I this my life:
    And since you leave me in the ocean thus
    To sink or swim, and put me to my shifts,
    I'll rouse my senses, and awake myself.
    Daughter, I have it: thou perceiv'st the plight
    Wherein these Christians have oppressed me:
    Be rul'd by me, for in extremity
    We ought to make bar of no policy.   270
Abigail. Father, whate'er it be, to injure them
    That have so manifestly wronged us,

243 portagues] gold coins, worth about £4 each   253 sect] sex   254 generally] without exception

What will not Abigail attempt?

Barabas.   Why, so.
  Then thus: thou told'st me they have turn'd my house
  Into a nunnery, and some nuns are there?

Abigail. I did.

Barabas.   Then, Abigail, there must my girl
  Entreat the abbess to be entertain'd.

Abigail. How! As a nun?

Barabas.   Ay, daughter; for religion
  Hides many mischiefs from suspicion.

Abigail. Ay, but, father, they will suspect me there.   280

Barabas. Let 'em suspect, but be thou so precise
  As they may think it done of holiness.
  Entreat 'em fair, and give them friendly speech,
  And seem to them as if thy sins were great,
  Till thou hast gotten to be entertain'd.

Abigail. Thus, father, shall I much dissemble.

Barabas.   Tush!
  As good dissemble that thou never mean'st
  As first mean truth, and then dissemble it:
  A counterfeit profession is better
  Than unseen hypocrisy.   290

Abigail. Well father, say I be entertain'd,
  What then shall follow?

Barabas.   This shall follow then.
  There have I hid, close underneath the plank
  That runs along the upper-chamber floor,
  The gold and jewels which I kept for thee.
  But here they come; be cunning, Abigail.

Abigail. Then, father, go with me.

Barabas. No, Abigail, in this
  It is not necessary I be seen;
  For I will seem offended with thee for't.   300
  Be close, my girl, for this must fetch my gold.

          [*Enter* Jacomo, Barnardine, Abbess, *and a* Nun.]

Jacomo. Sisters,
  We now are almost at the new-made nunnery.

Abbess. The better; for we love not to be seen.
  'Tis thirty winters long since some of us
  Did stray so far amongst the multitude.

Jacomo. But, madam, this house
  And quarters of this new-made nunnery

308 quarters] Ed. (waters Q)

Will much delight you.

Abbess. It may be so. But who comes here?   [Abigail *comes forward.*]

Abigail. Grave abbess, and you happy virgins' guide,   311
  Pity the state of a distressed maid.

Abbess. What art thou, daughter?

Abigail. The hopeless daughter of a hapless Jew,
  The Jew of Malta, wretched Barabas,
  Sometime the owner of a goodly house,
  Which they have now turn'd to a nunnery.

Abbess. Well, daughter, say, what is thy suit with us?

Abigail. Fearing the afflictions which my father feels
  Proceed from sin or want of faith in us,   320
  I'd pass away my life in penitence
  And be a novice in your nunnery,
  To make atonement for my labouring soul.

Jacomo. No doubt, brother, but this proceedeth of the spirit.

Barnardine. Ay, and of a moving spirit too, brother: but come, let us entreat
  she may be entertained.

Abbess. Well daughter, we admit you for a nun.

Abigail. First let me as a novice learn to frame
  My solitary life to your strait laws,
  And let me lodge where I was wont to lie.   330
  I do not doubt, by your divine precepts
  And mine own industry, but to profit much.

Barabas [*aside*]. As much, I hope, as all I hid is worth.

Abbess. Come, daughter, follow us.

Barabas [*coming forward*].   Why, how now, Abigail!
  What mak'st thou amongst these hateful Christians?

Jacomo. Hinder her not, thou man of little faith,
  For she has mortified herself.

Barabas.   How! Mortified?

Jacomo. And is admitted to the sisterhood.

Barabas. Child of perdition, and thy father's shame!
  What wilt thou do among these hateful fiends?   340
  I charge thee on my blessing that thou leave
  These devils and their damned heresy.

Abigail. Father, give me—

Barabas.   Nay, back, Abigail—   *Whispers to her.*
  And think upon the jewels and the gold;
  The board is marked thus that covers it.
  Away, accursed, from thy father's sight!

Jacomo. Barabas, although thou art in misbelief,
  And wilt not see thine own afflictions,

    Yet let thy daughter be no longer blind.

Barabas. Blind, friar, I reck not thy persuasions.   350
    [*Aside.*] The board is marked thus † that covers it.
    For I had rather die than see her thus.
    Wilt thou forsake me too in my distress,
    Seduced daughter? (*Aside to her.*) Go, forget not—
    Becomes it Jews to be so credulous?
    (*Aside to her.*) Tomorrow early I'll be at the door—
    No, come not at me, if thou wilt be damn'd,
    Forget me, see me not, and so be gone.
    (*Aside.*) Farewell, remember tomorrow morning.
    Out, out thou wretch.   *Exeunt* [*at different doors*].

Enter Mathias.

Mathias. Who's this? Fair Abigail, the rich Jew's daughter   361
    Become a nun! Her father's sudden fall
    Has humbled her and brought her down to this.
    Tut, she were fitter for a tale of love
    Than to be tired out with orisons;
    And better would she far become a bed
    Embraced in a friendly lover's arms,
    Than rise at midnight to a solemn mass.

Enter Lodowick.

Lodowick. Why, how now, Don Mathias, in a dump?

Mathias. Believe me, noble Lodowick, I have seen   370
    The strangest sight, in my opinion,
    That ever I beheld.

Lodowick.   What was't, I prithee?

Mathias. A fair young maid, scarce fourteen years of age,
    The sweetest flower in Cytherea's field,
    Cropp'd from the pleasures of the fruitful earth,
    And strangely metamorphos'd nun.

Lodowick. But say, what was she?

Mathias.   Why, the rich Jew's daughter.

Lodowick. What, Barabas, whose goods were lately seiz'd?
    Is she so fair?

Mathias.   And matchless beautiful;
    As had you seen her, 'twould have mov'd your heart,   380
    Though countermur'd with walls of brass, to love,
    Or at the least, to pity.

Lodowick. And if she be so fair as you report,

374 Cytherea] Venus   381 countermur'd] double-walled

    'Twere time well spent to go and visit her.
    How say you? Shall we?
Mathias. I must and will, sir, there's no remedy.
Lodowick. And so will I too, or it shall go hard.
    Farewell, Mathias.
Mathias.   Farewell, Lodowick.   *Exeunt.*

Actus Secundus [*Scaena 1*]

Enter Barabas *with a light.*

Barabas. Thus like the sad presaging raven that tolls
    The sick man's passport in her hollow beak,
    And in the shadow of the silent night
    Doth shake contagion from her sable wings,
    Vex'd and tormented runs poor Barabas
    With fatal curses towards these Christians.
    The incertain pleasures of swift-footed time
    Have ta'en their flight, and left me in despair;
    And of my former riches rests no more
    But bare remembrance, like a soldier's scar,   10
    That has no further comfort for his maim.
    O Thou, that with a fiery pillar led'st
    The sons of Israel through the dismal shades,
    Light Abraham's offspring, and direct the hand
    Of Abigail this night; or let the day
    Turn to eternal darkness after this!
    No sleep can fasten on my watchful eyes,
    Nor quiet enter my distemper'd thoughts,
    Till I have answer of my Abigail.

Enter Abigail *above.*

Abigail. Now have I happily espied a time   20
    To search the plank my father did appoint;
    And here, behold, unseen, where I have found
    The gold, the pearls, and jewels, which he hid.
Barabas. Now I remember those old women's words,
    Who in my wealth would tell me winter's tales,
    And speak of spirits and ghosts that glide by night
    About the place where treasure hath been hid.
    And now methinks that I am one of those;
    For whilst I live, here lives my soul's sole hope,

And when I die, here shall my spirit walk.   30
Abigail. Now that my father's fortune were so good
          As but to be about this happy place!
          'Tis not so happy: yet, when we parted last,
          He said he would attend me in the morn.
          Then, gentle Sleep, where'er his body rests,
          Give charge to Morpheus that he may dream
          A golden dream, and of the sudden walk,
          Come and receive the treasure I have found.
Barabas. Bueno para todos mi ganado no era;
          As good go on, as sit so sadly thus.   40
          But stay, what star shines yonder in the east?
          The loadstar of my life, if Abigail.
          Who's there?
Abigail.   Who's that?
Barabas. Peace, Abigail! 'Tis I.
Abigail. Then, father, here receive thy happiness.
Barabas. Hast thou't?
Abigail.   Here. (*Throws down bags.*) Hast thou't?
          There's more, and more, and more.
Barabas.   O my girl!
          My gold, my fortune, my felicity,
          Strength to my soul, death to mine enemy!
          Welcome the first beginner of my bliss!
          O Abigail, Abigail, that I had thee here too!   50
          Then my desires were fully satisfied:
          But I will practise thy enlargement thence.
          O girl! O gold! O beauty! O my bliss!   *Hugs his bags.*
Abigail. Father, it draweth towards midnight now,
          And 'bout this time the nuns begin to wake.
          To shun suspicion, therefore, let us part.
Barabas. Farewell my joy, and by my fingers take
          A kiss from him that sends it from his soul.
          Now Phoebus, ope the eyelids of the day,
          And for the raven, wake the morning lark,   60
          That I may hover with her in the air,
          Singing o'er these as she does o'er her young:
          Hermoso placer de los dineros.   *Exeunt.*

39 *Bueno . . . era*] 'My possessions were not good for everything'   63 *Hermoso . . . dineros*]
'The beautiful pleasure of money'

[*Scaena 2*]

Enter Ferneze, Martin del Bosco, *the* Knights [*and* Officers].

Ferneze. Now Captain, tell us whither thou art bound
 Whence is thy ship that anchors in our road?
 And why thou cam'st ashore without our leave?
Bosco. Governor of Malta, hither am I bound;
 My ship, the Flying Dragon, is of Spain,
 And so am I, del Bosco is my name,
 Vice-Admiral unto the Catholic king.
1 Knight. 'Tis true, my lord, therefore entreat him well.
Bosco. Our fraught is Grecians, Turks, and Afric Moors;
 For late upon the coast of Corsica,   10
 Because we vail'd not to the Turkish fleet,
 Their creeping galleys had us in the chase;
 But suddenly the wind began to rise,
 And then we luff'd and tack'd, and fought at ease.
 Some have we fir'd, and many have we sunk;
 But one amongst the rest became our prize:
 The captain's slain; the rest remain our slaves,
 Of whom we would make sale in Malta here.
Ferneze. Martin del Bosco, I have heard of thee.
 Welcome to Malta, and to all of us;   20
 But to admit a sale of these thy Turks,
 We may not, nay we dare not give consent,
 By reason of a tributary league.
1 Knight. Del Bosco, as thou lov'st and honour'st us,
 Persuade our governor against the Turk.
 This truce we have is but in hope of gold,
 And with that sum he craves might we wage war.
Bosco. Will Knights of Malta be in league with Turks,
 And buy it basely too for sums of gold?
 My lord, remember that, to Europe's shame,   30
 The Christian Isle of Rhodes, from whence you came,
 Was lately lost, and you were stated here
 To be at deadly enmity with Turks.
Ferneze. Captain we know it; but our force is small.
Bosco. What is the sum that Calymath requires?

11 vail'd] lowered sails 11 Turkish] Ed. (Spanish Q) 12 creeping] stealthy
31 Christian Isle of Rhodes] The Knights of the Order of the Hospital of St. John of
Jerusalem settled there *c.* 1309; they were expelled by the Turks in 1522, and came to
Malta. 32 stated] stationed

Ferneze. A hundred thousand crowns.

Bosco. My lord and king hath title to this isle,
　　And he means quickly to expel you hence.
　　Therefore be rul'd by me, and keep the gold:
　　I'll write unto his majesty for aid,   40
　　And not depart until I see you free.

Ferneze. On this condition shall thy Turks be sold.
　　Go, officers, and set them straight in show.   [*Exeunt* Officers.]
　　Bosco, thou shalt be Malta's general;
　　We and our warlike knights will follow thee
　　Against these barbarous mis-believing Turks.

Bosco. So shall you imitate those you succeed;
　　For when their hideous force environ'd Rhodes,
　　Small though the number was that kept the town,
　　They fought it out, and not a man surviv'd   50
　　To bring the hapless news to Christendom.

Ferneze. So will we fight it out. Come, let's away.
　　Proud-daring Calymath, instead of gold,
　　We'll send thee bullets wrapt in smoke and fire.
　　Claim tribute where thou wilt, we are resolv'd:
　　Honour is bought with blood, and not with gold.   *Exeunt*.

[*Scaena 3*]

Enter Officers *with* [Ithamore *and other*] Slaves.

1 Officer. This is the market-place, here let 'em stand:
　　Fear not their sale, for they'll be quickly bought.

2 Officer. Every one's price is written on his back,
　　And so much must they yield, or not be sold.

1 Officer. Here comes the Jew; had not his goods been seiz'd,
　　He'd give us present money for them all.

Enter Barabas.

Barabas. In spite of these swine-eating Christians
　　(Unchosen nation, never circumcis'd,
　　Such as, poor villains, were ne'er thought upon
　　Till Titus and Vespasian conquer'd us),   10
　　Am I become as wealthy as I was.
　　They hop'd my daughter would ha' been a nun;
　　But she's at home, and I have bought a house

10 Titus and Vespasian] The campaign against Judaea which began in 66 A.D. and ended
with the fall of Jerusalem in 70 A.D. was led first by Vespasian and then by his son Titus.

As great and fair as is the Governor's;
And there in spite of Malta will I dwell,
Having Ferneze's hand, whose heart I'll have;
Ay, and his son's too, or it shall go hard.
I am not of the tribe of Levi, I,
That can so soon forget an injury.
We Jews can fawn like spaniels when we please,   20
And when we grin we bite; yet are our looks
As innocent and harmless as a lamb's.
I learn'd in Florence how to kiss my hand,
Heave up my shoulders when they call me dog,
And duck as low as any bare-foot friar,
Hoping to see them starve upon a stall,
Or else be gather'd for in our synagogue,
That, when the offering-basin comes to me,
Even for charity I may spit into't.
Here comes Don Lodowick, the Governor's son,   30
One that I love for his good father's sake.

Enter Lodowick.

Lodowick. I hear the wealthy Jew walked this way.
  I'll seek him out, and so insinuate,
  That I may have a sight of Abigail,
  For Don Mathias tells me she is fair.
Barabas. Now will I show myself to have more of the serpent than the dove;
  that is, more knave than fool.
Lodowick. Yond' walks the Jew: now for fair Abigail.
Barabas. Ay, ay, no doubt but she's at your command.
Lodowick. Barabas, thou know'st I am the Governor's son.   40
Barabas. I would you were his father too, sir! that's all the harm I wish you.
  The slave looks like a hog's cheek new singed.
Lodowick. Whither walk'st thou, Barabas?
Barabas. No further. 'Tis a custom held with us,
  That when we speak with Gentiles like to you,
  We turn into the air to purge ourselves:
  For unto us the promise doth belong.
Lodowick. Well, Barabas, canst help me to a diamond?
Barabas. O, sir, your father had my diamonds.
  Yet I have one left that will serve your turn—   50
  (*Aside.*) I mean my daughter; but ere he shall have her
  I'll sacrifice her on a pile of wood:

47 the promise] of Jehovah, that Abraham and his sons should inherit the earth (Exodus 6: 8).

I ha' the poison of the city for him,
And the white leprosy.
Lodowick. What sparkle does it give without a foil?
Barabas. The diamond that I talk of ne'er was foil'd—
　　But, when he touches it, it will be foil'd—
　　Lord Lodowick, it sparkles bright and fair.
Lodowick. Is it square or pointed, pray let me know?
Barabas. Pointed it is, good sir, (*Aside.*) but not for you.　　　60
Lodowick. I like it much the better.
Barabas.　　　　　　　　So do I too.
Lodowick. How shows it by night?
Barabas.　　　　　　　　Outshines Cynthia's rays:
　　You'll like it better far o' nights than days.
Lodowick. And what's the price?
Barabas (*aside*).　　　　　Your life, and if you have it.
　　O my lord,
　　We will not jar about the price: come to my house,
　　And I will give't your honour (*Aside.*) with a vengeance.
Lodowick. No, Barabas, I will deserve it first.
Barabas. Good sir,
　　Your father has deserv'd it at my hands,　　　　　70
　　Who of mere charity and Christian ruth,
　　To bring me to religious purity,
　　And as it were in catechizing sort,
　　To make me mindful of my mortal sins,
　　Against my will, and whether I would or no,
　　Seiz'd all I had, and thrust me out-a-doors,
　　And made my house a place for nuns most chaste.
Lodowick. No doubt your soul shall reap the fruit of it.
Barabas. Ay, but my lord, the harvest is far off.
　　And yet I know the prayers of those nuns　　　　　80
　　And holy friars, having money for their pains,
　　Are wondrous; (*Aside.*) and indeed do no man good;
　　And, seeing they are not idle, but still doing,
　　'Tis likely they in time may reap some fruit,
　　I mean, in fullness of perfection
Lodowick. Good Barabas, glance not at our holy nuns.
Barabas. No, but I do it through a burning zeal—
　　Hoping ere long to set the house a-fire;
　　For, though they do a while increase and multiply,
　　I'll have a saying to that nunnery—　　　　　90
　　As for the diamond, sir, I told you of,

90 a saying to] a deal with

> Come home, and there's no price shall make us part,
> Even for your honourable father's sake—
> It shall go hard but I will see your death—
> But now I must be gone to buy a slave.

Lodowick. And, Barabas, I'll bear thee company.

Barabas. Come, then; here's the market-place. What's the price of this
slave? Two hundred crowns? Do the Turks weigh so much?

1 Officer. Sir, that's his price.

Barabas. What, can he steal, that you demand so much?   100
> Belike he has some new trick for a purse;
> And if he has, he is worth three hundred plats,
> So that, being bought, the town seal might be got
> To keep him for his lifetime from the gallows.
> The sessions-day is critical to thieves,
> And few or none escape but by being purg'd.

Lodowick. Rat'st thou this Moor but at two hundred plats?

1 Officer. No more, my lord.

Barabas. Why should this Turk be dearer than that Moor?

1 Officer. Because he is young, and has more qualities.   110

Barabas. What, hast the philosopher's stone? And thou hast, break my head
with it; I'll forgive thee.

Slave. No sir; I can cut and shave.

Barabas. Let me see, sirrah, are you not an old shaver?

Slave. Alas, sir, I am a very youth!

Barabas. A youth! I'll buy you, and marry you to Lady Vanity, if you do
well.

Slave. I will serve you, sir.

Barabas. Some wicked trick or other. It may be, under colour of shaving,
thou'lt cut my throat for my goods. Tell me, hast thou thy health well?

Slave. Ay, passing well.   121

Barabas. So much the worse; I must have one that's sickly, an't be but for
sparing victuals. 'Tis not a stone of beef a day will maintain you in these
chops; let me see one that's somewhat leaner.

1 Officer. Here's a leaner; how like you him?

Barabas. Where wast thou born?

Ithamore. In Thrace; brought up in Arabia.

Barabas. So much the better; thou art for my turn.

---

101 trick for a purse] means of stealing   102 plats] pieces of money   105–6 The sessions-
day... purg'd] As certain days were thought to be critical in medical matters (cf. *Tamburlaine*:
Part II, V. iii. 91–2), so the assizes held danger for thieves unless they could purge
their guilt by bribery.   111 philosopher's stone] the touchstone that would (when discovered) turn base metals into gold   114 shaver] cheat   116 Lady Vanity] character
in the Morality Plays who attempts to seduce Youth from Good Counsel

An hundred crowns? I'll have him; there's the coin.

1 Officer. Then mark him, sir, and take him hence.   130

Barabas. Ay, mark him, you were best; for this is he
    That by my help shall do much villainy.
    My lord, farewell. Come, sirrah, you are mine.
    As for the diamond, it shall be yours;
    I pray, sir, be no stranger at my house,
    All that I have shall be at your command.

Enter Mathias [*and* Katharine], *his mother.*

Mathias. What makes the Jew and Lodowick so private?
    I fear me 'tis about fair Abigail.

Barabas. Yonder comes Don Mathias; let us stay:
    He loves my daughter, and she holds him dear;   140
    But I have sworn to frustrate both their hopes,
    And be reveng'd upon the—Governor.   [*Exit* Lodowick.]

Katharine. This Moor is comeliest, is he not? Speak, son.

Mathias. No, this is the better, mother, view this well.

Barabas. Seem not to know me here before your mother,
    Lest she mistrust the match that is in hand.
    When you have brought her home, come to my house;
    Think of me as thy father. Son, farewell.

Mathias. But wherefore talk'd Don Lodowick with you?

Barabas. Tush, man, we talk'd of diamonds, not of Abigail.   150

Katharine. Tell me, Mathias, is not that the Jew?

Barabas. As for the comment on the Maccabees,
    I have it, sir, and 'tis at your command.

Mathias. Yes, madam, and my talk with him was about the borrowing of a
    book or two.

Katharine. Converse not with him; he is cast off from heaven.
    Thou hast thy crowns, fellow. Come, let's away.

Mathias. Sirrah Jew, remember the book.

Barabas. Marry will I, sir.   *Exeunt* [Katharine *and* Mathias, *with a* Slave].

1 Officer. Come, I have made a reasonable market; let's away.   160
                                        [*Exeunt* Officers *with* Slaves.]

Barabas. Now let me know thy name, and therewithal
    Thy birth, condition, and profession.

Ithamore. Faith, sir, my birth is but mean, my name's Ithamore, my pro-
    fession what you please.

Barabas. Hast thou no trade? Then listen to my words,
    And I will teach that shall stick by thee.
    First be thou void of these affections:
    Compassion, love, vain hope, and heartless fear;

    Be mov'd at nothing, see thou pity none,
    But to thyself smile when the Christians moan.   170
Ithamore. O, brave, master, I worship your nose for this.
Barabas. As for myself, I walk abroad a-nights,
    And kill sick people groaning under walls;
    Sometimes I go about and poison wells;
    And now and then, to cherish Christian thieves,
    I am content to lose some of my crowns,
    That I may, walking in my gallery,
    See 'em go pinion'd along by my door.
    Being young, I studied physic, and began
    To practise first upon the Italian;   180
    There I enrich'd the priests with burials,
    And always kept the sexton's arms in ure
    With digging graves and ringing dead men's knells.
    And after that, was I an engineer,
    And in the wars 'twixt France and Germany,
    Under the pretence of helping Charles the Fifth,
    Slew friend and enemy with my stratagems.
    Then after that was I an usurer,
    And with extorting, cozening, forfeiting,
    And tricks belonging unto brokery,   190
    I fill'd the gaols with bankrupts in a year,
    And with young orphans planted hospitals,
    And every moon made some or other mad,
    And now and then one hang himself for grief,
    Pinning upon his breast a long great scroll
    How I with interest tormented him.
    But mark how I am blest for plaguing them:
    I have as much coin as will buy the town.
    But tell me now, how hast thou spent thy time?
Ithamore. Faith, master,   200
    In setting Christian villages on fire,
    Chaining of eunuchs, binding galley-slaves.
    One time I was an hostler in an inn,
    And in the night time secretly would I steal
    To travellers' chambers, and there cut their throats;
    Once at Jerusalem, where the pilgrims kneel'd,
    I strewed powder on the marble stones,
    And therewithal their knees would rankle so,
    That I have laugh'd a-good to see the cripples
    Go limping home to Christendom on stilts.   210

182 in ure] in use

Barabas. Why, this is something: make account of me
  As of thy fellow; we are villains both:
  Both circumcised, we hate Christians both.
  Be true and secret, thou shalt want no gold.
  But stand aside, here comes Don Lodowick.

Enter Lodowick.

Lodowick. O, Barabas, well met.
  Where is the diamond you told me of?
Barabas. I have it for you, sir: please you walk in with me—
  What ho, Abigail! Open the door, I say!

Enter Abigail.

Abigail. In good time, father; here are letters come   220
  From Ormus, and the post stays here within.
Barabas. Give me the letters. Daughter, do you hear?
  Entertain Lodowick, the Governor's son,
  With all the courtesy you can afford,
  Provided that you keep your maidenhead.
  (*Aside.*) Use him as if he were a Philistine;
  Dissemble, swear, protest, vow to love him:
  He is not of the seed of Abraham.
  I am a little busy, sir; pray pardon me.
  Abigail, bid him welcome for my sake.   230
Abigail. For your sake and his own he's welcome hither.
Barabas. Daughter, a word more: kiss him, speak him fair,
  And like a cunning Jew so cast about,
  That ye be both made sure ere you come out.
Abigail. O father, Don Mathias is my love!
Barabas. I know it: yet, I say, make love to him;
  Do, it is requisite it should be so.
  Nay on my life, it is my factor's hand;
  But go you in, I'll think upon the account.

[*Exeunt* Abigail *and* Lodowick.]

  The account is made, for Lodowick dies.   240
  My factor sends me word a merchant's fled
  That owes me for a hundred tun of wine:
  I weigh it thus much; I have wealth enough;
  For now by this has he kiss'd Abigail,
  And she vows love to him, and he to her.
  And sure as heaven rain'd manna for the Jews,
  So sure shall he and Don Mathias die:

221 post] messenger   234 made sure] betrothed

His father was my chiefest enemy.

Enter Mathias.

Whither goes Don Mathias? Stay a while.

Mathias. Whither but to my fair love Abigail?   250

Barabas. Thou know'st, and heaven can witness it is true,
    That I intend my daughter shall be thine.

Mathias. Ay, Barabas, or else thou wrong'st me much.

Barabas. O, heaven forbid I should have such a thought!
    Pardon me though I weep: the Governor's son
    Will, whether I will or no, have Abigail;
    He sends her letters, bracelets, jewels, rings.

Mathias. Does she receive them?

Barabas. She! No, Mathias, no, but sends them back,
    And when he comes, she locks herself up fast;   260
    Yet through the key-hole will he talk to her,
    While she runs to the window looking out
    When you should come and hale him from the door.

Mathias. O treacherous Lodowick!

Barabas. Even now, as I came home, he slipt me in,
    And I am sure he is with Abigail.

Mathias. I'll rouse him thence.

Barabas. Not for all Malta; therefore sheathe your sword.
    If you love me, no quarrels in my house;
    But steal you in, and seem to see him not: 270
    I'll give him such a warning ere he goes,
    As he shall have small hopes of Abigail.
    Away, for here they come.

Enter Lodowick, Abigail.

Mathias. What, hand in hand! I cannot suffer this.

Barabas. Mathias, as thou lov'st me, not a word.

Mathias. Well, let it pass. Another time shall serve.   *Exit.*

Lodowick. Barabas, is not that the widow's son?

Barabas. Ay, and take heed, for he hath sworn your death.

Lodowick. My death! What, is the base-born peasant mad?

Barabas. No, no; but happily he stands in fear   280
    Of that which you, I think, ne'er dream upon,
    My daughter here, a paltry silly girl.

Lodowick. Why, loves she Don Mathias?

Barabas. Doth she not with her smiling answer you?

Abigail (aside). He has my heart; I smile against my will.

Lodowick. Barabas, thou know'st I have lov'd thy daughter long.

280 happily] perhaps

Barabas. And so has she done you, even from a child.
Lodowick. And now I can no longer hold my mind.
Barabas. Nor I the affection that I bear to you.
Lodowick. This is thy diamond. Tell me, shall I have it?   290
Barabas. Win it, and wear it; it is yet unsoil'd.
    O but I know your lordship would disdain
    To marry with the daughter of a Jew:
    And yet I'll give her many a golden cross,
    With Christian posies round about the ring.
Lodowick. 'Tis not thy wealth, but her that I esteem;
    Yet crave I thy consent.
Barabas. And mine you have; yet let me talk to her.
    (*Aside.*) This offspring of Cain, this Jebusite,
    That never tasted of the Passover,   300
    Nor e'er shall see the land of Canaan,
    Nor our Messias that is yet to come,
    This gentle maggot Lodowick I mean,
    Must be deluded: let him have thy hand,
    But keep thy heart till Don Mathias comes.
Abigail. What, shall I be betroth'd to Lodowick?
Barabas. It's no sin to deceive a Christian;
    For they themselves hold it a principle,
    Faith is not to be held with heretics:
    But all are heretics that are not Jews.   310
    This follows well, and therefore, daughter, fear not.
    I have entreated her, and she will grant.
Lodowick. Then gentle Abigail, plight thy faith to me.
Abigail. I cannot choose, seeing my father bids:
    Nothing but death shall part my love and me.
Lodowick. Now have I that for which my soul hath long'd.
Barabas (*aside*). So have not I; but yet I hope I shall.
Abigail (*aside*). O wretched Abigail, what hast thou done?
Lodowick. Why on the sudden is your colour chang'd?
Abigail. I know not: but farewell, I must be gone.   320
Barabas. Stay her, but let her not speak one word more.
Lodowick. Mute o' the sudden! Here's a sudden change.
Barabas. O, muse not at it; 'tis the Hebrews' guise,
    That maidens new-betroth'd should weep a while.
    Trouble her not; sweet Lodowick, depart;
    She is thy wife, and thou shalt be mine heir.
Lodowick. O, is't the custom? Then I am resolv'd:

294-5 golden cross . . . ring] coins, marked with a cross and bearing mottoes on the rim
313 gentle] with a pun on 'gentile'   321 Stay] Support   327 resolv'd] relaxed

But rather let the brightsome heavens be dim,
And nature's beauty choke with stifling clouds,
Than my fair Abigail should frown on me.   330
There comes the villain; now I'll be reveng'd.

Enter Mathias.

Barabas. Be quiet, Lodowick; it is enough
    That I have made thee sure to Abigail.
Lodowick. Well, let him go.   *Exit.*
Barabas. Well, but for me, as you went in at doors
    You had been stabb'd: but not a word on't now.
    Here must no speeches pass, nor swords be drawn.
Mathias. Suffer me, Barabas, but to follow him.
Barabas. No; so shall I, if any hurt be done,
    Be made an accessary of your deeds.   340
    Revenge it on him when you meet him next.
Mathias. For this I'll have his heart.
Barabas. Do so. Lo, here I give thee Abigail.
Mathias. What greater gift can poor Mathias have?
    Shall Lodowick rob me of so fair a love?
    My life is not so dear as Abigail.
Barabas. My heart misgives me, that to cross your love,
    He's with your mother; therefore after him.
Mathias. What, is he gone unto my mother?
Barabas. Nay, if you will, stay till she comes herself.   350
Mathias. I cannot stay; for, if my mother come,
    She'll die with grief.   *Exit.*
Abigail. I cannot take my leave of him for tears.
    Father, why have you thus incens'd them both?
Barabas. What's that to thee?
Abigail.   I'll make 'em friends again.
Barabas. You'll make 'em friends! Are there not Jews enow in Malta,
    But thou must dote upon a Christian?
Abigail. I will have Don Mathias; he is my love.
Barabas. Yes, you shall have him. Go, put her in.
Ithamore. Ay, I'll put her in.   [*Puts Abigail in.*]
Barabas. Now tell me, Ithamore, how lik'st thou this?   361
Ithamore. Faith, master, I think by this
    You purchase both their lives: is it not so?
Barabas. True, and it shall be cunningly perform'd.
Ithamore. O, master, that I might have a hand in this.
Barabas. Ay, so thou shalt: 'tis thou must do the deed.
    Take this, and bear it to Mathias straight.   [*Giving a letter.*]

And tell him that it comes from Lodowick.

Ithamore. 'Tis poison'd, is it not?

Barabas. No, no; and yet it might be done that way: 370
  It is a challenge feign'd from Lodowick.

Ithamore. Fear not, I'll so set his heart a-fire,
  That he shall verily think it comes from him.

Barabas. I cannot choose but like thy readiness;
  Yet be not rash, but do it cunningly.

Ithamore. As I behave myself in this, employ me hereafter.

Barabas. Away, then!   *Exit* [Ithamore].
  So, now will I go in to Lodowick,
  And like a cunning spirit feign some lie,
  Till I have set 'em both at enmity.   *Exit.*

Actus Tertius [Scaena 1]

Enter [Bellamira] a courtesan.

Bellamira. Since this town was besieg'd, my gain grows cold:
  The time has been, that but for one bare night
  A hundred ducats have been freely given;
  But now against my will I must be chaste;
  And yet I know my beauty doth not fail.
  From Venice merchants, and from Padua
  Were wont to come rare-witted gentlemen,
  Scholars I mean, learned and liberal;
  And now, save Pilia-Borza, comes there none,
  And he is very seldom from my house;   10
  And here he comes.

Enter Pilia-Borza.

Pilia-Borza. Hold thee, wench, there's something for thee to spend.

Bellamira. 'Tis silver; I disdain it.

Pilia-Borza. Ay, but the Jew has gold,
  And I will have it, or it shall go hard.

Bellamira. Tell me, how cam'st thou by this?

Pilia-Borza. Faith, walking the back lanes through the gardens, I chanced
  to cast mine eye up to the Jew's counting-house, where I saw some bags
  of money, and in the night I clambered up with my hooks; and as I was
  taking my choice, I heard a rumbling in the house; so I took only this,
  and run my way. But here's the Jew's man.   21

Enter Ithamore.

9 Pilia-Borza] 'Pickpocket'

Bellamira. Hide the bag.

Pilia-Borza. Look not towards him, let's away. Zoons, what a looking thou
    keep'st, thou'lt betray's anon.   [*Exeunt* Bellamira *and* Pilia-Borza.]

Ithamore. O the sweetest face that ever I beheld! I know she is a courtesan
    by her attire: now would I give a hundred of the Jew's crowns that I had
    such a concubine.

      Well, I have deliver'd the challenge in such sort,
      As meet they will, and fighting die; brave sport!   *Exit.*

[*Scaena 2*]

Enter Mathias [*reading*].

Mathias. This is the place; now Abigail shall see
    Whether Mathias holds her dear or no.

Enter Lodowick *reading.*

    What, dares the villain write in such base terms?

Lodowick. I did it; and revenge it if thou dar'st.   *Fight.*

Enter Barabas *above.*

Barabas. O bravely fought! and yet they thrust not home.
    Now Lodowick, now Mathias; so!   [*Both fall.*]
    So now they have show'd themselves to be tall fellows.

[*Voices*] *within.* Part 'em, part 'em!

Barabas. Ay, part 'em now they are dead. Farewell, farewell!   *Exit.*

Enter Ferneze, Katharine [*and* Attendants].

Ferneze. What sight is this? My Lodowick slain!   10
    These arms of mine shall be thy sepulchre.

Katharine. Who is this? My son Mathias slain!

Ferneze. O Lodowick, hadst thou perish'd by the Turk,
    Wretched Ferneze might have veng'd thy death!

Katharine. They son slew mine, and I'll revenge his death.

Ferneze. Look, Katharine, look, thy son gave mine these wounds.

Katharine. O leave to grieve me, I am griev'd enough.

Ferneze. O that my sighs could turn to lively breath,
    And these my tears to blood, that he might live.

Katharine. Who made them enemies?   20

Ferneze. I know not, and that grieves me most of all.

Katharine. My son lov'd thine.

Ferneze. And so did Lodowick him.

Katharine. Lend me that weapon that did kill my son,

---

s.d. [*reading*]] It appears from III. iii. 19 that faked challenges have been delivered to both
lovers.

And it shall murder me.

Ferneze. Nay, madam, stay; that weapon was my son's,
And on that rather should Ferneze die.

Katharine. Hold, let's inquire the causers of their deaths,
That we may venge their blood upon their heads.

Ferneze. Then take them up, and let them be interr'd   30
Within one sacred monument of stone,
Upon which altar I will offer up
My daily sacrifice of sighs and tears,
And with my prayers pierce impartial heavens,
Till they disclose the causers of our smarts,
Which forc'd their hands divide united hearts.
Come, Katharine, our losses equal are;
Then of true grief let us take equal share.   *Exeunt.*

[*Scaena 3*]

Enter Ithamore.

Ithamore. Why, was there ever seen such villainy,
So neatly plotted, and so well perform'd?
Both held in hand, and flatly both beguil'd.

Enter Abigail.

Abigail. Why, how now, Ithamore, why laugh'st thou so?

Ithamore. O mistress! Ha, ha, ha!

Abigail. Why, what ail'st thou?

Ithamore. O, my master!

Abigail. Ha?

Ithamore. O mistress, I have the bravest, gravest, secret, subtle, bottle-nosed
knave to my master, that ever gentleman had!   10

Abigail. Say, knave, why rail'st upon my father thus?

Ithamore. O, my master has the bravest policy!

Abigail. Wherein?

Ithamore. Why, know you not?

Abigail. Why, no.

Ithamore. Know you not of Mathias' and Don Lodowick's disaster?

Abigail. No, what was it?

Ithamore. Why, the devil invented a challenge, my master writ it, and I
carried it, first to Lodowick, and *imprimis* to Mathias:
And then they met, and as the story says,   20
In doleful wise they ended both their days.

35 they disclose the] Ed. (they the Q)   III. iii, 3 held in hand] led on

Abigail. And was my father furtherer of their deaths?

Ithamore. Am I Ithamore?

Abigail. Yes.

Ithamore. So sure did your father write, and I carry the challenge.

Abigail. Well, Ithamore, let me request thee this:
    Go to the new-made nunnery, and inquire
    For any of the friars of Saint Jacques,
    And say, I pray them come and speak with me.

Ithamore. I pray, mistress, will you answer me to one question?   30

Abigail. Well, sirrah, what is't?

Ithamore. A very feeling one: have not the nuns fine sport with the friars
now and then?

Abigail. Go to, Sirrah Sauce! Is this your question? Get ye gone.

Ithamore. I will forsooth, mistress.   *Exit.*

Abigail. Hard-hearted father, unkind Barabas!
    Was this the pursuit of thy policy,
    To make me show them favour severally,
    That by my favour they should both be slain?
    Admit thou lov'dst not Lodowick for his sire,   40
    Yet Don Mathias ne'er offended thee.
    But thou wert set upon extreme revenge,
    Because the Governor dispossess'd thee once,
    And couldst not venge it but upon his son;
    Nor on his son but by Mathias' means;
    Nor on Mathias but by murdering me.
    But I perceive there is no love on earth,
    Pity in Jews, nor piety in Turks.
    But here comes cursed Ithamore with the friar.

Enter Ithamore, *Friar* [Jacomo].

Jacomo. Virgo, salve.   50

Ithamore. When, duck you?

Abigail. Welcome, grave friar. Ithamore, be gone.   *Exit* [Ithamore].
    Know, holy sir, I am bold to solicit thee.

Jacomo. Wherein?

Abigail. To get me be admitted for a nun.

Jacomo. Why Abigail, it is not yet long since
    That I did labour thy admission,
    And then thou didst not like that holy life.

Abigail. Then were my thoughts so frail and unconfirm'd
    And I was chain'd to follies of the world;   60

40 Admit] Admittedly   50 *Virgo, salve*] 'Greetings, maiden'   51 When, duck you]
What, are you bowing and scraping

But now experience, purchased with grief,
Has made me see the difference of things.
My sinful soul, alas, hath pac'd too long
The fatal labyrinth of misbelief,
Far from the sun that gives eternal life.
Jacomo. Who taught thee this?
Abigail.   The abbess of the house,
Whose zealous admonition I embrace.
O therefore, Jacomo, let me be one,
Although unworthy, of that sisterhood!
Jacomo. Abigail, I will; but see thou change no more,   70
For that will be most heavy to thy soul.
Abigail. That was my father's fault.
Jacomo.   Thy father's! How?
Abigail. Nay, you shall pardon me. O Barabas,
Though thou deservest hardly at my hands,
Yet never shall these lips bewray thy life.
Jacomo. Come, shall we go?
Abigail.   My duty waits on you.   *Exeunt.*

[*Scaena 4*]

Enter Barabas *reading a letter.*
Barabas. What, Abigail become a nun again?
False and unkind! What, hast thou lost thy father?
And, all unknown and unconstrain'd of me,
Art thou again got to the nunnery?
Now here she writes, and wills me to repent:
Repentance? *Spurca!* What pretendeth this?
I fear she knows ('tis so) of my device
In Don Mathias' and Lodovico's deaths:
If so, 'tis time that it be seen into;
For she that varies from me in belief,
Gives great presumption that she loves me not;   10
Or loving, doth dislike of something done.
But who comes here?
                    [*Enter* Ithamore.]
                    O Ithamore, come near;
Come near, my love; come near, thy master's life,
My trusty servant, nay, my second self;
For I have now no hope but even in thee,

65 sun] Ed. (Sonne Q)   III. iv, 2 unkind] unnatural   6 *Spurca*] 'Filthy'

    And on that hope my happiness is built.
    When saw'st thou Abigail?
Ithamore. Today.
Barabas. With whom?   20
Ithamore. A friar.
Barabas. A friar! False villain, he hath done the deed.
Ithamore. How, sir!
Barabas. Why, made mine Abigail a nun.
Ithamore. That's no lie, for she sent me for him.
Barabas. O unhappy day!
    False, credulous, inconstant Abigail!
    But let 'em go: and, Ithamore, from hence
    Ne'er shall she grieve me more with her disgrace;
    Ne'er shall she live to inherit aught of mine,   30
    Be bless'd of me, nor come within my gates,
    But perish underneath my bitter curse,
    Like Cain by Adam for his brother's death.
Ithamore. O master!
Barabas. Ithamore, entreat not for her. I am mov'd,
    And she is hateful to my soul and me:
    And, 'less thou yield to this that I intreat,
    I cannot think but that thou hat'st my life.
Ithamore. Who I, master? Why, I'll run to some rock, and throw myself
    headlong into the sea; why, I'll do anything for your sweet sake.   40
Barabas. O trusty Ithamore; no servant, but my friend!
    I here adopt thee for mine only heir:
    All that I have is thine when I am dead;
    And whilst I live, use half; spend as myself.
    Here, take my keys—I'll give 'em thee anon.
    Go buy thee garments; but thou shalt not want.
    Only know this, that thus thou art to do:
    But first go fetch me in the pot of rice
    That for our supper stands upon the fire.
Ithamore. I hold my head, my master's hungry—I go, sir.   *Exit.*
Barabas. Thus every villain ambles after wealth,   51
    Although he ne'er be richer than in hope.
    But, husht!

Enter Ithamore *with the pot.*

Ithamore. Here 'tis, master.
Barabas. Well said, Ithamore! What, hast thou brought the ladle with thee
    too?

50 hold] bet

Ithamore. Yes, sir; the proverb says, he that eats with the devil had need of
a long spoon; I have brought you a ladle.

Barabas. Very well, Ithamore, then now be secret;
   And for thy sake, whom I so dearly love,   60
   Now shalt thou see the death of Abigail,
   That thou mayst freely live to be my heir.

Ithamore. Why, master, will you poison her with a mess of rice-porridge
that will preserve life, make her round and plump, and batten more than
you are aware?

Barabas. Ay, but Ithamore seest thou this?
   It is a precious powder that I bought
   Of an Italian in Ancona once,
   Whose operation is to bind, infect,
   And poison deeply, yet not appear   70
   In forty hours after it is ta'en.

Ithamore. How, master?

Barabas. Thus, Ithamore:
   This even they use in Malta here ('tis call'd
   Saint Jacques' Even) and then, I say, they use
   To send their alms unto the nunneries:
   Among the rest bear this, and set it there;
   There's a dark entry where they take it in,
   Where they must neither see the messenger,
   Nor make inquiry who hath sent it them.   80

Ithamore. How so?

Barabas. Belike there is some ceremony in't.
   There, Ithamore, must thou go place this pot:
   Stay, let me spice it first.

Ithamore. Pray do, and let me help you, master. Pray let me taste first.

Barabas. Prithee, do; what say'st thou now?

Ithamore. Troth, master, I'm loath such a pot of pottage should be spoiled.

Barabas. Peace, Ithamore! 'Tis better so than spar'd.
   Assure thyself thou shalt have broth by the eye.
   My purse, my coffer, and myself is thine.   90

Ithamore. Well, master, I go.

Barabas. Stay, first let me stir it, Ithamore.
   As fatal be it to her as the draught
   Of which great Alexander drunk and died;
   And with her let it work like Borgia's wine,
   Whereof his sire the Pope was poisoned.

---

89 by the eye] without limit   93-4 draught . . . died] Alexander the Great caught a
fatal fever after a drinking bout.   95-6 Borgia's wine . . . poisoned] Although he committed
other violent crimes, Cesare Borgia did not in fact poison his father, Pope Alexander VI.

In few, the blood of Hydra, Lerna's bane,
The juice of hebon, and Cocytus' breath,
And all the poisons of the Stygian pool,
Break from the fiery kingdom; and in this   100
Vomit your venom, and envenom her
That like a fiend hath left her father thus!

Ithamore. What a blessing has he given't! Was ever pot of rice-porridge so
sauced? What shall I do with it?

Barabas. O my sweet Ithamore, go set it down;
And come again as soon as thou hast done,
For I have other business for thee.

Ithamore. Here's a drench to poison a whole stable of Flanders mares: I'll
carry't to the nuns with a powder.

Barabas. And the horse-pestilence to boot. Away!   110

Ithamore. I am gone:
Pay me my wages, for my work is done.   *Exit.*

Barabas. I'll pay thee with a vengeance, Ithamore!   *Exit.*

[*Scaena 5*]

Enter Governor [Ferneze], [Martin del] Bosco, Knights [*meeting a*]
Basso.

Ferneze. Welcome, great Basso; how fares Calymath?
What wind drives you thus into Malta road?

Basso. The wind that bloweth all the world besides,
Desire of gold.

Ferneze.   Desire of gold, great sir!
That's to be gotten in the Western Inde:
In Malta are no golden minerals.

Basso. To you of Malta thus saith Calymath:
The time you took for respite is at hand;
For the performance of your promise pass'd,
And for the tribute money I am sent.   10

Ferneze. Basso, in brief, shalt have no tribute here,
Nor shall the heathens live upon our spoil:
First will we raze the city walls ourselves,
Lay waste the island, hew the temples down,
And, shipping off our goods to Sicily,
Open an entrance for the wasteful sea,

97 blood . . . bane] The blood of the Hydra from Lake Lerna was used to poison Hercules'
arrows.   98 hebon] yew   98 Cocytus] hell-mouth   108 drench] dose   109 with a
powder] in a hurry

Whose billows, beating the resistless banks,
Shall overflow it with their refluence.
Basso. Well, Governor, since thou hast broke the league
By flat denial of the promis'd tribute, 20
Talk not of razing down your city walls,
You shall not need trouble yourselves so far,
For Selim-Calymath shall come himself,
And with brass bullets batter down your towers,
And turn proud Malta to a wilderness,
For these intolerable wrongs of yours:
And so farewell.
Ferneze. Farewell. [*Exit* Basso.]
And now you men of Malta, look about,
And let's provide to welcome Calymath. 30
Close your portcullis, charge your basilisks,
And as you profitably take up arms,
So now courageously encounter them;
For by this answer broken is the league,
And naught is to be look'd for now but wars,
And naught to us more welcome is than wars. *Exeunt.*

[*Scaena 6*]

Enter two Friars [Jacomo *and* Barnardine].

Jacomo. O brother, brother, all the nuns are sick,
And physic will not help them; they must die.
Barnardine. The abbess sent for me to be confess'd.
O what a sad confession will there be!
Jacomo. And so did fair Maria send for me.
I'll to her lodging; hereabouts she lies. *Exit.*
Enter Abigail.
Barnardine. What, all dead save only Abigail?
Abigail. And I shall die too, for I feel death coming.
Where is the friar that convers'd with me?
Barnardine. O he is gone to see the other nuns. 10
Abigail. I sent for him, but seeing you are come,
Be you my ghostly father: and first know,
That in this house I liv'd religiously,
Chaste, and devout, much sorrowing for my sins;
But ere I came—

31 basilisks] cannon

Barnardine. What then?

Abigail. I did offend high heaven so grievously
    As I am almost desperate for my sins;
    And one offence torments me more than all.
    You knew Mathias and Don Lodowick?   20

Barnardine. Yes, what of them?

Abigail. My father did contract me to 'em both;
    First to Don Lodowick: him I never lov'd;
    Mathias was the man that I held dear,
    And for his sake did I become a nun.

Barnardine. So: say how was their end?

Abigail. Both jealous of my love, envied each other;
    And by my father's practice, which is there
    Set down at large, the gallants were both slain.   *[Gives a paper.]*

Barnardine. O monstrous villainy!   30

Abigail. To work my peace, this I confess to thee.
    Reveal it not, for then my father dies.

Barnardine. Know that confession must not be reveal'd;
    The canon law forbids it, and the priest
    That makes it known, being degraded first,
    Shall be condemn'd, and then sent to the fire.

Abigail. So I have heard; pray therefore keep it close.
    Death seizeth on my heart: ah, gentle friar,
    Convert my father that he may be sav'd,
    And witness that I die a Christian!   40
                                                     [Dies.]

Barnardine. Ay, and a virgin too; that grieves me most.
    But I must to the Jew, and exclaim on him,
    And make him stand in fear of me.

                    Enter first Friar [Jacomo].

Jacomo. O brother, all the nuns are dead; let's bury them.

Barnardine. First help to bury this; then go with me,
    And help me to exclaim against the Jew.

Jacomo. Why, what has he done?

Barnardine. A thing that makes me tremble to unfold.

Jacomo. What, has he crucified a child?

Barnardine. No, but a worse thing: 'twas told me in shrift.
    Thou know'st 'tis death, and if it be reveal'd.
    Come, let's away.   *Exeunt.*

42 exclaim on] denounce

Actus Quartus [*Scaena 1*]

Enter Barabas, Ithamore. *Bells within.*

Barabas. There is no music to a Christian's knell!
    How sweet the bells ring now the nuns are dead,
    That sound at other times like tinkers' pans!
    I was afraid the poison had not wrought,
    Or though it wrought, it would have done no good,
    For every year they swell, and yet they live;
    Now all are dead, not one remains alive.
Ithamore. That's brave, master; but think you it will not be known?
Barabas. How can it, if we two be secret?
Ithamore. For my part, fear you not.   10
Barabas. I'd cut thy throat, if I did.
Ithamore. And reason too.
    But here's a royal monastery hard by;
    Good master, let me poison all the monks.
Barabas. Thou shalt not need, for now the nuns are dead,
    They'll die with grief.
Ithamore. Do you not sorrow for your daughter's death?
Barabas. No, but I grieve because she liv'd so long;
    An Hebrew born, and would become a Christian:
    Cazzo diabole!   20
Ithamore. Look, look, master, here come two religious caterpillars.

Enter the two Friars [Jacomo *and* Barnardine].

Barabas. I smelt 'em ere they came.
Ithamore. God-a-mercy, nose; come, let's begone.
Barnardine. Stay wicked Jew; repent, I say, and stay.
Jacomo. Thou hast offended, therefore must be damn'd.
Barabas. I fear they know we sent the poison'd broth.
Ithamore. And so do I, master; therefore speak 'em fair.
Barnardine. Barabas, thou hast—
Jacomo. Ay, that thou hast—
Barabas. True, I have money; what though I have?
Barnardine. Thou art a—   30
Jacomo. Ay, that thou art, a—
Barabas. What needs all this? I know I am a Jew.
Barnardine. Thy daughter—
Jacomo. Ay, thy daughter—
Barabas. O, speak not of her, then I die with grief.

20 *Cazzo diabole*] 'Devil's prick'

Barnardinè. Remember that—
Jacomo. Ay, remember that—
Barabas. I must needs say that I have been a great usurer.
Barnardine. Thou hast committed—   40
Barabas. Fornication? But that was in another country, and besides the
    wench is dead.
Barnardine. Ay, but Barabas, remember Mathias and Don Lodowick.
Barabas. Why, what of them?
Barnardine. I will not say that by a forged challenge they met.
Barabas (*aside*). She has confess'd, and we are both undone,
    My bosom inmate! But I must dissemble.
    O holy friars, the burden of my sins
    Lie heavy on my soul; then pray you tell me,
    Is't not too late now to turn Christian?   50
    I have been zealous in the Jewish faith,
    Hard-hearted to the poor, a covetous wretch,
    That would for lucre's sake have sold my soul.
    A hundred for a hundred I have ta'en;
    And now for store of wealth may I compare
    With all the Jews in Malta: but what is wealth?
    I am a Jew, and therefore am I lost.
    Would penance serve for this my sin,
    I could afford to whip myself to death.
Ithamore. And so could I; but penance will not serve.   60
Barabas. To fast, to pray, and wear a shirt of hair,
    And on my knees creep to Jerusalem.
    Cellars of wine, and sollars full of wheat,
    Warehouses stuff'd with spices and with drugs,
    Whole chests of gold in bullion and in coin,
    Besides I know not how much weight in pearl,
    Orient and round, have I within my house;
    At Alexandria, merchandise unsold;
    But yesterday two ships went from this town,
    Their voyage will be worth ten thousand crowns.   70
    In Florence, Venice, Antwerp, London, Seville,
    Frankfort, Lubeck, Moscow, and where not,
    Have I debts owing; and in most of these
    Great sums of money lying in the banco.
    All this I'll give to some religious house,
    So I may be baptiz'd, and live therein.
Jacomo. O good Barabas, come to our house!
Barnardine. O no, good Barabas, come to our house!

54 A hundred for a hundred] 100 per cent interest   **63** sollars] lofts

And Barabas, you know—

Barabas. I know that I have highly sinn'd: 80
    You shall convert me, you shall have all my wealth.

Jacomo. O Barabas, their laws are strict!

Barabas. I know they are; and I will be with you.

Jacomo. They wear no shirts, and they go barefoot too.

Barabas. Then 'tis not for me; and I am resolv'd
    You shall confess me, and have all my goods.

Jacomo. Good Barabas, come to me.

Barabas. You see I answer him, and yet he stays;
    Rid him away, and go you home with me.

Jacomo. I'll be with you tonight.   90

Barabas. Come to my house at one o'clock this night.

Jacomo. You hear your answer, and you may be gone.

Barnardine. Why go, get you away.

Jacomo. I will not go for thee.

Barnardine. Not! Then I'll make thee, rogue.

Jacomo. How! Dost call me rogue?   *Fight.*

Ithamore. Part 'em, master, part 'em.

Barabas. This is mere frailty, brethren, be content.
    Friar Barnardine, go you with Ithamore.
    You know my mind; let me alone with him.   100

Jacomo. Why does he go to thy house? Let him be gone.

Barabas. I'll give him something, and so stop his mouth.

                        Exit [Ithamore *with* Barnardine].

    I never heard of any man but he
    Malign'd the order of the Jacobins;
    But do you think that I believe his words?
    Why, brother, you converted Abigail;
    And I am bound in charity to requite it,
    And so I will. O Jacomo, fail not, but come.

Jacomo. But Barabas, who shall be your godfathers?
    For presently you shall be shriv'd.   110

Barabas. Marry, the Turk shall be one of my godfathers,
    But not a word to any of your covent.

Jacomo. I warrant thee, Barabas.   *Exit.*

Barabas. So, now the fear is past, and I am safe;
    For he that shriv'd her is within my house.
    What if I murder'd him ere Jacomo comes?
    Now I have such a plot for both their lives,
    As never Jew nor Christian knew the like:
    One turn'd my daughter, therefore he shall die;

112 covent] convent

The other knows enough to have my life,   120
Therefore 'tis not requisite he should live.
But are not both these wise men, to suppose
That I will leave my house, my goods, and all,
To fast and be well whipp'd? I'll none of that.
Now Friar Barnardine, I come to you;
I'll feast you, lodge you, give you fair words,
And after that, I and my trusty Turk—
No more but so: it must and shall be done.

Enter Ithamore.

Ithamore, tell me, is the friar asleep?

Ithamore. Yes; and I know not what the reason is,   130
Do what I can, he will not strip himself,
Nor go to bed, but sleeps in his own clothes.
I fear me he mistrusts what we intend.

Barabas. No, 'tis an order which the friars use:
Yet if he knew our meanings, could he scape?

Ithamore. No, none can hear him, cry he ne'er so loud.

Barabas. Why, true; therefore did I place him there:
The other chambers open towards the street.

Ithamore. You loiter, master; wherefore stay we thus?
O how I long to see him shake his heels!   140

Barabas. Come on, sirrah, off with your girdle; make a handsome noose.
Friar, awake!

Barnardine. What, do you mean to strangle me?

Ithamore. Yes, 'cause you use to confess.

Barabas. Blame not us, but the proverb: Confess and be hanged. Pull hard!

Barnardine. What, will you have my life?

Barabas. Pull hard, I say. You would have had my goods.

Ithamore. Ay, and our lives too, therefore pull amain!
'Tis neatly done, sir; here's no print at all.

Barabas. Then is it as it should be. Take him up.   150

Ithamore. Nay, master, be ruled by me a little. So, let him lean upon his
staff. Excellent! He stands as if he were begging of bacon.

Barabas. Who would not think but that this friar liv'd? What time o' night
is't now, sweet Ithamore?

Ithamore. Towards one.

Barabas. Then will not Jacomo be long from hence.   *Exeunt.*

Enter Jacomo.

Jacomo. This is the hour wherein I shall proceed!
O happy hour, wherein I shall convert

128 s.d. *Enter* Ithamore] Ithamore enters from the inner stage, drawing back the curtain
to reveal Barnardine asleep.   157 proceed] prosper

An infidel, and bring his gold into our treasury!
But soft, is not this Barnardine? It is;   160
And understanding I should come this way,
Stands here o' purpose, meaning me some wrong,
And intercept my going to the Jew.
Barnardine!
Wilt thou not speak? Thou think'st I see thee not.
Away, I'd wish thee, and let me go by:
No, wilt thou not? Nay then, I'll force my way;
And see, a staff stands ready for the purpose.
As thou lik'st that, stop me another time!   *Strike him, he falls.*

Enter Barabas [*and* Ithamore].

Barabas. Why, how now Jacomo, what hast thou done?   170
Jacomo. Why, stricken him that would have struck at me.
Barabas. Who is it? Barnardine! Now, out, alas, he is slain!
Ithamore. Ay, master, he's slain; look how his brains drop out on's nose.
Jacomo. Good sirs, I have done't: but nobody knows it but you two; I may
    escape.
Barabas. So might my man and I hang with you for company.
Ithamore. No, let us bear him to the magistrates.
Jacomo. Good Barabas, let me go.
Barabas. No, pardon me, the law must have his course.
    I must be forc'd to give in evidence,   180
    That being importun'd by this Barnardine
    To be a Christian, I shut him out,
    And there he sate. Now I, to keep my word,
    And give my goods and substance to your house,
    Was up thus early, with intent to go
    Unto your friary, because you stay'd.
Ithamore. Fie upon 'em! Master, will you turn Christian, when holy friars
    turn devils and murder one another?
Barabas. No, for this example I'll remain a Jew.
    Heaven bless me! What, a friar a murderer?   190
    When shall you see a Jew commit the like?
Ithamore. Why, a Turk could ha' done no more.
Barabas. Tomorrow is the sessions; you shall to it.
    Come Ithamore, let's help to take him hence.
Jacomo. Villains, I am a sacred person; touch me not.
Barabas. The law shall touch you, we'll but lead you, we.
    'Las, I could weep at your calamity!
    Take in the staff too, for that must be shown:
    Law wills that each particular be known.   *Exeunt.*

[*Scaena 2*]

Enter Courtesan [Bellamira] *and* Pilia-Borza.

Bellamira. Pilia-Borza, didst thou meet with Ithamore?

Pilia-Borza. I did.

Bellamira. And didst thou deliver my letter?

Pilia-Borza. I did.

Bellamira. And what think'st thou? Will he come?

Pilia-Borza. I think so, and yet I cannot tell; for at the reading of the letter, he looked like a man of another world.

Bellamira. Why so?

Pilia-Borza. That such a base slave as he should be saluted by such a tall   10
man as I am, from such a beautiful dame as you.

Bellamira. And what said he?

Pilia-Borza. Not a wise word; only gave me a nod, as who should say, 'Is it even so?'; and so I left him, being driven to a non-plus at the critical aspect of my terrible countenance.

Bellamira. And where didst meet him?

Pilia-Borza. Upon mine own freehold, within forty foot of the gallows, conning his neck-verse, I take it, looking of a friar's execution; whom I saluted with an old hempen proverb, *Hodie tibi, cras mihi*, and so I left him to the mercy of the hangman; but the exercise being done, see where he comes.   20

Enter Ithamore.

Ithamore. I never knew a man take his death so patiently as this friar. He was ready to leap off ere the halter was about his neck; and, when the hangman had put on his hempen tippet, he made such haste to his prayers, as if he had had another cure to serve. Well, go whither he will, I'll be none of his followers in haste. And now I think on't, going to the execution, a fellow met me with a muschatoes like a raven's wing, and a dagger with a hilt like a warming pan; and he gave me a letter from one Madam Bellamira, saluting me in such sort as if he had meant to make clean my boots with his lips. The effect was, that I should come to her house. I wonder what the reason is; it may be she sees more in me than I can find in myself; for she writes further, that she loves me ever since she saw me, and who would not requite such love? Here's her house; and here

13 critical aspect] as of some malignant star   16 mine own freehold] his 'patch', the
land where he picks pockets   17 conning his neck-verse] The beginning of Psalm 51 was
read aloud by a criminal to entitle him to benefit of clergy; illiterates, by attending executions,
might learn the words by heart.   18 *Hodie tibi, cras mihi*] 'You today and me tomorrow'
26 muschatoes] moustache

she comes. And now would I were gone! I am not worthy to look upon her.

Pilia-Borza. This is the gentleman you writ to.

Ithamore. Gentleman! He flouts me: what gentry can be in a poor Turk of tenpence? I'll be gone.

Bellamira. Is't not a sweet-faced youth, Pilia?

Ithamore. Again, sweet youth! Did not you, sir, bring the sweet youth a letter?   40

Pilia-Borza. I did, sir, and from this gentlewoman, who, as myself and the rest of the family, stand or fall at your service.

Bellamira. Though woman's modesty should hale me back,
      I can withhold no longer; welcome, sweet love.

Ithamore. Now am I clean, or rather foully, out of the way.

Bellamira. Whither so soon?

Ithamore. I'll go steal some money from my master to make me handsome. Pray pardon me; I must go see a ship discharged.

Bellamira. Canst thou be so unkind to leave me thus?

Pilia-Borza. And ye did but know how she loves you, sir!   50

Ithamore. Nay, I care not how much she loves me. Sweet Allamira, would I had my master's wealth for thy sake!

Pilia-Borza. And you can have it, sir, and if you please.

Ithamore. If 'twere above ground, I could and would have it; but he hides and buries it up as partridges do their eggs, under the earth.

Pilia-Borza. And is't not possible to find it out?

Ithamore. By no means possible.

Bellamira (*aside to* Pilia-Borza). What shall we do with this base villain, then?   59

Pilia-Borza. Let me alone; do but you speak him fair:—But you know some secrets of the Jew, which, if they were reveal'd, would do him harm.

Ithamore. Ay, and such as—go to, no more! I'll make him send me half he has, and glad he scapes so too. Pen and ink: I'll write unto him; we'll have money straight.

Pilia-Borza. Send for a hundred crowns at least.

Ithamore. Ten hundred thousand crowns.   *He writes.*
      'Master Barabas—'

Pilia-Borza. Write not so submissively, but threatening him.

Ithamore. 'Sirrah Barabas, send me a hundred crowns.'

Pilia-Borza. Put in two hundred at least.   70

Ithamore. 'I charge thee send me three hundred by this bearer, and this shall be your warrant: if you do not—no more but so.'

Pilia-Borza. Tell him you will confess.

Ithamore. 'Otherwise I'll confess all.' Vanish, and return in a twinkle.

---

72 no more but so] A vague threat, which Pilia-Borza converts into a more precise one.

Pilia-Borza. Let me alone; I'll use him in his kind.
Ithamore. Hang him, Jew!   *Exit* [Pilia-Borza].
Bellamira. Now, gentle Ithamore, lie in my lap.
    Where are my maids? Provide a running banquet;
    Send to the merchant, bid him bring me silks;
    Shall Ithamore my love go in such rags?   80
Ithamore. And bid the jeweller come hither too.
Bellamira. I have no husband, sweet; I'll marry thee.
Ithamore. Content: but we will leave this paltry land,
    And sail from hence to Greece, to lovely Greece.
    I'll be thy Jason, thou my golden fleece;
    Where painted carpets o'er the meads are hurl'd,
    And Bacchus' vineyards overspread the world;
    Where woods and forests go in goodly green;
    I'll be Adonis, thou shalt be Love's Queen;
    The meads, the orchards, and the primrose-lanes,   90
    Instead of sedge and reed, bear sugar-canes:
    Thou in those groves, by Dis above,
    Shalt live with me and be my love.
Bellamira. Whither will I not go with gentle Ithamore?

Enter Pilia-Borza.

Ithamore. How now? Hast thou the gold?
Pilia-Borza. Yes.
Ithamore. But came it freely? Did the cow give down her milk freely?
Pilia-Borza. At reading of the letter, he stared and stamped, and turned
    aside. I took him by the beard, and looked upon him thus; told him he
    were best to send it. Then he hugged and embraced me.   100
Ithamore. Rather for fear than love.
Pilia-Borza. Then like a Jew he laughed and jeered, and told me he loved
    me for your sake, and said what a faithful servant you had been.
Ithamore. The more villain he to keep me thus: here's goodly 'parel, is
    there not?
Pilia-Borza. To conclude, he gave me ten crowns.
Ithamore. But ten? I'll not leave him worth a grey groat. Give me a ream
    of paper: we'll have a kingdom of gold for't.
Pilia-Borza. Write for five hundred crowns.
Ithamore. 'Sirrah Jew, as you love your life, send me five hundred crowns,
    and give the bearer a hundred.' Tell him I must have't.   111
Pilia-Borza. I warrant your worship shall have't.

75 in his kind] as he deserves   78 running banquet] light banquet   92 Dis] god of
the underworld. The lines are a parody of Marlowe's own verses, 'The Passionate
Shepherd to his Love'.

Ithamore. And if he ask why I demand so much, tell him I scorn to write a
line under a hundred crowns.

Pilia-Borza. You'd make a rich poet, sir. I am gone.   *Exit.*

Ithamore. Take thou the money; spend it for my sake.

Bellamira. 'Tis not thy money, but thyself I weigh.

    Thus Bellamira esteems of gold;   [*Throw it aside.*]
                  But thus of thee.   *Kiss him.*

Ithamore. That kiss again! She runs division of my lips. What an eye she
casts on me! It twinkles like a star.   120

Bellamira. Come, my dear love, let's in and sleep together.

Ithamore. O, that ten thousand nights were put in one, that we might sleep
seven years together afore we wake!

Bellamira. Come, amorous wag, first banquet, and then sleep.   [*Exeunt.*]

[*Scaena* 3]

Enter Barabas, *reading a letter.*

Barabas. 'Barabas, send me three hundred crowns'—
    Plain Barabas! O that wicked courtesan!
    He was not wont to call me Barabas—
    'Or else I will confess'—ay, there it goes:
    But, if I get him, *coupe de gorge* for that.
    He sent a shaggy, totter'd, staring slave,
    That when he speaks, draws out his grisly beard,
    And winds it twice or thrice about his ear;
    Whose face has been a grindstone for men's swords;
    His hands are hack'd, some fingers cut quite off,   10
    Who when he speaks, grunts like a hog, and looks
    Like one that is employ'd in catzery
    And cross-biting; such a rogue
    As is the husband to a hundred whores:
    And I by him must send three hundred crowns!
    Well, my hope is, he will not stay there still;
    And when he comes—O, that he were but here!

             Enter Pilia-Borza.

Pilia-Borza. Jew, I must ha' more gold.

Barabas. Why, want'st thou any of thy tale?

Pilia-Borza. No, but three hundred will not serve his turn.   20

---

119 runs division] plays swiftly (as on a musical instrument)   IV, iii, 4 *coupe de gorge*]
'cut his throat'   6 totter'd] ragged   12 catzery] bawdry   13 cross-biting] swindling
19 tale] sum

Barabas. Not serve his turn, sir?

Pilia-Borza. No, sir; and therefore I must have five hundred more.

Barabas. I'll rather—

Pilia-Borza. O, good words, sir, and send it you were best; see, there's his letter.

Barabas. Might he not as well come as send? Pray, bid him come and fetch it: what he writes for you, ye shall have straight.

Pilia-Borza. Ay, and the rest too, or else—

Barabas [*aside*]. I must make this villain away—Please you dine with me, sir, and you shall be most heartily (*Aside.*) poisoned.　30

Pilia-Borza. No, God-a-mercy; shall I have these crowns?

Barabas. I cannot do it; I have lost my keys.

Pilia-Borza. O, if that be all, I can pick ope your locks.

Barabas. Or climb up to my counting-house window: you know my meaning.

Pilia-Borza. I know enough, and therefore talk not to me of your counting-house. The gold, or know, Jew, it is in my power to hang thee.

Barabas. I am betray'd.
　'Tis not five hundred crowns that I esteem;
　I am not mov'd at that: this angers me,
　That he, who knows I love him as myself,　40
　Should write in this imperious vein. Why sir,
　You know I have no child, and unto whom
　Should I leave all, but unto Ithamore?

Pilia-Borza. Here's many words, but no crowns: the crowns!

Barabas. Commend me to him, sir, most humbly,
　And unto your good mistress as unknown.

Pilia-Borza. Speak, shall I have 'em, sir?

Barabas. Sir, here they are.
　[*Aside.*] O, that I should part with so much gold!—
　Here, take 'em, fellow, with as good a will—　50
　[*Aside.*] As I would see thee hang'd!—O, love stops my breath!
　Never lov'd man servant as I do Ithamore.

Pilia-Borza. I know it, sir.

Barabas. Pray when, sir, shall I see you at my house?

Pilia-Borza. Soon enough to your cost, sir. Fare you well. 　*Exit.*

Barabas. Nay to thine own cost, villain, if thou com'st!
　Was ever Jew tormented as I am?
　To have a shag-rag knave to come convey
　Three hundred crowns, and then five hundred crowns!
　Well, I must seek a means to rid 'em all,　60
　And presently; for in his villainy

46 as unknown] as yet unknown to me　58 come convey] Ed. (come Q). Another word has to be supplied and 'convey', meaning steal as well as carry, seems appropriate.

He will tell all he knows, and I shall die for't.
I have it:
I will in some disguise go see the slave,
And how the villain revels with my gold.   *Exit.*

[*Scaena 4*]

Enter Courtesan [Bellamira], Ithamore, Pilia-Borza.

Bellamira. I'll pledge thee, love, and therefore drink it off.
Ithamore. Say'st thou me so? Have at it! And, do you hear ...
                                                          [*Whispers to her.*]
Bellamira. Go to, it shall be so.
Ithamore. Of that condition I will drink it up: here's to thee.
Bellamira. Nay, I'll have all or none.
Ithamore. There, if thou lov'st me, do not leave a drop.
Bellamira. Love thee! Fill me three glasses.
Ithamore. Three and fifty dozen: I'll pledge thee.
Pilia-Borza. Knavely spoke, and like a knight-at-arms.
Ithamore. Hey, *Rivo Castiliano!* A man's a man.   10
Bellamira. Now to the Jew.
Ithamore. Ha! To the Jew; and send me money you were best.
Pilia-Borza. What wouldst thou do, if he should send thee none?
Ithamore. Do nothing. But I know what I know: he's a murderer.
Bellamira. I had not thought he had been so brave a man.
Ithamore. You knew Mathias and the Governor's son? He and I killed 'em
  both, and yet never touched 'em.
Pilia-Borza. O bravely done!
Ithamore. I carried the broth that poisoned the nuns; and he and I—snicle!
  hand to! fast!—strangled a friar.   20
Bellamira. You two alone?
Ithamore. We two; and 'twas never known, nor never shall be for me.
Pilia-Borza [*aside to* Bellamira]. This shall with me unto the Governor.
Bellamira [*aside to* Pilia-Borza]. And fit it should: but first let's ha' more
  gold.
     Come, gentle Ithamore, lie in my lap.
Ithamore. Love me little, love me long: let music rumble,
     Whilst I in thy incony lap do tumble.
                    Enter Barabas *with a lute, disguised.*
Bellamira. A French musician! Come, let's hear your skill.
Barabas. Must tuna my lute for sound, twang twang first.   30

10 *Rivo Castiliano*] 'Let the drink flow'   19 snicle . . . fast] Ithamore's acted version of
the murder.   28 incony] loving

Ithamore. Wilt drink, Frenchman? Here's to thee with a—Pox on this drun-
    ken hiccup!

Barabas. Gramercy, monsieur.

Bellamira. Prithee, Pilia-Borza, bid the fiddler give me the posy in his hat
    there.

Pilia-Borza. Sirrah, you must give my mistress your posy.

Barabas. A votre commandement, madame.

Bellamira. How sweet, my Ithamore, the flowers smell!

Ithamore. Like thy breath, sweetheart; no violet like 'em.

Pilia-Borza. Foh! Methinks they stink like a hollyhock.   40

Barabas [*aside*]. So, now I am reveng'd upon 'em all.
       The scent thereof was death; I poison'd it.

Ithamore. Play, fiddler, or I'll cut your cat's guts into chitterlings.

Barabas. Pardonnez moi, be no in tune yet; so, now, now all be in.

Ithamore. Give him a crown, and fill me out more wine.

Pilia-Borza. There's two crowns for thee; play.

Barabas (*aside*). How liberally the villain gives me mine own gold!

                                          [*He plays.*]

Pilia-Borza. Methinks he fingers very well.

Barabas (*aside*). So did you when you stole my gold.

Pilia-Borza. How swift he runs!   50

Barabas (*aside*). You run swifter when you threw my gold out of my window.

Bellamira. Musician, hast been in Malta long?

Barabas. Two, three, four month, madam.

Ithamore. Dost not know a Jew, one Barabas?

Barabas. Very mush, monsieur, you no be his man?

Pilia-Borza. His man?

Ithamore. I scorn the peasant: tell him so.

Barabas [*aside*]. He knows it already.

Ithamore. 'Tis a strange thing of that Jew: he lives upon pickled grass-
    hoppers and sauced mushrooms.   60

Barabas (*aside*). What a slave's this! The Governor feeds not as I do.

Ithamore. He never put on clean shirt since he was circumcised.

Barabas (*aside*). O rascal! I change myself twice a day.

Ithamore. The hat he wears, Judas left under the elder when he hanged
    himself.

Barabas (*aside*). 'Twas sent me for a present from the Great Cham.

Pilia-Borza. A masty slave he is. Whither now, fiddler?

Barabas. Pardonnez moi, monsieur; me be no well.   *Exit.*

Pilia-Borza. Farewell, fiddler. One letter more to the Jew.

Bellamira. Prithee sweet love, one more, and write it sharp.   70

Ithamore. No, I'll send by word of mouth now. Bid him deliver thee a

66 Great Cham] Emperor of Tartary   67 masty] swinish

thousand crowns, by the same token that the nuns loved rice, that Friar
Barnardine slept in his own clothes; any of 'em will do it.

Pilia-Borza. Let me alone to urge it, now I know the meaning.

Ithamore. The meaning has a meaning. Come, let's in:

   To undo a Jew is charity, and not sin.   *Exeunt.*

Actus Quintus   [Scaena 1]

Enter Governor [Ferneze], *Knights, Martin del Bosco* [*and* Officers].

Ferneze. Now, gentlemen, betake you to your arms,
   And see that Malta be well fortified;
   And it behoves you to be resolute,
   For Calymath, having hover'd here so long,
   Will win the town, or die before the walls.

1 Knight. And die he shall: for we will never yield.

Enter Courtesan [Bellamira] *and* Pilia-Borza.

Bellamira. O bring us to the Governor!

Ferneze. Away with her! She is a courtesan.

Bellamira. Whate'er I am, yet Governor, hear me speak.
   I bring thee news by whom thy son was slain: 10
   Mathias did it not; it was the Jew.

Pilia-Borza. Who, besides the slaughter of these gentlemen,
   Poison'd his own daughter and the nuns,
   Strangled a friar, and I know not what
   Mischief beside.

Ferneze.   Had we but proof of this—

Bellamira. Strong proof, my lord: his man's now at my lodging
   That was his agent; he'll confess it all.

Ferneze. Go fetch him straight.   [*Exeunt* Officers.]
                  I always fear'd that Jew.

Enter [Officers *with*] Barabas *and* Ithamore.

Barabas. I'll go alone; dogs, do not hale me thus.   19

Ithamore. Nor me neither; I cannot outrun you, constable. O, my belly!

Barabas. One dram of powder more had made all sure:
   What a damn'd slave was I!

Ferneze. Make fires, heat irons, let the rack be fetch'd.

1 Knight. Nay stay, my lord; 't may be he will confess.

Barabas. Confess! What mean you, lords? Who should confess?

Ferneze. Thou and thy Turk; 'twas you that slew my son.

Ithamore. Guilty, my lord, I confess. Your son and Mathias were both con-
tracted unto Abigail: 'a forged a counterfeit challenge.
Barabas. Who carried that challenge?
Ithamore. I carried it, I confess; but who writ it? Marry, even he that
strangled Barnardine, poisoned the nuns and his own daughter.   31
Ferneze. Away with him! His sight is death to me.
Barabas. For what? You men of Malta, hear me speak.
    She is a courtesan, and he a thief,
    And he my bondman; let me have law,
    For none of this can prejudice my life.
Ferneze. Once more, away with him! You shall have law.
Barabas. Devils, do your worst! I'll live in spite of you.
    As these have spoke, so be it to their souls!—
    [*Aside.*] I hope the poison'd flowers will work anon.   40

            [*Exeunt* Officers *with* Barabas *and* Ithamore;
            Bellamira, *and* Pilia-Borza.]

        Enter Katharine.

Katharine. Was my Mathias murder'd by the Jew?
    Ferneze, 'twas thy son that murder'd him.
Ferneze. Be patient, gentle madam; it was he;
    He forg'd the daring challenge made them fight.
Katharine. Where is the Jew? Where is that murderer?
Ferneze. In prison, till the law has pass'd on him.

        Enter Officer.

Officer. My lord, the courtesan and her man are dead;
    So is the Turk and Barabas the Jew.
Ferneze. Dead?
Officer. Dead, my lord, and here they bring his body.   50
Bosco. This sudden death of his is very strange.

    [*Enter* Officers, *carrying* Barabas *as dead.*]

Ferneze. Wonder not at it, sir; the heavens are just.
    Their deaths were like their lives; then think not of 'em.
    Since they are dead, let them be buried.
    For the Jew's body, throw that o'er the walls,
    To be a prey for vultures and wild beasts.
    So, now away and fortify the town.   [*Exeunt leaving* Barabas.]
Barabas. What, all alone? Well fare, sleepy drink!
    I'll be reveng'd on this accursed town;
    For by my means Calymath shall enter in.   60
    I'll help to slay their children and their wives,

55 o'er the walls] Barabas' 'body' may be thrown to the front of the stage, remaining there
until he rises. Ferneze's 'So' suggests that his order has been carried out.

To fire the churches, pull their houses down,
Take my goods too, and seize upon my lands.
I hope to see the Governor a slave,
And, rowing in a galley, whipp'd to death.

Enter Calymath, Bassoes, Turks.

Calymath. Whom have we there? A spy?
Barabas. Yes, my good lord, one that can spy a place
Where you may enter, and surprise the town.
My name is Barabas; I am a Jew.
Calymath. Art thou that Jew whose goods we heard were sold   70
For tribute money?
Barabas.   The very same, my lord:
And since that time they have hir'd a slave, my man,
To accuse me of a thousand villainies.
I was imprisoned, but scap'd their hands,
Calymath. Didst break prison?
Barabas. No, no:
I drank of poppy and cold mandrake juice;
And being asleep, belike they thought me dead,
And threw me o'er the walls: so, or how else,
The Jew is here, and rests at your command.   80
Calymath. 'Twas bravely done. But tell me, Barabas,
Canst thou, as thou report'st, make Malta ours?
Barabas. Fear not, my lord, for here, against the trench,
The rock is hollow, and of purpose digg'd,
To make a passage for the running streams
And common channels of the city.
Now, whilst you give assault unto the walls,
I'll lead five hundred soldiers through the vault,
And rise with them i' the middle of the town,
Open the gates for you to enter in,
And by this means the city is your own.   90
Calymath. If this be true, I'll make thee Governor.
Barabas. And if it be not true, then let me die.
Calymath. Thou'st doom'd thyself. Assault it presently.   *Exeunt.*

83 trench] Ed. (truce Q)   86 channels] sewers

[*Scaena 2*]

Alarms. Enter [Calymath *and other*] Turks, Barabas; *Governor*
[Ferneze] *and* Knights *prisoners*.

Calymath. Now vail your pride, you captive Christians,
    And kneel for mercy to your conquering foe.
    Now where's the hope you had of haughty Spain?
    Ferneze, speak; had it not been much better
    T' have kept thy promise than be thus surpris'd?
Ferneze. What should I say? We are captives, and must yield.
Calymath. Ay, villains, you must yield, and under Turkish yokes
    Shall groaning bear the burden of our ire.
    And Barabas, as erst we promis'd thee,
    For thy desert we make thee Governor;   10
    Use them at thy discretion.
Barabas.   Thanks, my lord.
Ferneze. O fatal day, to fall into the hands
    Of such a traitor and unhallow'd Jew!
    What greater misery could heaven inflict?
Calymath. 'Tis our command; and, Barabas, we give,
    To guard thy person, these our janizaries:
    Intreat them well, as we have used thee.
    And now, brave bassoes, come; we'll walk about
    The ruin'd town, and see the wrack we made.
    Farewell brave Jew, farewell great Barabas!   20
                        Exeunt [Calymath *and* Bassoes].
Barabas. May all good fortune follow Calymath!
    And now, as entrance to our safety,
    To prison with the Governor and these
    Captains, his consorts and confederates.
Ferneze. O villain, heaven will be reveng'd on thee.
                        Exeunt [*all except* Barabas].
Barabas. Away, no more; let him not trouble me.
    Thus hast thou gotten, by thy policy,
    No simple place, no small authority:
    I now am Governor of Malta; true,
    But Malta hates me, and in hating me   30
    My life's in danger; and what boots it thee,
    Poor Barabas, to be the Governor,
    Whenas thy life shall be at their command?
    No, Barabas, this must be look'd into;
    And, since by wrong thou got'st authority,

Maintain it bravely by firm policy;
At least, unprofitably lose it not.
For he that liveth in authority,
And neither gets him friends nor fills his bags,
Lives like the ass that Æsop speaketh of,   40
That labours with a load of bread and wine,
And leaves it off to snap on thistle-tops.
But Barabas will be more circumspect.
Begin betimes; occasion's bald behind:
Slip not thine opportunity, for fear too late
Thou seek'st for much, but canst not compass it.
Within here!

     Enter [Ferneze] *with a* Guard.

Ferneze.   My lord?
Barabas.   Ay, *lord*; thus slaves will learn.
Now, Governor—stand by there, wait within. [*Exeunt* Guard.]
This is the reason that I sent for thee:
Thou seest thy life and Malta's happiness   50
Are at my arbitrement; and Barabas
At his discretion may dispose of both.
Now tell me, Governor, and plainly too,
What think'st thou shall become of it and thee?
Ferneze. This Barabas: since things are in thy power,
I see no reason but of Malta's wrack,
Nor hope of thee but extreme cruelty.
Nor fear I death, nor will I flatter thee.
Barabas. Governor, good words, be not so furious.
'Tis not thy life which can avail me aught;   60
Yet you do live, and live for me you shall.
And as for Malta's ruin, think you not
'Twere slender policy for Barabas
To dispossess himself of such a place?
For sith, as once you said, within this isle,
In Malta here, that I have got my goods,
And in this city still have had success,
And now at length am grown your Governor,
Yourselves shall see it shall not be forgot;
For as a friend not known but in distress,   70
I'll rear up Malta now remediless.
Ferneze. Will Barabas recover Malta's loss?
Will Barabas be good to Christians?
Barabas. What wilt thou give me, Governor, to procure
A dissolution of the slavish bands

Wherein the Turk hath yok'd your land and you?
What will you give me if I render you
The life of Calymath, surprise his men,
And in an out-house of the city shut
His soldiers, till I have consum'd 'em all with fire?   80
What will you give him that procureth this?
Ferneze. Do but bring this to pass which thou pretend'st,
    Deal truly with us as thou intimat'st,
    And I will send amongst the citizens,
    And by my letters privately procure
    Great sums of money for thy recompense:
    Nay more, do this, and live thou Governor still.
Barabas. Nay, do thou this, Ferneze, and be free.
    Governor, I enlarge thee. Live with me;
    Go walk about the city, see thy friends.   90
    Tush, send not letters to 'em; go thy self,
    And let me see what money thou canst make.
    Here is my hand that I'll set Malta free.
    And thus we cast it: to a solemn feast
    I will invite young Selim-Calymath,
    Where be thou present, only to perform
    One stratagem that I'll impart to thee,
    Wherein no danger shall betide thy life,
    And I will warrant Malta free for ever.
Ferneze. Here is my hand; believe me, Barabas,   100
    I will be there, and do as thou desirest.
    When is the time?
Barabas.   Governor, presently.
    For Calymath, when he hath view'd the town,
    Will take his leave and sail toward Ottoman.
Ferneze. Then will I, Barabas, about this coin,
    And bring it with me to thee in the evening.
Barabas. Do so, but fail not. Now farewell, Ferneze.   [*Exit* Ferneze.]
    And thus far roundly goes the business:
    Thus loving neither, will I live with both,
    Making a profit of my policy;   110
    And he from whom my most advantage comes,
    Shall be my friend.
    This is the life we Jews are us'd to lead;
    And reason too, for Christians do the like.
    Well, now about effecting this device:
    First, to surprise great Selim's soldiers,

79 out-house of the city] house in the suburbs

And then to make provision for the feast,
That at one instant all things may be done.
My policy detests prevention.
To what event my secret purpose drives,
I know; and they shall witness with their lives.   120

Exit.

[*Scaena 3*]

Enter Calymath, Bassoes.

Calymath. Thus have we view'd the city, seen the sack,
And caus'd the ruins to be new-repair'd,
Two lofty turrets that command the town,
Which with our bombards' shot and basilisk
We rent in sunder at our entry:
And now I see the situation,
And how secure this conquer'd island stands,
Environ'd with the Mediterranean sea,
Strong countermur'd with other petty isles
And towards Calabria, back'd by Sicily   10
Where Syracusian Dionysius reign'd.
I wonder how it could be conquered thus.

Enter a Messenger.

Messenger. From Barabas, Malta's Governor, I bring
A message unto mighty Calymath:
Hearing his sovereign was bound for sea,
To sail to Turkey, to great Ottoman,
He humbly would entreat your majesty
To come and see his homely citadel,
And banquet with him ere thou leav'st the isle.

Calymath. To banquet with him in his citadel?   20
I fear me, messenger, to feast my train
Within a town of war so lately pillag'd,
Will be too costly and too troublesome;
Yet would I gladly visit Barabas,
For well has Barabas deserv'd of us.

Messenger. Selim, for that, thus saith the Governor:
That he hath in store a pearl so big,
So precious, and withal so orient,
As be it valu'd but indifferently,
The price thereof will serve to entertain   30

28 orient] precious

    Selim and all his soldiers for a month.
    Therefore he humbly would entreat your highness
    Not to depart till he has feasted you.
Calymath. I cannot feast my men in Malta walls,
    Except he place his tables in the streets.
Messenger. Know, Selim, that there is a monastery
    Which standeth as an out-house to the town;
    There will he banquet them but thee at home,
    With all thy bassoes and brave followers.
Calymath. Well, tell the Governor we grant his suit;   40
    We'll in this summer evening feast with him.
Messenger. I shall, my lord.   *Exit.*
Calymath. And now, bold bassoes, let us to our tents,
    And meditate how we may grace us best,
    To solemnize our Governor's great feast.   *Exeunt.*

[*Scaena 4*]

    Enter Governor [Ferneze], *Knights,* [Martin] *del Bosco.*

Ferneze. In this, my countrymen, be rul'd by me:
    Have special care that no man sally forth
    Till you shall hear a culverin discharg'd
    By him that bears the linstock, kindled thus;
    Then issue out and come to rescue me,
    For happily I shall be in distress,
    Or you released of this servitude.
1 Knight. Rather than thus to live as Turkish thralls,
    What will we not adventure?
Ferneze. On, then; be gone.   10
Knights. Farewell, grave Governor.   [*Exeunt.*]

[*Scaena 5*]

    Enter [Barabas] *with a hammer, above, very busy* [*and* Carpenters].

Barabas. How stand the cords? How hang these hinges, fast?
    Are all the cranes and pulleys sure?
Carpenter. All fast.
Barabas. Leave nothing loose, all levell'd to my mind.
    Why, now I see that you have art indeed.

V. iv, 3 culverin] cannon   4 linstock] long stick with light

There, carpenters, divide that gold amongst you.
Go, swill in bowls of sack and muscadine;
Down to the cellar, taste of all my wines.
Carpenter. We shall, my lord, and thank you. *Exeunt.*
Barabas. And, if you like them, drink your fill and die; 10
For so I live, perish may all the world.
Now Selim-Calymath, return me word
That thou wilt come, and I am satisfied.

Enter Messenger.

Now, sirrah; what, will he come?
Messenger. He will; and has commanded all his men
To come ashore, and march through Malta streets,
That thou mayst feast them in thy citadel.
Barabas. Then now are all things as my wish would have 'em;
There wanteth nothing but the Governor's pelf;
And see, he brings it. 20

Enter Ferneze.

Now, Governor, the sum.
Ferneze. With free consent, a hundred thousand pounds.
Barabas. Pounds say'st thou, Governor? Well, since it is no more,
I'll satisfy myself with that; nay, keep it still,
For if I keep not promise, trust not me.
And Governor, now partake my policy:
First, for his army, they are sent before,
Enter'd the monastery, and underneath
In several places are field-pieces pitch'd,
Bombards, whole barrels full of gunpowder, 30
That on the sudden shall dissever it
And batter all the stones about their ears,
Whence none can possibly escape alive.
Now as for Calymath and his consorts,
Here have I made a dainty gallery,
The floor whereof, this cable being cut,
Doth fall asunder, so that it doth sink
Into a deep pit past recovery.
Here, hold that knife; and when thou seest he comes,
And with his bassoes shall be blithely set, 40
A warning-piece shall be shot off from the tower,
To give thee knowledge when to cut the cord,
And fire the house. Say, will not this be brave?
Ferneze. O, excellent! Here, hold thee, Barabas;
I trust thy word; take what I promis'd thee.

Barabas. No, Governor, I'll satisfy thee first.
    Thou shalt not live in doubt of anything.
    Stand close, for here they come.   [Ferneze *retires.*]
                                Why, is not this
        A kingly kind of trade, to purchase towns   50
        By treachery, and sell 'em by deceit?
        Now tell me, worldlings, underneath the sun
        If greater falsehood ever has been done.

                    Enter Calymath *and* Bassoes.

Calymath. Come, my companion bassoes: see I pray,
        How busy Barabas is there above
        To entertain us in his gallery.
        Let us salute him. Save thee, Barabas!
Barabas. Welcome, great Calymath!
Ferneze. How the slave jeers at him!
Barabas. Will't please thee, mighty Selim-Calymath,   60
        To ascend our homely stairs?
Calymath.   Ay, Barabas.
        Come, bassoes, ascend.
Ferneze [*coming forward*].   Stay, Calymath;
        For I will show thee greater courtesy
        Than Barabas would have afforded thee.
Knight [*within*]. Sound a charge there!
    A charge, the cable cut. A cauldron discovered [*into which* Barabas *falls*].
Calymath. How now! What means this?
Barabas. Help, help me, Christians, help!
Ferneze. See, Calymath, this was devis'd for thee.
Calymath. Treason, treason! Bassoes, fly!
Ferneze. No, Selim, do not fly.   70
        See his end first, and fly then if thou canst.
Barabas. O help me, Selim! Help me, Christians!
        Governor, why stand you all so pitiless?
Ferneze. Should I in pity of thy plaints or thee,
        Accursed Barabas, base Jew, relent?
        No, thus I'll see thy treachery repaid,
        But wish thou hadst behav'd thee otherwise.
Barabas. You will not help me, then?
Ferneze.   No, villain, no.
Barabas. And villains, know you cannot help me now.
        Then Barabas, breathe forth thy latest fate,   80
        And in the fury of thy torments strive

65 charge] trumpet signal

To end thy life with resolution.
Know, Governor, 'twas I that slew thy son;
I fram'd the challenge that did make them meet.
Know, Calymath, I aim'd thy overthrow:
And had I but escap'd this stratagem,
I would have brought confusion on you all,
Damn'd Christians, dogs, and Turkish infidels!
But now begins the extremity of heat
To pinch me with intolerable pangs.   90
Die life! Fly soul! Tongue curse thy fill, and die!   [*Dies.*]

Calymath. Tell me, you Christians, what doth this portend?
Ferneze. This train he laid to have entrapp'd thy life.
Now Selim, note the unhallow'd deeds of Jews:
Thus he determin'd to have handled thee,
But I have rather chose to save thy life.

Calymath. Was this the banquet he prepar'd for us?
Let's hence, lest further mischief be pretended.

Ferneze. Nay, Selim, stay, for since we have thee here,
We will not let thee part so suddenly.   100
Besides, if we should let thee go, all's one,
For with thy galleys couldst thou not get hence,
Without fresh men to rig and furnish them.

Calymath. Tush, Governor, take thou no care for that.
My men are all aboard,
And do attend my coming there by this.

Ferneze. Why, heard'st thou not the trumpet sound a charge?
Calymath. Yes, what of that?
Ferneze.   Why, then the house was fir'd,
Blown up, and all thy soldiers massacred.

Calymath. O monstrous treason!
Ferneze.   A Jew's courtesy.   110
For he that did by treason work our fall,
By treason hath deliver'd thee to us.
Know therefore, till thy father hath made good
The ruins done to Malta and to us,
Thou canst not part; for Malta shall be freed,
Or Selim ne'er return to Ottoman.

Calymath. Nay rather, Christians, let me go to Turkey,
In person there to mediate your peace.
To keep me here will naught advantage you.

Ferneze. Content thee, Calymath, here thou must stay,   120
And live in Malta prisoner; for come all the world

93 train] snare   98 pretended] intended

  To rescue thee, so will we guard us now;
As sooner shall they drink the ocean dry,
Than conquer Malta, or endanger us.
So march away; and let due praise be given,
Neither to Fate nor Fortune, but to Heaven.   *[Exeunt.]*

       FINIS.

Edward II

The text of this play is based on the Octavo of 1594, perhaps the first but certainly the earliest surviving edition. Only one copy of this is now known to exist (in Zurich), but I have been able to use a photographic reprint of another, formerly in the Landesbibliothek of Cassel, Germany, which was destroyed in the bombing of that city. According to the title-page of this edition, the play was 'sundrie times publiquely acted' in London by the Servants of the Earl of Pembroke, a patron of Marlowe's in 1591.

Marlowe's chief source for this play was the standard Elizabethan history, Holinshed's *Chronicles of England*. Other historians provided him with minor details—the Bannockburn ballad (II.ii.189–94) might have come from Fabyan's *Chronycle*, and the episode of the shaving with puddle-water (V.iii.25 ff.) is to be found in Stow's *Annales*. The historical events which Marlowe compresses into the two hours' traffic of his stage stretch over twenty-three years, from the accession of Edward II in 1307 to the trial and execution of Mortimer in 1330, three years after the murder of the King.

The troublesome

raigne and lamentable death of
Edward *the second, King of*
England : with the tragicall
fall of proud Mortimer:

As it was sundrie times publiquely acted
in the honourable citie of London *, by the*
sight honourable the Earle of Pem-
brooke *his seruants.*

Written by Chri. Marlow *Gent.*

Imprinted at London for. *William* Iones,
dwelling neere Holbourne conduit at the
signe of the Gunne *,* 1594

[DRAMATIS PERSONAE

King Edward II
Prince Edward, his son; later *King Edward III*
Edmund Earl of Kent, the King's brother
Piers de Gaveston
The Earls of
   Warwick
   Lancaster
   Pembroke
   Arundel
   Leicester
   Berkeley
Mortimer (of Wigmore)
Mortimer Senior (of Chirk), his uncle
Spencer
Spencer the Father
Baldock
The Bishops of
   Coventry
   Canterbury
   Winchester
Beaumont
James, one of Pembroke's men
Levune
Sir John of Hainault
Rice ap Howell
Mayor of Bristol
Trussel
Gurney
Matrevis
Lightborn
Three Poor Men
Herald
Abbot
A Mower
Champion

Isabella, Queen to Edward II
Lady Margaret de Clare, betrothed to Gaveston

Lords, Ladies, Messengers, Soldiers, Attendants, Monks]

[Act I Scene i]

Enter Gaveston *reading on a letter that was brought him from the King.*

Gaveston. 'My father is deceas'd, come Gaveston,
    And share the kingdom with thy dearest friend.'
    Ah, words that make me surfeit with delight!
    What greater bliss can hap to Gaveston
    Than live and be the favourite of a king?
    Sweet prince I come; these, these thy amorous lines
    Might have enforc'd me to have swum from France,
    And like Leander, gasp'd upon the sand,
    So thou wouldst smile and take me in thy arms.
    The sight of London to my exil'd eyes   10
    Is as Elysium to a new-come soul:
    Not that I love the city or the men,
    But that it harbours him I hold so dear,
    The King, upon whose bosom let me die,
    And with the world be still at enmity.
    What need the arctic people love star-light
    To whom the sun shines both by day and night?
    Farewell base stooping to the lordly peers;
    My knee shall bow to none but to the King
    As for the multitude, that are but sparks   20
    Rak'd up in embers of their poverty,
    Tanti! I'll fan first on the wind,
    That glanceth at my lips and flieth away.
    But how now, what are these?

Enter three Poor Men.

Poor Men. Such as desire your worship's service.
Gaveston. What canst thou do?
1 Poor Man. I can ride.
Gaveston. But I have no horses. What art thou?
2 Poor Man. A traveller.
Gaveston. Let me see, thou wouldst do well to wait at my trencher and tell
    me lies at dinner-time; and as I like your discoursing, I'll have you. And
    what art thou?   32
3 Poor Man. A soldier, that hath serv'd against the Scot.
Gaveston. Why, there are hospitals for such as you;
    I have no war, and therefore, sir, be gone.
3 Poor Man. Farewell, and perish by a soldier's hand,

14 die] swoon   22 *Tanti*] 'So much for them'   34 hospitals] workhouses

> That wouldst reward them with an hospital.

Gaveston. Ay, ay. These words of his move me as much
>> As if a goose should play the porpintine,
>> And dart her plumes, thinking to pierce my breast.   40
>> But yet it is no pain to speak men fair;
>> I'll flatter these, and make them live in hope.
>> You know that I came lately out of France,
>> And yet I have not view'd my lord the King;
>> If I speed well, I'll entertain you all.

Poor Men. We thank your worship.

Gaveston. I have some business; leave me to myself.

Poor Men. We will wait here about the court.   *Exeunt.*

Gaveston. Do. These are not men for me;
>> I must have wanton poets, pleasant wits.   50
>> Musicians, that with touching of a string
>> May draw the pliant King which way I please;
>> Music and poetry is his delight:
>> Therefore I'll have Italian masques by night,
>> Sweet speeches, comedies, and pleasing shows;
>> And in the day, when he shall walk abroad,
>> Like sylvan nymphs my pages shall be clad;
>> My men like satyrs grazing on the lawns
>> Shall with their goat-feet dance an antic hay;
>> Sometime a lovely boy in Dian's shape,   60
>> With hair that gilds the water as it glides,
>> Crownets of pearl about his naked arms,
>> And in his sportful hands an olive tree
>> To hide those parts which men delight to see,
>> Shall bathe him in a spring; and there hard by,
>> One like Actaeon peeping through the grove,
>> Shall by the angry goddess be transform'd,
>> And running in the likeness of an hart,
>> By yelping hounds pull'd down, and seem to die.
>> Such things as these best please his majesty.   70
>> My lord! Here comes the King and the nobles
>> From the parliament; I'll stand aside.

> *Enter the King* [Edward], *Lancaster, Mortimer Senior, Mortimer,*
>> *Edmund Earl of* Kent, *Guy Earl of* Warwick, [*and* Lords] *etc.*

Edward. Lancaster.

---

39 porpintine] porcupine   59 antic hay] grotesque country dance   60 Dian's shape]
in the appearance of Diana who was spied upon while she was bathing by Actaeon

Lancaster. My lord?

Gaveston. That Earl of Lancaster do I abhor.

Edward. Will you not grant me this? [*Aside.*] In spite of them
    I'll have my will, and these two Mortimers
    That cross me thus shall know I am displeas'd.

Mortimer Senior. If you love us, my lord, hate Gaveston.

Gaveston. That villain Mortimer, I'll be his death.   80

Mortimer. Mine uncle here, this earl, and I myself,
    Were sworn to your father at his death
    That he should ne'er return into the realm;
    And know, my lord, ere I will break my oath,
    This sword of mine that should offend your foes
    Shall sleep within the scabbard at thy need,
    And underneath thy banners march who will,
    For Mortimer will hang his armour up.

Gaveston. Mort Dieu!

Edward. Well Mortimer, I'll make thee rue these words;   90
    Beseems it thee to contradict thy king?
    Frownst thou thereat, aspiring Lancaster?
    The sword shall plane the furrows of thy brows,
    And hew these knees that now are grown so stiff.
    I will have Gaveston; and you shall know
    What danger 'tis to stand against your king.

Gaveston. Well done Ned.

Lancaster. My lord, who do you thus incense your peers,
    That naturally would love and honour you
    But for that base and obscure Gaveston?   100
    Four earldoms have I besides Lancaster—
    Derby, Salisbury, Lincoln, Leicester;
    These will I sell to give my soldiers pay
    Ere Gaveston shall stay within the realm.
    Therefore if he be come, expel him straight.

Kent. Barons and earls, your pride hath made me mute,
    But now I'll speak, and to the proof I hope.
    I do remember in my father's days,
    Lord Percy of the north, being highly moved,
    Brav'd Mowbery in presence of the King;   110
    For which, had not his highness lov'd him well,
    He should have lost his head; but with his look
    The undaunted spirit of Percy was appeas'd,
    And Mowbery and he were reconcil'd:
    Yet dare you brave the King unto his face.
    Brother, revenge it; and let these their heads

Preach upon poles for trespass of their tongues.

Warwick. O our heads!

Edward. Ay, yours; and therefore I would wish you grant.

Warwick. Bridle thy anger, gentle Mortimer.   120

Mortimer. I cannot nor I will not; I must speak.

Cousin, our hands I hope shall fence our heads,
And strike off his that makes you threaten us.
Come uncle, let us leave the brainsick King,
And henceforth parley with our naked swords.

Mortimer Senior. Wiltshire hath men enough to save our heads.

Warwick. All Warwickshire will love him for my sake.

Lancaster. And northward Gaveston hath many friends.

Adieu my lord; and either change your mind,
Or look to see the throne where you should sit   130
To float in blood, and at thy wanton head
The glozing head of thy base minion thrown.   *Exeunt Nobiles.*

Edward. I cannot brook these haughty menaces:
Am I a king and must be overrul'd?
Brother, display my ensigns in the field;
I'll bandy with the barons and the earls,
And either die or live with Gaveston.

Gaveston. I can no longer keep me from my lord.   [*Comes forward.*]

Edward. What, Gaveston, welcome! Kiss not my hand,
Embrace me Gaveston as I do thee: 140
Why shouldst thou kneel? Know'st thou not who I am?
Thy friend, thy self, another Gaveston!
Not Hylas was more mourn'd of Hercules
Than thou hast been of me since thy exile.

Gaveston. And since I went from hence, no soul in hell
Hath felt more torment than poor Gaveston.

Edward. I know it. Brother, welcome home my friend.
Now let the treacherous Mortimers conspire,
And that high-minded Earl of Lancaster:
I have my wish, in that I joy thy sight,   150
And sooner shall the sea o'erwhelm my land
Than bear the ship that shall transport thee hence!
I here create thee Lord High Chamberlain,
Chief Secretary to the state and me,
Earl of Cornwall, King and Lord of Man.

117 Preach upon poles] As a warning to others, the heads of executed traitors were displayed
on poles.   132 glozing] flattering   136 bandy] volley (as at tennis)   143 Hylas]
kidnapped from the Argonauts at Mysia   155 King . . . Man] Rulers of the Isle of Man
had certain sovereign rights until 1829.

Gaveston. My lord, these titles far exceed my worth.
Kent. Brother, the least of these may well suffice
    For one of greater birth than Gaveston.
Edward. Cease brother, for I cannot brook these words.
    Thy worth, sweet friend, is far above my gifts,   160
    Therefore to equal it, receive my heart.
    If for these dignities thou be envied
    I'll give thee more, for but to honour thee
    Is Edward pleas'd with kingly regiment.
    Fear'st thou thy person? Thou shalt have a guard.
    Wants thou gold? Go to my treasury.
    Wouldst thou be lov'd and fear'd? Receive my seal;
    Save or condemn, and in our name command
    Whatso thy mind affects or fancy likes.
Gaveston. It shall suffice me to enjoy your love,   170
    Which whiles I have, I think myself as great
    As Caesar riding in the Roman street
    With captive kings at his triumphant car.

Enter the Bishop of Coventry.

Edward. Whither goes my lord of Coventry so fast?
Coventry. To celebrate your father's exequies.
    But is that wicked Gaveston return'd?
Edward. Ay priest; and lives to be reveng'd on thee
    That wert the only cause of his exile.
Gaveston. 'Tis true, and but for reverence of these robes
    Thou shouldst not plod one foot beyond this place.   180
Coventry. I did no more than I was bound to do;
    And Gaveston, unless thou be reclaim'd,
    As then I did incense the parliament,
    So will I now, and thou shalt back to France.
Gaveston. Saving your reverence, you must pardon me.
Edward. Throw off his golden mitre, rend his stole,
    And in the channel christen him anew.
Kent. Ah brother, lay not violent hands on him,
    For he'll complain unto the See of Rome
Gaveston. Let him complain unto the See of Hell;   190
    I'll be reveng'd on him for my exile.
Edward. No, spare his life, but seize upon his goods;
    Be thou Lord Bishop and receive his rents,
    And make him serve thee as thy chaplain;
    I give him thee. Here, use him as thou wilt.

182 reclaim'd] reformed   187 channel] gutter

Gaveston. He shall to prison, and there die in bolts.

Edward. Ay, to the Tower, the Fleet, or where thou wilt.

Coventry. For this offence be thou accurst of God.

Edward. Who's there? Convey this priest to the Tower.

Coventry. True, true!   [*Exit Bishop guarded.*]

Edward. But in the meantime, Gaveston, away
  And take possession of his house and goods;
  Come, follow me, and thou shalt have my guard
  To see it done and bring thee safe again.

Gaveston. What should a priest do with so fair a house?
  A prison may beseem his holiness.   [*Exeunt.*]

[Scene ii]

Enter [*on one side*] *both the* Mortimers, [*on the other*] Warwick *and*
Lancaster.

Warwick. 'Tis true, the Bishop is in the Tower,
  And goods and body given to Gaveston.

Lancaster. What, will they tyrannize upon the Church?
  Ah wicked King, accursed Gaveston!
  This ground which is corrupted with their steps
  Shall be their timeless sepulchre, or mine.

Mortimer. Well, let that peevish Frenchman guard him sure;
  Unless his breast be sword-proof he shall die.

Mortimer Senior. How now, why droops the Earl of Lancaster?

Mortimer. Wherefore is Guy of Warwick discontent?   10

Lancaster. That villain Gaveston is made an earl.

Mortimer Senior. An earl!

Warwick. Ay, and besides, Lord Chamberlain of the realm,
  And Secretary too, and Lord of Man.

Mortimer Senior. We may not, nor we will not, suffer this.

Mortimer. Why post we not from hence to levy men?

Lancaster. 'My lord of Cornwall' now at every word;
  And happy is the man whom he vouchsafes,
  For vailing of his bonnet, one good look.
  Thus arm in arm the King and he doth march—   20
  Nay more, the guard upon his lordship waits,
  And all the court begins to flatter him.

Warwick. Thus leaning on the shoulder of the King,
  He nods, and scorns, and smiles at those that pass.

197 the Fleet] the Fleet prison 199 Convey] The word has a slang sense, to steal, which
the Bishop points in his rejoinder. I. ii, 19 vailing] doffing

Mortimer Senior. Doth no man take exceptions at the slave?
Lancaster. All stomach him, but none dare speak a word.
Mortimer. Ah, that bewrays their baseness, Lancaster.
    Were all the earls and barons of my mind,
    We'll hale him from the bosom of the King,
    And at the court gate hang the peasant up,   30
    Who, swoln with venom of ambitious pride,
    Will be the ruin of the realm and us.

      Enter the Bishop of Canterbury [*talking to an* Attendant].

Warwick. Here comes my lord of Canterbury's grace.
Lancaster. His countenance bewrays he is displeas'd.
Canterbury. First were his sacred garments rent and torn,
    Then laid they violent hands upon him, next
    Himself imprison'd and his goods asseiz'd;
    This certify the Pope; away, take horse.   [*Exit* Attendant.]
Lancaster. My lord, will you take arms against the King?
Canterbury. What need I? God himself is up in arms   40
    When violence is offer'd to the Church.
Mortimer. Then will you join with us that be his peers
    To banish or behead that Gaveston?
Canterbury. What else my lords, for it concerns me near;
    The bishopric of Coventry is his.

      Enter the Queen [Isabella].

Mortimer. Madam, whither walks your majesty so fast?
Isabella. Unto the forest, gentle Mortimer,
    To live in grief and baleful discontent;
    For now my lord the King regards me not,
    But dotes upon the love of Gaveston.   50
    He claps his cheeks and hangs about his neck,
    Smiles in his face, and whispers in his ears;
    And when I come, he frowns, as who should say,
    'Go whither thou wilt, seeing I have Gaveston.'
Mortimer Senior. Is it not strange that he is thus bewitch'd?
Mortimer. Madam, return unto the court again:
    That sly inveigling Frenchman we'll exile,
    Or lose our lives; and yet ere that day come,
    The King shall lose his crown—for we have power,
    And courage too, to be reveng'd at full.   60
Canterbury. But yet lift not your swords against the King.
Lancaster. No, but we'll lift Gaveston from hence.
Warwick. And war must be the means, or he'll stay still.

26 stomach] resent

Isabella. Then let him stay; for rather than my lord
    Shall be oppress'd by civil mutinities,
    I will endure a melancholy life,
    And let him frolic with his minion.
Canterbury. My lords, to ease all this but hear me speak:
    We and the rest that are his counsellors
    Will meet, and with a general consent   70
    Confirm his banishment with our hands and seals.
Lancaster. What we confirm the King will frustrate.
Mortimer. Then may we lawfully revolt from him.
Warwick. But say my lord, where shall this meeting be?
Canterbury. At the New Temple.
Mortimer. Content.
Canterbury. And in the meantime I'll entreat you all
    To cross to Lambeth, and there stay with me.
Lancaster. Come then, let's away.
Mortimer. Madam, farewell.   80
Isabella. Farewell sweet Mortimer; and for my sake
    Forbear to levy arms against the King.
Mortimer. Ay, if words will serve; if not, I must.   [*Exeunt different ways.*]

[Scene iii]

Enter Gaveston *and the Earl of* Kent.

Gaveston. Edmund, the mighty prince of Lancaster,
    That hath more earldoms than an ass can bear,
    And both the Mortimers—two goodly men—
    With Guy of Warwick, that redoubted knight,
    Are gone towards Lambeth; there let them remain.   *Exeunt.*

[Scene iv]

Enter Nobiles [Lancaster, Warwick, Pembroke, Mortimer Senior,
Mortimer, *Bishop of* Canterbury].

Lancaster. Here is the form of Gaveston's exile:
    May it please your lordship to subscribe your name.
Canterbury. Give me the paper.
Lancaster. Quick, quick my lord; I long to write my name.
Warwick. But I long more to see him banish'd hence.
Mortimer. The name of Mortimer shall fright the King

Unless he be declin'd from that base peasant.

Enter the King and Gaveston [*and* Kent].

Edward. What, are you mov'd that Gaveston sits here?
 It is our pleasure; we will have it so.
Lancaster. Your grace doth well to place him by your side,   10
 For nowhere else the new earl is so safe.
Mortimer Senior. What man of noble birth can brook this sight?
 Quam male conveniunt!
 See what a scornful look the peasant casts.
Pembroke. Can kingly lions fawn on creeping ants?
Warwick. Ignoble vassal, that like Phaeton
 Aspir'st unto the guidance of the sun.
Mortimer. Their downfall is at hand, their forces down;
 We will not thus be fac'd and over-peer'd.
Edward. Lay hands on that traitor Mortimer.   20
Mortimer Senior. Lay hands on that traitor Gaveston.

[*They draw their swords.*]

Kent. Is this the duty that you owe your king?
Warwick. We know our duties; let him know his peers.

[*They seize* Gaveston.]

Edward. Whither will you bear him? Stay, or ye shall die.
Mortimer Senior. We are no traitors, therefore threaten not.
Gaveston. No, threaten not, my lord, but pay them home.
 Were I a king——
Mortimer. Thou villain, wherefore talkst thou of a king,
 That hardly art a gentleman by birth?
Edward. Were he a peasant, being my minion,   30
 I'll make the proudest of you stoop to him.
Lancaster. My lord, you may not thus disparage us.
 Away I say with hateful Gaveston.
Mortimer Senior. And with the Earl of Kent that favours him.

[Attendants *remove* Kent *and* Gaveston.]

Edward. Nay, then lay violent hands upon your king!
 Here Mortimer, sit thou in Edward's throne;
 Warwick and Lancaster, wear you my crown.
 Was ever king thus overrul'd as I?
Lancaster. Learn then to rule us better, and the realm.
Mortimer. What we have done, our heart-blood shall maintain.   40
Warwick. Think you that we can brook this upstart pride?
Edward. Anger and wrathful fury stops my speech.

13 *Quam . . . conveniunt*] 'How ill they suit'   16 Phaeton] who attempted to drive the
sun's chariot and would have destroyed the earth if Zeus had not intervened

Canterbury. Why are you mov'd? Be patient, my lord,
    And see what we your counsellors have done.
                [*Gives* Edward *the form for* Gaveston's *exile*.]
Mortimer. My lords, now let us all be resolute,
    And either have our wills or lose our lives.
Edward. Meet you for this, proud over-daring peers?
    Ere my sweet Gaveston shall part from me,
    This isle shall fleet upon the ocean
    And wander to the unfrequented Inde.   50
Canterbury. You know that I am legate to the Pope;
    On your allegiance to the See of Rome
    Subscribe, as we have done, to his exile.
Mortimer. Curse him if he refuse; and then may we
    Depose him, and elect another king.
Edward. Ay, there it goes; but yet I will not yield.
    Curse me; depose me; do the worst you can.
Lancaster. Then linger not, my lord, but do it straight.
Canterbury. Remember how the Bishop was abus'd.
    Either banish him that was the cause thereof,   60
    Or I will presently discharge these lords
    Of duty and allegiance due to thee.
Edward. It boots me not to threat; I must speak fair,
    The legate of the Pope will be obeyed.
    My lord, you shall be Chancellor of the realm;
    Thou, Lancaster, High Admiral of our fleet;
    Young Mortimer and his uncle shall be earls,
    And you, Lord Warwick, President of the North,
    And thou of Wales. If this content you not,
    Make several kingdoms of this monarchy   70
    And share it equally amongst you all—
    So I may have some nook or corner left
    To frolic with my dearest Gaveston.
Canterbury. Nothing shall alter us; we are resolv'd.
Lancaster. Come, come, subscribe.
Mortimer. Why should you love him whom the world hates so?
Edward. Because he loves me more than all the world.
    Ah, none but rude and savage-minded men
    Would seek the ruin of my Gaveston;
    You that be noble born should pity him.   80
Warwick. You that are princely born should shake him off.
    For shame subscribe, and let the lown depart.
Mortimer Senior. Urge him, my lord.

54 Curse] Excommunicate   82 lown] peasant

Canterbury. Are you content to banish him the realm?
Edward. I see I must, and therefore am content;
    Instead of ink I'll write it with my tears.   [*Subscribes*.]
Mortimer. The King is love-sick for his minion.
Edward. 'Tis done; and now accursed hand fall off.
Lancaster. Give it me; I'll have it publish'd in the streets.
Mortimer. I'll see him presently dispatched away.   90
Canterbury. Now is my heart at ease.
Warwick.   And so is mine.
Pembroke. This will be good news to the common sort.
Mortimer Senior. Be it or no, he shall not linger here.   *Exeunt Nobiles*.
Edward. How fast they run to banish him I love;
    They would not stir, were it to do me good.
    Why should a king be subject to a priest?
    Proud Rome, that hatchest such imperial grooms,
    For these thy superstitious taper-lights
    Wherewith thy antichristian churches blaze,
    I'll fire thy crazed buildings, and enforce   100
    The papal towers to kiss the lowly ground;
    With slaughter'd priests make Tiber's channel swell,
    And banks rais'd higher with their sepulchres.
    As for the peers that back the clergy thus,
    If I be king, not one of them shall live.

Enter Gaveston.

Gaveston. My lord, I hear it whisper'd everywhere,
    That I am banish'd and must fly the land.
Edward. 'Tis true sweet Gaveston—O were it false!
    The legate of the Pope will have it so,
    And thou must hence or I shall be depos'd.   110
    But I will reign to be reveng'd of them,
    And therefore, sweet friend, take it patiently.
    Live where thou wilt—I'll send thee gold enough;
    And long thou shalt not stay; or if thou dost
    I'll come to thee; my love shall ne'er decline.
Gaveston. Is all my hope turned to this hell of grief?
Edward. Rend not my heart with thy too-piercing words.
    Thou from this land, I from my self am banish'd.
Gaveston. To go from hence grieves not poor Gaveston,
    But to forsake you, in whose gracious looks   120
    The blessedness of Gaveston remains,
    For nowhere else seeks he felicity.

90 presently] immediately

Edward. And only this torments my wretched soul,
That whether I will or no thou must depart.
Be Governor of Ireland in my stead,
And there abide till fortune call thee home.
Here, take my picture, and let me wear thine.
O might I keep thee here, as I do this,
Happy were I, but now most miserable.

Gaveston. 'Tis something to be pitied of a king.　　　　　　130

Edward. Thou shalt not hence; I'll hide thee, Gaveston.

Gaveston. I shall be found, and then 'twill grieve me more.

Edward. Kind words and mutual talk makes our grief greater,
Therefore with dumb embracement let us part.
Stay Gaveston—I cannot leave thee thus.

Gaveston. For every look, my lord, drops down a tear.
Seeing I must go, do not renew my sorrow.

Edward. The time is little that thou hast to stay,
And therefore give me leave to look my fill.
But come sweet friend, I'll bear thee on thy way.　　　140

Gaveston. The peers will frown.

Edward. I pass not for their anger; come, let's go.
O that we might as well return as go.

Enter Queen Isabella.

Isabella. Whither goes my lord?

Edward. Fawn not on me, French strumpet; get thee gone.

Isabella. On whom but on my husband should I fawn?

Gaveston. On Mortimer; with whom, ungentle Queen—
I say no more. . . . Judge you the rest, my lord.

Isabella. In saying this, thou wrongst me Gaveston.
Is't not enough that thou corrupts my lord,　　　　　150
And art a bawd to his affections,
But thou must call mine honour thus in question?

Gaveston. I mean not so; your grace must pardon me.

Edward. Thou art too familiar with that Mortimer,
And by thy means is Gaveston exil'd;
But I would wish thee reconcile the lords,
Or thou shalt ne'er be reconcil'd to me.

Isabella. Your highness knows it lies not in my power.

Edward. Away then, touch me not; come Gaveston.

Isabella. Villain, 'tis thou that robb'st me of my lord.　　160

Gaveston. Madam, 'tis you that rob me of my lord.

Edward. Speak not unto her, let her droop and pine.

142 pass] care

Isabella. Wherein, my lord, have I deserv'd these words?
  Witness the tears that Isabella sheds,
  Witness this heart, that sighing for thee breaks,
  How dear my lord is to poor Isabel.
Edward. And witness heaven how dear thou art to me.
  There weep; for till my Gaveston be repeal'd,
  Assure thyself, thou com'st not in my sight.
          Exeunt Edward *and* Gaveston.

Isabella. O miserable and distressed Queen!   170
  Would when I left sweet France and was embark'd,
  That charming Circes walking on the waves
  Had chang'd my shape; or at the marriage-day
  The cup of Hymen had been full of poison;
  Or with those arms that twin'd about my neck
  I had been stifl'd, and not liv'd to see
  The King my lord thus to abandon me.
  Like frantic Juno will I fill the earth
  With ghastly murmur of my sighs and cries;
  For never doted Jove on Ganymede   180
  So much as he on cursed Gaveston.
  But that will more exasperate his wrath;
  I must entreat him, I must speak him fair,
  And be a means to call home Gaveston:
  And yet he'll ever dote on Gaveston,
  And so am I for ever miserable.

  Enter the Nobles [Warwick, Lancaster, Pembroke, Mortimer Senior,
       Mortimer] *to the Queen.*

Lancaster. Look where the sister of the King of France
  Sits wringing of her hands and beats her breast.
Warwick. The King I fear hath ill intreated her.
Pembroke. Hard is the heart that injures such a saint.   190
Mortimer. I know 'tis 'long of Gaveston she weeps.
Mortimer Senior. Why? He is gone.
Mortimer.   Madam, how fares your grace?
Isabella. Ah Mortimer! Now breaks the King's hate forth,
  And he confesseth that he loves me not.
Mortimer. Cry quittance, Madam then; and love not him.
Isabella. No, rather will I die a thousand deaths;
  And yet I love in vain, he'll ne'er love me.

172–3 charming Circes . . . shape] Circe transformed her rival, Scylla, into a monster.
178–80 Juno . . . Ganymede] Juno was jealous of her husband's love for this boy (cf.
Dido, induction).

Lancaster. Fear ye not, Madam; now his minion's gone
    His wanton humour will be quickly left.

Isabella. O never, Lancaster! I am enjoin'd   200
    To sue unto you all for his repeal:
    This wills my lord, and this must I perform,
    Or else be banish'd from his highness' presence.

Lancaster. For his repeal! Madam, he comes not back
    Unless the sea cast up his shipwrack body.

Warwick. And to behold so sweet a sight as that
    There's none here but would run his horse to death.

Mortimer. But Madam, would you have us call him home?

Isabella. Ay Mortimer, for till he be restor'd
    The angry King hath banish'd me the court;   210
    And therefore as thou lov'st and tendrest me,
    Be thou my advocate unto these peers.

Mortimer. What, would ye have me plead for Gaveston?

Mortimer Senior. Plead for him he that will; I am resolv'd.

Lancaster. And so am I my lord; dissuade the Queen.

Isabella. O Lancaster, let him dissuade the King,
    For 'tis against my will he should return.

Warwick. Then speak not for him; let the peasant go.

Isabella. 'Tis for myself I speak, and not for him.

Pembroke. No speaking will prevail, and therefore cease.   220

Mortimer. Fair Queen, forbear to angle for the fish
    Which, being caught, strikes him that takes it dead—
    I mean that vile torpedo, Gaveston,
    That now, I hope, floats on the Irish seas.

Isabella. Sweet Mortimer, sit down by me a while,
    And I will tell thee reasons of such weight
    As thou wilt soon subscribe to his repeal.

Mortimer. It is impossible; but speak your mind.

Isabella. Then thus—but none shall hear it but ourselves.

          [Isabella *and* Mortimer *retire to back of stage.*]

Lancaster. My lords, albeit the Queen win Mortimer,   230
    Will you be resolute and hold with me?

Mortimer Senior. Not I against my nephew.

Pembroke. Fear not, the Queen's words cannot alter him.

Warwick. No? Do but mark how earnestly she pleads.

Lancaster. And see how coldly his looks make denial.

Warwick. She smiles! Now for my life his mind is chang'd!

Lancaster. I'll rather lose his friendship, I, than grant.

Mortimer. Well, of necessity it must be so.   [*Comes forward.*]

223 torpedo] electric ray fish

  My lords, that I abhor base Gaveston

  I hope your honours make no question;   240

  And therefore though I plead for his repeal,

  'Tis not for his sake, but for our avail—

  Nay, for the realm's behoof and for the King's.

Lancaster. Fie Mortimer, dishonour not thyself!

  Can this be true, 'twas good to banish him?

  And is this true, to call him home again?

  Such reasons make white black, and dark night day.

Mortimer. My lord of Lancaster, mark the respect.

Lancaster. In no respect can contraries be true.

Isabella. Yet, good my lord, hear what he can allege.   250

Warwick. All that he speaks is nothing. We are resolv'd.

Mortimer. Do you not wish that Gaveston were dead?

Pembroke. I would he were.

Mortimer. Why then, my lord, give me but leave to speak.

Mortimer Senior. But nephew, do not play the sophister.

Mortimer. This which I urge is of a burning zeal

  To mend the King and do our country good:

  Know you not Gaveston hath store of gold

  Which may in Ireland purchase him such friends

  As he will front the mightiest of us all?   260

  And whereas he shall live and be belov'd,

  'Tis hard for us to work his overthrow.

Warwick. Mark you but that, my lord of Lancaster?

Mortimer. But were he here, detested as he is,

  How easily might some base slave be suborn'd

  To greet his lordship with a poniard;

  And none so much as blame the murderer,

  But rather praise him for that brave attempt,

  And in the chronicle enrol his name

  For purging of the realm of such a plague.   270

Pembroke. He saith true.

Lancaster. Ay, but how chance this was not done before?

Mortimer. Because, my lords, it was not thought upon.

  Nay more—when he shall know it lies in us

  To banish him, and then to call him home,

  'Twill make him vail the topflag of his pride,

  And fear t'offend the meanest nobleman.

Mortimer Senior. But how if he do not, nephew?

Mortimer. Then may we with some colour rise in arms.

  For howsoever we have borne it out,   280

255 sophister] casuist 261 whereas] whilst 279 colour] justification

'Tis treason to be up against the King;
So shall we have the people of our side,
Which for his father's sake lean to the King,
But cannot brook a night-grown mushrump,
Such a one as my lord of Cornwall is,
Should bear us down of the nobility;
And when the commons and the nobles join,
'Tis not the King can buckler Gaveston;
We'll pull him from the strongest hold he hath.
My lords, if to perform this I be slack,   290
Think me as base a groom as Gaveston.

Lancaster. On that condition Lancaster will grant.
Pembroke. And so will Pembroke.
Warwick.   And I.
Mortimer Senior.   And I.
Mortimer. In this I count me highly gratified,
And Mortimer will rest at your command.
Isabella. And when this favour Isabel forgets,
Then let her live abandon'd and forlorn.
But see, in happy time, my lord the King,
Having brought the Earl of Cornwall on his way,
Is new return'd; this news will glad him much,   300
Yet not so much as me; I love him more
Than he can Gaveston—would he lov'd me
But half so much, then were I treble blest.

                Enter King Edward *mourning [attended by* Beaumont].

Edward. He's gone, and for his absence thus I mourn.
Did never sorrow go so near my heart
As doth the want of my sweet Gaveston;
And could my crown's revenue bring him back
I would freely give it to his enemies,
And think I gain'd, having bought so dear a friend.
Isabella. Hark how he harps upon his minion.   310
Edward. My heart is as an anvil unto sorrow,
Which beats upon it like the Cyclops' hammers,
And with the noise turns up my giddy brain,
And makes me frantic for my Gaveston;
Ah, had some bloodless Fury rose from hell,
And with my kingly sceptre struck me dead,
When I was forc'd to leave my Gaveston!
Lancaster. Diablo! What passions call you these?

312 Cyclops] labourers in Vulcan's forge

Isabella. My gracious lord, I come to bring you news.

Edward. That you have parley'd with your Mortimer.   320

Isabella. That Gaveston, my lord, shall be repeal'd.

Edward. Repeal'd! The news is too sweet to be true.

Isabella. But will you love me, if you find it so?

Edward. If it be so, what will not Edward do?

Isabella. For Gaveston, but not for Isabel.

Edward. For thee, fair Queen, if thou lov'st Gaveston;
    I'll hang a golden tongue about thy neck,
    Seeing thou hast pleaded with so good success.

Isabella. No other jewels hang about my neck
    Than these, my lord, nor let me have more wealth,   330
    Than I may fetch from this rich treasury.   *[Kisses him.]*
    O how a kiss revives poor Isabel.

Edward. Once more receive my hand; and let this be
    A second marriage 'twixt thyself and me.

Isabella. And may it prove more happy than the first.
    My gentle lord, bespeak these nobles fair
    That wait attendance for a gracious look,
    And on their knees salute your majesty.

Edward. Courageous Lancaster, embrace thy king,
    And as gross vapours perish by the sun,   340
    Even so let hatred with thy sovereign's smile:
    Live thou with me as my companion.

Lancaster. This salutation overjoys my heart.

Edward. Warwick shall be my chiefest counsellor:
    These silver hairs will more adorn my court,
    Than gaudy silks or rich embroidery.
    Chide me, sweet Warwick, if I go astray.

Warwick. Slay me, my lord, when I offend your grace.

Edward. In solemn triumphs and in public shows
    Pembroke shall bear the sword before the King.   350

Pembroke. And with this sword Pembroke will fight for you.

Edward. But wherefore walks young Mortimer aside?
    Be thou commander of our royal fleet,
    Or if that lofty office like thee not,
    I make thee here Lord Marshal of the realm.

Mortimer. My lord, I'll marshal so your enemies
    As England shall be quiet and you safe.

Edward. And as for you, lord Mortimer of Chirk,
    Whose great achievements in our foreign war
    Deserves no common place nor mean reward,   360

330 these] i.e. Edward's arms   350 the sword] the sword of state

    Be you the general of the levied troops,
    That now are ready to assail the Scots.
Mortimer Senior. In this your grace hath highly honour'd me,
    For with my nature war doth best agree.
Isabella. Now is the King of England rich and strong,
    Having the love of his renowned peers.
Edward. Ay Isabel, ne'er was my heart so light.
    Clerk of the crown, direct our warrant forth
    For Gaveston to Ireland; Beaumont fly,
    As fast as Iris, or Jove's Mercury.   370
Beaumont. It shall be done, my gracious lord.   [*Exit.*]
Edward. Lord Mortimer, we leave you to your charge.
    Now let us in and feast it royally.
    Against our friend the Earl of Cornwall comes
    We'll have a general tilt and tournament,
    And then his marriage shall be solemniz'd;
    For wot you not that I have made him sure
    Unto our cousin, the Earl of Gloucester's heir?
Lancaster. Such news we hear, my lord.
Edward. That day, if not for him, yet for my sake,   380
    Who in the triumph will be challenger,
    Spare for no cost; we will requite your love.
Warwick. In this, or aught, your highness shall command us.
Edward. Thanks gentle Warwick. Come, let's in and revel.
              Exeunt [*except the* Mortimers].
Mortimer Senior. Nephew, I must to Scotland; thou stay'st here.
    Leave now to oppose thyself against the King.
    Thou seest by nature he is mild and calm,
    And seeing his mind so dotes on Gaveston,
    Let him without controlment have his will.
    The mightiest kings have had their minions: 390
    Great Alexander lov'd Hephaestion;
    The conquering Hercules for Hylas wept;
    And for Patroclus stern Achilles droop'd:
    And not kings only, but the wisest men:
    The Roman Tully lov'd Octavius;
    Great Socrates, wild Alcibiades.
    Then let his grace, whose youth is flexible,
    And promiseth as much as we can wish,
    Freely enjoy that vain light-headed earl,
    For riper years will wean him from such toys.   400

370 Iris . . . Mercury] messengers for Juno and Jupiter   377 made him sure] betrothed
395 Roman Tully] Cicero

Mortimer. Uncle, his wanton humour grieves not me,
    But this I scorn, that one so basely born
    Should by his sovereign's favour grow so pert,
    And riot it with treasure of the realm
    While soldiers mutiny for want of pay.
    He wears a lord's revenue on his back,
    And Midas-like he jets it in the court
    With base outlandish cullions at his heels,
    Whose proud fantastic liveries make such show
    As if that Proteus, god of shapes, appear'd.   410
    I have not seen a dapper jack so brisk;
    He wears a short Italian hooded cloak
    Larded with pearl; and in his Tuscan cap
    A jewel of more value than the crown.
    Whiles other walk below, the King and he
    From out a window laugh at such as we,
    And flout our train, and jest at our attire.
    Uncle, 'tis this that makes me impatient.
Mortimer Senior. But nephew, now you see the King is chang'd.
Mortimer. Then so am I, and live to do him service: 420
    But whiles I have a sword, a hand, a heart,
    I will not yield to any such upstart.
    You know my mind. Come uncle, let's away.   *Exeunt.*

[Act II   Scene i]

Enter Spencer *and* Baldock.

Baldock. Spencer,
    Seeing that our lord th' Earl of Gloucester's dead,
    Which of the nobles dost thou mean to serve?
Spencer. Not Mortimer, nor any of his side,
    Because the King and he are enemies.
    Baldock, learn this of me: a factious lord
    Shall hardly do himself good, much less us;
    But he that hath the favour of a king
    May with one word advance us while we live.
    The liberal Earl of Cornwall is the man   10
    On whose good fortune Spencer's hope depends.
Baldock. What, mean you then to be his follower?
Spencer. No, his companion, for he loves me well,

407 Midas-like] clad in gold   408 cullions] rascals

And would have once preferred me to the King.
Baldock. But he is banish'd; there's small hope of him.
Spencer. Aȳ for a while; but Baldock, mark the end:
    A friend of mine told me in secrecy,
    That he's repeal'd, and sent for back again;
    And even now, a post came from the court
    With letters to our lady from the King,   20
    And as she read, she smil'd; which makes me think
    It is about her lover, Gaveston.
Baldock. 'Tis like enough, for since he was exil'd
    She neither walks abroad, nor comes in sight.
    But I had thought the match had been broke off,
    And that his banishment had chang'd her mind.
Spencer. Our lady's first love is not wavering:
    My life for thine, she will have Gaveston.
Baldock. Then hope I by her means to be preferr'd,
    Having read unto her since she was a child.   30
Spencer. Then, Baldock, you must cast the scholar off,
    And learn to court it like a gentleman.
    'Tis not a black coat and a little band,
    A velvet-cap'd cloak, fac'd before with serge,
    And smelling to a nosegay all the day,
    Or holding of a napkin in your hand,
    Or saȳing a long grace at a table's end,
    Or making low legs to a nobleman,
    Or looking downward, with your eyelids close,
    And saying 'truly, an't may please your honour',   40
    Can get you any favour with great men.
    You must be proud, bold, pleasant, resolute—
    And now and then, stab as occasion serves.
Baldock. Spencer, thou knowest I hate such formal toys,
    And use them but of mere hypocrisy.
    Mine old lord, whiles he liv'd, was so precise
    That he would take exceptions at my buttons,
    And, being like pins' heads, blame me for the bigness,
    Which made me curate-like in mine attire,
    Though inwardly licentious enough   50
    And apt for any kind of villainy.
    I am none of these common pedants, I,
    That cannot speak without '*propterea quod*'.
Spencer. But one of those that saith '*quandoquidem*',

14 preferred] recommended   38 making . . . legs] bows   53-4 '*propterea quod*' . . .
'*quandoquidem*'] Both phrases mean 'because', but the latter is the more elegant.

And hath a special gift to form a verb!
Baldock. Leave off this jesting—here my lady comes.

     Enter the Lady [Margaret de Clare].

Lady Margaret. The grief for his exile was not so much,
 As is the joy of his returning home.
 This letter came from my sweet Gaveston.   [*She reads it.*]
 What needst thou, love, thus to excuse thyself?   60
 I know thou couldst not come and visit me.
 'I will not long be from thee, though I die':
 This argues the entire love of my lord;
 'When I forsake thee, death seize on my heart'.
 But rest thee here where Gaveston shall sleep.
       [*Puts the letter in her bosom.*]
 Now to the letter of my lord the King. [*She reads the other letter.*]
 He wills me to repair unto the court,
 And meet my Gaveston! Why do I stay,
 Seeing that he talks thus of my marriage-day?
 Who's there? Baldock?   70
 See that my coach be ready, I must hence.
Baldock. It shall be done, madam.   *Exit.*
Lady Margaret. And meet me at the park pale presently.
 Spencer, stay you and bear me company,
 For I have joyful news to tell thee of:
 My lord of Cornwall is a-coming over,
 And will be at the court as soon as we.
Spencer. I knew the King would have him home again.
Lady Margaret. If all things sort out, as I hope they will,
 Thy service, Spencer, shall be thought upon.   80
Spencer. I humbly thank your ladyship.
Lady Margaret. Come lead the way; I long till I am there. [*Exeunt.*]

[Scene ii]

Enter Edward, *the Queen,* Lancaster, Mortimer, Warwick, Pembroke,
Kent, Attendants.

Edward. The wind is good, I wonder why he stays.
 I fear me he is wracked upon the sea.
Isabella. Look Lancaster, how passionate he is,
 And still his mind runs on his minion.
Lancaster. My lord——

55 to form a verb] A joke is clearly intended—but its point is now lost.

Edward. How now, what news? Is Gaveston arriv'd?
Mortimer. Nothing but Gaveston! What means your grace?
 You have matters of more weight to think upon;
 The King of France sets foot in Normandy.
Edward. A trifle; we'll expel him when we please.   10
 But tell me Mortimer, what's thy device
 Against the stately triumph we decreed?
Mortimer. A homely one, my lord, not worth the telling.
Edward. Prithee let me know it.
Mortimer. But seeing you are so desirous, thus it is:
 A lofty cedar tree fair flourishing,
 On whose top branches kingly eagles perch,
 And by the bark a canker creeps me up,
 And gets unto the highest bough of all:
 The motto: *Æque tandem.*   20
Edward. And what is yours, my lord of Lancaster?
Lancaster. My lord, mine's more obscure than Mortimer's.
 Pliny reports, there is a flying fish
 Which all the other fishes deadly hate,
 And therefore being pursu'd, it takes the air;
 No sooner is it up, but there's a fowl
 That seizeth it: this fish, my lord, I bear;
 The motto this: *Undique mors est.*
Edward. Proud Mortimer! Ungentle Lancaster!
 Is this the love you bear your sovereign?   30
 Is this the fruit your reconcilement bears?
 Can you in words make show of amity,
 And in your shields display your rancorous minds?
 What call you this but private libelling
 Against the Earl of Cornwall and my brother?
Isabella. Sweet husband be content, they all love you.
Edward. They love me not that hate my Gaveston.
 I am that cedar; shake me not too much.
 And you the eagles; soar ye ne'er so high,
 I have the jesses that will pull you down,   40
 And *Æque tandem* shall that canker cry
 Unto the proudest peer of Britainy.
 Though thou compar'st him to a flying fish,
 And threat'nest death whether he rise or fall,
 'Tis not the hugest monster of the sea
 Nor foulest harpy that shall swallow him.

18 canker] caterpillar 20 *Æque tandem*] 'Equal at length' 28 *Undique mors est*] 'Death is on all sides' 35 my brother] Gaveston (not Kent) referred to affectionately

Mortimer. If in his absence thus he favours him,
  What will he do whenas he shall be present?
Lancaster. That shall we see; look where his lordship comes.

Enter Gaveston.

Edward. My Gaveston!   50
  Welcome to Tynemouth, welcome to thy friend!
  Thy absence made me droop and pine away,
  For as the lovers of fair Danäe,
  When she was lock'd up in a brazen tower,
  Desir'd her more, and wax'd outrageous,
  So did it sure with me; and now thy sight
  Is sweeter far than was thy parting hence
  Bitter and irksome to my sobbing heart.
Gaveston. Sweet lord and King, your speech preventeth mine,
  Yet have I words left to express my joy: 60
  The shepherd nipp'd with biting winter's rage
  Frolics not more to see the painted spring,
  Than I do to behold your majesty.
Edward. Will none of you salute my Gaveston?
Lancaster. Salute him? Yes! Welcome Lord Chamberlain.
Mortimer. Welcome is the good Earl of Cornwall.
Warwick. Welcome Lord Governor of the Isle of Man.
Pembroke. Welcome Master Secretary.
Kent. Brother, do you hear them?
Edward. Still will these earls and barons use me thus!   70
Gaveston. My lord, I cannot brook these injuries.
Isabella. Ay me, poor soul, when these begin to jar.
Edward. Return it to their throats; I'll be thy warrant.
Gaveston. Base leaden earls that glory in your birth,
  Go sit at home and eat your tenants' beef,
  And come not here to scoff at Gaveston,
  Whose mounting thoughts did never creep so low,
  As to bestow a look on such as you.
Lancaster. Yet I disdain not to do this for you.   [*Draws his sword.*]
Edward. Treason, treason! Where's the traitor?   80
Pembroke. Here, here!
Edward. Convey hence Gaveston; they'll murder him.
Gaveston. The life of thee shall salve this foul disgrace.
Mortimer. Villain, thy life, unless I miss mine aim.   [*Wounds Gaveston.*]
Isabella. Ah furious Mortimer, what hast thou done?

53 Danäe] who was locked in a tower of brass, to which Jove gained access by transforming himself into a shower of gold (cf. III. iii. 81 ff.)   59 preventeth] anticipates

Mortimer. No more than I would answer were he slain.

                                   [*Exit* Gaveston *with* Attendants.]

Edward. Yes, more than thou canst answer, though he live;

    Dear shall you both aby this riotous deed.

    Out of my presence! Come not near the court.

Mortimer. I'll not be barr'd the court for Gaveston.   90

Lancaster. We'll hale him by the ears unto the block.

Edward. Look to your own heads; his is sure enough.

Warwick. Look to your own crown, if you back him thus.

Kent. Warwick, these words do ill beseem thy years.

Edward. Nay, all of them conspire to cross me thus;

    But if I live, I'll tread upon their heads

    That think with high looks thus to tread me down.

    Come Edmund let's away and levy men;

    'Tis war that must abate these barons' pride.

                          Exit the King [*with Queen and* Kent].

Warwick. Let's to our castles, for the King is mov'd.   100

Mortimer. Mov'd may he be, and perish in his wrath.

Lancaster. Cousin, it is no dealing with him now;

    He means to make us stoop by force of arms,

    And therefore let us jointly here protest

    To prosecute that Gaveston to the death.

Mortimer. By heaven, the abject villain shall not live.

Warwick. I'll have his blood, or die in seeking it.

Pembroke. The like oath Pembroke takes.

Lancaster. And so doth Lancaster.

    Now send our heralds to defy the King,   110

    And make the people swear to put him down.

                        Enter a Post.

Mortimer. Letters? From whence?

Post. From Scotland, my lord.

Lancaster. Why how now, cousin, how fares all our friends?

Mortimer [*reading letter*]. My uncle's taken prisoner by the Scots.

Lancaster. We'll have him ransom'd, man; be of good cheer.

Mortimer. They rate his ransom at five thousand pound.

    Who should defray the money but the King,

    Seeing he is taken prisoner in his wars?

    I'll to the King.   120

Lancaster. Do cousin, and I'll bear thee company.

Warwick. Meantime my lord of Pembroke and myself

    Will to Newcastle here, and gather head.

88 aby] pay for

Mortimer. About it then, and we will follow you.

Lancaster. Be resolute and full of secrecy.

Warwick. I warrant you.   [*Exeunt all but* Mortimer *and* Lancaster.]

Mortimer. Cousin, and if he will not ransom him,

 I'll thunder such a peal into his ears,

 As never subject did unto his king.

Lancaster. Content, I'll bear my part. Holla! Who's there!   130

[Enter Guard.]

Mortimer. Ay, marry, such a guard as this doth well.

Lancaster. Lead on the way.

Guard. Whither will your lordships?

Mortimer. Whither else but to the King?

Guard. His highness is dispos'd to be alone.

Lancaster. Why, so he may, but we will speak to him.

Guard. You may not in, my lord.

Mortimer. May we not!

[Enter Edward and Kent.]

Edward. How now, what noise is this? Who have we there? Is't you?

Mortimer. Nay, stay my lord, I come to bring you news;   140

 Mine uncle's taken prisoner by the Scots.

Edward. Then ransom him.

Lancaster. 'Twas in your wars, you should ransom him.

Mortimer. And you shall ransom him, or else——

Kent. What Mortimer, you will not threaten him!

Edward. Quiet yourself; you shall have the broad seal

 To gather for him thoroughout the realm.

Lancaster. Your minion Gaveston hath taught you this.

Mortimer. My lord, the family of the Mortimers

 Are not so poor but, would they sell their land,   150

 Would levy men enough to anger you.

 We never beg, but use such prayers as these.

[Lays hold of his sword.]

Edward. Shall I still be haunted thus?

Mortimer. Nay, now you are here alone, I'll speak my mind.

Lancaster. And so will I, and then, my lord, farewell.

Mortimer. The idle triumphs, masques, lascivious shows

 And prodigal gifts bestow'd on Gaveston,

 Have drawn thy treasure dry, and made thee weak,

 The murmuring commons overstretched hath.

Lancaster. Look for rebellion, look to be depos'd: 160

---

146 broad seal] Authority under the Great Seal was necessary for the legal raising of money.

Thy garrisons are beaten out of France,
And lame and poor lie groaning at the gates;
The wild O'Neill, with swarms of Irish kerns,
Lives uncontroll'd within the English Pale;
Unto the walls of York the Scots made road,
And unresisted drave away rich spoils.

Mortimer. The haughty Dane commands the narrow seas,
  While in the harbour ride thy ships unrigg'd.

Lancaster. What foreign prince sends thee ambassadors?

Mortimer. Who loves thee but a sort of flatterers?   170

Lancaster. Thy gentle queen, sole sister to Valois,
  Complains that thou hast left her all forlorn.

Mortimer. Thy court is naked, being bereft of those
  That makes a king seem glorious to the world—
  I mean the peers, whom thou shouldst dearly love;
  Libels are cast against thee in the streets,
  Ballads and rimes made of thy overthrow.

Lancaster. The Northren borderers, seeing the houses burnt,
  Their wives and children slain, run up and down
  Cursing the name of thee and Gaveston.   180

Mortimer. When wert thou in the field with banner spread?
  But once! And then thy soldiers marched like players,
  With garish robes, not armour; and thyself,
  Bedaub'd with gold, rode laughing at the rest,
  Nodding and shaking of thy spangled crest,
  Where women's favours hung like labels down.

Lancaster. And thereof came it that the fleering Scots,
  To England's high disgrace, have made this jig:
        Maids of England, sore may you mourn
        For your lemans you have lost at Bannocks bourne.   190
              With a heave and a ho.
        What weeneth the King of England,
        So soon to have won Scotland?
              With a rombelow.

Mortimer. Wigmore shall fly, to set my uncle free.

Lancaster. And when 'tis gone, our swords shall purchase more.
  If ye be mov'd, revenge it as you can:
  Look next to see us with our ensigns spread.   *Exeunt Nobiles.*

Edward. My swelling heart for very anger breaks!
  How oft have I been baited by these peers,   200

163 kerns] foot-soldiers   164 the English Pale] that part of Ireland where the English
had authority   186 labels] document-seals   190 lemans] sweethearts   195 Wigmore]
Mortimer's castle

And dare not be reveng'd, for their power is great?
Yet shall the crowing of these cockerels
Affright a lion? Edward, unfold thy paws,
And let their lives' blood slake thy fury's hunger;
If I be cruel and grow tyrannous,
Now let them thank themselves, and rue too late.
Kent. My lord, I see your love to Gaveston
    Will be the ruin of the realm and you,
    For now the wrathful nobles threaten wars;
    And therefore, brother, banish him for ever.   210
Edward. Art thou an enemy to my Gaveston?
Kent. Ay, and it grieves me that I favour'd him.
Edward. Traitor, be gone; whine thou with Mortimer.
Kent. So will I, rather than with Gaveston.
Edward. Out of my sight, and trouble me no more.
Kent. No marvel though thou scorn thy noble peers,
    When I thy brother am rejected thus.   *Exit.*
Edward. Away!
    Poor Gaveston, that hast no friend but me,
    Do what they can, we'll live in Tynemouth here,   220
    And so I walk with him about the walls,
    What care I though the earls begirt us round?
    Here comes she that's cause of all these jars.

Enter the Queen, Ladies 3 [Margaret de Clare *and* Ladies *in Waiting*],
                Baldock *and* Spencer [*and* Gaveston].

Isabella. My lord, 'tis thought the earls are up in arms.
Edward. Ay, and 'tis likewise thought you favour him.
Isabella. Thus do you still suspect me without cause.
Lady Margaret. Sweet uncle, speak more kindly to the Queen.
Gaveston. My lord, dissemble with her, speak her fair.
Edward. Pardon me, sweet, I forgot myself.
Isabella. Your pardon is quickly got of Isabel.   230
Edward. The younger Mortimer is grown so brave,
    That to my face he threatens civil wars.
Gaveston. Why do you not commit him to the Tower?
Edward. I dare not, for the people love him well.
Gaveston. Why then, we'll have him privily made away.
Edward. Would Lancaster and he had both carous'd
    A bowl of poison to each other's health:
    But let them go, and tell me what are these?
Lady Margaret. Two of my father's servants whilst he liv'd;

225 him] i.e. Mortimer

May't please your grace to entertain them now.   240

Edward. Tell me, where wast thou born? What is thine arms?

Baldock. My name is Baldock, and my gentry
    I fetch'd from Oxford, not from heraldry.

Edward. The fitter art thou, Baldock, for my turn;
    Wait on me, and I'll see thou shalt not want.

Baldock. I humbly thank your majesty.

Edward. Knowest thou him, Gaveston?

Gaveston.   Ay my lord;
    His name is Spencer, he is well allied.
    For my sake let him wait upon your grace;
    Scarce shall you find a man of more desert.   250

Edward. Then, Spencer, wait upon me; for his sake
    I'll grace thee with a higher style ere long.

Spencer. No greater titles happen unto me
    Than to be favour'd of your majesty.

Edward. Cousin, this day shall be your marriage feast,
    And Gaveston, think that I love thee well
    To wed thee to our niece, the only heir
    Unto the Earl of Gloucester late deceas'd.

Gaveston. I know, my lord, many will stomach me,
    But I respect neither their love nor hate.   260

Edward. The headstrong barons shall not limit me;
    He that I list to favour shall be great.
    Come, let's away; and when the marriage ends,
    Have at the rebels and their complices.   *Exeunt omnes.*

[Scene iii]

Enter Lancaster, Mortimer, Warwick, Pembroke, Kent.

Kent. My lords, of love to this our native land
    I come to join with you and leave the King;
    And in your quarrel and the realm's behoof
    Will be the first that shall adventure life.

Lancaster. I fear me you are sent of policy
    To undermine us with a show of love.

Warwick. He is your brother, therefore have we cause
    To cast the worst, and doubt of your revolt.

Kent. Mine honour shall be hostage of my truth;
    If that will not suffice, farewell my lords.   10

Mortimer. Stay Edmund; never was Plantagenet

242 gentry] condition as a gentleman   II. iii, 5 of policy] as a trick

    False of his word and therefore trust we thee.

Pembroke. But what's the reason you should leave him now?

Kent. I have inform'd the Earl of Lancaster.

Lancaster. And it sufficeth. Now, my lords, know this,
    That Gaveston is secretly arriv'd
    And here in Tynemouth frolics with the King.
    Let us with these our followers scale the walls,
    And suddenly surprise them unawares.

Mortimer. I'll give the onset.

Warwick.   And I'll follow thee.   20

Mortimer. This totter'd ensign of my ancestors,
    Which swept the desert shore of that dead sea,
    Whereof we got the name of Mortimer,
    Will I advance upon this castle walls.
    Drums strike alarum! Raise them from their sport,
    And ring aloud the knell of Gaveston.

Lancaster. None be so hardy as to touch the King;
    But neither spare you Gaveston nor his friends.   *Exeunt.*

[Scene iv]

Enter the King and Spencer, *to them* Gaveston [*the Queen*, Margaret
de Clare].

Edward. O tell me Spencer, where is Gaveston?

Spencer. I fear me he is slain, my gracious lord.

Edward. No, here he comes! Now let them spoil and kill.
    Fly, fly my lords, the earls have got the hold.
    Take shipping and away to Scarborough;
    Spencer and I will post away by land.

Gaveston. O stay, my lord, they will not injure you.

Edward. I will not trust them, Gaveston. Away!

Gaveston. Farewell, my lord.

Edward. Lady, farewell.   10

Lady Margaret. Farewell, sweet uncle, till we meet again.

Edward. Farewell, sweet Gaveston, and farewell, niece.

Isabella. No farewell to poor Isabel, thy queen?

Edward. Yes, yes—for Mortimer your lover's sake.

                 Exeunt omnes, manet Isabella.

Isabella. Heavens can witness, I love none but you.
    From my embracements thus he breaks away;

21 totter'd] tattered   22–3 dead sea . . . Mortimer] The traditional (but incorrect)
etymology of the name Mortimer was *de mortuo mari.*

O that mine arms could close this isle about,
That I might pull him to me where I would;
Or that these tears that drizzle from mine eyes
Had power to mollify his stony heart,   20
That when I had him we might never part.

Enter the Barons [Lancaster, Warwick, Mortimer]. *Alarums* [*within*].

Lancaster. I wonder how he scap'd?
Mortimer.   Who's this? The Queen!
Isabella. Ay Mortimer, the miserable Queen,
    Whose pining heart her inward sighs have blasted,
    And body with continual mourning wasted;
    These hands are tired with haling of my lord
    From Gaveston, from wicked Gaveston,
    And all in vain; for when I speak him fair,
    He turns away and smiles upon his minion.
Mortimer. Cease to lament, and tell us where's the King.   30
Isabella. What would you with the King? Is't him you seek?
Lancaster. No Madam, but that cursed Gaveston.
    Far be it from the thought of Lancaster
    To offer violence to his sovereign.
    We would but rid the realm of Gaveston;
    Tell us where he remains, and he shall die.
Isabella. He's gone by water unto Scarborough:
    Pursue him quickly, and he cannot scape;
    The King hath left him, and his train is small.
Warwick. Forslow no time sweet Lancaster; let's march.   40
Mortimer. How comes it that the King and he is parted?
Isabella. That this your army, going several ways,
    Might be of lesser force, and with the power
    That he intendeth presently to raise
    Be easily suppress'd; and therefore be gone.
Mortimer. Here in the river rides a Flemish hoy;
    Let's all aboard and follow him amain.
Lancaster. The wind that bears him hence will fill our sails;
    Come, come aboard; 'tis but an hour's sailing.
Mortimer. Madam, stay you within this castle here.   50
Isabella. No Mortimer, I'll to my lord the King.
Mortimer. Nay, rather sail with us to Scarborough.
Isabella. You know the King is so suspicious,
    As if he hear I have but talk'd with you
    Mine honour will be call'd in question;

40 Forslow] Waste   46 hoy] fishing boat

And therefore, gentle Mortimer, be gone.
Mortimer. Madam, I cannot stay to answer you,
    But think of Mortimer as he deserves.   *[Exeunt all but* Isabella.]
Isabella. So well hast thou deserv'd, sweet Mortimer,
    As Isabel could live with thee for ever.   60
    In vain I look for love at Edward's hand,
    Whose eyes are fix'd on none but Gaveston.
    Yet once more I'll importune him with prayers;
    If he be strange and not regard my words,
    My son and I will over into France,
    And to the King my brother there complain
    How Gaveston hath robb'd me of his love.
    But yet I hope my sorrows will have end,
    And Gaveston this blessed day be slain.   *Exit.*

[Scene v]

Enter Gaveston *pursued.*

Gaveston. Yet, lusty lords, I have escap'd your hands,
    Your threats, your larums, and your hot pursuits;
    And though divorced from King Edward's eyes,
    Yet liveth Piers of Gaveston unsurpris'd,
    Breathing, in hope (*malgrado* all your beards,
    That muster rebels thus against your king)
    To see his royal sovereign once again.

Enter the Nobles [Lancaster, Warwick, Pembroke, Mortimer,] [Soldiers].

Warwick. Upon him soldiers! Take away his weapons.
Mortimer. Thou proud disturber of thy country's peace,
    Corrupter of thy king, cause of these broils,   10
    Base flatterer, yield! And were it not for shame,
    Shame and dishonour to a soldier's name,
    Upon my weapon's point here shouldst thou fall,
    And welter in thy gore.
Lancaster.   Monster of men,
    That, like the Greekish strumpet, train'd to arms
    And bloody wars so many valiant knights,
    Look for no other fortune, wretch, than death.
    King Edward is not here to buckler thee.
Warwick. Lancaster, why talkst thou to the slave?
    Go, soldiers, take him hence, for by my sword,   20

5 *malgrado*] 'in spite of'   15 train'd] decoyed

His head shall off. Gaveston, short warning
Shall serve thy turn: it is our country's cause
That here severely we will execute
Upon thy person. Hang him at a bough!
Gaveston. My lord——
Warwick. Soldiers, have him away.
But for thou wert the favourite of a king,
Thou shalt have so much honour at our hands.
Gaveston. I thank you all, my lords. Then I perceive
That heading is one, and hanging is the other,   30
And death is all.

Enter Earl of Arundel.

Lancaster. How now, my lord of Arundel?
Arundel. My lords, King Edward greets you all by me.
Warwick. Arundel, say your message.
Arundel.   His majesty,
Hearing that you had taken Gaveston,
Entreateth you by me, yet but he may
See him before he dies; for why, he says,
And sends you word, he knows that die he shall;
And if you gratify his grace so far,
He will be mindful of the courtesy.   40
Warwick. How now?
Gaveston.   Renowmed Edward, how thy name
Revives poor Gaveston.
Warwick.   No, it needeth not.
Arundel, we will gratify the King
In other matters; he must pardon us in this.
Soldiers, away with him.
Gaveston. Why, my lord of Warwick,
Will not these delays beget my hopes?
I know it, lords, it is this life you aim at,
Yet grant King Edward this.
Mortimer.   Shalt thou appoint
What we shall grant? Soldiers, away with him!   50
Thus we'll gratify the King:
We'll send his head by thee; let him bestow
His tears on that, for that is all he gets
Of Gaveston, or else his senseless trunk.
Lancaster. Not so my lord, lest he bestow more cost
In burying him, than he hath ever earned.

28 so much honour] i.e. to be executed like a gentleman and not hung as a felon

Arundel. My lords, it is his majesty's request;
    And in the honour of a king he swears
    He will but talk with him and send him back.
Warwick. When, can you tell? Arundel, no; we wot   60
    He that the care of realm remits,
    And drives his nobles to these exigents
    For Gaveston, will, if he seize him once,
    Violate any promise to possess him.
Arundel. Then if you will not trust his grace in keep,
    My lords, I will be pledge for his return.
Mortimer. It is honourable in thee to offer this,
    But for we know thou art a noble gentleman
    We will not wrong thee so, to make away
    A true man for a thief.   70
Gaveston. How mean'st thou Mortimer? That is over-base.
Mortimer. Away, base groom, robber of king's renowm,
    Question with thy companions and thy mates.
Pembroke. My lord Mortimer, and you my lords each one,
    To gratify the King's request therein,
    Touching the sending of this Gaveston;
    Because his majesty so earnestly
    Desires to see the man before his death,
    I will upon mine honour undertake
    To carry him, and bring him back again;   80
    Provided this, that you my lord of Arundel
    Will join with me.
Warwick.   Pembroke, what wilt thou do?
    Cause yet more bloodshed? Is it not enough
    That we have taken him, but must we now
    Leave him on 'had I wist', and let him go?
Pembroke. My lords, I will not over-woo your honours,
    But if you dare trust Pembroke with the prisoner,
    Upon mine oath I will return him back.
Arundel. My lord of Lancaster, what say you in this?
Lancaster. Why, I say, let him go on Pembroke's word.   90
Pembroke. And you, lord Mortimer?
Mortimer. How say you, my lord of Warwick?
Warwick. Nay, do your pleasures; I know how 'twill prove.
Pembroke. Then give him me.
Gaveston.   Sweet sovereign, yet I come
    To see thee ere I die.

65 in keep] with the custody   85 'had I wist'] 'if only I had known'; the exclamation
of one who repents when it is too late

Warwick [*aside*].   Yet not, perhaps,
   If Warwick's wit and policy prevail.
Mortimer. My lord of Pembroke, we deliver him you;
   Return him on your honour. Sound away!   *Exeunt.*
       Manent Pembroke, [Arundel,] Gaveston, *and Pembroke's Men*
                    [James *and three* Soldiers].
Pembroke. My lord, you shall go with me;
   My house is not far hence, out of the way   100
   A little, but our men shall go along.
   We that have pretty wenches to our wives,
   Sir, must not come so near and balk their lips.
Arundel. 'Tis very kindly spoke, my lord of Pembroke:
   Your honour hath an adamant of power
   To draw a prince.
Pembroke.   So, my lord. Come hither James.
   I do commit this Gaveston to thee;
   Be thou this night his keeper; in the morning
   We will discharge thee of thy charge. Be gone.
Gaveston. Unhappy Gaveston, whither goest thou now?   110
                        Exit cum servis Pem.
Pembroke. My lord, we'll quickly be at Cobham.   *Exeunt ambo.*

[Act III   Scene i]

   Enter Gaveston *mourning*, [James,] *and the Earl of Pembroke's Men.*
Gaveston. O treacherous Warwick, thus to wrong thy friend!
James. I see it is your life these arms pursue.
Gaveston. Weaponless must I fall, and die in bands.
   O! Must this day be period of my life,
   Centre of all my bliss? And ye be men,
   Speed to the King.
          Enter Warwick *and his Company.*
Warwick.   My lord of Pembroke's men,
   Strive you no longer; I will have that Gaveston.
James. Your lordship doth dishonour to yourself,
   And wrong our lord, your honourable friend.

105 adamant] magnet   110 f.] O gives the last line to 'Horseboy', and most editors
assume that he is speaking to Gaveston, Pembroke having already left the stage with his
servants. But if Gaveston departs (with Pembroke's servants) on his own line, the last line
can be given to Pembroke, addressing Arundel. The allusion to Cobham is unexplained,
however—Pembroke's seat was Deddington.

Warwick. No James, it is my country's cause I follow.   10
    Go, take the villain; soldiers, come away,
    We'll make quick work. Commend me to your master,
    My friend, and tell him that I watch'd it well.
    Come, let thy shadow parley with King Edward.
Gaveston. Treacherous earl, shall I not see the King?
Warwick. The king of heaven perhaps, no other king.
    Away!

                         Exeunt Warwick *and his Men, with* Gaveston.
                                Manent James *cum caeteris.*

James. Come fellows, it booted not for us to strive.
    We will in haste go certify our lord.   *Exeunt.*

[Scene ii]

Enter King Edward *and* Spencer [*and* Baldock], *with Drums and Fifes.*

Edward. I long to hear an answer from the barons
    Touching my friend, my dearest Gaveston.
    Ah Spencer, not the riches of my realm
    Can ransom him; ah, he is mark'd to die.
    I know the malice of the younger Mortimer;
    Warwick I know is rough; and Lancaster
    Inexorable; and I shall never see
    My lovely Piers, my Gaveston, again.
    The barons overbear me with their pride.
Spencer. Were I King Edward, England's sovereign,   10
    Son to the lovely Eleanor of Spain,
    Great Edward Longshanks' issue—would I bear
    These braves, this rage, and suffer uncontroll'd
    These barons thus to beard me in my land,
    In mine own realm? My lord, pardon my speech.
    Did you retain your father's magnanimity,
    Did you regard the honour of your name,
    You would not suffer thus your majesty
    Be counterbuff'd of your nobility.
    Strike off their heads, and let them preach on poles;   20
    No doubt such lessons they will teach the rest,
    As by their preachments they will profit much,
    And learn obedience to their lawful king.
Edward. Yea, gentle Spencer, we have been too mild,

17 s.d. *cum caeteris*] 'with the rest'   III. ii, 12 Edward Longshanks] Edward I, nicknamed
for his long legs

Too kind to them; but now have drawn our sword,
And if they send me not my Gaveston
We'll steel it on their crest, and poll their tops.

Baldock. This haught resolve becomes your majesty,
Not to be tied to their affection,
As though your highness were a schoolboy still,   30
And must be aw'd and govern'd like a child.

Enter Hugh Spencer *an old man, father to the young Spencer, with*
his truncheon and Soldiers.

Spencer the Father. Long live my sovereign, the noble Edward,
In peace triumphant, fortunate in wars.

Edward. Welcome, old man. Com'st thou in Edward's aid?
Then tell thy prince of whence and what thou art.

Spencer the Father. Lo, with a band of bowmen and of pikes,
Brown bills and targeteers, four hundred strong,
Sworn to defend King Edward's royal right,
I come in person to your majesty;
Spencer, the father of Hugh Spencer there,   40
Bound to your highness everlastingly
For favours done in him unto us all.

Edward. Thy father, Spencer?

Spencer. True, and it like your grace,
That pours in lieu of all your goodness shown,
His life, my lord, before your princely feet.

Edward. Welcome ten thousand times, old man, again.
Spencer, this love, this kindness to thy king
Argues thy noble mind and disposition;
Spencer, I here create thee Earl of Wiltshire,
And daily will enrich thee with our favour,   50
That as the sunshine shall reflect o'er thee.
Beside, the more to manifest our love,
Because we hear lord Bruce doth sell his land,
And that the Mortimers are in hand withal,
Thou shalt have crowns of us, t'outbid the barons,
And Spencer, spare them not but lay it on.
Soldiers, a largesse; and thrice welcome all.

Spencer. My lord, here comes the Queen.

Enter the Queen and her son [Prince Edward], *and* Levune
a Frenchman.

27 poll their tops] prune their heads (like trees) and set them on poles (like traitors)
29 affection] will   37 Brown bills] Foot-soldiers armed with bronzed halberds
37 targeteers] shield-bearers   54 in hand withal] engaged in the transaction

Edward.   Madam, what news?
Isabella. News of dishonour, lord, and discontent:
    Our friend Levune, faithful and full of trust,   60
    Informeth us, by letters and by words,
    That lord Valois our brother, King of France,
    Because your highness hath been slack in homage,
    Hath seized Normandy into his hands;
    These be the letters, this the messenger.
Edward. Welcome Levune. Tush Sib, if this be all,
    Valois and I will soon be friends again.
    But to my Gaveston—shall I never see,
    Never behold thee now? Madam, in this matter
    We will employ you and your little son;   70
    You shall go parley with the King of France.
    Boy, see you bear you bravely to the King,
    And do your message with a majesty.
Prince Edward. Commit not to my youth things of more weight
    Than fits a prince so young as I to bear,
    And fear not, lord and father, heaven's great beams
    On Atlas' shoulder shall not lie more safe
    Than shall your charge committed to my trust.
Isabella. Ah boy, this towardness makes thy mother fear
    Thou art not mark'd to many days on earth.   80
Edward. Madam, we will that you with speed be shipp'd,
    And this our son; Levune shall follow you
    With all the haste we can dispatch him hence.
    Choose of our lords to bear you company,
    And go in peace; leave us in wars at home.
Isabella. Unnatural wars, where subjects brave their king:
    God end them once. My lord, I take my leave
    To make my preparation for France.
                       [*Exit Queen and* Prince Edward.]

                Enter Arundel.

Edward. What, lord Arundel, dost thou come alone?
Arundel. Yea my good lord, for Gaveston is dead.   90
Edward. Ah, traitors, have they put my friend to death?
    Tell me, Arundel, died he ere thou cam'st,
    Or didst thou see my friend to take his death?
Arundel. Neither, my lord; for as he was surpris'd,
    Begirt with weapons, and with enemies round,
    I did your highness' message to them all,

79 towardness] precociousness   87 once] once for all

    Demanding him of them, entreating rather,
    And said, upon the honour of my name,
    That I would undertake to carry him
    Unto your highness, and to bring him back.   100
Edward. And tell me, would the rebels deny me that?
Spencer. Proud recreants!
Edward.   Yea Spencer, traitors all.
Arundel. I found them at the first inexorable;
    The Earl of Warwick would not bide the hearing,
    Mortimer hardly; Pembroke and Lancaster
    Spake least. And when they flatly had denied,
    Refusing to receive me pledge for him,
    The Earl of Pembroke mildly thus bespake:
    'My lords, because our sovereign sends for him
    And promiseth he shall be safe return'd,   110
    I will this undertake, to have him hence,
    And see him re-deliver'd to your hands.'
Edward. Well, and how fortunes that he came not?
Spencer. Some treason or some villainy was cause.
Arundel. The Earl of Warwick seiz'd him on his way.
    For being deliver'd unto Pembroke's men,
    Their lord rode home, thinking his prisoner safe;
    But ere he came, Warwick in ambush lay,
    And bare him to his death, and in a trench
    Strake off his head, and march'd unto the camp.   120
Spencer. A bloody part, flatly against law of arms.
Edward. O, shall I speak, or shall I sigh and die!
Spencer. My lord, refer your vengeance to the sword
    Upon these barons; hearten up your men.
    Let them not unreveng'd murder your friends.
    Advance your standard, Edward, in the field,
    And march to fire them from their starting-holes.
Edward (*kneels, and saith*). By earth, the common mother of us all,
    By heaven, and all the moving orbs thereof,
    By this right hand and by my father's sword,   130
    And all the honours 'longing to my crown,
    I will have heads and lives for him, as many
    As I have manors, castles, towns and towers.
    Treacherous Warwick! Traitorous Mortimer!
    If I be England's king, in lakes of gore
    Your headless trunks, your bodies will I trail,
    That you may drink your fill, and quaff in blood,
    And stain my royal standard with the same;

That so my bloody colours may suggest
Remembrance of revenge immortally   140
On your accursed traitorous progeny,
You villains that have slain my Gaveston.
And in this place of honour and of trust,
Spencer, sweet Spencer, I adopt thee here,
And merely of our love we do create thee
Earl of Gloucester and Lord Chamberlain,
Despite of times, despite of enemies.
Spencer. My lord, here is a messenger from the barons
      Desires access unto your majesty.
Edward. Admit him near.   150

>   *Enter the* Herald *from the barons, with his coat of arms.*

Herald. Long live King Edward, England's lawful lord.
Edward. So wish not they, I wis, that sent thee hither;
      Thou com'st from Mortimer and his complices—
      A ranker rout of rebels never was.
      Well, say thy message.
Herald. The barons up in arms, by me salute
      Your highness with long life and happiness;
      And bid me say as plainer to your grace,
      That if without effusion of blood
      You will this grief have ease and remedy,   160
      That from your princely person you remove
      This Spencer, as a putrefying branch
      That deads the royal vine, whose golden leaves
      Empale your princely head, your diadem,
      Whose brightness such pernicious upstarts dim;
      Say they; and lovingly advise your grace
      To cherish virtue and nobility,
      And have old servitors in high esteem,
      And shake off smooth dissembling flatterers.
      This granted, they, their honours and their lives,   170
      Are to your highness vow'd and consecrate.
Spencer. Ah traitors, will they still display their pride?
Edward. Away! Tarry no answer but be gone.
      Rebels, will they appoint their sovereign
      His sports, his pleasures, and his company?
      Yet ere thou go, see how I do divorce   *Embrace* Spencer.
      Spencer from me. Now get thee to thy lords,
      And tell them I will come to chastise them

145 merely] for no other reason   158 plainer] plaintiff

For murdering Gaveston. Hie thee, get thee gone;
Edward with fire and sword follows at thy heels.   180

[*Exit* Herald.]

My lord, perceive you how these rebels swell?
Soldiers, good hearts, defend your sovereign's righ t,
For now, even now, we march to make them stoop.
Away!   *Exeunt.*

[Scene iii]

Alarums, excursions, a great fight, and a retreat. Enter the King,
Spencer the Father, Spencer, *and Noblemen of the King's side.*

Edward. Why do we sound retreat? Upon them, lords!
    This day I shall pour vengeance with my sword
    On those proud rebels that are up in arms,
    And do confront and countermand their king.
Spencer. I doubt it not, my lord; right will prevail.
Spencer the Father. 'Tis not amiss, my liege, for either part
    To breathe awhile; our men, with sweat and dust
    All chok'd well near, begin to faint for heat;
    And this retire refresheth horse and man.
Spencer. Here come the rebels.   10

Enter the Barons, Mortimer, Lancaster, [Kent,] Warwick, Pembroke,
                          cum caeteris.

Mortimer. Look Lancaster, yonder is Edward
    Among his flatterers.
Lancaster.   And there let him be,
    Till he pay dearly for their company.
Warwick. And shall, or Warwick's sword shall smite in vain.
Edward. What, rebels, do you shrink and sound retreat?
Mortimer. No, Edward, no; thy flatterers faint and fly.
Lancaster. Th'ad best betimes forsake them and their trains,
    For they'll betray thee, traitors as they are.
Spencer. Traitor on thy face, rebellious Lancaster.
Pembroke. Away, base upstart; brav'st thou nobles thus?   20
Spencer the Father. A noble attempt and honourable deed
    Is it not, trow ye, to assemble aid
    And levy arms against your lawful king?
Edward. For which ere long, their heads shall satisfy
    T'appease the wrath of their offended king.
Mortimer. Then Edward, thou wilt fight it to the last,

And rather bathe thy sword in subjects' blood
Than banish that pernicious company?
Edward. Ay, traitors all! Rather than thus be brav'd,
    Make England's civil towns huge heaps of stones   30
    And ploughs to go about our palace gates.
Warwick. A desperate and unnatural resolution.
    Alarum to the fight! St. George for England
    And the barons' right.
Edward. St. George for England and King Edward's right.
                            [Exeunt both parties different ways.]

    [Alarums.] Enter Edward *[the two* Spencers, Baldock *and* Levune*]*
      with the Barons [Kent, Warwick, Lancaster, Mortimer] *captives.*

Edward. Now, lusty lords, now, not by chance of war,
    But justice of the quarrel and the cause,
    Vail'd is your pride. Methinks you hang the heads,
    But we'll advance them, traitors! Now 'tis time
    To be aveng'd on you for all your braves,   40
    And for the murder of my dearest friend,
    To whom right well you knew our soul was knit,
    Good Piers of Gaveston, my sweet favourite—
    Ah rebels, recreants, you made him away!
Kent. Brother, in regard of thee and of thy land
    Did they remove that flatterer from thy throne.
Edward. So sir, you have spoke; away, avoid our presence.   *[Exit* Kent.*]*
    Accursed wretches, was't in regard of us,
    When we had sent our messenger to request
    He might be spar'd to come to speak with us,   50
    And Pembroke undertook for his return,
    That thou, proud Warwick, watch'd the prisoner,
    Poor Piers, and headed him against law of arms?
    For which thy head shall overlook the rest
    As much as thou in rage out-went'st the rest.
Warwick. Tyrant, I scorn thy threats and menaces;
    'Tis but temporal that thou canst inflict.
Lancaster. The worst is death, and better die to live,
    Than live in infamy under such a king.
Edward. Away with them; my lord of Winchester,   60
    These lusty leaders, Warwick and Lancaster,
    I charge you roundly, off with both their heads.
    Away!

57 but temporal] only physical (not spiritual) torture   60 lord of Winchester] i.e.
Spencer the father, who was given that title in 1322

Warwick. Farewell, vain world.
Lancaster.   Sweet Mortimer, farewell.
                                 [*Exeunt* Warwick *and* Lancaster
                                      with Spencer the Father.]
Mortimer. England, unkind to thy nobility,
  Groan for this grief, behold how thou art maim'd.
Edward. Go take that haughty Mortimer to the Tower,
  There see him safe bestow'd; and for the rest,
  Do speedy execution on them all.
  Be gone.   70
Mortimer. What, Mortimer! Can ragged stony walls
  Immure thy virtue that aspires to heaven?
  No Edward, England's scourge, it may not be;
  Mortimer's hope surmounts his fortune far.   [*Exit, guarded.*]
Edward. Sound drums and trumpets! March with me, my friends;
  Edward this day hath crown'd him king anew.   [*Exit.*]
                          Manent Spencer, Levune *and* Baldock.
Spencer. Levune, the trust that we repose in thee
  Begets the quiet of King Edward's land;
  Therefore be gone in haste, and with advice
  Bestow that treasure on the lords of France,   80
  That therewithal enchanted, like the guard
  That suffered Jove to pass in showers of gold
  To Danäe, all aid may be denied
  To Isabel the Queen, that now in France
  Makes friends, to cross the seas with her young son,
  And step into his father's regiment.
Levune. That's it these barons and the subtile Queen
  Long levell'd at?
Baldock.   Yea, but Levune, thou seest
  These barons lay their heads on blocks together;
  What they intend, the hangman frustrates clean.   90
Levune. Have you no doubts, my lords; I'll clap so close
  Among the lords of France with England's gold,
  That Isabel shall make her plaints in vain,
  And France shall be obdurate with her tears.
Spencer. Then make for France amain; Levune, away,
  Proclaim King Edward's wars and victories.   *Exeunt omnes.*

88 levell'd] aimed   95 amain] with speed

[Act IV   Scene i]

Enter Kent.

Kent. Fair blows the wind for France; blow gentle gale
    Till Edmund be arriv'd for England's good.
    Nature, yield to my country's cause in this:
    A brother—no, a butcher of thy friends—
    Proud Edward, dost thou banish me thy presence?
    But I'll to France, and cheer the wronged queen,
    And certify what Edward's looseness is.
    Unnatural king, to slaughter noble men
    And cherish flatterers! Mortimer, I stay
    Thy sweet escape; stand gracious, gloomy night,   10
    To his device.

                Enter Mortimer *disguised.*

Mortimer.   Holla! Who walketh there?
    Is't you, my lord?
Kent.   Mortimer, 'tis I;
    But hath thy potion wrought so happily?
Mortimer. It hath, my lord: the warders all asleep,
    I thank them, gave me leave to pass in peace.
    But hath your grace got shipping into France?
Kent. Fear it not.   *Exeunt.*

[Scene ii]

Enter the Queen and her son.

Isabella. Ah boy, our friends do fail us all in France;
    The lords are cruel and the King unkind.
    What shall we do?
Prince Edward.   Madam, return to England,
    And please my father well, and then a fig
    For all my uncle's friendship here in France.
    I warrant you, I'll win his highness quickly;
    'A loves me better than a thousand Spencers.
Isabella. Ah boy, thou art deceiv'd at least in this,
    To think that we can yet be tun'd together;
    No, no, we jar too far. Unkind Valois!   10
    Unhappy Isabel, when France rejects;
    Whither, O whither dost thou bend thy steps?
            Enter Sir John of Hainault.

Sir John. Madam, what cheer?

Isabella.   Ah, good Sir John of Hainault,
          Never so cheerless, nor so far distress'd.

Sir John. I hear, sweet lady, of the King's unkindness,
          But droop not, Madam; noble minds contemn
          Despair. Will your grace with me to Hainault
          And there stay time's advantage with your son?
          How say you, my lord, will you go with your friends,
          And shake off all our fortunes equally?   20

Prince Edward. So pleaseth the Queen my mother, me it likes.
          The King of England nor the court of France
          Shall have me from my gracious mother's side
          Till I be strong enough to break a staff;
          And then have at the proudest Spencer's head.

Sir John. Well said, my lord.

Isabella. Oh my sweet heart, how do I moan thy wrongs,
          Yet triumph in the hope of thee, my joy.
          Ah sweet Sir John, even to the utmost verge
          Of Europe, or the shore of Tanaïs
          Will we with thee; to Hainault, so we will.   30
          The marquis is a noble gentleman;
          His grace, I dare presume, will welcome me.
          But who are these?

                    Enter Kent *and* Mortimer.

Kent.   Madam, long may you live
          Much happier than your friends in England do.

Isabella. Lord Edmund and lord Mortimer alive!
          Welcome to France! The news was here, my lord,
          That you were dead, or very near your death.

Mortimer. Lady, the last was truest of the twain;
          But Mortimer, reserv'd for better hap,   40
          Hath shaken off the thraldom of the Tower
          And lives t'advance your standard, good my lord.

Prince Edward. How mean you, and the King my father lives?
          No, my lord Mortimer, not I, I trow.

Isabella. Not, son! Why not? I would it were no worse;
          But, gentle lords, friendless we are in France.

Mortimer. Monsieur le Grand, a noble friend of yours,
          Told us at our arrival all the news,
          How hard the nobles, how unkind the King
          Hath show'd himself. But, Madam, right makes room   50

30 Tanaïs] the river Don, believed to divide Europe from Asia

Where weapons want; and though a many friends
Are made away, as Warwick, Lancaster,
And others of our party and faction,
Yet have we friends, assure your grace, in England
Would cast up caps and clap their hands for joy,
To see us there appointed for our foes.

Kent. Would all were well, and Edward well reclaim'd,
For England's honour, peace and quietness.

Mortimer. But by the sword, my lord, it must be deserv'd;
The King will ne'er forsake his flatterers.   60

Sir John. My lords of England, sith the ungentle King
Of France refuseth to give aid of arms
To this distressed queen his sister here,
Go you with her to Hainault; doubt ye not,
We will find comfort, money, men and friends
Ere long, to bid the English King a base.
How say, young Prince, what think you of the match?

Prince Edward. I think King Edward will out-run us all.

Isabella. Nay son, not so; and you must not discourage
Your friends that are so forward in your aid.   70

Kent. Sir John of Hainault, pardon us, I pray;
These comforts that you give our woeful Queen
Bind us in kindness all at your command.

Isabella. Yea, gentle brother; and the God of Heaven
Prosper your happy motion, good Sir John.

Mortimer. This noble gentleman, forward in arms,
Was born, I see, to be our anchor-hold.
Sir John of Hainault, be it thy renown
That England's Queen and nobles in distress
Have been by thee restor'd and comforted.   80

Sir John. Madam, along, and you my lord with me,
That England's peers may Hainault's welcome see.   [*Exeunt.*]

[Scene iii]

Enter the King, Arundel, *the two* Spencers, *with others.*

Edward. Thus after many threats of wrathful war,
Triumpheth England's Edward with his friends;
And triumph Edward with his friends uncontroll'd.
My lord of Gloucester, do you hear the news?

Spencer. What news, my lord?

Edward. Why man, they say there is great execution

66 to bid . . . a base] to challenge (from the game of prisoners' base)

Done through the realm; my lord of Arundel,
You have the note, have you not?
Arundel. From the lieutenant of the Tower, my lord.
Edward. I pray let us see it. What have we there?   10
Read it, Spencer.   Spencer *reads their names.*
Why so; they bark'd apace a month ago,
Now on my life they'll neither bark nor bite.
Now sirs, the news from France: Gloucester, I trow
The lords of France love England's gold so well
As Isabel gets no aid from thence.
What now remains? Have you proclaim'd, my lord,
Reward for them can bring in Mortimer?
Spencer. My lord, we have, and if he be in England
'A will be had ere long, I doubt it not.   20
Edward. If, dost thou say? Spencer, as true as death
He is in England's ground; our port-masters
Are not so careless of their king's command.

Enter a Post.

How now, what news with thee? From whence come these?
Post. Letters, my lord, and tidings forth of France
To you, my lord of Gloucester, from Levune.
Edward. Read.   Spencer *reads the letter.*
Spencer. 'My duty to your honour promised, &c. I have according to instructions in that behalf, dealt with the King of France his lords, and
effected that the Queen, all discontented and discomforted, is gone;
whither, if you ask, with Sir John of Hainault, brother to the marquis,
into Flanders; with them are gone lord Edmund and the lord Mortimer,
having in their company divers of your nation, and others; and, as constant
report goeth, they intend to give King Edward battle in England sooner
than he can look for them. This is all the news of import.
                                        Your honour's in all service, Levune.'
Edward. Ah villains, hath that Mortimer escap'd?
With him is Edmund gone associate?
And will Sir John of Hainault lead the round?
Welcome, a God's name, Madam and your son;   40
England shall welcome you and all your rout.
Gallop apace bright Phoebus through the sky,
And dusky night, in rusty iron car,
Between you both, shorten the time, I pray,
That I may see that most desired day

---

12 s.d. *their names*] The list read out here could have been compiled from Holinshed—or
the names invented.   39 round] dance

When we may meet these traitors in the field.
Ah, nothing grieves me but my little boy
Is thus misled to countenance their ills.
Come, friends, to Bristow, there to make us strong;
And winds, as equal be to bring them in   50
As you injurious were to bear them forth.   [*Exeunt.*]

[Scene iv]

Enter the Queen, her son, [Kent,] Mortimer *and* Sir John.

Isabella. Now lords, our loving friends and countrymen,
  Welcome to England all; with prosperous winds
  Our kindest friends in Belgia have we left,
  To cope with friends at home. A heavy case,
  When force to force is knit, and sword and glaive
  In civil broils makes kin and countrymen
  Slaughter themselves in others, and their sides
  With their own weapons gor'd. But what's the help?
  Misgovern'd kings are cause of all this rack;
  And Edward, thou art one among them all   10
  Whose looseness hath betray'd thy land to spoil,
  And made the channels overflow with blood;
  Of thine own people patron shouldst thou be,
  But thou——
Mortimer. Nay Madam, if you be a warrior,
  You must not grow so passionate in speeches.
  Lords, sith that we are by sufferance of heaven
  Arriv'd and armed in this prince's right,
  Here for our country's cause swear we to him
  All homage, fealty and forwardness.   20
  And for the open wrongs and injuries
  Edward hath done to us, his queen and land,
  We come in arms to wreck it with the sword,
  That England's Queen in peace may repossess
  Her dignities and honours; and withal
  We may remove these flatterers from the King,
  That havocs England's wealth and treasury.
Sir John. Sound trumpets, my lord, and forward let us march;
  Edward will think we come to flatter him.
Kent. I would he never had been flattered more.   30
                                                   [*Exeunt.*]

49 Bristow] Bristol

[Scene v]

Enter the King, Baldock *and* Spencer, *flying about the stage.*

Spencer. Fly, fly, my lord! The Queen is over-strong,
    Her friends do multiply and yours do fail.
    Shape we our course to Ireland, there to breathe.
Edward. What, was I born to fly and run away,
    And leave the Mortimers conquerors behind?
    Give me my horse, and let's r'enforce our troops,
    And in this bed of honour die with fame.
Baldock. Oh no, my lord, this princely resolution
    Fits not the time; away, we are pursu'd.   [*Exeunt.*]

Enter Kent *alone with a sword and target.*

Kent. This way he fled, but I am come too late.   10
    Edward alas, my heart relents for thee.
    Proud traitor Mortimer, why dost thou chase
    Thy lawful king, thy sovereign, with thy sword?
    Vilde wretch, and why hast thou of all unkind,
    Borne arms against thy brother and thy king?
    Rain showers of vengeance on my cursed head,
    Thou God, to whom in justice it belongs
    To punish this unnatural revolt.
    Edward, this Mortimer aims at thy life;
    O fly him then! But Edmund, calm this rage;   20
    Dissemble or thou diest; for Mortimer
    And Isabel do kiss while they conspire,
    And yet she bears a face of love, forsooth;
    Fie on that love that hatcheth death and hate!
    Edmund, away; Bristow to Longshanks' blood
    Is false. Be not found single for suspect;
    Proud Mortimer pries near into thy walks.

Enter the Queen, Mortimer, *the young* Prince, *and* Sir John of Hainault.

Isabella. Successful battles gives the God of kings
    To them that fight in right and fear his wrath;
    Since then successfully we have prevail'd,   30
    Thanks be heaven's great architect, and you.
    Ere farther we proceed, my noble lords,
    We here create our well-beloved son,
    Of love and care unto his royal person,
    Lord Warden of the realm; and sith the fates

26 for suspect] for fear of being suspected

    Have made his father so infortunate,
    Deal you my lords in this, my loving lords,
    As to your wisdoms fittest seems in all.
Kent. Madam, without offence if I may ask,
    How will you deal with Edward in his fall?   40
Prince Edward. Tell me good uncle, what Edward do you mean?
Kent. Nephew, your father; I dare not call him King.
Mortimer. My lord of Kent, what needs these questions?
    'Tis not in her controlment, nor in ours;
    But as the realm and parliament shall please,
    So shall your brother be disposed of.
    [*Aside to the Queen.*] I like not this relenting mood in Edmund,
    Madam; 'tis good to look to him betimes.
Isabella. My lord, the mayor of Bristow knows our mind?
Mortimer. Yea Madam, and they scape not easily.   50
    That fled the field.
Isabella.   Baldock is with the King;
    A goodly chancellor, is he not, my lord?
Sir John. So are the Spencers, the father and the son.
Kent. This Edward is the ruin of the realm.

      Enter Rice ap Howell *and the* Mayor *of Bristow, with* Spencer the
                                  Father.

Rice ap Howell. God save Queen Isabel and her princely son!
    Madam, the mayor and citizens of Bristow,
    In sign of love and duty to this presence,
    Present by me this traitor to the state,
    Spencer, the father to that wanton Spencer,
    That like the lawless Catiline of Rome   60
    Revelled in England's wealth and treasury.
Isabella. We thank you all.
Mortimer.   Your loving care in this
    Deserveth princely favours and rewards.
    But where's the King and the other Spencer fled?
Rice ap Howell. Spencer the son, created earl of Gloucester,
    Is with that smooth-tongu'd scholar Baldock gone,
    And shipp'd but late for Ireland with the King.
Mortimer. Some whirlwind fetch them back or sink them all!
    They shall be started thence, I doubt it not.
Prince Edward. Shall I not see the King my father yet?   70
Kent [*aside*]. Unhappy's Edward, chas'd from England's bounds.
Sir John. Madam, what resteth, why stand ye in a muse?
Isabella. I rue my lord's ill fortune, but, alas,

  Care of my country called me to this war.

Mortimer. Madam, have done with care and sad complaint;
  Your king hath wrong'd your country and himself,
  And we must seek to right it as we may.
  Meanwhile, have hence this rebel to the block;
  Your lordship cannot privilege your head.

Spencer the Father. Rebel is he that fights against his prince, 80
  So fought not they that fought in Edward's right.

Mortimer. Take him away, he prates. [*Exit* Spencer the Father, *guarded.*]
      You, Rice ap Howell,
  Shall do good service to her majesty,
  Being of countenance in your country here,
  To follow these rebellious runagates.
  We in meanwhile, Madam, must take advice
  How Baldock, Spencer, and their complices
  May in their fall be follow'd to their end.   *Exeunt omnes.*

[Scene vi]

Enter the Abbot, Monks, Edward, Spencer *and* Baldock.

Abbot. Have you no doubt, my lord, have you no fear;
  As silent and as careful will we be
  To keep your royal person safe with us,
  Free from suspect and fell invasion
  Of such as have your majesty in chase—
  Yourself, and those your chosen company—
  As danger of this stormy time requires.

Edward. Father, thy face should harbour no deceit.
  O, hadst thou ever been a king, thy heart
  Pierced deeply with sense of my distress, 10
  Could not but take compassion of my state.
  Stately and proud, in riches and in train,
  Whilom I was powerful and full of pomp;
  But what is he, whom rule and empery
  Have not in life or death made miserable?
  Come Spencer, come Baldock, come sit down by me;
  Make trial now of that philosophy
  That in our famous nurseries of arts
  Thou suck'dst from Plato and from Aristotle.
  Father, this life contemplative is heaven— 20

84 of countenance] influential IV. vi, 13 Whilom] Once

O that I might this life in quiet lead!
But we alas are chas'd; and you, my friends,
Your lives and my dishonour they pursue.
Yet gentle monks, for treasure, gold nor fee,
Do you betray us and our company.

Monks. Your grace may sit secure, if none but we
Do wot of your abode.

Spencer. Not one alive; but shrewdly I suspect
A gloomy fellow in a mead below.
'A gave a long look after us, my lord,   30
And all the land, I know, is up in arms,
Arms that pursue our lives with deadly hate.

Baldock. We were embark'd for Ireland, wretched we,
With awkward winds and sore tempests driven
To fall on shore, and here to pine in fear
Of Mortimer and his confederates.

Edward. Mortimer! Who talks of Mortimer?
Who wounds me with the name of Mortimer,
That bloody man? Good father, on thy lap
Lay I this head, laden with mickle care.   40
O might I never open these eyes again,
Never again lift up this drooping head,
O never more lift up this dying heart.

Spencer. Look up my lord. Baldock, this drowsiness
Betides no good. Here even we are betray'd.

Enter with Welsh hooks Rice ap Howell, *a* Mower, *and the Earl of*
Leicester.

Mower. Upon my life, those be the men ye seek.

Rice ap Howell. Fellow, enough. My lord, I pray be short,
A fair commission warrants what we do.

Leicester. The Queen's commission, urg'd by Mortimer;
What cannot gallant Mortimer with the Queen?   50
Alas, see where he sits and hopes unseen
T'escape their hands that seek to reave his life.
Too true it is: *quem dies vidit veniens superbum,*
Hunc dies vidit fugiens iacentem.
But Leicester, leave to grow so passionate.
Spencer and Baldock, by no other names,
I arrest you of high treason here;
Stand not on titles, but obey th'arrest;

52 reave] take away   53–4 *quem . . . iacentem*] 'the same man that the morning saw in
his pride, the evening saw in lowliness'   56 by no other names] i.e. he will not recite
their titles

'Tis in the name of Isabel the Queen.
My lord, why droop you thus?   60
Edward. O day, the last of all my bliss on earth,
Centre of all misfortune! O my stars!
Why do you lour unkindly on a king?
Comes Leicester then in Isabella's name
To take my life, my company, from me?
Here man, rip up this panting breast of mine
And take my heart, in rescue of my friends.
Rice ap Howell. Away with them.
Spencer.   It may become thee yet
To let us take our farewell of his grace.
Abbot. My heart with pity earns to see this sight;   70
A king to bear these words and proud commands!
Edward. Spencer, ah sweet Spencer; thus then must we part?
Spencer. We must, my lord, so will the angry heavens.
Edward. Nay, so will hell and cruel Mortimer;
The gentle heavens have not to do in this.
Baldock. My lord, it is in vain to grieve or storm;
Here humbly of your grace we take our leaves;
Our lots are cast. I fear me, so is thine.
Edward. In heaven we may, in earth never shall we meet.
And Leicester say, what shall become of us?   80
Leicester. Your majesty must go to Killingworth.
Edward. Must! 'Tis somewhat hard when kings must go.
Leicester. Here is a litter ready for your grace
That waits your pleasure; and the day grows old.
Rice ap Howell. As good be gone, as stay and be benighted.
Edward. A litter hast thou? Lay me in a hearse,
And to the gates of hell convey me hence;
Let Pluto's bells ring out my fatal knell,
And hags howl for my death at Charon's shore,
For friends hath Edward none, but these, and these,
And these must die under a tyrant's sword.   90
Rice ap Howell. My lord, be going; care not for these,
For we shall see them shorter by the heads.
Edward. Well, that shall be, shall be; part we must,
Sweet Spencer, gentle Baldock, part we must.
Hence feigned weeds, unfeigned are my woes.
Father, farewell. Leicester, thou stay'st for me
And go I must. Life, farewell with my friends.

Exeunt Edward *and* Leicester.

70 earns] grieves   81 Killingworth] Kenilworth

Spencer. O is he gone! Is noble Edward gone,
    Parted from hence, never to see us more?   100
    Rent sphere of heaven, and fire forsake thy orb,
    Earth melt to air, gone is my sovereign,
    Gone, gone, alas, never to make return.
Baldock. Spencer, I see our souls are fleeted hence,
    We are depriv'd the sunshine of our life.
    Make for a new life, man, throw up thy eyes,
    And heart and hand to heaven's immortal throne,
    Pay nature's debt with cheerful countenance;
    Reduce we all our lessons unto this:
    To die, sweet Spencer, therefore live we all;   110
    Spencer, all live to die, and rise to fall.
Rice ap Howell. Come, come, keep these preachments till you come to the
    place appointed. You, and such as you are, have made wise work in
    England. Will your lordships away?
Mower. Your worship, I trust, will remember me?
Rice ap Howell. Remember thee, fellow? What else? Follow me to the town.
                                      [Exeunt.]

[Act V   Scene i]

Enter the King, Leicester, *with the Bishop* [*of* Winchester, *and* Trussel]
for the crown.

Leicester. Be patient, good my lord, cease to lament;
    Imagine Killingworth Castle were your court,
    And that you lay for pleasure here a space,
    Not of compulsion or necessity.
Edward. Leicester, if gentle words might comfort me,
    Thy speeches long ago had eas'd my sorrows,
    For kind and loving hast thou always been.
    The griefs of private men are soon allay'd,
    But not of kings: the forest deer being struck
    Runs to an herb that closeth up the wounds,   10
    But when the imperial lion's flesh is gor'd
    He rends and tears it with his wrathful paw,
    And highly scorning that the lowly earth
    Should drink his blood, mounts up into the air:
    And so it fares with me, whose dauntless mind
    The ambitious Mortimer would seek to curb,
    And that unnatural queen, false Isabel,
    That thus hath pent and mew'd me in a prison;

For such outrageous passions cloy my soul
As with the wings of rancour and disdain   20
Full often am I soaring up to heaven
To plain me to the gods against them both.
But when I call to mind I am a king,
Methinks I should revenge me of the wrongs
That Mortimer and Isabel have done.
But what are kings, when regiment is gone,
But perfect shadows in a sunshine day?
My nobles rule, I bear the name of king;
I wear the crown; but am controll'd by them,
By Mortimer and my unconstant queen   30
Who spots my nuptial bed with infamy,
Whilst I am lodg'd within this cave of care,
Where sorrow at my elbow still attends
To company my heart with sad laments,
That bleeds within me for this strange exchange.
But tell me, must I now resign my crown
To make usurping Mortimer a king?
Winchester. Your grace mistakes; it is for England's good,
And princely Edward's right we claim the crown.
Edward. No, 'tis for Mortimer, not Edward's head;   40
For he's a lamb encompassed by wolves
Which in a moment will abridge his life.
But if proud Mortimer do wear this crown,
Heavens turn it to a blaze of quenchless fire,
Or like the snaky wreath of Tisiphon
Engirt the temples of his hateful head;
So shall not England's vines be perished,
But Edward's name survives, though Edward dies.
Leicester. My lord, why waste you thus your time away?
They stay your answer: will you yield your crown?   50
Edward. Ah Leicester, weigh how hardly I can brook
To lose my crown and kingdom without cause,
To give ambitious Mortimer my right,
That like a mountain overwhelms my bliss;
In which extreme my mind here murder'd is.
But what the heavens appoint, I must obey.
Here, take my crown, the life of Edward too:
Two kings in England cannot reign at once.
But stay awhile, let me be King till night,
That I may gaze upon this glittering crown;   60

45 Tisiphon] one of the Furies, who had snakes for hair

So shall my eyes receive their last content,
My head the latest honour due to it,
And jointly both yield up their wished right.
Continue ever, thou celestial sun,
Let never silent night possess this clime;
Stand still, you watches of the element,
All times and seasons, rest you at a stay,
That Edward may be still fair England's king.
But day's bright beams doth vanish fast away,
And needs I must resign my wished crown.   70
Inhuman creatures, nurs'd with tiger's milk,
Why gape you for your sovereign's overthrow—
My diadem, I mean, and guiltless life?
See, monsters, see, I'll wear my crown again!
What, fear you not the fury of your king?
But hapless Edward, thou art fondly led;
They pass not for thy frowns as late they did,
But seeks to make a new elected king;
Which fills my mind with strange despairing thoughts;
Which thoughts are martyred with endless torments;   80
And in this torment, comfort find I none
But that I feel the crown upon my head.
And therefore let me wear it yet awhile.
Trussel. My lord, the parliament must have present news,
    And therefore say: will you resign or no?   *The King rageth.*
Edward. I'll not resign, but whilst I live—
    Traitors, be gone, and join you with Mortimer.
    Elect, conspire, install; do what you will,
    Their blood and yours shall seal these treacheries.
Winchester. This answer we'll return and so farewell.   90
Leicester. Call them again, my lord, and speak them fair,
    For if they go the Prince shall lose his right.
Edward. Call thou them back; I have no power to speak.
Leicester. My lord, the King is willing to resign.
Winchester. If he be not, let him choose—
Edward. O would I might! But heavens and earth conspire
    To make me miserable. Here, receive my crown.
    Receive it? No, these innocent hands of mine
    Shall not be guilty of so foul a crime.
    He of you all that most desires my blood,   100
    And will be called the murderer of a king,
    Take it. What, are you mov'd? Pity you me?
    Then send for unrelenting Mortimer

And Isabel, whose eyes been turn'd to steel
Will sooner sparkle fire than shed a tear.
Yet stay; for rather than I will look on them,
Here, here!   *[Gives the crown.]*
           Now, sweet God of Heaven,
Make we despise this transitory pomp,
And sit for aye enthronized in heaven.
Come death, and with thy fingers close my eyes,   110
Or if I live, let me forget myself.
Winchester. My lord——
Edward. Call me not lord! Away—out of my sight!
  Ah, pardon me, grief makes me lunatic.
  Let not that Mortimer protect my son;
  More safety is there in a tiger's jaws
  Than his embracements. Bear this to the Queen,
              [Gives Bishop a handkerchief.]
  Wet with my tears, and dried again with sighs;
  If with the sight thereof she be not mov'd,
  Return it back, and dip it in my blood.   120
  Commend me to my son, and bid him rule
  Better than I. Yet how have I transgress'd,
  Unless it be with too much clemency?
Trussel. And thus, most humbly, do we take our leave.
            [Exeunt Bishop and Trussel.]
Edward. Farewell. I know the next news that they bring
  Will be my death, and welcome shall it be;
  To wretched men death is felicity
Leicester. Another post! What news brings he?

Enter Berkeley.

Edward. Such news as I expect. Come, Berkeley, come,
  And tell thy message to my naked breast.   130
Berkeley. My lord, think not a thought so villainous
  Can harbour in a man of noble birth.
  To do your highness service and devoir,
  And save you from your foes, Berkeley would die.
Leicester [*reading letter*]. My lord, the council of the Queen commands
  That I resign my charge.
Edward. And who must keep me now? Must you, my lord?
Berkeley. Ay, my most gracious lord, so 'tis decreed.
Edward [*taking the letter.*] By Mortimer, whose name is written here.
              [Tears up the paper.]

115 protect] be Protector to   133 devoir] duty

Well may I rent his name, that rends my heart!   140
This poor revenge hath something eas'd my mind;
So may his limbs be torn, as is this paper:
Hear me, immortal Jove, and grant it too.
Berkeley. Your grace must hence with me to Berkeley straight.
Edward. Whither you will; all places are alike,
And every earth is fit for burial.
Leicester. Favour him, my lord, as much as lieth in you.
Berkeley. Even so betide my soul as I use him.
Edward. Mine enemy hath pitied my estate,
And that's the cause that I am now remov'd.   150
Berkeley. And thinks your grace that Berkeley will be cruel?
Edward. I know not; but of this am I assur'd,
That death ends all, and I can die but once.
Leicester, farewell.
Leicester. Not yet, my lord; I'll bear you on your way.   *Exeunt omnes.*

[Scene ii]

Enter Mortimer *and* Queen *Isabel.*

Mortimer. Fair Isabel, now have we our desire.
The proud corrupters of the light-brain'd King
Have done their homage to the lofty gallows,
And he himself lies in captivity.
Be rul'd by me, and we will rule the realm.
In any case, take heed of childish fear,
For now we hold an old wolf by the ears
That if he slip will seize upon us both,
And gripe the sorer being grip'd himself.
Think therefore, Madam, that imports us much   10
To erect your son with all the speed we may,
And that I be Protector over him;
For our behoof will bear the greater sway
Whenas a king's name shall be underwrit.
Isabella. Sweet Mortimer, the life of Isabel,
Be thou persuaded that I love thee well,
And therefore, so the Prince my son be safe,
Whom I esteem as dear as these mine eyes,
Conclude against his father what thou wilt,
And I myself will willingly subscribe.   20
Mortimer. First would I hear news that he were depos'd,
And then let me alone to handle him.

Enter Messenger.

Letters, from whence?

Messenger.   From Killingworth, my lord.

Isabella. How fares my lord the King?

Messenger. In health Madam, but full of pensiveness.

Isabella. Alas, poor soul, would I could ease his grief.

                    [*Enter the Bishop of* Winchester *with the crown.*]

Thanks, gentle Winchester. Sirra be gone.   [*Exit* Messenger.]

Winchester. The King hath willingly resigned his crown.

Isabella. O happy news! Send for the Prince my son.

Winchester. Further, ere this letter was seal'd, Lord Berkeley came,   30
  So that he now is gone from Killingworth;
  And we have heard that Edmund laid a plot
  To set his brother free; no more but so.
  The lord of Berkeley is so pitiful
  As Leicester that had charge of him before.

Isabella. Then let some other be his guardian.

Mortimer. Let me alone—here is the privy seal.

                              [*Exit Bishop of* Winchester.]

Who's there? Call hither Gurney and Matrevis!
  To dash the heavy-headed Edmund's drift
  Berkeley shall be discharg'd, the King remov'd,   40
  And none but we shall know where he lieth.

Isabella. But Mortimer, as long as he survives
  What safety rests for us, or for my son?

Mortimer. Speak, shall he presently be dispatch'd and die?

Isabella. I would he were, so it were not by my means.

                    Enter Matrevis *and* Gurney.

Mortimer. Enough.
  Matrevis, write a letter presently
  Unto the lord of Berkeley from ourself,
  That he resign the king to thee and Gurney;
  And when 'tis done we will subscribe our name.   50

Matrevis. It shall be done, my lord.

Mortimer.   Gurney.

Gurney.   My lord?

Mortimer. As thou intend'st to rise by Mortimer,
  Who now makes Fortune's wheel turn as he please,
  Seek all the means thou canst to make him droop,
  And neither give him kind word nor good look.

Gurney. I warrant you, my lord.

Mortimer. And this above the rest, because we hear
  That Edmund casts to work his liberty,

Remove him still from place to place by night,
And at the last he come to Killingworth,   60
And then from thence to Berkeley back again;
And by the way, to make him fret the more,
Speak curstly to him; and in any case
Let no man comfort him, if he chance to weep,
But amplify his grief with bitter words.
Matrevis. Fear not, my lord, we'll do as you command.
Mortimer. So now away, post thitherwards amain.
Isabella. Whither goes this letter? To my lord the King?
    Commend me humbly to his majesty
    And tell him that I labour all in vain   70
    To ease his grief and work his liberty;
    And bear him this, as witness of my love.   [*Gives some token.*]
Matrevis. I will, Madam.   *Exeunt* Matrevis *and* Gurney.
                                              Manent Isabel *and* Mortimer.

        Enter the young Prince *and the Earl of* Kent *talking with him.*

Mortimer. Finely dissembl'd, do so still, sweet Queen.
    Here comes the young Prince, with the Earl of Kent.
Isabella. Something he whispers in his childish ears.
Mortimer. If he have such access unto the Prince
    Our plots and stratagems will soon be dash'd.
Isabella. Use Edmund friendly, as if all were well.
Mortimer. How fares my honourable lord of Kent?   80
Kent. In health, sweet Mortimer. How fares your grace?
Isabella. Well—if my lord your brother were enlarg'd.
Kent. I hear of late he hath depos'd himself.
Isabella. The more my grief.
Mortimer.   And mine.
Kent.   Ah, they do dissemble.
Isabella. Sweet son, come hither, I must talk with thee.
Mortimer. Thou being his uncle and the next of blood
    Do look to be Protector over the Prince?
Kent. Not I, my lord; who should protect the son
    But she that gave him life—I mean, the Queen?
Prince Edward. Mother, persuade me not to wear the crown;   90
    Let him be King. I am too young to reign.
Isabella. But be content, seeing it his highness' pleasure.
Prince Edward. Let me but see him first, and then I will.
Kent. Ay, do, sweet nephew.
Isabella. Brother, you know it is impossible.
Prince Edward. Why, is he dead?

Isabella. No, God forbid!

Kent. I would these words proceeded from your heart.

Mortimer. Inconstant Edmund, dost thou favour him,
That wast a cause of his imprisonment?   100

Kent. The more cause have I now to make amends.

Mortimer. I tell thee 'tis not meet that one so false
Should come about the person of a prince.
My lord, he hath betray'd the King his brother,
And therefore trust him not.

Prince Edward. But he repents, and sorrows for it now.

Isabella. Come son, and go with this gentle lord and me.

Prince Edward. With you I will, but not with Mortimer.

Mortimer. Why youngling, 'sdain'st thou so of Mortimer?
Then I will carry thee by force away.   110

Prince Edward. Help, uncle Kent! Mortimer will wrong me.

Isabella. Brother Edmund, strive not; we are his friends;
Isabel is nearer than the Earl of Kent.

Kent. Sister, Edward is my charge; redeem him.

Isabella. Edward is my son and I will keep him.

Kent. Mortimer shall know that he hath wronged me.
Hence will I haste to Killingworth castle,
And rescue aged Edward from his foes
To be reveng'd on Mortimer and thee.   *Exeunt omnes.*

[Scene iii]

Enter Matrevis *and* Gurney *with the King* [*and* Soldiers].

Matrevis. My lord, be not pensive, we are your friends.
Men are ordain'd to live in misery;
Therefore come, dalliance dangereth our lives.

Edward. Friends, whither must unhappy Edward go?
Will hateful Mortimer appoint no rest?
Must I be vexed like the nightly bird
Whose sight is loathsome to all winged fowls?
When will the fury of his mind assuage?
When will his heart be satisfied with blood?
If mine will serve, unbowel straight this breast
And give my heart to Isabel and him;   10
It is the chiefest mark they level at.

Gurney. Not so, my liege, the Queen hath given this charge
To keep your grace in safety;
Your passions make your dolours to increase.

Edward. This usage makes my misery increase.

But can my air of life continue long
When all my senses are annoy'd with stench?
Within a dungeon England's king is kept,
Where I am starv'd for want of sustenance;   20
My daily diet is heart-breaking sobs
That almost rents the closet of my heart.
Thus lives old Edward, not reliev'd by any;
And so must die, though pitied by many.
O water, gentle friends, to cool my thirst,
And clear my body from foul excrements.

Matrevis. Here's channel water, as our charge is given;
   Sit down, for we'll be barbers to your grace.
Edward. Traitors, away! What, will you murder me,
   Or choke your sovereign with puddle water?   30
Gurney. No, but wash your face and shave away your beard,
   Lest you be known and so be rescued.
Matrevis. Why strive you thus? Your labour is in vain.
Edward. The wren may strive against the lion's strength,
   But all in vain; so vainly do I strive
   To seek for mercy at a tyrant's hand.

                     They wash him with puddle water, and shave his
                                    beard away.

Immortal powers, that knows the painful cares
That waits upon my poor distressed soul,
O level all your looks upon these daring men,
That wrongs their liege and sovereign, England's king.   40
O Gaveston, it is for thee that I am wrong'd!
For me, both thou and both the Spencers died;
And for your sakes, a thousand wrongs I'll take.
The Spencers' ghosts, wherever they remain,
Wish well to mine; then tush, for them I'll die.

Matrevis. 'Twixt theirs and yours shall be no enmity.
   Come, come away; now put the torches out;
   We'll enter in by darkness to Killingworth.

                   Enter Kent.

Gurney. How now, who comes there?
Matrevis. Guard the King sure, it is the Earl of Kent.   50
Edward. O gentle brother, help to rescue me.
Matrevis. Keep them asunder; thrust in the King.
Kent. Soldiers, let me but talk to him one word.
Gurney. Lay hands upon the Earl for this assault.
Kent. Lay down your weapons! Traitors, yield the King.

320   EDWARD II [Act V]

Matrevis. Edmund, yield thyself, or thou shalt die.
Kent. Base villains, wherefore do you gripe me thus?
Gurney. Bind him, and so convey him to the court.
Kent. Where is the court but here? Here is the King,
    And I will visit him; why stay you me?   60
Matrevis. The court is where lord Mortimer remains,
    Thither shall your honour go. And so farewell.
            Exeunt Matrevis *and* Gurney *with the King.*
Kent. O miserable is that commonweal
    Where lords keep courts and kings are lock'd in prison!
Soldier. Wherefore stay we? On sirs, to the court.
Kent. Ay, lead me whither you will, even to my death,
    Seeing that my brother cannot be releas'd.   *Exeunt omnes.*

[Scene iv]

Enter Mortimer *alone.*

Mortimer. The King must die, or Mortimer goes down.
    The commons now begin to pity him.
    Yet he that is the cause of Edward's death
    Is sure to pay for it when his son is of age;
    And therefore will I do it cunningly.
    This letter, written by a friend of ours,
    Contains his death yet bids them save his life:
    '*Edwardum occidere nolite timere bonum est*';
    Fear not to kill the king, 'tis good he die.
    But read it thus, and that's another sense: 10
    '*Edwardum occidere nolite timere bonum est*';
    Kill not the king, 'tis good to fear the worst.
    Unpointed as it is, thus shall it go,
    That, being dead, if it chance to be found,
    Matrevis and the rest may bear the blame,
    And we be quit that caus'd it to be done.
    Within this room is lock'd the messenger
    That shall convey it and perform the rest;
    And by a secret token that he bears
    Shall he be murder'd when the deed is done.   20
    Lightborn, come forth.

            [*Enter* Lightborn.]
    Art thou as resolute as thou wast?

13 Unpointed] Unpunctuated

Lightborn. What else, my lord? And far more resolute.
Mortimer. And hast thou cast how to accomplish it?
Lightborn. Ay, ay; and none shall know which way he died.
Mortimer. But at his looks, Lightborn, thou wilt relent.
Lightborn. Relent, ha, ha! I use much to relent.
Mortimer. Well, do it bravely, and be secret.
Lightborn. You shall not need to give instructions;
 'Tis not the first time I have kill'd a man.   30
 I learn'd in Naples how to poison flowers;
 To strangle with a lawn thrust through the throat;
 To pierce the windpipe with a needle's point;
 Or whilst one is asleep, to take a quill
 And blow a little powder in his ears,
 Or open his mouth and pour quicksilver down.
 But yet I have a braver way than these.
Mortimer. What's that?
Lightborn. Nay, you shall pardon me; none shall know my tricks.
Mortimer. I care not how it is, so it be not spied.   40
 Deliver this to Gurney and Matrevis.   *[Gives him a letter.]*
 At every ten miles' end thou hast a horse.
 Take this.   *[Gives token.]*
    Away, and never see me more.
Lightborn. No?
Mortimer. No,
 Unless thou bring me news of Edward's death.
Lightborn. That will I quickly do. Farewell, my lord. *[Exit Lightborn.]*
Mortimer. The Prince I rule, the Queen do I command,
 And with a lowly congé to the ground
 The proudest lords salute me as I pass.   50
 I seal, I cancel, I do what I will;
 Fear'd am I more than lov'd: let me be fear'd,
 And when I frown, make all the court look pale.
 I view the Prince with Aristarchus' eyes,
 Whose looks were as a breeching to a boy.
 They thrust upon me the Protectorship,
 And sue to me for that that I desire:
 While at the council-table, grave enough
 And not unlike a bashful puritan,
 First I complain of imbecility,   60
 Saying it is *onus quam gravissimum*,
 Till being interrupted by my friends,

49 congé] bow 54 Aristarchus] an early grammarian and schoolmaster 60 imbecility]
weakness 61 *onus quam gravissimum*] 'an exceedingly heavy burden'

Suscepi that *provinciam*, as they term it;
And, to conclude, I am Protector now.
Now all is sure: the Queen and Mortimer
Shall rule the realm, the King and none rule us.
Mine enemies will I plague, my friends advance,
And what I list command, who dare control?
Maior sum quam cui possit fortuna nocere.
And that this be the coronation day   70
It pleaseth me, and Isabel the Queen.
The trumpets sound; I must go take my place.

Enter the young King [Edward III], *Bishop of* Canterbury, Champion,
Nobles, Queen.

Canterbury. Long live King Edward, by the grace of God
King of England and Lord of Ireland.
Champion. If any Christian, heathen, Turk or Jew
Dares but affirm that Edward's not true king,
And will avouch his saying with the sword,
I am the Champion that will combat him.
Mortimer. None comes. Sound trumpets.
Edward III.   Champion, here's to thee.
                    [*Drinks a toast and gives* Champion *the goblet.*]
Isabella. Lord Mortimer, now take him to your charge.   80

Enter Soldiers *with the Earl of* Kent *prisoner.*

Mortimer. What traitor have we there, with blades and bills?
Soldier. Edmund the Earl of Kent.
Edward III.   What hath he done?
Soldier. 'A would have taken the King away perforce
As we were bringing him to Killingworth.
Mortimer. Did you attempt his rescue, Edmund? Speak.
Kent. Mortimer, I did. He is our king;
And thou compell'st this prince to wear the crown.
Mortimer. Strike off his head! He shall have martial law.
Kent. Strike off my head? Base traitor, I defy thee.
Edward III. My lord, he is my uncle, and shall live.   90
Mortimer. My lord, he is your enemy, and shall die.
Kent. Stay, villains!
Edward III. Sweet mother, if I cannot pardon him,
Entreat my lord Protector for his life.
Isabella. Son, be content, I dare not speak a word.
Edward III. Nor I, and yet methinks I should command.

63 *Suscepi* that *provinciam*] 'I undertook that duty'   69 *Maior . . . nocere*] 'I am great
beyond Fortune's harm'

But seeing I cannot, I'll entreat for him:
    My lord, if you will let my uncle live,
    I will requite it when I come to age.
Mortimer. 'Tis for your highness' good, and for the realm's.   100
    How often shall I bid you bear him hence?
Kent. Art thou king? Must I die at thy command?
Mortimer. At our command. Once more, away with him.
Kent. Let me but stay and speak; I will not go.
    Either my brother or his son is king,
    And none of both them thirst for Edmund's blood;
    And therefore soldiers, whither will you hale me?
                They hale Kent *away, and carry him to be beheaded.*
Edward III. What safety may I look for at his hands
    If that my uncle shall be murder'd thus?
Isabella. Fear not, sweet boy, I'll guard thee from thy foes;   110
    Had Edmund liv'd, he would have sought thy death.
    Come son, we'll ride a-hunting in the park.
Edward III. And shall my uncle Edmund ride with us?
Isabella. He is a traitor; think not on him. Come.   *Exeunt omnes.*

[Scene v]

Enter Matrevis *and* Gurney.

Matrevis. Gurney, I wonder the King dies not,
    Being in a vault up to the knees in water,
    To which the channels of the castle run,
    From whence a damp continually ariseth,
    That were enough to poison any man,
    Much more a king, brought up so tenderly.
Gurney. And so do I, Matrevis; yesternight
    I open'd but the door to throw him meat,
    And I was almost stifl'd with the savour.
Matrevis. He hath a body able to endure   10
    More than we can inflict; and therefore now
    Let us assail his mind another while.
Gurney. Send for him out thence and I will anger him.
Matrevis. But stay—who's this?

Enter Lightborn.

Lightborn.   My lord Protector greets you.
                                 [Gives the letter.]

Gurney. What's here? I know not how to conster it.

3 channels] sewers   15 conster] construe

Matrevis. Gurney, it was left unpointed for the nonce:
    '*Edwardum occidere nolite timere*'—
    That's his meaning.
Lightborn. Know you this token? [*Shows the token.*] I must have the King.
Matrevis. Ay, stay awhile, thou shalt have answer straight.   20
    This villain's sent to make away the King.
Gurney. I thought as much.
Matrevis.   And when the murder's done,
    See how he must be handled for his labour:
    Pereat iste. Let him have the King,
    What else? Here is the keys, this is the lake;
    Do as you are commanded by my lord.
Lightborn. I know what I must do; get you away—
    Yet be not far off, I shall need your help.
    See that in the next room I have a fire,
    And get me a spit, and let it be red-hot.   30
Matrevis. Very well.
Gurney. Need you anything besides?
Lightborn. What else? A table and a featherbed.
Gurney. That's all?
Lightborn. Ay, ay, so when I call you, bring it in.
Matrevis. Fear not you that.
Gurney. Here's a light to go into the dungeon.
                     [*Exeunt* Matrevis *and* Gurney.]
Lightborn. So now must I about this gear; ne'er was there any
    So finely handl'd as this king shall be.
    Foh! Here's a place indeed, with all my heart.   40
                     [*Reveal* Edward *in prison.*]
Edward. Who's there? What light is that? Wherefore comes thou?
Lightborn. To comfort you and bring you joyful news.
Edward. Small comfort finds poor Edward in thy looks;
    Villain, I know thou com'st to murder me.
Lightborn. To murder you, my most gracious lord?
    Far is it from my heart to do you harm.
    The Queen sent me, to see how you were us'd,
    For she relents at this your misery.
    And what eyes can refrain from shedding tears
    To see a king in this most piteous state?   50
Edward. Weep'st thou already? List awhile to me,
    And then thy heart, were it as Gurney's is,
    Or as Matrevis', hewn from the Caucasus,

16 for the nonce] on purpose   24 *Pereat iste*] 'Let him [Lightborn] die'   25 lake]
dungeon   38 gear] job

        Yet will it melt ere I have done my tale.
        This dungeon where they keep me is the sink
        Wherein the filth of all the castle falls.
Lightborn. O villains!
Edward. And there in mire and puddle have I stood
        This ten days' space, and lest that I should sleep,
        One plays continually upon a drum;   60
        They give me bread and water, being a king;
        So that for want of sleep and sustenance
        My mind's distemper'd and my body's numb'd,
        And whether I have limbs or no, I know not.
        O would my blood dropp'd out from every vein
        As doth this water from my tatter'd robes;
        Tell Isabel the Queen, I look'd not thus
        When for her sake I ran at tilt in France,
        And there unhors'd the duke of Cleremont.
Lightborn. O speak no more, my lord; this breaks my heart.   70
        Lie on this bed and rest yourself awhile.
Edward. These looks of thine can harbour nought but death;
        I see my tragedy written in thy brows.
        Yet stay awhile, forbear thy bloody hand,
        And let me see the stroke before it comes,
        That even then when I shall lose my life
        My mind may be more steadfast on my God.
Lightborn. What means your highness to mistrust me thus?
Edward. What means thou to dissemble with me thus?
Lightborn. These hands were never stain'd with innocent blood,   80
        Nor shall they now be tainted with a king's.
Edward. Forgive my thought, for having such a thought.
        One jewel have I left; receive thou this.
        Still fear I, and I know not what's the cause,
        But every joint shakes as I give it thee:
        O, if thou harbour'st murder in thy heart,
        Let this gift change thy mind, and save thy soul.
        Know that I am a king—— O, at that name
        I feel a hell of grief! Where is my crown?
        Gone, gone; and do I remain alive?   90
Lightborn. You're overwatch'd, my lord; lie down and rest.
Edward. But that grief keeps me waking, I should sleep,
        For not these ten days have these eyes' lids clos'd;
        Now as I speak they fall: and yet with fear
        Open again. O wherefore sits thou here?

91 overwatch'd] exhausted from lack of sleep

Lightborn. If you mistrust me I'll be gone, my lord.
Edward. No, no; for if thou mean'st to murder me
      Thou wilt return again; and therefore stay.
Lightborn. He sleeps.
Edward. O let me not die! Yet stay, O stay awhile.   100
Lightborn. How now my lord?
Edward. Something still buzzeth in mine ears,
      And tells me, if I sleep I never wake;
      This fear is that which makes me tremble thus,
      And therefore tell me, wherefore art thou come?
Lightborn. To rid thee of thy life. Matrevis, come!

                     [*Enter* Matrevis.]

Edward. I am too weak and feeble to resist;
      Assist me, sweet God, and receive my soul.
Lightborn. Run for the table.

                                   [Matrevis *fetches in* Gurney, *with table and spit.*]
Edward. O spare me—or dispatch me in a trice.   110
Lightborn. So, lay the table down and stamp on it,
      But not too hard, lest that you bruise his body.
                          [*They assault* Edward, *who screams and dies.*]
Matrevis. I fear me that this cry will raise the town,
      And therefore let us take horse and away.
Lightborn. Tell me sirs, was it not bravely done?
Gurney. Excellent well: take this for thy reward.

                                   Then Gurney *stabs* Lightborn.

      Come, let us cast the body in the moat,
      And bear the King's to Mortimer our lord.
      Away!   *Exeunt omnes.*

                        [Scene vi]

                Enter Mortimer *and* Matrevis.

Mortimer. Is't done, Matrevis, and the murderer dead?
Matrevis. Ay my good lord. I would it were undone.
Mortimer. Matrevis, if thou now grow'st penitent,
      I'll be thy ghostly father; therefore choose,
      Whether thou wilt be secret in this,
      Or else die by the hand of Mortimer.
Matrevis. Gurney, my lord, is fled, and will I fear
      Betray us both; therefore let me fly.
Mortimer. Fly to the savages!

4 ghostly father] confessor (a euphemism here for murderer)

Matrevis. I humbly thank your honour.   10

                                           [Exit.]

Mortimer. As for myself, I stand as Jove's huge tree,
    And others are but shrubs compared to me;
    All tremble at my name, and I fear none;
    Let's see who dare impeach me for his death.

                   Enter the Queen.

Isabella. Ah Mortimer, the King my son hath news
    His father's dead, and we have murder'd him.
Mortimer. What if we have? The King is yet a child.
Isabella. Ay, ay, but he tears his hair and wrings his hands,
    And vows to be reveng'd upon us both;
    Into the council-chamber he is gone,   20
    To crave the aid and succour of his peers.
    Ay me! See where he comes, and they with him;
    Now, Mortimer, begins our tragedy.

        Enter King Edward III *with the* Lords.

1 Lord. Fear not, my lord, know that you are a king.
Edward III. Villain!
Mortimer. How now, my lord?
Edward III. Think not that I am frighted with thy words.
    My father's murder'd through thy treachery,
    And thou shalt die, and on his mournful hearse
    Thy hateful and accursed head shall lie,   30
    To witness to the world, that by thy means
    His kingly body was too soon interr'd.
Isabella. Weep not, sweet son.
Edward III. Forbid not me to weep, he was my father;
    And had you lov'd him half so well as I,
    You could not bear his death thus patiently.
    But you, I fear, conspir'd with Mortimer.
2 Lord. Why speak you not unto my lord the King?
Mortimer. Because I think scorn to be accus'd.
    Who is the man dare say I murder'd him?   40
Edward III. Traitor, in me my loving father speaks,
    And plainly saith, 'twas thou that murd'redst him.
Mortimer. But hath your grace no other proof than this?
Edward III. Yes, if this be the hand of Mortimer.   *[Shows token.]*
Mortimer. False Gurney hath betray'd me and himself.
Isabella. I fear'd as much; murder cannot be hid.
Mortimer. 'Tis my hand. What gather you by this?

11 Jove's huge tree] the oak

Edward III. That thither thou didst send a murderer.
Mortimer. What murderer? Bring forth the man I sent.
Edward III. Ah Mortimer, thou know'st that he is slain,   50
  And so shalt thou be too. Why stays he here?
  Bring him unto a hurdle, drag him forth,
  Hang him, I say, and set his quarters up,
  But bring his head back presently to me.
Isabella. For my sake, sweet son, pity Mortimer.
Mortimer. Madam, entreat not; I will rather die
  Than sue for life unto a paltry boy.
Edward III. Hence with the traitor, with the murderer.
Mortimer. Base Fortune, now I see, that in thy wheel
  There is a point, to which when men aspire,   60
  They tumble headlong down; that point I touch'd,
  And seeing there was no place to mount up higher,
  Why should I grieve at my declining fall?
  Farewell, fair Queen, weep not for Mortimer,
  That scorns the world, and as a traveller
  Goes to discover countries yet unknown.
Edward III. What, suffer you the traitor to delay?

  [*Exit* Mortimer *with first* Lord.]

Isabella. As thou receiv'dst thy life from me,
  Spill not the blood of gentle Mortimer.
Edward III. This argues that you spilt my father's blood;   70
  Else would you not entreat for Mortimer.
Isabella. I spill his blood? No!
Edward III. Ay Madam, you, for so the rumour runs.
Isabella. That rumour is untrue; for loving thee
  Is this report raised on poor Isabel.
Edward III. I do not think her so unnatural.
3 Lord. My lord, I fear me it will prove too true.
Edward III. Mother, you are suspected for his death,
  And therefore we commit you to the Tower
  Till further trial may be made thereof.   80
  If you be guilty, though I be your son,
  Think not to find me slack or pitiful.
Isabella. Nay, to my death, for too long have I liv'd
  Whenas my son thinks to abridge my days.
Edward III. Away with her, her words enforce these tears,
  And I shall pity her if she speak again.
Isabella. Shall I not mourn for my beloved lord,

52 hurdle] sledge on which traitors were dragged through the streets to the place of
execution

And with the rest accompany him to his grave?
2 Lord. Thus Madam, 'tis the King's will you shall hence.
Isabella. He hath forgotten me! Stay, I am his mother.   90
3 Lord. That boots not, therefore, gentle Madam, go.
Isabella. Then come, sweet death, and rid me of this grief. [*Exit, attended.*]

  [*Enter first* Lord *with the head of* Mortimer.]

1 Lord. My lord, here is the head of Mortimer.
Edward III. Go fetch my father's hearse, where it shall lie,
  And bring my funeral robes.   [*Exit* Lord.]
                        Accursed head,
Could I have rul'd thee then, as I do now,
Thou hadst not hatch'd this monstrous treachery.
Here comes the hearse; help me to mourn, my lords.

  [*Enter* Attendants *with the hearse and funeral robes.*]

Sweet father here, unto thy murder'd ghost,
I offer up this wicked traitor's head;   100
And let these tears distilling from mine eyes
Be witness of my grief and innocency.   [*Exeunt omnes.*]

                    FINIS.

Doctor Faustus

Marlowe's most famous play is also, for an editor, his most perplexing. *Doctor Faustus* exists in two very different versions. The earlier, known as the A Text, was printed in 1604 and reprinted twice before its place was taken in 1616 by the longer B Text. While A shows signs of having been reconstructed from memory by an actor, B contains stage directions that (in my view) point to a basis in a theatrical prompt-book. B presents certain scenes, mainly comic, which are either expanded versions of similar episodes in A (e.g. IV. ii), or else additions (such as the scene between the Pope and Bruno, III.i.90 ff.). It is still a vexed question whether these scenes were, if not written by Marlowe, at least planned by him in the original form of the work. Or are they the 'adicyones' for which Henslowe paid £4 in 1602? The parts of the play where Marlowe's hand is unmistakable are substantially the same in A and B; but there are many verbal differences. Often the A Text is superior; it was produced before the 1606 Act of Abuses which imposed a heavy fine for blasphemy uttered on stage. Thereafter the actors, to avoid the fine, expurgated any words, however innocently used, that might put them in danger. So at v.ii.143-5 A reads

> O Ile leape vp to my God: who pulles me downe?
> See see where Christs blood streames in the firmament,
> One drop would saue my soule.

B has been severely cut:

> O I'le leape vp to heauen: who puls me downe?
> One drop of bloud will saue me.

Absolute trust can be given to neither the A nor the B Text, and a modern edition must be an amalgam of the two. The present edition is based on the B Text, but readings from A are adopted whenever they seem justified. In some of the comic scenes it is impossible to reconcile the two; B's versions of II. iii, III. iii, IV. i and iv, and the Old Man's speech from v. i (ll. 36-52) are offered in the body of the play, and A's are printed as an Appendix.

The date of *Doctor Faustus* is also a problem. Arguments for an early date —about 1589, between *Tamburlaine* and *The Jew of Malta*—are based on the play's style and technique, and on possible echoes of *Doctor Faustus* in early plays by other dramatists. Opposition arguments stress the date of the play's undoubted source, *The Historie of the damnable life, and deserved death of Doctor John Faustus*. This *Historie*, a combination of tract and jest-book, was published in Frankfurt in 1587; an English version appeared in 1592. The translator, one P.F., added minor details to his German original, details which are present in the play. Until—and unless—an earlier text of the translation can be traced, *Doctor Faustus* must be regarded as Marlowe's last play.

The Tragicall History
of the Life and Death
of *Doctor Faustus.*

Written by *Ch. Mar.*

LONDON,
Printed for *Iohn Wright*, and are to be fold at his fhop
without Newgate, at the f.... .f the
Bib.. 1616.

[DRAMATIS PERSONAE

Chorus

Dr. John Faustus
Wagner, his servant, a student
Valdes ⎱
Cornelius ⎰ his friends, magicians
Three Scholars, students under Faustus
Old Man

Pope Adrian
Raymond, King of Hungary
Bruno, the rival Pope
Cardinals of France and Padua
Archbishop of Rheims

Charles V, Emperor of Germany
Martino ⎱
Frederick ⎬ knights at the Emperor's court
Benvolio ⎰
Duke of Saxony

Duke of Vanholt
Duchess of Vanholt

Robin
Dick
Vintner
Horse-courser
Carter
Hostess

Good Angel
Bad Angel (Spirit)
Mephostophilis
Lucifer
Belzebub
Spirits presenting The Seven Deadly Sins
           Alexander the Great
           Alexander's Paramour
           Darius, King of Persia
           Helen of Troy

Devils, Cupids, Bishops, Monks, Friars, Lords, Soldiers, Attendants]

[Prologue]

Chorus.

Not marching in the fields of Thrasimene,
Where Mars did mate the warlike Carthagens,
Nor sporting in the dalliance of love
In courts of kings where state is overturn'd,
Nor in the pomp of proud audacious deeds,
Intends our muse to vaunt his heavenly verse.
Only this, Gentles, we must now perform
The form of Faustus' fortunes, good or bad.
And now to patient judgements we appeal,
And speak for Faustus in his infancy.   10
Now is he born, of parents base of stock,
In Germany, within a town called Rhode.
At riper years to Wittenberg he went,
Whereas his kinsmen chiefly brought him up.
So much he profits in divinity,
The fruitful plot of scholarism grac'd,
That shortly he was grac'd with doctor's name,
Excelling all whose sweet delight disputes
In heavenly matters of theology.
Till swol'n with cunning, of a self-conceit,   20
His waxen wings did mount above his reach,
And melting, heavens conspir'd his overthrow.
For falling to a devilish exercise,
And glutted now with learning's golden gifts,
He surfeits upon cursed necromancy;
Nothing so sweet as magic is to him,
Which he prefers before his chiefest bliss:
And this the man that in his study sits.   *Exit.*

1–2 Thrasimene . . . Carthagens] Lake Trasimene, scene of one of Hannibal's most famous
victories in 217 B.C.; 'mate' here must have the sense of 'ally himself with'.   12 Rhode]
Stadtroda, in central Gerrmany   20 cunning] knowledge (but with overtones of knowledge misapplied)   21 His waxen wings] like those of Icarus who flew too near the sun

[Act I Scene i]

Faustus in his study.

Faustus. Settle thy studies, Faustus, and begin
     To sound the depth of that thou wilt profess.
     Having commenc'd, be a divine in show,
     Yet level at the end of every art
     And live and die in Aristotle's works.
     Sweet Analytics, 'tis thou hast ravish'd me.
     Bene disserere est finis logices. ——— *cater ref. Ren.*
     Is to dispute well logic's chiefest end?
     Affords this art no greater miracle?
     Then read no more, thou hast attained that end.   10
     A greater subject fitteth Faustus' wit:
     Bid *on kai me on* farewell; Galen, come.
     Seeing, *ubi desinit philosophus, ibi incipit medicus.*
     Be a physician Faustus, heap up gold
     And be eterniz'd for some wondrous cure.
     Summum bonum medicinae sanitas:
     The end of physic is our body's health.
     Why Faustus, hast thou not attain'd that end?
     Is not thy common talk sound aphorisms?
     Are not thy bills hung up as monuments,   20
     Whereby whole cities have escap'd the plague,
     And thousand desperate maladies been cur'd?
     Yet art thou still but Faustus, and a man.
     Couldst thou make men to live eternally,   *like the gods*
     Or being dead, raise them to life again,
     Then this profession were to be esteem'd.
     Physic, farewell. Where is Justinian?
     Si una eademque res legatur duobus,
     Alter rem, alter valorem rei—etc.,
     A petty case of paltry legacies!   30
     Exhaereditare filium non potest pater, nisi—
     Such is the subject of the Institute

---

4 level at the end] consider the purpose   12 *on kai me on*] 'being and not being'
13 *ubi . . . medicus*] 'where the philosopher ends, the doctor starts' (Aristotle, *de sensu*,
436a)   16 *Summum . . . sanitas*] Aristotle, *Nicomachean Ethics*, 1094.a.8   19 aphorisms]
medical precepts (after the *Aphorisms* of Hippocrates)   20 bills] prescriptions
28–9 *Si . . . rei*] 'If one and the same thing is bequeathed to two persons, one shall have the
thing itself, the other the value of the thing' (Justinian, *Institutes*, ii. 20)   31 *Exhaereditare
. . . nisi—*] 'A father cannot disinherit his son unless—' (*Institutes*, ii. 13)

And universal body of the law.
This study fits a mercenary drudge,
Who aims at nothing but external trash,
Too servile and illiberal for me.
When all is done, divinity is best.
Jerome's Bible, Faustus, view it well.
Stipendium peccati mors est. Ha! *Stipendium, etc.,*
The reward of sin is death. That's hard.   40
Si pecasse negamus, fallimur, et nulla est in nobis veritas.
If we say that we have no sin we deceive ourselves, and there is no truth
in us. Why then, belike we must sin, and so consequently die.
Ay, we must die an everlasting death.
What doctrine call you this? *Che sera, sera.*
What will be, shall be. Divinity, adieu!
These metaphysics of magicians
And necromantic books are heavenly;
Lines, circles, signs, letters and characters:
Ay, these are those that Faustus most desires.   50
O what a world of profit and delight,
Of power, of honour, of omnipotence,
Is promis'd to the studious artisan!
All things that move between the quiet poles
Shall be at my command. Emperors and kings
Are but obey'd in their several provinces.
Nor can they raise the wind or rend the clouds.
But his dominion that exceeds in this
Stretcheth as far as doth the mind of man:
A sound magician is a demi-god.   60
Here, tire my brains to get a deity.

Enter Wagner.

Wagner, commend me to my dearest friends,
The German Valdes and Cornelius.
Request them earnestly to visit me.
Wagner. I will sir.   *Exit.*
Faustus. Their conference will be a greater help to me
Than all my labours, plod I ne'er so fast.

Enter the Angel *and* Spirit.

Good Angel. O Faustus, lay that damned book aside,
And gaze not on it lest it tempt thy soul,

38 Jerome's Bible] the Vulgate   39 *Stipendium . . . est*] Romans 6: 23   41 *Si . . . veritas*]
John 1: 8   67 s.d. Spirit] i.e. Bad Angel; to the Elizabethans 'spirit' and 'devil' were
synonymous. See Introduction p. xxii.

And heap God's heavy wrath upon thy head.   70
Read, read the scriptures: that is blasphemy.
Bad Angel. Go forward, Faustus, in that famous art
   Wherein all nature's treasury is contain'd.
   Be thou on earth as Jove is in the sky,
   Lord and commander of these elements.   *Exeunt* Angels.
Faustus. How am I glutted with conceit of this!
   Shall I make spirits fetch me what I please,
   Resolve me of all ambiguities,
   Perform what desperate enterprise I will?
   I'll have them fly to India for gold,   80
   Ransack the ocean for orient pearl,
   And search all corners of the new-found world
   For pleasant fruits and princely delicates;
   I'll have them read me strange philosophy,
   And tell the secrets of all foreign kings;
   I'll have them wall all Germany with brass,
   And make swift Rhine circle fair Wittenberg;
   I'll have them fill the public schools with silk,
   Wherewith the students shall be bravely clad;
   I'll levy soldiers with the coin they bring,   90
   And chase the Prince of Parma from our land,
   And reign sole king of all the provinces.
   Yea, stranger engines for the brunt of war
   Than was the fiery keel at Antwerp's bridge
   I'll make my servile spirits to invent.
   Come, German Valdes and Cornelius,
   And make me blest with your sage conference.

Enter Valdes *and* Cornelius.

   Valdes, sweet Valdes and Cornelius!
   Know that your words have won me at the last
   To practise magic and concealed arts.   100
   Yet not your words only but mine own fantasy
   That will receive no object for my head,
   But ruminates on necromantic skill.
   Philosophy is odious and obscure,
   Both law and physic are for petty wits;

86 wall . . . brass] Bacon, in Greene's *Friar Bacon and Friar Bungay*, planned to do this for England.   88 public schools] university lecture rooms   88 silk] Ed. (skill Q). In Marlowe's day undergraduates were ordered to dress soberly.   91–2 Prince . . . provinces] The Prince of Parma governed the provinces of the Netherlands 1579–92.   94 fiery keel . . . bridge] A fire-ship destroyed a bridge across the Scheldt in 1585.

Divinity is basest of the three,
Unpleasant, harsh, contemptible and vile.
'Tis magic, magic that hath ravish'd me.
Then, gentle friends, aid me in this attempt,
And I, that have with concise syllogisms   110
Gravell'd the pastors of the German church
And made the flowering pride of Wittenberg
Swarm to my problems as the infernal spirits
On sweet Musaeus when he came to hell,
Will be as cunning as Agrippa was,
Whose shadows made all Europe honour him.

Valdes. Faustus, these books, thy wit and our experience
    Shall make all nations to canonize us.
    As Indian Moors obey their Spanish lords,
    So shall the spirits of every element   120
    Be always serviceable to us three.
    Like lions shall they guard us when we please,
    Like Almain rutters with their horsemen's staves,
    Or Lapland giants trotting by our sides;
    Sometimes like women or unwedded maids,
    Shadowing more beauty in their airy brows
    Than has the white breasts of the Queen of Love.
    From Venice shall they drag huge argosies,
    And from America the golden fleece
    That yearly stuffs old Philip's treasury,   130
    If learned Faustus will be resolute.

Faustus. Valdes, as resolute am I in this
    As thou to live, therefore object it not.

Cornelius. The miracles that magic will perform
    Will make thee vow to study nothing else.
    He that is grounded in astrology,
    Enrich'd with tongues, well seen in minerals,
    Hath all the principles magic doth require.
    Then doubt not, Faustus, but to be renown'd,
    And more frequented for this mystery   140
    Than heretofore the Delphian oracle.
    The spirits tell me they can dry the sea,
    And fetch the treasure of all foreign wrecks—
    Ay, all the wealth that our forefathers hid

106–7 Divinity . . . vile] Omitted in B   114 Musaeus] a legendary bard often confused
(as here) with Orpheus   115 Agrippa] magician and necromancer (1486–1535)
123 Almain rutters] German cavalry   130 old Philip] Philip II of Spain; he died in
1598 and the B Text has changed 'stuffs' to 'stuff'd'.   137 seen in] informed about

Within the massy entrails of the earth
Then tell me, Faustus, what shall we three want?
Faustus. Nothing, Cornelius! O, this cheers my soul.
    Come, show me some demonstrations magical,
    That I may conjure in some lusty grove,
    And have these joys in full possession.   150
Valdes. Then haste thee to some solitary grove,
    And bear wise Bacon's and Abanus' works,
    The Hebrew Psalter and New Testament;
    And whatsoever else is requisite
    We will inform thee ere our conference cease.
Cornelius. Valdes, first let him know the words of art,
    And then, all other ceremonies learn'd,
    Faustus may try his cunning by himself.
Valdes. First I'll instruct thee in the rudiments,
    And then wilt thou be perfecter than I.   160
Faustus. Then come and dine with me, and after meat
    We'll canvass every quiddity thereof,
    For ere I sleep, I'll try what I can do.
    This night I'll conjure, though I die therefore.   *Exeunt omnes.*

[Scene ii]

Enter two Scholars.

1 Scholar. I wonder what's become of Faustus, that was wont to make our
schools ring with *sic probo*.

Enter Wagner.

2 Scholar. That shall we presently know. Here comes his boy.

1 Scholar. How now, sirrah, where's thy master?

Wagner. God in heaven knows.

2 Scholar. Why, dost not thou know then?

Wagner. Yes, I know, but that follows not.

1 Scholar. Go to, sirrah, leave your jesting and tell us where he is.

Wagner. That follows not by force of argument, which you, being licentiates,
should stand upon; therefore acknowledge your error and be attentive.

2 Scholar. Then you will not tell us?   11

Wagner. You are deceived, for I will tell you. Yet if you were not dunces,

---

152-3 bear . . . Testament] Roger Bacon and Pietro d'Abano were both popularly supposed
to have been magicians; as well as their works, Faustus would need certain Psalms (especially 22 and 51) and the opening words of St. John's Gospel for his conjuring.   I. ii, 2 *sic
probo*] 'thus I prove it'

you would never ask me such a question. For is he not *corpus naturale*?
And is not that *mobile*? Then wherefore should you ask me such a question? But that I am by nature phlegmatic, slow to wrath and prone to
lechery (to love, I would say), it were not for you to come within forty
foot of the place of execution, although I do not doubt but to see you
both hanged the next sessions. Thus, having triumphed over you, I will
set my countenance like a precisian, and begin to speak thus: Truly, my
dear brethren, my master is within at dinner with Valdes and Cornelius,
as this wine, if it could speak, would inform your worships. And so the
Lord bless you, preserve you and keep you, my dear brethren.   *Exit.*

1 Scholar. O Faustus, then I fear that which I have long suspected   23
    That thou art fallen into that damned art
    For which they two are infamous through the world.
2 Scholar. Were he a stranger, not allied to me,
    The danger of his soul would make me mourn.
    But come, let us go and inform the Rector;
    It may be his grave counsel may reclaim him.
1 Scholar. I fear me nothing will reclaim him now.
2 Scholar. Yet let us see what we can do.   *Exeunt.*

[Scene iii]

*Thunder. Enter Lucifer and four Devils [above]. Faustus to them
                        with this speech.*

Faustus. Now that the gloomy shadow of the night,
    Longing to view Orion's drizzling look,
    Leaps from th'antarctic world unto the sky,
    And dims the welkin with her pitchy breath,
    Faustus, begin thine incantations
    And try if devils will obey thy hest,
    Seeing thou hast pray'd and sacrific'd to them.
    Within this circle is Jehovah's name
    Forward and backward anagrammatiz'd:
    Th' abbreviated names of holy saints,   10
    Figures of every adjunct to the heavens,
    And characters of signs and erring stars
    By which the spirits are enforc'd to rise.

13-14 *corpus naturale . . . mobile*] The phrase *corpus naturale seu mobile* ('a natural body and
as such capable of movement'), adapted from Aristotle, was used to describe the subject-
matter of physics.   19 precisian] puritan   I. iii, 11 adjunct] heavenly body   12 characters
of signs] symbols of the Zodiac   12 erring stars] planets (distinguishing them from the
fixed stars joined to the firmament)

Then fear not, Faustus, to be resolute
And try the utmost magic can perform.   *Thunder.*
Sint mihi dei Acherontis propitii; valeat numen triplex Jehovae; ignei,
aerii, aquatici, terreni spiritus salvete! Orientis princeps, Belzebub inferni
ardentis monarcha, et Demogorgon, propitiamus vos, ut appareat, et surgat,
Mephostophilis.   *Dragon.*
Quid tu moraris? Per Jehovam, Gehennam, et consecratam aquam quam
nunc spargo; signumque crucis quod nunc facio; et per vota nostra, ipse nunc
surgat nobis dicatus Mephostophilis.   22

Enter a Devil.

I charge thee to return and change thy shape,
Thou art too ugly to attend on me.
Go, and return an old Franciscan friar,
That holy shape becomes a devil best.   *Exit* Devil.
I see there's virtue in my heavenly words!
Who would not be proficient in this art?
How pliant is this Mephostophilis,
Full of obedience and humility,   30
Such is the force of magic and my spells.
Now, Faustus, thou art conjurer laureate,
That canst command great Mephostophilis.
Quin redis, Mephostophilis, fratris imagine!

Enter Mephostophilis.

Mephostophilis. Now Faustus, what wouldst thou have me do?
Faustus. I charge thee wait upon me whilst I live,
To do whatever Faustus shall command,
Be it to make the moon drop from her sphere,
Or the ocean to overwhelm the world.
Mephostophilis. I am a servant to great Lucifer,   40
And may not follow thee without his leave;
No more than he commands must we perform.
Faustus. Did not he charge thee to appear to me?
Mephostophilis. No, I came now hither of mine own accord.
Faustus. Did not my conjuring speeches raise thee? Speak.

16–22 *Sint . . . Mephostophilis*] 'May the gods of Acheron be favourable to me; farewell to
the spirit of the threefold Jehovah; hail spirits of fire, air, water and earth. O prince of the
East [Lucifer], Belzebub monarch of burning hell, and Demogorgon, we beseech you that
Mephostophilis should appear and rise. Why do you delay? By Jehovah, Gehenna, and the
holy water that I now sprinkle; and by the sign of the cross that I now make; and by our
vows, may Mephostophilis himself now rise, compelled to obey us'   19 s.d. *Dragon*] an
anticipatory direction to the property-man to prepare his dragon for the devil's appearance
at l. 22 (see 1616 title-page illustration)   34 *Quin . . . imagine*] 'Why do you not return,
Mephostophilis, in the likeness of a friar'

Mephostophilis. That was the cause, but yet *per accidens;*
    For when we hear one rack the name of God,
    Abjure the scriptures and his saviour Christ,
    We fly in hope to get his glorious soul;
    Nor will we come unless he use such means   50
    Whereby he is in danger to be damn'd.
    Therefore the shortest cut for conjuring
    Is stoutly to abjure the Trinity
    And pray devoutly to the prince of hell.
Faustus. So Faustus hath already done, and holds this principle:
    There is no chief but only Belzebub,
    To whom Faustus doth dedicate himself.
    This word 'damnation' terrifies not him,
    For he confounds hell in Elysium.
    His ghost be with the old philosophers.   60
    But leaving these vain trifles of men's souls,
    Tell me, what is that Lucifer, thy lord?
Mephostophilis. Arch-regent and commander of all spirits.
Faustus. Was not that Lucifer an angel once?
Mephostophilis. Yes Faustus, and most dearly loved of God.
Faustus. How comes it then that he is prince of devils?
Mephostophilis. O, by aspiring pride and insolence,
    For which God threw him from the face of heaven.
Faustus. And what are you that live with Lucifer?
Mephostophilis. Unhappy spirits that fell with Lucifer,   70
    Conspir'd against our God with Lucifer,
    And are for ever damn'd with Lucifer.
Faustus. Where are you damn'd?
Mephostophilis. In hell.
Faustus. How comes it then that thou art out of hell?
Mephostophilis. Why, this is hell, nor am I out of it.
    Think'st thou that I who saw the face of God
    And tasted the eternal joys of heaven,
    Am not tormented with ten thousand hells
    In being depriv'd of everlasting bliss?   80
    O Faustus, leave these frivolous demands,
    Which strikes a terror to my fainting soul.
Faustus. What, is great Mephostophilis so passionate
    For being deprived of the joys of heaven?
    Learn thou of Faustus manly fortitude,
    And scorn those joys thou never shalt possess.

46 *per accidens*] 'only in appearance'   53 the Trinity] A (all godliness B)   60 His . . .
philosophers] a saying of Averroës, '*sit anima mea cum philosophis*'. See Introduction p. xxi.

Go, bear these tidings to great Lucifer,
Seeing Faustus hath incurr'd eternal death
By desperate thoughts against Jove's deity.
Say he surrenders up to him his soul,   90
So he will spare him four and twenty years,
Letting him live in all voluptuousness,
Having thee ever to attend on me,
To give me whatsoever I shall ask,
To tell me whatsoever I demand,
To slay mine enemies and aid my friends
And always be obedient to my will.
Go, and return to mighty Lucifer,
And meet me in my study at midnight,
And then resolve me of thy master's mind.   100
Mephostophilis. I will, Faustus.   *Exit.*
Faustus. Had I as many souls as there be stars,
I'd give them all for Mephostophilis.
By him I'll be great emperor of the world,
And make a bridge through the moving air
To pass the ocean with a band of men;
I'll join the hills that bind the Afric shore,
And make that country continent to Spain,
And both contributory to my crown.
The Emperor shall not live but by my leave,   110
Nor any potentate of Germany.
Now that I have obtain'd what I desire
I'll live in speculation of this art
Till Mephostophilis return again.
                                                                   Exit.
                                    [*Exeunt* Lucifer *and* Devils.]

[Scene iv]

Enter Wagner *and the Clown* [Robin].

Wagner. Come hither, sirrah boy.

Robin. Boy? O disgrace to my person! Zounds, boy in your face! You
have seen many boys with such pickadevants, I am sure.

Wagner. Sirrah, hast thou no comings in?

Robin. Yes, and goings out too, you may see, sir.

Wagner. Alas, poor slave, see how poverty jests in his nakedness. I know
the villain's out of service and so hungry that I know he would give his
soul to the devil for a shoulder of mutton, though it were blood-raw.

3 pickadevants] pointed beards   4 comings in] income

Robin. Not so neither. I had need to have it well roasted, and good sauce to
it, if I pay so dear, I can tell you.   10

Wagner. Sirrah, wilt thou be my man and wait on me? And I will make thee
go like *Qui mihi discipulus.*

Robin. What, in verse?

Wagner. No, slave, in beaten silk and stavesacre.

Robin. Stavesacre? That's good to kill vermin; then belike if I serve you I
shall be lousy.

Wagner. Why, so thou shalt be whether thou dost it or no; for, sirrah, if
thou dost not presently bind thyself to me for seven years, I'll turn all
the lice about thee into familiars and make them tear thee in pieces.

Robin. Nay sir, you may save yourself a labour, for they are as familiar with
me as if they paid for their meat and drink, I can tell you.   21

Wagner. Well sirrah, leave your jesting and take these guilders.

Robin. Yes, marry sir, and I thank you too.

Wagner. So, now thou art to be at an hour's warning, whensoever and
wheresoever the devil shall fetch thee.

Robin. Here, take your guilders, I'll none of 'em.

Wagner. Not I, thou art pressed; prepare thyself, for I will presently raise
up two devils to carry thee away. Banio! Belcher!

Robin. Belcher? And Belcher come here, I'll belch him! I am not afraid of a
devil.   30

Enter two Devils, *and the Clown runs up and down crying.*

Wagner. How now, sir, will you serve me now?

Robin. Ay, good Wagner; take away the devil then.

Wagner. Spirits, away!   *Exeunt* [Devils].
              Now, sirrah, follow me.

Robin. I will sir. But hark you master, will you teach me this conjuring
occupation?

Wagner. Ay sirrah, I'll teach thee to turn thyself to a dog, or a cat, or a
mouse, or a rat, or anything.

Robin. A dog, or a cat, or a mouse, or a rat! O brave, Wagner.

Wagner. Villain, call me Master Wagner, and see that you walk attentively,
and let your right eye be always diametrally fixed upon my left heel, that
thou may'st *quasi vestigiis nostris insistere.*   41

Robin. Well sir, I warrant you.   *Exeunt.*

---

12 *Qui mihi discipulus*] 'You who are my pupil' (the opening words of a didactic poem for
schoolboys) 14 beaten . . . stavesacre] Silk was embroidered with beaten gold; stavesacre
(prepared from delphinium seeds) a flea-powder. 'In effect Wagner promises to dress his
servant (or rather to dress him down) in silk—and adds that plenty of Keating's powder
will be needed' (Greg) 41 *quasi . . . insistere*] 'as it were follow in our footsteps'

[Act II   Scene i]

Enter Faustus *in his study.*

Faustus. Now, Faustus, must thou needs be damn'd?
　　And canst thou not be sav'd.
　　What boots it then to think on God or heaven?
　　Away with such vain fancies, and despair;
　　Despair in God, and trust in Belzebub.
　　Now go not backward; no, Faustus, be resolute.
　　Why waver'st thou? O something soundeth in mine ears,
　　'Abjure this magic, turn to God again.'
　　Ay, and Faustus will turn to God again.
　　To God? He loves thee not.   10
　　The God thou serv'st is thine own appetite,
　　Wherein is fix'd the love of Belzebub.
　　To him, I'll build an altar and a church,
　　And offer lukewarm blood of new-born babes.

Enter the two Angels.

Good Angel. Sweet Faustus, leave that execrable art.
Faustus. Contrition, prayer, repentance, what of these?
Good Angel. O they are means to bring thee unto heaven.
Bad Angel. Rather illusions, fruits of lunacy,
　　That makes men foolish that do trust them most.
Good Angel. Sweet Faustus, think of heaven and heavenly things.   20
Bad Angel. No, Faustus, think of honour and of wealth.   *Exeunt Angels.*
Faustus. Of wealth!
　　Why, the signory of Emden shall be mine!
　　When Mephostophilis shall stand by me,
　　What God can hurt me? Faustus, thou art safe;
　　Cast no more doubts. Mephostophilis, come,
　　And bring glad tidings from great Lucifer.
　　Is't not midnight? Come Mephostophilis!
　　Veni, veni, Mephostophile!

Enter Mephostophilis.

　　Now tell me, what saith Lucifer, thy lord?   30
Mephostophilis. That I shall wait on Faustus whilst he lives,
　　So he will buy my service with his soul.
Faustus. Already Faustus hath hazarded that for thee.

23 Emden] a port on the mouth of the Ems, trading extensively with England   25 God]
A (power B)   29 *Veni, veni Mephostophile*] 'Come, O come Mephostophilis'

Mephostophilis. But now thou must bequeath it solemnly,
    And write a deed of gift with thine own blood,
    For that security craves Lucifer.
    If thou deny it, I must back to hell.
Faustus. Stay, Mephostophilis, and tell me
    What good will my soul do thy lord?
Mephostophilis. Enlarge his kingdom.   40
Faustus. Is that the reason why he tempts us thus?
Mephostophilis. Solamen miseris, socios habuisse doloris.
Faustus. Why, have you any pain, that torture other?
Mephostophilis. As great as have the human souls of men.
    But tell me, Faustus, shall I have thy soul?
    And I will be thy slave and wait on thee,
    And give thee more than thou hast wit to ask.
Faustus. Ay, Mephostophilis, I'll give it him.
Mephostophilis. Then, Faustus, stab thy arm courageously,
    And bind thy soul, that at some certain day   50
    Great Lucifer may claim it as his own,
    And then be thou as great as Lucifer.
Faustus. Lo, Mephostophilis, for love of thee
    Faustus hath cut his arm, and with his proper blood
    Assures his soul to be great Lucifer's,
    Chief lord and regent of perpetual night.
    View here this blood that trickles from mine arm,
    And let it be propitious for my wish.
Mephostophilis. But, Faustus,
    Write it in manner of a deed of gift.   60
Faustus. Ay, so I will. But, Mephostophilis,
    My blood congeals and I can write no more!
Mephostophilis. I'll fetch thee fire to dissolve it straight.   *Exit.*
Faustus. What might the staying of my blood portend?
    Is it unwilling I should write this bill?
    Why streams it not that I may write afresh?
    'Faustus gives to thee his soul': ah, there it stayed!
    Why shouldst thou not? Is not thy soul thine own?
    Then write again: 'Faustus gives to thee his soul'.

          Enter Mephostophilis *with the chafer of fire.*

Mephostophilis. See Faustus, here is fire; set it on.   70
Faustus. So, now the blood begins to clear again;
    Now will I make an end immediately.
Mephostophilis. What will not I do to obtain his soul!

42 *Solamen . . . doloris*] 'It is a comfort to the wretched to have companions in distress'

Faustus. Consummatum est: this bill is ended,
    And Faustus hath bequeath'd his soul to Lucifer.
    But what is this inscription on mine arm?
    Homo fuge! Whither should I flie?
    If unto God, he'll throw me down to hell.
    My senses are deceiv'd: here's nothing writ!
    O yes, I see it plain. Even here is writ   80
    Homo fuge! Yet shall not Faustus fly.
Mephostophilis. I'll fetch him somewhat to delight his mind.   *Exit.*

Enter Devils, *giving crowns and rich apparel to* Faustus; *they dance
    and then depart. Enter* Mephostophilis.

Faustus. What means this show? Speak, Mephostophilis.
Mephostophilis. Nothing, Faustus, but to delight thy mind,
    And let thee see what magic can perform.
Faustus. But may I raise such spirits when I please?
Mephostophilis. Ay, Faustus, and do greater things than these.
Faustus. Then Mephostophilis, receive this scroll,
    A deed of gift, of body and of soul:
    But yet conditionally, that thou perform   90
    All covenants and articles between us both.
Mephostophilis. Faustus, I swear by hell and Lucifer
    To effect all promises between us made.
Faustus. Then hear me read it, Mephostophilis.
    On these conditions following:
    'First, that Faustus may be a spirit in form and substance.
    'Secondly, that Mephostophilis shall be his servant, and at his command.
    'Thirdly, that Mephostophilis shall do for him, and bring him whatsoever.   100
    'Fourthly, that he shall be in his chamber or house invisible.
    'Lastly, that he shall appear to the said John Faustus at all times, in what form or shape soever he please.
    'I, John Faustus of Wittenberg, doctor, by these presents, do give both body and soul to Lucifer, Prince of the East, and his minister Mephostophilis, and furthermore grant unto them that, four-and-twenty years being expired, the articles above written inviolate, full power to fetch or carry the said John Faustus, body and soul, flesh, blood or goods, into their habitation wheresoever.
    By me John Faustus.'   110
Mephostophilis. Speak, Faustus, do you deliver this as your deed?

74 *Consummatum est*] 'It is finished' (the last words of Christ on the cross)   77 *Homo fuge*] 'Fly O man'   78 God] A (heaven B)   96 spirit] See Introduction p. xxii.

Faustus. Ay, take it, and the devil give thee good on't.

Mephostophilis. Now, Faustus, ask what thou wilt.

Faustus. First will I question with thee about hell.
    Tell me, where is the place that men call hell?

Mephostophilis. Under the heavens.

Faustus. Ay, so are all things else; but whereabouts?

Mephostophilis. Within the bowels of these elements,
    Where we are tortur'd and remain for ever.
    Hell hath no limits, nor is circumscrib'd   120
    In one self place, but where we are is hell,
    And where hell is, there must we ever be.
    And to be short, when all the world dissolves
    And every creature shall be purified,
    All places shall be hell that is not heaven.

Faustus. I think hell's a fable.

Mephostophilis. Ay, think so still, till experience change thy mind.

Faustus. Why, dost thou think that Faustus shall be damn'd?

Mephostophilis. Ay, of necessity, for here's the scroll
    In which thou hast given thy soul to Lucifer.   130

Faustus. Ay, and body too, but what of that?
    Think'st thou that Faustus is so fond to imagine
    That after this life there is any pain?
    Tush, these are trifles and mere old wives' tales.

Mephostophilis. But I am an instance to prove the contrary,
    For I tell thee I am damn'd, and now in hell.

Faustus. Nay, and this be hell, I'll willingly be damn'd.
    What, sleeping, eating, walking and disputing?
    But leaving this, let me have a wife, the fairest maid in Germany, for I
    am wanton and lascivious, and cannot live without a wife.   140

Mephostophilis. How, a wife? I prithee, Faustus, talk not of a wife.

Faustus. Nay, sweet Mephostophilis, fetch me one, for I will have one.

Mephostophilis. Well, thou wilt have one. Sit there till I come: I'll fetch thee
    a wife in the devil's name.   [*Exit.*]

        Enter with a Devil *dressed like a woman, with fireworks.*
    Tell me, Faustus, how dost thou like thy wife?

Faustus. A plague on her for a hot whore.

Mephostophilis. Marriage is but a ceremonial toy,
    And if thou lov'st me, think no more of it.
    I'll cull thee out the fairest courtesans
    And bring them every morning to thy bed: 150
    She whom thine eye shall like, thy heart shall have,
    Were she as chaste as was Penelope,

152 Penelope] the faithful wife of Ulysses

As wise as Saba, or as beautiful
As was bright Lucifer before his fall.
Hold, take this book, peruse it thoroughly:
The iterating of these lines brings gold,
The framing of this circle on the ground
Brings thunder, whirlwinds, storm and lightning.
Pronounce this thrice devoutly to thyself
And men in harness shall appear to thee,   160
Ready to execute what thou command'st.

Faustus. Thanks, Mephostophilis. Yet fain would I have a book wherein I
might behold all spells and incantations, that I might raise up spirits when
I please.

Mephostophilis. Here they are in this book.   *There turn to them.*

Faustus. Now would I have a book where I might see all characters and
planets of the heavens, that I might know their motions and dispositions.

Mephostophilis. Here they are too.   *Turn to them.*

Faustus. Nay, let me have one book more, and then I have done, wherein I
might see all plants, herbs and trees that grow upon the earth.   170

Mephostophilis. Here they be.

Faustus. Oh thou art deceived.

Mephostophilis. Tut, I warrant thee.   *Turn to them.*
                                                                    Exeunt.

[Scene ii]

Enter Faustus *in his study, and* Mephostophilis.

Faustus. When I behold the heavens then I repent,
        And curse thee, wicked Mephostophilis,
        Because thou hast depriv'd me of those joys.

Mephostophilis. 'Twas thine own seeking, Faustus, thank thyself.
        But think'st thou heaven is such a glorious thing?
        I tell thee, Faustus, it is not half so fair
        As thou or any man that breathes on earth.

Faustus. How prov'st thou that?

Mephostophilis. 'Twas made for man; then he's more excellent.

Faustus. If heaven was made for man, 'twas made for me.   10
        I will renounce this magic and repent.

                        Enter the two Angels.

Good Angel. Faustus, repent; yet God will pity thee.

153 Saba] Queen of Sheba   160 harness] armour   Scene ii] A scene must have been
lost between the ending of Scene i and the beginning of Scene ii; the Elizabethans would
not take two characters off stage to bring them on again immediately. Greg suggests a
comic interlude showing the Clown stealing one of the conjuring books.

Bad Angel. Thou art a spirit; God cannot pity thee.
Faustus. Who buzzeth in mine ears I am a spirit?
    Be I a devil, yet God may pity me;
    Yea, God will pity me if I repent.
Bad Angel. Ay, but Faustus never shall repent.   *Exeunt Angels.*
Faustus. My heart's so harden'd I cannot repent.
    Scarce can I name salvation, faith or heaven,
    But fearful echoes thunders in mine ears   20
    'Faustus, thou art damn'd'; then swords and knives,
    Poison, guns, halters and envenom'd steel
    Are laid before me to dispatch myself.
    And long ere this I should have done the deed,
    Had not sweet pleasure conquer'd deep despair.
    Have not I made blind Homer sing to me
    Of Alexander's love and Oenon's death?
    And hath not he, that built the walls of Thebes
    With ravishing sound of his melodious harp,
    Made music with my Mephostophilis?   30
    Why should I die then, or basely despair?
    I am resolv'd, Faustus shall not repent.
    Come, Mephostophilis, let us dispute again,
    And reason of divine astrology.
    Speak, are there many spheres above the moon?
    Are all celestial bodies but one globe,
    As is the substance of this centric earth?
Mephostophilis. As are the elements, such are the heavens,
    Even from the moon unto the empyreal orb,
    Mutually folded in each other's spheres,   40
    And jointly move upon one axle-tree,
    Whose termine is termed the world's wide pole.
    Nor are the names of Saturn, Mars or Jupiter
    Feigned, but are erring stars.
Faustus. But have they all one motion, both *situ et tempore?*
Mephostophilis. All move from east to west in four and twenty hours upon
    the poles of the world, but differ in their motions upon the poles of the
    zodiac.
Faustus. These slender questions Wagner can decide!
    Hath Mephostophilis no greater skill?   50

27 Of Alexander's . . . death] Paris (Alexander) loved Oenone before he met Helen.
28–9 he . . . harp] At the sound of Amphion's harp the stones rose voluntarily to build the
walls of Thebes.   37 this centric earth] the earth as the centre of the universe
45 But . . . *tempore*] Do all the planets move in the same way, in the same direction and at
the same speed

Who knows not the double motion of the planets,
    That the first is finish'd in a natural day,
The second thus: Saturn in thirty years, Jupiter in twelve, Mars in four,
the Sun, Venus and Mercury in a year, the Moon in twenty-eight days.
These are freshmen's suppositions. But tell me, hath every sphere a
dominion or *intelligentia*?

Mephostophilis. Ay.

Faustus. How many heavens or spheres are there?

Mephostophilis. Nine, the seven planets, the firmament, and the empyreal
    heaven.   60

Faustus. But is there not *coelum igneum*? *et cristallinum*?

Mephostophilis. No, Faustus, they be but fables.

Faustus. Resolve me then in this one question. Why are not conjunctions,
    oppositions, aspects, eclipses, all at one time, but in some years we have
    more, in some less?

Mephostophilis. Per inaequalem motum, respectu totius.

Faustus. Well, I am answered. Now tell me, who made the world?

Mephostophilis. I will not.

Faustus. Sweet Mephostophilis, tell me.

Mephostophilis. Move me not, Faustus.

Faustus. Villain, have not I bound thee to tell me anything?   70

Mephostophilis. Ay, that is not against our kingdom:
    This is. Thou art damn'd, think thou of hell.

Faustus. Think, Faustus, upon God, that made the world.

Mephostophilis. Remember this—   *Exit.*

Faustus. Ay, go, accursed spirit to ugly hell.
    'Tis thou hast damn'd distressed Faustus' soul.
    Is't not too late?

                    Enter the two Angels.

Bad Angel. Too late.

Good Angel. Never too late, if Faustus will repent.   80

Bad Angel. If thou repent, devils will tear thee in pieces.

Good Angel. Repent, and they shall never raze thy skin.   *Exeunt Angels.*

Faustus. Ah, Christ my saviour, my saviour,
    Help to save distressed Faustus' soul.

            Enter Lucifer, Belzebub, *and* Mephostophilis.

Lucifer. Christ cannot save thy soul, for he is just;
    There's none but I have interest in the same.

55 freshmen's suppositions] elementary facts given to first-year undergraduates
56 *intelligentia*] the guiding spirit of a planet   61 *coelum . . . cristallinum*] The spheres
of fire and of crystal were added to the Aristotelian concept of the universe, but were not
always accepted.   66 *Per . . . totius*] 'Because of an unequal movement with respect to
the whole'

Faustus. O what art thou that look'st so terribly?

Lucifer. I am Lucifer, and this is my companion prince in hell.

Faustus. O Faustus, they are come to fetch thy soul.

Belzebub. We are come to tell thee thou dost injure us. 90

Lucifer. Thou call'st on Christ contrary to thy promise.

Belzebub. Thou shouldst not think on God.

Lucifer. Think on the devil.

Belzebub. And his dam too.

Faustus. Nor will I henceforth. Pardon me in this,
    And Faustus vows never to look to heaven,
    Never to name God or to pray to him,
    To burn his scriptures, slay his ministers,
    And make my spirits pull his churches down.

Lucifer. So shalt thou show thyself an obedient servant, 100
    And we will highly gratify thee for it.

Belzebub. Faustus, we are come from hell in person to show thee some
pastime. Sit down and thou shalt behold the Seven Deadly Sins appear
to thee in their own proper shapes and likeness.

Faustus. That sight will be as pleasant to me as Paradise was to Adam the
first day of his creation.

Lucifer. Talk not of Paradise or Creation, but mark the show. Go, Mephostophilis, fetch them in.

Enter the Seven Deadly Sins.

Belzebub. Now, Faustus, question them of their names and dispositions.

Faustus. That shall I soon. What art thou, the first? 110

Pride. I am Pride. I disdain to have any parents. I am like to Ovid's flea, I
can creep into every corner of a wench; sometimes like a periwig I sit
upon her brow; next, like a necklace I hang about her neck; then, like a
fan of feathers, I kiss her; and then, turning myself to a wrought smock,
do what I list. But fie, what a smell is here! I'll not speak another word,
unless the ground be perfumed and covered with cloth of arras.

Faustus. Thou art a proud knave indeed. What art thou, the second?

Covetousness. I am Covetousness, begotten of an old churl in a leather bag;
and might I now obtain my wish, this house, you and all, should turn to
gold, that I might lock you safe into my chest. O my sweet gold! 120

Faustus. And what art thou, the third?

Envy. I am Envy, begotten of a chimney-sweeper and an oyster-wife. I
cannot read and therefore wish all books burned. I am lean with seeing
others eat: O that there would come a famine over all the world, that all

111 Ovid's flea] The poet of 'The Song of the Flea' (probably medieval but attributed to
Ovid) envies the flea for its freedom of movement over his mistress' body.   122 begotten
. . . wife] 'and therefore black and malodorous' (Wheeler)

might die, and I live alone; then thou shouldst see how fat I'd be. But must thou sit and I stand? Come down, with a vengeance!

Faustus. Out, envious wretch. But what art thou, the fourth?

Wrath. I am Wrath. I had neither father nor mother. I leapt out of a lion's mouth when I was scarce an hour old, and ever since have run up and down the world with these case of rapiers, wounding myself when I could get none to fight withal. I was born in hell, and look to it, for some of you shall be my father.   132

Faustus. And what art thou, the fifth?

Gluttony. I am Gluttony. My parents are all dead, and the devil a penny they have left me, but a small pension, and that buys me thirty meals a day and ten bevers: a small trifle to suffice nature. I come of a royal pedigree: my father was a gammon of bacon and my mother was a hogshead of claret wine. My godfathers were these: Peter Pickle-herring and Martin Martlemas-beef. But my godmother, O, she was an ancient gentlewoman, and well-beloved in every good town and city; her name was Mistress Margery March-beer. Now, Faustus, thou hast heard all my progeny, wilt thou bid me to supper?   142

Faustus. No, I'll see thee hanged; thou wilt eat up all my victuals.

Gluttony. Then the devil choke thee.

Faustus. Choke thyself, Glutton. What art thou, the sixth?

Sloth. Hey ho, I am Sloth. I was begotten on a sunny bank, where I have lain ever since, and you have done me great injury to bring me from thence. Let me be carried thither again by Gluttony and Lechery. Hey ho! I'll not speak a word more for a king's ransom.

Faustus. And what are you, Mistress Minx, the seventh and last?   150

Lechery. Who, I, sir? I am one that loves an inch of raw mutton better than an ell of fried stockfish, and the first letter of my name begins with Lechery.

Lucifer. Away to hell! Away, on, piper!   *Exeunt the* Seven Sins.

Faustus. O how this sight doth delight my soul.

Lucifer. But Faustus, in hell is all manner of delight.

Faustus. O might I see hell and return again safe, how happy were I then!

Lucifer. Faustus, thou shalt; at midnight I will send for thee. Meanwhile, peruse this book and view it throughly, and thou shalt turn thyself into what shape thou wilt.   160

Faustus. Thanks, mighty Lucifer; this will I keep as chary as my life.

Lucifer. Now, Faustus, farewell.

Faustus. Farewell, great Lucifer. Come, Mephostophilis.

                                            Exeunt omnes, several ways.

___

136 bevers] snacks   151–2 one that . . . stockfish] i.e., one who prefers a small quantity of virility to a large extent of impotence

[Scene iii]

Enter the Clown [Robin].

Robin. What, Dick, look to the horses there till I come again. I have gotten
one of Doctor Faustus' conjuring books, and now we'll have such knavery
as't passes.

Enter Dick.

Dick. What, Robin, you must come away and walk the horses.

Robin. I walk the horses? I scorn't, 'faith. I have other matters in hand. Let
the horses walk themselves and they will. *A per se a, t.h.e. the: o per se o,
deny orgon, gorgon.* Keep further from me, O thou illiterate and unlearned
hostler.

Dick. 'Snails, what hast thou got there? A book? Why, thou can'st not tell
ne'er a word on't.   10

Robin. That thou shalt see presently. Keep out of the circle, I say, lest I send
you into the hostry with a vengeance.

Dick. That's like, 'faith. You had best leave your foolery, for an my master
come, he'll conjure you, 'faith!

Robin. My master conjure me? I'll tell thee what, an my master come here,
I'll clap as fair a pair of horns on's head as e'er thou sawest in thy life.

Dick. Thou need'st not do that, for my mistress hath done it.

Robin. Ay, there be of us here, that have waded as deep into matters as other
men, if they were disposed to talk.

Dick. A plague take you! I thought you did not sneak up and down after
her for nothing. But I prithee tell me, in good sadness, Robin, is that a
conjuring book?   22

Robin. Do but speak what thou'lt have me to do, and I'll do't. If thou'lt
dance naked, put off thy clothes and I'll conjure thee about presently.
Or if thou'lt go but to the tavern with me, I'll give thee white wine, red
wine, claret wine, sack, muscadine, malmesey and whippincrust, hold—
belly—hold, and we'll not pay one penny for it.

Dick. O brave! Prithee, let's to it presently, for I am as dry as a dog.

Robin. Come, then, let's away.   *Exeunt.*

Scene iii] A's version of this scene is printed in the Appendix, p. 393.   3 as't passes]
as beats everything   6 *A per se a*] 'a by itself spells a'   26 whippincrust] hippocras,
a spiced wine

[Chorus 1]

Chorus.

Learned Faustus,
To find the secrets of astronomy
Graven in the book of Jove's high firmament,
Did mount him up to scale Olympus top,
Where sitting in a chariot burning bright,
Drawn by the strength of yoked dragons' necks,
He views the clouds, the planets, and the stars,
The tropics, zones, and quarters of the sky,
From the bright circle of the horned moon,
Even to the height of *Primum Mobile*.   10
And whirling round with this circumference,
Within the concave compass of the pole,
From east to west his dragons swiftly glide,
And in eight days did bring him home again.
Not long he stay'd within his quiet house,
To rest his bones after his weary toil,
But new exploits do hale him out again,
And mounted then upon a dragon's back,
That with his wings did part the subtle air,
He now is gone to prove cosmography,   20
That measures coasts and kingdoms of the earth;
And as I guess will first arrive at Rome,
To see the Pope and manner of his court,
And take some part of holy Peter's feast,
The which this day is highly solemniz'd.   *Exit.*

[Act III   Scene i]

Enter Faustus *and* Mephostophilis.

Faustus. Having now, my good Mephostophilis,
    Pass'd with delight the stately town of Trier,
    Environ'd round with airy mountain tops,
    With walls of flint, and deep-entrenched lakes,
    Not to be won by any conquering prince;
    From Paris next, coasting the realm of France,

25 this day] 29th June is the feast of St. Peter.

We saw the river Main fall into Rhine,
Whose banks are set with groves of fruitful vines;
Then up to Naples, rich Campania,
With buildings fair and gorgeous to the eye,   10
Whose streets straight forth and paved with finest brick,
Quarters the town in four equivalents.
There saw we learned Maro's golden tomb,
The way he cut, an English mile in length,
Thorough a rock of stone in one night's space.
From thence to Venice, Padua and the rest,
In midst of which a sumptuous temple stands,
That threats the stars with her aspiring top,
Whose frame is pav'd with sundry colour'd stones,
And roof'd aloft with curious work in gold.   20
Thus hitherto hath Faustus spent his time.
But tell me now, what resting place is this?
Hast thou, as erst I did command,
Conducted me within the walls of Rome?
Mephostophilis. I have, my Faustus, and for proof thereof,
    This is the goodly palace of the Pope;
    And 'cause we are no common guests,
    I choose his privy chamber for our use.
Faustus. I hope his Holiness will bid us welcome.
Mephostophilis. All's one, for we'll be bold with his venison.   30
    But now, my Faustus, that thou may'st perceive
    What Rome contains for to delight thine eyes,
    Know that this city stands upon seven hills,
    That underprop the groundwork of the same;
    Just through the midst runs flowing Tiber's stream,
    With winding banks that cut it in two parts,
    Over the which four stately bridges lean,
    That make safe passage to each part of Rome.
    Upon the bridge called Ponte Angelo
    Erected is a castle passing strong,   40
    Where thou shalt see such store of ordinance
    As that the double cannons forg'd of brass
    Do match the number of the days contain'd
    Within the compass of one complete year;
    Beside the gates and high pyramides,
    That Julius Caesar brought from Africa.

13–15 There . . . space] The tomb of Virgil (Publius Virgilius Maro) stands at the end of the promontory of Posilippo; legend ascribes the tunnel running through this promontory to Virgil's magic.

Faustus. Now by the kingdoms of infernal rule,
    Of Styx, of Acheron, and the fiery lake
    Of ever-burning Phlegethon, I swear
    That I do long to see the monuments   50
    And situation of bright-splendent Rome.
    Come, therefore, let's away.
Mephostophilis. Nay stay, my Faustus. I know you'd see the Pope,
    And take some part of holy Peter's feast,
    The which in state and high solemnity
    This day is held through Rome and Italy
    In honour of the Pope's triumphant victory.
Faustus. Sweet Mephostophilis, thou pleasest me.
    Whilst I am here on earth let me be cloy'd
    With all things that delight the heart of man.   60
    My four-and-twenty years of liberty
    I'll spend in pleasure and in dalliance,
    That Faustus' name, whilst this bright frame doth stand,
    May be admired through the furthest land.
Mephostophilis. 'Tis well said, Faustus. Come then, stand by me,
    And thou shalt see them come immediately.
Faustus. Nay stay, my gentle Mephostophilis,
    And grant me my request, and then I go.
    Thou know'st within the compass of eight days
    We view'd the face of heaven, of earth and hell;   70
    So high our dragons soar'd into the air,
    That looking down, the earth appear'd to me
    No bigger than my hand in quantity.
    There did we view the kingdoms of the world,
    And what might please mine eye, I there beheld.
    Then in this show let me an actor be,
    That this proud Pope may Faustus' cunning see.
Mephostophilis. Let it be so, my Faustus, but first stay
    And view their triumphs as they pass this way.
    And then devise what best contents thy mind   80
    By cunning in thine art to cross the Pope,
    Or dash the pride of this solemnity,
    To make his monks and abbots stand like apes,
    And point like antics at his triple crown,
    To beat the beads about the friars' pates,
    Or clape huge horns upon the cardinals' heads,
    Or any villainy thou canst devise,
    And I'll perform it, Faustus. Hark, they come!
    This day shall make thee be admir'd in Rome.

Enter the Cardinals *and* Bishops, *some bearing crosiers, some the pillars;*
　　Monks *and* Friars *singing their procession. Then the* Pope *and*
　　　Raymond *King of Hungary with* Bruno *led in chains.*

Pope. Cast down our footstool.
Raymond.　　　　　　　　　Saxon Bruno, stoop,　　　　　　90
　　Whilst on thy back his Holiness ascends
　　Saint Peter's chair and state pontifical.
Bruno. Proud Lucifer, that state belongs to me:
　　But thus I fall to Peter, not to thee.
Pope. To me and Peter shalt thou grovelling lie,
　　And crouch before the papal dignity.
　　Sound trumpets then, for thus Saint Peter's heir
　　From Bruno's back ascends Saint Peter's chair.
　　　　　　　　　　　　　　　A flourish while he ascends.
　　Thus, as the gods creep on with feet of wool
　　Long ere with iron hands they punish men,　　　　　　100
　　So shall our sleeping vengeance now arise,
　　And smite with death thy hated enterprise.
　　Lord cardinals of France and Padua,
　　Go forthwith to our holy consistory,
　　And read amongst the statutes decretal,
　　What by the holy council held at Trent
　　The sacred synod hath decreed for him
　　That doth assume the papal government,
　　Without election and a true consent.
　　Away, and bring us word with speed!　　　　　　110
1 Cardinal. We go, my lord.
　　　　　　　　　　　　　　　　　　Exeunt Cardinals.
Pope. Lord Raymond.　　　　　　[*The* Pope *and* Raymond *converse.*]
Faustus. Go, haste thee, gentle Mephostophilis,
　　Follow the cardinals to the consistory,
　　And as they turn their superstitious books,
　　Strike them with sloth and drowsy idleness,
　　And make them sleep so sound that in their shapes
　　Thyself and I may parley with this Pope,
　　This proud confronter of the Emperor,
　　And in despite of all his holiness　　　　　　120
　　Restore this Bruno to his liberty
　　And bear him to the states of Germany.
Mephostophilis. Faustus, I go.
Faustus.　　　　　　　　　Dispatch it soon,
　　The Pope shall curse that Faustus came to Rome.
　　　　　　　　　　　　　Exeunt Faustus *and* Mephostophilis.

Bruno. Pope Adrian, let me have some right of law:
    I was elected by the Emperor.
Pope. We will depose the Emperor for that deed,
    And curse the people that submit to him.
    Both he and thou shalt stand excommunicate,
    And interdict from Church's privilege   130
    And all society of holy men.
    He grows too proud in his authority,
    Lifting his lofty head above the clouds
    And like a steeple overpeers the Church.
    But we'll pull down his haughty insolence,
    And as Pope Alexander, our progenitor,
    Stood on the neck of German Frederick,
    Adding this golden sentence to our praise,
    That Peter's heirs should tread on emperors
    And walk upon the dreadful adder's back,   140
    Treading the lion and the dragon down,
    And fearless spurn the killing basilisk,
    So will we quell that haughty schismatic,
    And by authority apostolical
    Depose him from his regal government.
Bruno. Pope Julius swore to princely Sigismund,
    For him and the succeeding popes of Rome,
    To hold the emperors their lawful lords.
Pope. Pope Julius did abuse the Church's rites,
    And therefore none of his decrees can stand.   150
    Is not all power on earth bestow'd on us?
    And therefore though we would we cannot err.
    Behold this silver belt, whereto is fix'd
    Seven golden keys fast seal'd with seven seals,
    In token of our seven-fold power from heaven,
    To bind or loose, lock fast, condemn or judge,
    Resign or seal, or whatso pleaseth us.
    Then he and thou, and all the world, shall stoop,
    Or be assured of our dreadful curse,
    To light as heavy as the pains of hell.   160

        Enter Faustus *and* Mephostophilis, *like the cardinals*.

Mephostophilis. Now tell me, Faustus, are we not fitted well?
Faustus. Yes, Mephostophilis, and two such cardinals
    Ne'er served a holy pope as we shall do.

136–7 Pope Alexander . . . Frederick] Alexander III compelled the Emperor Frederick
Barbarossa to acknowledge papal supremacy.

But whilst they sleep within the consistory,
Let us salute his reverend Fatherhood.
Raymond. Behold, my lord, the cardinals are return'd.
Pope. Welcome, grave fathers, answer presently:
What have our holy council there decreed
Concerning Bruno and the Emperor,
In quittance of their late conspiracy   170
Against our state and papal dignity?
Faustus. Most sacred patron of the Church of Rome,
By full consent of all the synod
Of priests and prelates, it is thus decreed:
That Bruno and the German Emperor
Be held as lollards and bold schismatics
And proud disturbers of the Church's peace.
And if that Bruno by his own assent,
Without enforcement of the German peers,
Did seek to wear the triple diadem   180
And by your death to climb Saint Peter's chair,
The statutes decretal have thus decreed:
He shall be straight condemn'd of heresy
And on a pile of faggots burnt to death.
Pope. It is enough. Here, take him to your charge,
And bear him straight to Ponte Angelo,
And in the strongest tower enclose him fast.
Tomorrow, sitting in our consistory
With all our college of grave cardinals,
We will determine of his life or death.   190
Here, take his triple crown along with you,
And leave it in the Church's treasury.
Make haste again, my good lord cardinals,
And take our blessing apostolical.
Mephostophilis. So, so, was never devil thus bless'd before.
Faustus. Away, sweet Mephostophilis, be gone:
The cardinals will be plagu'd for this anon.
             Exeunt Faustus *and* Mephostophilis [*with* Bruno].
Pope. Go presently and bring a banquet forth
That we may solemnize Saint Peter's feast,
And with Lord Raymond, King of Hungary,   200
Drink to our late and happy victory.   *Exeunt.*

176 lollards] heretics (originally the followers of Wyclif)

[Scene ii]

A sennet while the banquet is brought in; and then enter Faustus *and*
Mephostophilis *in their own shapes.*

Mephostophilis. Now, Faustus, come prepare thyself for mirth;
    The sleepy cardinals are hard at hand
    To censure Bruno, that is posted hence,
    And on a proud-pac'd steed as swift as thought
    Flies o'er the Alps to fruitful Germany,
    There to salute the woeful Emperor.

Faustus. The Pope will curse them for their sloth today,
    That slept both Bruno and his crown away.
    But now, that Faustus may delight his mind,
    And by their folly make some merriment,   10
    Sweet Mephostophilis, so charm me here,
    That I may walk invisible to all,
    And do what e'er I please unseen of any.

Mephostophilis. Faustus, thou shalt. Then kneel down presently:
    Whilst on thy head I lay my hand,
    And charm thee with this magic wand.
    First wear this girdle, then appear
    Invisible to all are here.
    The planets seven, the gloomy air,
    Hell, and the Furies' forked hair,   20
    Pluto's blue fire and Hecat's tree,
    With magic spells so compass thee,
    That no eye may thy body see.
    So, Faustus, now for all their holiness,
    Do what thou wilt, thou shalt not be discern'd.

Faustus. Thanks, Mephostophilis. Now, friars, take heed
    Lest Faustus make your shaven crowns to bleed.

Mephostophilis. Faustus, no more; see where the cardinals come.

Enter Pope *and all the* Lords [*and* Archbishop of Rheims]. *Enter the*
Cardinals *with a book.*

Pope. Welcome, lord cardinals. Come, sit down.
    Lord Raymond, take your seat. Friars, attend,   30
    And see that all things be in readiness
    As best beseems this solemn festival.

1 Cardinal. First, may it please your sacred holiness

s.d. *sennet*] flourish on trumpets   20 forked hair] the tongues of the snakes on the
Furies' heads   21 Pluto's . . . fire] the sulphurous smoke of hell   21 Hecat's tree]
the gallows-tree

  To view the sentence of the reverend synod
  Concerning Bruno and the Emperor?
Pope. What needs this question? Did I not tell you
  Tomorrow we would sit i'the consistory
  And there determine of his punishment?
  You brought us word even now, it was decreed
  That Bruno and the cursed Emperor   40
  Were by the holy Council both condemn'd
  For loathed lollards and base schismatics.
  Then wherefore would you have me view that book?
1 Cardinal. Your grace mistakes. You gave us no such charge.
Raymond. Deny it not; we all are witnesses
  That Bruno here was late deliver'd you,
  With his rich triple crown to be reserv'd
  And put into the Church's treasury.
Both Cardinals. By holy Paul, we saw them not.
Pope. By Peter, you shall die   50
  Unless you bring them forth immediately.
  Hale them to prison, lade their limbs with gyves!
  False prelates, for this hateful treachery,
  Curs'd be your souls to hellish misery.   [*Exit* Cardinals, *guarded.*]
Faustus. So, they are safe. Now Faustus, to the feast;
  The Pope had never such a frolic guest.
Pope. Lord Archbishop of Rheims, sit down with us.
Archbishop. I thank your holiness.
Faustus. Fall to; the devil choke you an you spare.
Pope. Who's that spoke? Friars, look about.   60
Friars. Here's nobody, if it like your holiness.
Pope. Lord Raymond, pray fall to. I am beholding
  To the Bishop of Milan for this so rare a present.
Faustus. I thank you, sir.   *Snatch it.*
Pope. How now? Who snatch'd the meat from me?
  Villains, why speak you not?
  My good Lord Archbishop, here's a most dainty dish
  Was sent me from a cardinal in France.
Faustus. I'll have that too.   [*Snatch it.*]
Pope. What lollards do attend our holiness   70
  That we receive such great indignity? Fetch me some wine.
Faustus. Ay, pray do, for Faustus is a-dry.
Pope. Lord Raymond, I drink unto your grace.
Faustus. I pledge your grace.   [*Snatch the cup.*]
Pope. My wine gone too? Ye lubbers, look about
  And find the man that doth this villainy,

    Or by our sanctitude you all shall die.
    I pray, my lords, have patience at this
    Troublesome banquet.
Archbishop. Please it your holiness, I think it be some ghost crept out of
    purgatory, and now is come unto your holiness for his pardon.   81
Pope. It may be so.
    Go, then, command our priests to sing a dirge
    To lay the fury of this same troublesome ghost.
                                The Pope *crosseth himself.*
Faustus. How now? Must every bit be spiced with a cross? Nay then, take
    that.   Faustus *hits him a box of the ear.*
Pope. Oh, I am slain! Help me, my lords.
    Oh come, and help to bear my body hence.
    Damn'd be this soul for ever for this deed!
                                Exeunt the Pope *and his train.*
Mephostophilis. Now, Faustus, what will you do now? For I can tell you,
    you'll be cursed with bell, book and candle.   91
Faustus. Bell, book and candle, candle, book and bell,
    Forward and backward, to curse Faustus to hell.

      Enter the Friars *with bell, book and candle, for the dirge.*

Friar. Come, brethren, let's about our business with good devotion.
                                          Sing this.

        Cursed be he that stole his holiness' meat from the table.
                Maledicat Dominus!
        Cursed be he that struck his holiness a blow on the face.
                Maledicat Dominus!
        Cursed be he that took Friar Sandelo a blow on the pate.
                Maledicat Dominus!   100
        Cursed be he that disturbeth our holy dirge.
                Maledicat Dominus!
        Cursed be he that took away his holiness' wine.
                Maledicat Dominus!
                [Faustus *and* Mephostophilis] *beat the* Friars, *fling*
                      fireworks among them, and exeunt [*omnes*].

96 *Maledicat Dominus*] 'May God curse him'   104 s.d. *exeunt*] A concludes this scene
with '*Et omnes sancti, amen*' ('and all the saints, amen'); the formality seems at odds with
the general disorder of the fireworks.

[Scene iii]

Enter Clown [Robin] *and* Dick, *with a cup.*

Dick. Sirrah, Robin we were best look that your devil can answer the stealing
of this same cup, for the vintner's boy follows us at the hard heels.

Robin. 'Tis no matter, let him come; an he follow us, I'll so conjure him,
as he was never conjured in his life, I warrant him. Let me see the cup.

Enter Vintner.

Dick. Here 'tis. Yonder he comes! Now Robin, now or never show thy
cunning.

Vintner. O, are you here? I am glad I have found you. You are a couple of
fine companions! Pray where's the cup you stole from the tavern?

Robin. How, how? We steal a cup? Take heed of what you say; we look not
like cup-stealers, I can tell you.   10

Vintner. Never deny't, for I know you have it, and I'll search you.

Robin. Search me? Ay, and spare not. [*Aside.*] Hold the cup, Dick. Come,
come, search me, search me.   [Vintner *searches him.*]

Vintner. Come on sirrah, let me search you now.

Dick. Ay, ay, do, do. [*Aside.*] Hold the cup, Robin. I fear not your search-
ing; we scorn to steal your cups, I can tell you.   [Vintner *searches him.*]

Vintner. Never outface me for the matter, for sure the cup is between you
two.

Robin. Nay, there you lie; 'tis beyond us both.

Vintner. A plague take you! I thought 'twas your knavery to take it away.
Come, give it me again.   21

Robin. Ay, much! When, can you tell? Dick, make me a circle, and stand
close at my back, and stir not for thy life. Vintner, you shall have your
cup back anon. Say nothing, Dick. *O per se, o; Demogorgon, Belcher and
Mephostophilis!*

Enter Mephostophilis.

Mephostophilis. You princely legions of infernal rule,
How am I vexed by these villains' charms!
From Constantinople have they brought me now,
Only for pleasure of these damned slaves.   [*Exit* Vintner.]

Robin. By lady sir, you have had a shrewd journey of it. Will it please you
to take a shoulder of mutton to supper, and a tester in your purse, and go
back again?   32

Dick. Ay, I pray you heartily, sir, for we called you but in jest, I promise
you.

Scene iii] A's version of this scene is printed in the Appendix, p. 394.   19 beyond us
both] The clowns have juggled with the cup so that neither holds it.   31 tester] sixpence

Mephostophilis. To purge the rashness of this cursed deed
    First, be thou turned to this ugly shape,
    For apish deeds transformed to an ape.

Robin. O brave, an ape! I pray sir, let me have the carrying of him about to
    show some tricks.

Mephostophilis. And so thou shalt: be thou transformed to a dog, and carry
    him upon thy back. Away, be gone!   41

Robin. A dog? That's excellent: let the maids look well to their porridge-pots,
    for I'll into the kitchen presently. Come, Dick, come.

                                       Exeunt the two Clowns.

Mephostophilis. Now with the flames of ever-burning fire
    I'll wing myself and forthwith fly amain
    Unto my Faustus to the great Turk's court.   *Exit.*

[Chorus 2]

Chorus.

When Faustus had with pleasure ta'en the view
Of rarest things and royal courts of kings,
He stay'd his course and so returned home,
Where such as bare his absence but with grief—
I mean his friends and near'st companions—
Did gratulate his safety with kind words;
And in their conference of what befell,
Touching his journey through the world and air,
They put forth questions of astrology,
Which Faustus answered with such learned skill   10
As they admir'd and wonder'd at his wit.
Now is his fame spread forth in every land:
Amongst the rest, the Emperor is one,
Carolus the Fifth, at whose palace now
Faustus is feasted 'mongst his noblemen.
What there he did in trial of his art,
I leave untold: your eyes shall see perform'd.   *Exit.*

Chorus 2] This Chorus, which is not in B, precedes the clowns' scene with the goblet in A.

[Act IV   Scene i]

Enter Martino *and* Frederick *at several doors.*

Martino. What ho, officers, gentlemen!
    Hie to the presence to attend the Emperor.
    Good Frederick, see the rooms be voided straight,
    His majesty is coming to the hall;
    Go back, and see the state in readiness.
Frederick. But where is Bruno, our elected Pope,
    That on a fury's back came post from Rome?
    Will not his grace consort the Emperor?
Martino. Oh yes, and with him comes the German conjurer,
    The learned Faustus, fame of Wittenberg,   10
    The wonder of the world for magic art;
    And he intends to show great Carolus
    The race of all his stout progenitors,
    And bring in presence of his majesty
    The royal shapes and warlike semblances
    Of Alexander and his beauteous paramour.
Frederick. Where is Benvolio?
Martino. Fast asleep, I warrant you.
    He took his rouse with stoups of Rhenish wine
    So kindly yesternight to Bruno's health,   20
    That all this day the sluggard keeps his bed.
Frederick. See, see, his window's ope. We'll call to him.
Martino. What ho, Benvolio?

Enter Benvolio *above at a window in his nightcap, buttoning.*

Benvolio. What a devil ail you two?
Martino. Speak softly, sir, lest the devil hear you;
    For Faustus at the court is late arriv'd,
    And at his heels a thousand furies wait
    To accomplish whatsoever the doctor please.
Benvolio. What of this?
Martino. Come, leave thy chamber first, and thou shalt see   30
    This conjurer perform such rare exploits
    Before the Pope and royal Emperor
    As never yet was seen in Germany.
Benvolio. Has not the Pope enough of conjuring yet?
    He was upon the devil's back late enough,
    And if he be so far in love with him,
    I would he would post with him to Rome again.

2 presence] audience-chamber   5 state] throne   19 took his rouse] drank heavily

Frederick. Speak, wilt thou come and see this sport?

Benvolio. Not I.

Martino. Wilt thou stand in thy window and see it, then?   40

Benvolio. Ay, and I fall not asleep i' the meantime.

Martino. The Emperor is at hand, who comes to see
  What wonders by black spells may compass'd be.

Benvolio. Well, go you attend the Emperor. I am content for this once to
  thrust my head out at a window, for they say if a man be drunk overnight
  the devil cannot hurt him in the morning. If that be true, I have a charm
  in my head shall control him as well as the conjurer, I warrant you.

  A sennet. [*Enter*] *Charles the German* Emperor, Bruno, [*Duke of*]
  Saxony, Faustus, Mephostophilis, *and* Attendants.

Emperor. Wonder of men, renowned magician,
  Thrice-learned Faustus, welcome to our court.
  This deed of thine, in setting Bruno free   50
  From his and our professed enemy,
  Shall add more excellence unto thine art,
  Than if by powerful necromantic spells
  Thou couldst command the world's obedience.
  For ever be belov'd of Carolus;
  And if this Bruno thou hast late redeem'd,
  In peace possess the triple diadem
  And sit in Peter's chair, despite of chance,
  Thou shalt be famous through all Italy,
  And honour'd of the German Emperor.   60

Faustus. These gracious words, most royal Carolus,
  Shall make poor Faustus to his utmost power
  Both love and serve the German Emperor,
  And lay his life at holy Bruno's feet.
  For proof whereof, if so your grace be pleas'd,
  The doctor stands prepar'd by power of art
  To cast his magic charms that shall pierce through
  The ebon gates of ever-burning hell,
  And hale the stubborn furies from their caves,
  To compass whatsoe'er your grace commands.   70

Benvolio. Blood, he speaks terribly! But for all that, I do not greatly believe
  him; he looks as like a conjurer as the Pope to a costermonger.

Emperor. Then, Faustus, as thou late didst promise us,
  We would behold that famous conqueror,

---

47 s.d. *sennet*] Most editors start a new scene here. But since Frederick and Martino are
already present, and Benvolio remains at his window, there seems no necessity for it. A's
version of the following episode is printed in the Appendix, p. 395.

> Great Alexander, and his paramour,
> In their true shapes and state majestical,
> That we may wonder at their excellence.

Faustus. Your majesty shall see them presently.
> Mephostophilis, away!
> And with a solemn noise of trumpets' sound,   80
> Present before this royal Emperor
> Great Alexander and his beauteous paramour.

Mephostophilis. Faustus, I will.   *Exit* Mephostophilis.

Benvolio. Well, master doctor, an your devils come not away quickly, you shall have me asleep presently. Zounds, I could eat myself for anger, to think I have been such an ass all this while, to stand gaping after the devil's governor, and can see nothing.

Faustus. I'll make you feel something anon, if my art fail me not.
> My lord, I must forewarn your majesty
> That when my spirits present the royal shapes   90
> Of Alexander and his paramour,
> Your grace demand no questions of the king,
> But in dumb silence let them come and go.

Emperor. Be it as Faustus please, we are content.

Benvolio. Ay, ay, and I am content too. And thou bring Alexander and his paramour before the Emperor, I'll be Actaeon and turn myself to a stag.

Faustus. And I'll play Diana, and send you the horns presently.

> *Sennet. Enter at one door the Emperor* Alexander, *at the other* Darius;
> *they meet;* Darius *is thrown down;* Alexander *kills him, takes off*
> *his crown, and, offering to go out, his* Paramour *meets him;*
> *he embraceth her and sets* Darius' *crown upon her head,*
> *and coming back, both salute the* Emperor, *who, leaving*
> *his state, offers to embrace them, which* Faustus *seeing,*
> *suddenly stays him. Then trumpets cease and music sounds.*

> My gracious lord, you do forget yourself;
> These are but shadows, not substantial.

Emperor. O pardon me, my thoughts are so ravished   100
> With sight of this renowned emperor,
> That in mine arms I would have compass'd him.
> But, Faustus, since I may not speak to them,
> To satisfy my longing thoughts at full,
> Let me this tell thee: I have heard it said
> That this fair lady, whilst she liv'd on earth,
> Had on her neck a little wart or mole;
> How may I prove that saying to be true?

Faustus. Your majesty may boldly go and see.

96 Actaeon] who was turned into a stag when he spied on Diana when she was bathing

Emperor. Faustus, I see it plain,   110
    And in this sight thou better pleasest me
    Than if I gain'd another monarchy.

Faustus. Away, be gone.   *Exit Show.*
    See, see, my gracious lord, what strange beast is yon, that thrusts his
    head out at window?

Emperor. O, wondrous sight! See, Duke of Saxony,
    Two spreading horns most strangely fastened
    Upon the head of young Benvolio!

Saxony. What, is he asleep or dead?

Faustus. He sleeps, my lord, but dreams not of his horns.   120

Emperor. This sport is excellent. We'll call and wake him.
    What ho, Benvolio!

Benvolio. A plague upon you! Let me sleep awhile.

Emperor. I blame thee not to sleep much, having such a head of thine own.

Saxony. Look up, Benvolio, 'tis the Emperor calls.

Benvolio. The Emperor? Where? O, zounds, my head!

Emperor. Nay, and thy horns hold, 'tis no matter for thy head, for that's
    armed sufficiently.

Faustus. Why, how now, sir knight? What, hanged by the horns? This
    is most horrible! Fie, fie, pull in your head for shame, let not all the
    world wonder at you.   131

Benvolio. Zounds, doctor, is this your villainy?

Faustus. O say not so, sir. The doctor has no skill,
    No art, no cunning, to present these lords
    Or bring before this royal Emperor
    The mighty monarch, warlike Alexander.
    If Faustus do it, you are straight resolv'd
    In bold Actaeon's shape to turn a stag.
    And therefore, my lord, so please your majesty,
    I'll raise a kennel of hounds shall hunt him so   140
    As all his footmanship shall scarce prevail
    To keep his carcass from their bloody fangs.
    Ho, Belimote, Argiron, Asterote!

Benvolio. Hold, hold! Zounds, he'll raise up a kennel of devils, I think,
    anon. Good my lord, entreat for me. 'Sblood, I am never able to endure
    these torments.

Emperor. Then, good master doctor,
    Let me entreat you to remove his horns:
    He has done penance now sufficiently.   149

Faustus. My gracious lord, not so much for injury done to me, as to delight
    your majesty with some mirth, hath Faustus justly requited this injurious

141 footmanship] skill in running

knight; which being all I desire, I am content to remove his horns.
Mephostophilis, transform him. And hereafter, sir, look you speak well
of scholars.

Benvolio. Speak well of ye? 'Sblood, and scholars be such cuckold-makers
to clap horns of honest men's heads o' this order, I'll ne'er trust smooth
faces and small ruffs more. But an I be not revenged for this, would I
might be turned to a gaping oyster and drink nothing but salt water.

Emperor. Come, Faustus, while the Emperor lives,
    In recompense of this thy high desert,   160
    Thou shalt command the state of Germany,
    And live belov'd of mighty Carolus.   *Exeunt omnes.*

[Scene ii]

Enter Benvolio, Martino, Frederick, *and* Soldiers.

Martino. Nay, sweet Benvolio, let us sway thy thoughts
    From this attempt against the conjurer.

Benvolio. Away, you love me not, to urge me thus.
    Shall I let slip so great an injury,
    When every servile groom jests at my wrongs,
    And in their rustic gambols proudly say
    'Benvolio's head was grac'd with horns today'?
    O may these eyelids never close again
    Till with my sword I have that conjurer slain.
    If you will aid me in this enterprise,   10
    Then draw your weapons and be resolute;
    If not, depart: here will Benvolio die,
    But Faustus' death shall quit my infamy.

Frederick. Nay, we will stay with thee, betide what may,
    And kill that doctor if he come this way.

Benvolio. Then, gentle Frederick, hie thee to the grove,
    And place our servants and our followers
    Close in an ambush there behind the trees.
    By this, I know, the conjurer is near:
    I saw him kneel and kiss the Emperor's hand,   20
    And take his leave, laden with rich rewards.
    Then, soldiers, boldly fight; if Faustus die,
    Take you the wealth, leave us the victory.

Frederick. Come, soldiers, follow me unto the grove.
    Who kills him shall have gold and endless love.

                        Exit Frederick *with the* Soldiers.

6 proudly] insolently   13 But] Unless

Benvolio. My head is lighter than it was by th'horns,
    But yet my heart's more ponderous than my head,
    And pants until I see that conjurer dead.
Martino. Where shall we place ourselves, Benvolio?
Benvolio. Here will we stay to bide the first assault.   30
    O were that damned hell-hound but in place,
    Thou soon shouldst see me quit my foul disgrace.

Enter Frederick.

Frederick. Close, close! The conjurer is at hand,
    And all alone comes walking in his gown.
    Be ready then, and strike the peasant down.
Benvolio. Mine be that honour, then; now sword, strike home.
    For horns he gave, I'll have his head anon.

Enter Faustus *with the false head*.

Martino. See, see, he comes.
Benvolio.   No words. This blow ends all.
    Hell take his soul; his body thus must fall.

[*Strikes* Faustus.]

Faustus. O!
Frederick. Groan you, master doctor?   40
Benvolio. Break may his heart with groans! Dear Frederick, see,
    Thus will I end his griefs immediately.   [*Cuts off his head*.]
Martino. Strike with a willing hand; his head is off.
Benvolio. The devil's dead; the Furies now may laugh.
Frederick. Was this that stern aspect, that awful frown,
    Made the grim monarch of infernal spirits
    Tremble and quake at his commanding charms?
Martino. Was this that damned head, whose heart conspir'd
    Benvolio's shame before the Emperor?   50
Benvolio. Ay, that's the head, and here the body lies,
    Justly rewarded for his villainies.
Frederick. Come, let's devise how we may add more shame
    To the black scandal of his hated name.
Benvolio. First, on his head, in quittance of my wrongs,
    I'll nail huge forked horns, and let them hang
    Within the window where he yok'd me first,
    That all the world may see my just revenge.
Martino. What use shall we put his beard to?
Benvolio. We'll sell it to a chimney-sweeper; it will wear out ten birchen
    brooms, I warrant you.   61
Frederick. What shall his eyes do?

Benvolio. We'll put out his eyes, and they shall serve for buttons to his lips,
  to keep his tongue from catching cold.

Martino. An excellent policy! And now, sirs, having divided him, what shall
  the body do?   [Faustus *stands up.*]

Benvolio. Zounds, the devil's alive again!

Frederick. Give him his head, for God's sake!

Faustus. Nay, keep it. Faustus will have heads and hands,

    Ay, all your hearts to recompense this deed.   70

    Knew you not, traitors, <u>I was limited</u>

    For four-and-twenty years to breathe on earth?

    And had you cut my body with your swords,

    Or hew'd this flesh and bones as small as sand,

    Yet in a minute had my spirit return'd,

    And I had breath'd a man made free from harm.

    But wherefore do I dally my revenge?

    Asteroth, Belimoth, Mephostophilis!

Enter Mephostophilis and other Devils.

    Go, horse these traitors on your fiery backs,

    And mount aloft with them as high as heaven;   80

    Thence pitch them headlong to the lowest hell.

    Yet stay, the world shall see their misery,

    And hell shall after plague their treachery.

    Go, Belimoth, and take this caitiff hence,

    And hurl him in some lake of mud and dirt.

    Take thou this other, drag him through the woods

    Amongst the pricking thorns and sharpest briars,

    Whilst with my gentle Mephostophilis,

    This traitor flies unto some steepy rock,

    That rolling down may break the villain's bones   90

    As he intended to dismember me.

    Fly hence, dispatch my charge immediately.

Frederick. Pity us, gentle Faustus! Save our lives!

Faustus. Away!

Frederick.   He must needs go that the devil drives.

Exeunt Spirits with the Knights.

Enter the ambushed Soldiers.

1 Soldier. Come, sirs, prepare yourselves in readiness.

    Make haste to help these noble gentlemen.

    I heard them parley with the conjurer.

2 Soldier. See where he comes; dispatch and kill the slave.

Faustus. What's here? An ambush to betray my life!

    Then Faustus, try thy skill. Base peasants, stand!   100

For lo, these trees remove at my command,
And stand as bulwarks twixt yourselves and me,
To shield me from your hated treachery.
Yet, to encounter this your weak attempt,
Behold an army comes incontinent.

Faustus *strikes the door, and enter a* Devil *playing on a drum; after*
him another bearing an ensign; and divers with weapons;
Mephostophilis *with fireworks. They set upon the* Soldiers *and*
drive them out.

[*Exit* Faustus.]

[Scene iii]

Enter at several doors Benvolio, Frederick, *and* Martino, *their heads*
and faces bloody and besmeared with mud and dirt, all having
horns on their heads.

Martino. What ho, Benvolio!
Benvolio. Here, what, Frederick, ho!
Frederick. O help me, gentle friend; where is Martino?
Martino. Dear Frederick, here,
    Half smother'd in a lake of mud and dirt,
    Through which the furies dragged me by the heels.
Frederick. Martino, see, Benvolio's horns again!
Martino. O misery! How now, Benvolio?
Benvolio. Defend me, heaven! Shall I be haunted still?
Martino. Nay, fear not, man; we have no power to kill.   10
Benvolio. My friends transformed thus! O hellish spite!
    Your heads are all set with horns!
Frederick.   You hit it right:
    It is your own you mean; feel on your head.
Benvolio. Zounds, horns again!
Martino.   Nay, chafe not, man, we all are sped.
Benvolio. What devil attends this damn'd magician,
    That, spite of spite, our wrongs are doubled?
Frederick. What may we do, that we may hide our shames?
Benvolio. If we should follow him to work revenge,
    He'd join long asses' ears to these huge horns,
    And make us laughing stocks to all the world.   20
Martino. What shall we then do, dear Benvolio?
Benvolio. I have a castle joining near these woods,
    And thither we'll repair and live obscure,

Till time shall alter these our brutish shapes.
Sith black disgrace hath thus eclips'd our fame,
We'll rather die with grief, than live with shame.   *Exeunt omnes.*

[Scene iv]

Enter Faustus *and the* Horse-courser *and* Mephostophilis.

Horse-courser. I beseech your worship accept of these forty dollars.

Faustus. Friend, thou canst not buy so good a horse for so small a price;
I have no great need to sell him, but if thou likest him for ten dollars more,
take him, because I see thou hast a good mind to him.

Horse-courser. I beseech you sir, accept of this. I am a very poor man, and
have lost very much of late by horse-flesh, and this bargain will set me up
again.

Faustus. Well, I will not stand with thee, give me the money. Now sirrah,
I must tell you, that you may ride him o'er hedge and ditch, and spare
him not; but, do you hear, in any case, ride him not into the water.   10

Horse-courser. How sir, not into the water? Why, will he not drink of all
waters?

Faustus. Yes, he will drink of all waters, but ride him not into the water;
o'er hedge and ditch or where thou wilt, but not into the water. Go bid
the ostler deliver him unto you—and remember what I say.

Horse-courser. I warrant you, sir. O joyful day! Now am I a made man for
ever.   *Exit.*

Faustus. What art thou, Faustus, but a man condemn'd to die?
Thy fatal time draws to a final end.
Despair doth drive distrust into my thoughts;   20
Confound these passions with a quiet sleep.
Tush, Christ did call the thief upon the cross,
Then rest thee, Faustus, quiet in conceit.   *He sits to sleep.*

Enter the Horse-courser, *wet.*

Horse-courser. O what a cozening doctor was this! I, riding my horse into
the water, thinking some hidden mystery had been in the horse, I had
nothing under me but a little straw, and had much ado to escape drowning.
Well, I'll go rouse him, and make him give me my forty dollars again.
Ho, sirrah doctor, you cozening scab! Master doctor, awake, and rise, and
give me my money again, for your horse is turned to a bottle of hay.
Master doctor!   *He pulls off his leg.*

Scene iv] A's version of this scene is printed in the Appendix, p. 397.   10 not into the
water] Running water (but not the stagnant water of a ditch) will break a witch's spell.
11 drink of all waters] go anywhere

Alas, I am undone; what shall I do? I have pulled off his leg.   31
Faustus. O help, help! The villain hath murdered me.
Horse-courser. Murder or not murder, now he has but one leg I'll outrun
    him, and cast this leg into some ditch or other.   [*Exit.*]
Faustus. Stop him, stop him, stop him—ha, ha, ha! Faustus hath his leg
    again, and the horse-courser a bundle of hay for his forty dollars.

Enter Wagner.

How now Wagner, what news with thee?
Wagner. If it please you, the Duke of Vanholt doth earnestly entreat your
    company, and hath sent some of his men to attend you with provision
    fit for your journey.   40
Faustus. The Duke of Vanholt's an honourable gentleman, and one to whom
    I must be no niggard of my cunning. Come away.   *Exeunt.*

[Scene v]

Enter Clown [Robin], Dick, Horse-courser, *and a* Carter.

Carter. Come, my masters, I'll bring you to the best beer in Europe. What
    ho, hostess. Where be these whores?

Enter Hostess.

Hostess. How now, what lack you? What, my old guests, welcome!
Robin. Sirrah Dick, dost thou know why I stand so mute?
Dick. No, Robin, why is't?
Robin. I am eighteen pence on the score; but say nothing, see if she have
    forgotten me.
Hostess. Who's this, that stands so solemnly by himself? What, my old
    guest!
Robin. Oh, hostess, how do you? I hope my score stands still.   10
Hostess. Ay, there's no doubt of that, for methinks you make no haste to
    wipe it out.
Dick. Why, hostess, I say, fetch us some beer.
Hostess. You shall presently. Look up into the hall there, ho!   *Exit.*
Dick. Come, sirs, what shall we do now till mine hostess comes?
Carter. Marry, sir, I'll tell you the bravest tale how a conjurer served me.
    You know Doctor Fauster?
Horse-courser. Ay, a plague take him. Here's some on's have cause to know
    him. Did he conjure thee too?   19
Carter. I'll tell you how he served me. As I was going to Wittenberg t'other
    day, with a load of hay, he met me and asked me what he should give me
    for as much hay as he could eat. Now, sir, I, thinking that a little would
    serve his turn, bade him take as much as he would for three-farthings.

So he presently gave me my money and fell to eating; and, as I am a cursen man, he never left eating till he had eat up all my load of hay.

All. O monstrous, eat a whole load of hay!

Robin. Yes, yes, that may be, for I have heard of one that h'as eat a load of logs.   28

Horse-courser. Now, sirs, you shall hear how villainously he served me. I went to him yesterday to buy a horse of him, and he would by no means sell him under forty dollars. So, sir, because I knew him to be such a horse as would run over hedge and ditch and never tire, I gave him his money. So when I had my horse, Doctor Fauster bade me ride him night and day and spare him no time. 'But', quoth he, 'in any case ride him not into the water'. Now, sir, I thinking the horse had some quality that he would not have me know of, what did I but rid him into a great river, and when I came just in the midst, my horse vanished away, and I sat straddling upon a bottle of hay.

All. O brave doctor!   39

Horse-courser. But you shall hear how bravely I served him for it: I went me home to his house, and there I found him asleep. I kept a-hallowing and whooping in his ears, but all could not wake him. I, seeing that, took him by the leg and never rested pulling, till I had pulled me his leg quite off, and now 'tis at home in mine hostry.

Robin. And has the doctor but one leg, then? That's excellent, for one of his devils turned me into the likeness of an ape's face.

Carter. Some more drink, hostess.

Robin. Hark you, we'll into another room and drink a while, and then we'll go seek out the doctor.   *Exeunt omnes.*

[Scene vi]

Enter the Duke of Vanholt, *his* Duchess, [Servants,] Faustus *and* Mephostophilis.

Duke. Thanks, master doctor, for these pleasant sights. Nor know I how sufficiently to recompense your great deserts in erecting that enchanted castle in the air, the sight whereof so delighted me, as nothing in the world could please me more.

Faustus. I do think myself, my good lord, highly recompensed in that it pleaseth your grace to think but well of that which Faustus hath performed. But, gracious lady, it may be that you have taken no pleasure in those sights; therefore, I pray you tell me, what is the thing you most desire to have: be it in the world, it shall be yours. I have

25 cursen] christened (a dialect form)   Scene vi] A's version of this scene does not include the intrusion of the clowns.

heard that great-bellied women do long for things are rare and dainty.

Duchess. True, master doctor, and since I find you so kind, I will make known
unto you what my heart desires to have; and were it now summer, as it is
January, a dead time of the winter, I would request no better meat than
a dish of ripe grapes.   14

Faustus. This is but a small matter; go, Mephostophilis, away.

Exit Mephostophilis.

Madame, I will do more than this for your content.

Enter Mephostophilis *again with the grapes.*

Here, now taste ye these; they should be good, for they come from a far
country, I can tell you.

Duke. This makes me wonder more than all the rest, that at this time of the
year, when every tree is barren of his fruit, from whence you had these ripe
grapes.   21

Faustus. Please it your grace, the year is divided into two circles over
the whole world, so that when it is winter with us, in the contrary circle
it is likewise summer with them, as in India, Saba and such countries
that lie far east, where they have fruit twice a year. From whence, by
means of a swift spirit that I have, I had these grapes brought as you
see.

Duchess. And trust me, they are the sweetest grapes that e'er I tasted.

The Clowns bounce at the gate within.

Duke. What rude disturbers have we at the gate?
Go, pacify their fury. Set it ope,   30
And then demand of them what they would have.

They knock again and call out to talk with Faustus.

Servant. Why, how now, masters? What a coil is there? What is the reason
you disturb the Duke?

Dick. We have no reason for it, therefore a fig for him.

Servant. Why, saucy varlets, dare you be so bold?

Horse-courser. I hope, sir, we have wit enough to be more bold than welcome.

Servant. It appears so. Pray be bold elsewhere, and trouble not the Duke.

Duke. What would they have?

Servant. They all cry out to speak with Doctor Faustus.

Carter. Ay, and we will speak with him.   40

Duke. Will you, sir? Commit the rascals.

Dick. Commit with us! He were as good commit with his father as commit
with us.

Faustus. I do beseech your grace let them come in.

28 s.d. *bounce*] beat. At the end of IV.v. the clowns were to step to 'another room'—but
it appears that Faustus has brought them, unawares, to the Duke's court.   32 coil]
disturbance   34 fig] Dick makes a pun on reason/raisin.   41 Commit] Take to prison
and Commit fornication

They are good subject for a merriment.

Duke. Do as thou wilt, Faustus; I give thee leave.

Faustus. I thank your grace.

Enter the Clown [Robin], Dick, Carter, *and* Horse-courser.

Why, how now, my good friends?

Faith, you are too outrageous, but come near;

I have procur'd your pardons. Welcome all.   49

Robin. Nay, sir, we will be welcome for our money, and we will pay for
what we take. What ho! Give's half-a-dozen of beer here, and be hanged.

Faustus. Nay, hark you, can you tell me where you are?

Carter. Ay, marry can I; we are under heaven.

Servant. Ay, but, sir sauce-box, know you in what place?

Horse-courser. Ay, ay, the house is good enough to drink in. Zounds, fill us
some beer or we'll break all the barrels in the house and dash out all your
brains with your bottles.

Faustus. Be not so furious; come, you shall have beer.

My lord, beseech you give me leave awhile.

I'll gage my credit, 'twill content your grace.   60

Duke. With all my heart, kind doctor, please thyself;

Our servants and our court's at thy command.

Faustus. I humbly thank your grace. Then fetch some beer.

Horse-courser. Ay, marry, there spake a doctor indeed, and, 'faith, I'll drink
a health to thy wooden leg for that word.

Faustus. My wooden leg? What dost thou mean by that?

Carter. Ha, ha, ha! Dost thou hear him, Dick? He has forgot his leg.

Horse-courser. Ay, ay, he does not stand much upon that.

Faustus. No, 'faith, not much upon a wooden leg.

Carter. Good Lord, that flesh and blood should be so frail with your worship!
Do not you remember a horse-courser you sold a horse to?   71

Faustus. Yes, I remember I sold one a horse.

Carter. And do you remember you bid he should not ride into the water?

Faustus. Yes, I do very well remember that.

Carter. And do you remember nothing of your leg?

Faustus. No, in good sooth.

Carter. Then I pray remember your curtsy.

Faustus. I thank you, sir.   [*He bows.*]

Carter. 'Tis not so much worth; I pray you, tell me one thing.

Faustus. What's that?   80

Carter. Be both your legs bedfellows every night together?

Faustus. Wouldst thou make a colossus of me, that thou askest me such
questions?

60 gage] stake

Carter. No, truly, sir; I would make nothing of you, but I would fain know
that.

Enter Hostess *with drink*.

Faustus. Then I assure thee certainly they are.

Carter. I thank you, I am fully satisfied.

Faustus. But wherefore dost thou ask?

Carter. For nothing, sir—but methinks you should have a wooden bedfellow
of one of 'em.   90

Horse-courser. Why, do you hear, sir, did not I pull off one of your legs
when you were asleep?

Faustus. But I have it again now I am awake. Look you here, sir.

All. O horrible! Had the doctor three legs?

Carter. Do you remember, sir, how you cozened me and eat up my load
of—   Faustus *charms him dumb*.

Dick. Do you remember how you made me wear an ape's—

Horse-courser. You whoreson conjuring scab, do you remember how you
cozened me with a ho—   99

Robin. Ha' you forgotten me? You think to carry it away with your hey-
pass and re-pass. Do you remember the dog's fa—   *Exeunt Clowns*.

Hostess. Who pays for the ale? Hear you, master doctor, now you have sent
away my guests, I pray who shall pay me for my a—   *Exit* Hostess.

Duchess. My lord,
     We are much beholding to this learned man.

Duke. So are we, madam, which we will recompense
     With all the love and kindness that we may.
     His artful sport drives all sad thoughts away.   *Exeunt*.

[Act V   Scene i]

Thunder and lightning. Enter Devils *with covered dishes*.
Mephostophilis *leads them into* Faustus' *study. Then enter* Wagner.

Wagner. I think my master means to die shortly.
     He hath made his will, and given me his wealth,
     His house, his goods, and store of golden plate,
     Besides two thousand ducats ready coin'd.
     And yet methinks, if that death were near,
     He would not banquet and carouse and swill
     Amongst the students, as even now he doth,
     Who are at supper with such belly-cheer
     As Wagner ne'er beheld in all his life.

    See where they come; belike the feast is ended.   10

                                                              Exit.

             Enter Faustus, Mephostophilis, *and two or three* Scholars.

1 Scholar. Master Doctor Faustus, since our conference about fair ladies, which was the beautifullest in all the world, we have determined with ourselves that Helen of Greece was the admirablest lady that ever lived. Therefore master doctor, if you will do us so much favour, as to let us see that peerless dame of Greece, whom all the world admires for majesty, we should think ourselves much beholding unto you.

Faustus. Gentlemen,

    For that I know your friendship is unfeign'd,
    And Faustus custom is not to deny
    The just requests of those that wish him well,   20
    You shall behold that peerless dame of Greece,
    No otherways for pomp and majesty,
    Than when Sir Paris cross'd the seas with her,
    And brought the spoils to rich Dardania.
    Be silent then, for danger is in words.

        Music sounds. Mephostophilis *brings in* Helen; *she passeth over the stage.*

2 Scholar. Too simple is my wit to tell her praise,
    Whom all the world admires for majesty.
3 Scholar. No marvel though the angry Greeks pursu'd
    With ten years war the rape of such a queen,
    Whose heavenly beauty passeth all compare.   30
1 Scholar. Since we have seen the pride of nature's works,
    And only paragon of excellence,
    Let us depart; and for this glorious deed
    Happy and blest be Faustus evermore.

               Enter an Old Man.

Faustus. Gentlemen, farewell: the same wish I to you.   *Exeunt* Scholars.
Old Man. O gentle Faustus, leave this damned art,
    This magic, that will charm thy soul to hell,
    And quite bereave thee of salvation.
    Though thou hast now offended like a man,
    Do not persever in it like a devil.   40
    Yet, yet, thou hast an amiable soul,
    If sin by custom grow not into nature:
    Then, Faustus, will repentance come too late,
    Then thou art banish'd from the sight of heaven;
    No mortal can express the pains of hell.

24 Dardania] Troy   36–52] A's version of these lines is printed in the Appendix, p. 400.

It may be this my exhortation
Seems harsh and all unpleasant; let it not,
For, gentle son, I speak it not in wrath,
Or envy of thee, but in tender love,
And pity of thy future misery;   50
And so have hope, that this my kind rebuke,
Checking thy body, may amend thy soul.

Faustus. Where art thou, Faustus? Wretch, what hast thou done?
Damn'd art thou, Faustus, damn'd: despair and die.
Hell claims his right, and with a roaring voice
Says 'Faustus, come, thine hour is almost come'
                                        Mephostophilis *gives him a dagger.*
And Faustus now will come to do thee right.

Old Man. O stay, good Faustus, stay thy desperate steps!
I see an angel hovers o'er thy head,
And with a vial full of precious grace,   60
Offers to pour the same into thy soul.
Then call for mercy and avoid despair.

Faustus. O friend, I feel thy words
To comfort my distressed soul.
Leave me awhile to ponder on my sins.

Old Man. Faustus, I leave thee, but with grief of heart,
Fearing the ruin of thy hapless soul.   *Exit.*

Faustus. Accursed Faustus, where is mercy now?
I do repent, and yet I do despair.
Hell strives with grace for conquest in my breast;   70
What shall I do to shun the snares of death?

Mephostophilis. Thou traitor, Faustus, I arrest thy soul
For disobedience to my sovereign lord.
Revolt, or I'll in piecemeal tear thy flesh.

Faustus. I do repent I e'er offended him.
Sweet Mephostophilis, entreat thy lord
To pardon my unjust presumption,
And with my blood again I will confirm
The former vow I made to Lucifer.

Mephostophilis. Do it then, Faustus, with unfeigned heart,   80
Lest greater dangers do attend thy drift.

Faustus. Torment, sweet friend, that base and crooked age
That durst dissuade me from thy Lucifer,
With greatest torment that our hell affords.

Mephostophilis. His faith is great: I cannot touch his soul,
But what I may afflict his body with
I will attempt, which is but little worth.

Faustus. One thing, good servant, let me crave of thee,
    To glut the longing of my heart's desire,
    That I may have unto my paramour   90
    That heavenly Helen which I saw of late,
    Whose sweet embracings may extinguish clear
    Those thoughts that do dissuade me from my vow,
    And keep mine oath I made to Lucifer.
Mephostophilis. This, or what else my Faustus shall desire,
    Shall be perform'd in twinkling of an eye.

        Enter Helen *again, passing over between two* Cupids.

Faustus. Was this the face that launch'd a thousand ships,
    And burnt the topless towers of Ilium?
    Sweet Helen, make me immortal with a kiss:
    Her lips suck forth my soul, see where it flies.   100
    Come, Helen, come, give me my soul again.
    Here will I dwell, for heaven is in these lips,
    And all is dross that is not Helena.

             Enter Old Man.

    I will be Paris, and for love of thee
    Instead of Troy shall Wittenberg be sack'd,
    And I will combat with weak Menelaus,
    And wear thy colours on my plumed crest.
    Yea, I will wound Achilles in the heel,
    And then return to Helen for a kiss.
    O, thou art fairer than the evening's air,   110
    Clad in the beauty of a thousand stars.
    Brighter art thou than flaming Jupiter,
    When he appear'd to hapless Semele:
    More lovely than the monarch of the sky,
    In wanton Arethusa's azur'd arms,
    And none but thou shalt be my paramour.

             Exeunt [Faustus *and* Helen].

Old Man. Accursed Faustus, miserable man,
    That from thy soul exclud'st the grace of heaven,
    And fliest the throne of his tribunal seat.

           Enter the Devils.

    Satan begins to sift me with his pride,   120
    As in this furnace God shall try my faith.
    My faith, vile hell, shall triumph over thee!

112-13 flaming . . . Semele] The appearance of Jupiter, divinely bright, was Semele's destruction.   115 Arethusa] the nymph changed into a fountain; this may be a reference to the sun reflected in water

Ambitious fiends, see how the heavens smiles
At your repulse, and laughs your state to scorn.
Hence, hell, for hence I fly unto my God.   *Exeunt.*

[Scene ii]

Thunder. Enter Lucifer, Belzebub, *and* Mephostophilis [*above*].

Lucifer. Thus from infernal Dis do we ascend
  To view the subjects of our monarchy,
  Those souls which sin seals the black sons of hell,
  'Mong which as chief, Faustus, we come to thee,
  Bringing with us lasting damnation
  To wait upon thy soul; the time is come
  Which makes it forfeit.
Mephostophilis.   And this gloomy night,
  Here in this room will wretched Faustus be.
Belzebub. And here we'll stay,
  To mark him how he doth demean himself.   10
Mephostophilis. How should he, but in desperate lunacy?
  Fond worldling, now his heart-blood dries with grief,
  His conscience kills it, and his labouring brain
  Begets a world of idle fantasies
  To overreach the devil. But all in vain:
  His store of pleasures must be sauc'd with pain.
  He and his servant Wagner are at hand.
  Both come from drawing Faustus' latest will.
  See where they come.

Enter Faustus *and* Wagner.

Faustus. Say, Wagner, thou hast perus'd my will: 20
  How dost thou like it?
Wagner.   Sir, so wondrous well,
  As in all humble duty I do yield
  My life and lasting service for your love.

Enter the Scholars.

Faustus. Gramercies, Wagner. Welcome, gentlemen.   [*Exit* Wagner.]
1 Scholar. Now, worthy Faustus, methinks your looks are changed.
Faustus. Ah gentlemen!
2 Scholar. What ails Faustus?
Faustus. Ah, my sweet chamber-fellow, had I lived with thee, then had I

Scene ii] Lines 1–23 and 80–125 are present only in B.   1 Dis] the underworld

lived still, but now must die eternally. Look, sirs, comes he not, comes he
not?   30

1 Scholar. O my dear Faustus, what imports this fear?

2 Scholar. Is all our pleasure turned to melancholy?

3 Scholar. He is not well with being over-solitary.

2 Scholar. If it be so, we'll have physicians, and Faustus shall be cured.

3 Scholar. 'Tis but a surfeit, sir, fear nothing.

Faustus. A surfeit of deadly sin, that hath damned both body and soul.

2 Scholar. Yet Faustus, look up to heaven, and remember God's mercy is
infinite.   38

Faustus. But Faustus' offence can ne'er be pardoned; the serpent that temp-
ted Eve may be saved, but not Faustus. O gentlemen, hear with patience
and tremble not at my speeches. Though my heart pants and quivers to
remember that I have been a student here these thirty years—O would I
had never seen Wittenberg, never read book! And what wonders I have
done all Germany can witness, yea all the world—for which Faustus hath
lost both Germany and the world, yea heaven itself, heaven, the seat of
God, the throne of the blessed, the kingdom of joy, and must remain in
hell for ever. Hell, ah hell for ever! Sweet friends, what shall become of
Faustus, being in hell for ever?

2 Scholar. Yet Faustus, call on God.   49

Faustus. On God, whom Faustus hath abjured? On God, whom Faustus
hath blasphemed? Ah my God—I would weep, but the devil draws in
my tears. Gush forth blood instead of tears, yea, life and soul! O, he stays
my tongue. I would lift up my hands, but see, they hold them, they hold
them.

All. Who, Faustus?

Faustus. Why, Lucifer and Mephostophilis: Ah gentlemen, I gave them my
soul for my cunning.

All. God forbid.

Faustus. God forbade it indeed, but Faustus hath done it. For the vain
pleasure of four-and-twenty years hath Faustus lost eternal joy and felicity.
I writ them a bill with mine own blood; the date is expired; this is the
time, and he will fetch me.   62

1 Scholar. Why did not Faustus tell us of this before, that divines might have
prayed for thee?

Faustus. Oft have I thought to have done so, but the devil threatened to tear
me in pieces if I named God, to fetch me body and soul if I once gave
ear to divinity; and now 'tis too late. Gentlemen, away, lest you perish
with me.

2 Scholar. Oh what may we do to save Faustus?

Faustus. Talk not of me, but save yourselves and depart.   70

3 Scholar. God will strengthen me. I will stay with Faustus.

1 Scholar. Tempt not God, sweet friend, but let us into the next room and
   pray for him.

Faustus. Ay, pray for me, pray for me. And what noise soever you hear,
   come not unto me, for nothing can rescue me.

2 Scholar. Pray thou, and we will pray, that God may have mercy upon thee.

Faustus. Gentlemen, farewell. If I live till morning, I'll visit you. If not,
   Faustus is gone to hell.

All. Faustus, farewell.   *Exeunt* Scholars.

Mephostophilis. Ay, Faustus, now thou hast no hope of heaven,   80
      Therefore despair, think only upon hell,
      For that must be thy mansion, there to dwell.

Faustus. Oh, thou bewitching fiend, 'twas thy temptation
      Hath robb'd me of eternal happiness.

Mephostophilis. I do confess it, Faustus, and rejoice.
      'Twas I that, when thou were't i' the way to heaven,
      Damm'd up thy passage; when thou took'st the book
      To view the scriptures, then I turn'd the leaves
      And led thine eye.
      What, weep'st thou? 'Tis too late, despair. Farewell.   90
      Fools that will laugh on earth, must weep in hell.   *Exit.*

         Enter the Good *and the* Bad Angel *at several doors.*

Good Angel. O Faustus, if thou hadst given ear to me
      Innumerable joys had follow'd thee.
      But thou didst love the world.

Bad Angel.   Gave ear to me,
      And now must taste hell's pains perpetually.

Good Angel. O, what will all thy riches, pleasures, pomps,
      Avail thee now?

Bad Angel.   Nothing but vex thee more,
      To want in hell, that had on earth such store.
                              Music while the throne descends.

Good Angel. O, thou hast lost celestial happiness,
      Pleasures unspeakable, bliss without end.   100
      Hadst thou affected sweet divinity,
      Hell, or the devil, had had no power on thee.
      Hadst thou kept on that way, Faustus, behold
      In what resplendent glory thou hadst sat
      In yonder throne, like those bright shining saints,
      And triumph'd over hell. That hast thou lost,
      And now, poor soul, must thy good angel leave thee:
      The jaws of hell are open to receive thee.   *Exit* [*the throne ascends*].
                              Hell is discovered.

Bad Angel. Now, Faustus, let thine eyes with horror stare
        Into that vast perpetual torture-house.   110
        There are the furies tossing damned souls
        On burning forks; there bodies boil in lead;
        There are live quarters broiling on the coals
        That ne'er can die; this ever-burning chair
        Is for o'er-tortured souls to rest them in;
        These, that are fed with sops of flaming fire,
        Were gluttons, and loved only delicates,
        And laugh'd to see the poor starve at their gates.
        But yet all these are nothing: thou shalt see
        Then thousand tortures that more horrid be.   120
Faustus. O, I have seen enough to torture me.
Bad Angel. Nay, thou must feel them, taste the smart of all:
        He that loves pleasure must for pleasure fall.
        And so I leave thee, Faustus, till anon:
        Then wilt thou tumble in confusion.   *Exit [Hell is concealed].*
                                                         The clock strikes eleven.

Faustus. Ah Faustus,
        Now hast thou but one bare hour to live,
        And then thou must be damn'd perpetually.
        Stand still, you ever-moving spheres of heaven,
        That time may cease and midnight never come.   130
        Fair nature's eye, rise, rise again, and make
        Perpetual day; or let this hour be but
        A year, a month, a week, a natural day,
        That Faustus may repent and save his soul.
        O lente, lente, currite noctis equi!
        The stars move still, time runs, the clock will strike.
        The devil will come, and Faustus must be damn'd.
        O I'll leap up to my God! Who pulls me down?
        See, see, where Christ's blood streams in the firmament!
        One drop would save my soul, half a drop. Ah, my Christ!   140
        Rend not my heart for naming of my Christ!
        Yet will I call on him. O spare me, Lucifer!
        Where is it now? 'Tis gone:
        And see where God stretcheth out his arm,
        And bends his ireful brows.
        Mountains and hills, come, come, and fall on me,
        And hide me from the heavy wrath of God.
        No, no!

135 *O lente . . . equi*] 'O run slowly, slowly, horses of the night'; the words are those of Ovid
the lover (*Amores* I.xiii.40) wishing to prolong the night in his mistress's arms.

Then will I headlong run into the earth.
Earth, gape! O no, it will not harbour me.   150
You stars that reign'd at my nativity,
Whose influence hath allotted death and hell,
Now draw up Faustus like a foggy mist
Into the entrails of yon labouring cloud,
That when you vomit forth into the air
My limbs may issue from your smoky mouths,
So that my soul may but ascend to heaven.   *The watch strikes.*
Ah, half the hour is past, 'twill all be past anon.
O God,
If thou wilt not have mercy on my soul,   160
Yet for Christ's sake whose blood hath ransom'd me,
Impose some end to my incessant pain:
Let Faustus live in hell a thousand years,
A hundred thousand, and at last be sav'd.
O, no end is limited to damned souls.
Why wert thou not a creature wanting soul?
Or why is this immortal that thou hast?
Ah, Pythagoras' *metempsychosis*, were that true,
This soul should fly from me, and I be chang'd
Unto some brutish beast.   170
All beasts are happy, for when they die
Their souls are soon dissolv'd in elements,
But mine must live still to be plagu'd in hell.
Curs'd be the parents that engender'd me!
No, Faustus, curse thyself, curse Lucifer,
That hath depriv'd thee of the joys of heaven.
                                     The clock striketh twelve.
It strikes, it strikes! Now body turn to air,
Or Lucifer will bear thee quick to hell.   *Thunder and lightning.*
O soul, be chang'd into little water drops
And fall into the ocean, ne'er be found.   180
            Thunder, and enter the Devils.
My God, my God! Look not so fierce on me.
Adders and serpents, let me breathe awhile.
Ugly hell, gape not! Come not, Lucifer!
I'll burn my books. Ah, Mephostophilis!   *Exeunt with him.*

159–60 O God . . . soul] A (O if my soul must suffer for my sin B)   168 Pythagoras'
metempsychosis] the theory that at the death of the body the human soul adopted some
other form of life

[Scene iii]

Enter the Scholars.

1 Scholar. Come gentlemen, let us go visit Faustus,
  For such a dreadful night was never seen
  Since first the world's creation did begin.
  Such fearful shrieks and cries were never heard;
  Pray heaven the doctor have escap'd the danger.
2 Scholar. Oh help us, heaven! See, here are Faustus' limbs,
  All torn asunder by the hand of death.
3 Scholar. The devils whom Faustus serv'd have torn him thus:
  For 'twixt the hours of twelve and one, methought
  I heard him shriek and call aloud for help,   10
  At which self time the house seem'd all on fire
  With dreadful horror of these damned fiends.
2 Scholar. Well, gentlemen, though Faustus' end be such
  As every Christian heart laments to think on,
  Yet, for he was a scholar once admir'd
  For wondrous knowledge in our German schools,
  We'll give his mangl'd limbs due burial,
  And all the students cloth'd in mourning black
  Shall wait upon his heavy funeral.   *Exeunt.*

[Epilogue]

Chorus.

Cut is the branch that might have grown full straight,
And burned is Apollo's laurel bough,
That sometime grew within this learned man.
Faustus is gone: regard his hellish fall,
Whose fiendful fortune may exhort the wise
Only to wonder at unlawful things,
Whose deepness doth entice such forward wits,
To practise more than heavenly power permits.   *[Exit.]*

Terminat hora diem, terminat Author opus.

FINIS.

Scene iii] This scene is not to be found in A. Ep. 8 *Terminat . . . opus*] 'The hour ends
the day, the author ends his work'

THE
TRAGICALL

History of D. Faustus.

As it hath bene Acted by the Right
Honorable the Earle of Nottingham his seruants.

Written by Ch. Marl.

LONDON

Printed by V. S. for Thomas Bushell. 1604.

Appendix
Major variants in the A Text

[Act II   Scene iii]

Enter Robin *the ostler with a book in his hand.*

Robin. O this is admirable! Here I ha' stol'n one of Doctor Faustus' conjuring books, and, i'faith, I mean to search some circles for my own use. Now will I make all the maidens in our parish dance at my pleasure stark naked before me, and so by that means I shall see more than e'er I felt or saw yet.

Enter Rafe *calling* Robin.

Rafe. Robin, prithee come away! There's a gentleman tarries to have his horse, and he would have his things rubbed and made clean; he keeps such a chafing with my mistress about it, and she has sent me to look thee out. Prithee, come away!   9

Robin. Keep out, keep out, or else you are blown up, you are dismembered, Rafe; keep out, for I am about a roaring piece of work.

Rafe. Come, what dost thou with that same book? Thou canst not read.

Robin. Yes, my master and mistress shall find that I can read, he for his forehead, she for her private study; she's born to bear with me, or else my art fails.

Rafe. Why, Robin, what book is that?

Robin. What book? Why, the most intolerable book for conjuring that e'er was invented by any brimstone devil.

Rafe. Canst thou conjure with it?   19

Robin. I can do all these things easily with it. First, I can make thee drunk with hippocras at any tavern in Europe, for nothing—that's one of my conjuring works.

Rafe. Our master parson says that's nothing.

Robin. True, Rafe, and more, Rafe, if thou hast any mind to Nan Spit, our kitchenmaid, then turn her and wind her to thy own use as often as thou wilt, and at midnight.

Rafe. O brave Robin! Shall I have Nan Spit, and to mine own use? On that condition, I'll feed thy devil with horsebread as long as he lives, of free cost.   29

Robin. No more, sweet Rafe. Let's go and make clean our boots which lie foul upon our hands; and then to our conjuring, in the devil's name.

Exeunt.

[Act III   Scene iii]

Enter Robin *and* Rafe *with a silver goblet.*

Robin. Come, Rafe, did not I tell thee we were for ever made by this Doctor
Faustus' book? *Ecce signum*, here's a simple purchase for horse-keepers;
our horses shall eat no hay as long as this lasts.

Enter the Vintner.

Rafe. But, Robin, here comes the vintner.

Robin. Hush, I'll gull him supernaturally. Drawer, I hope all is paid. God
be with you. Come, Rafe.

Vintner. Soft, sir, a word with you. I must yet have a goblet paid from you
ere you go.

Robin. I, a goblet? Rafe, I a goblet? I scorn you, and you are but a etc. I,
a goblet? Search me.   10

Vintner. I mean so, sir, with your favour.

Robin. How say you now?

Vintner. I must say somewhat to your fellow—you, sir.

Rafe. Me, sir? Me, sir? Search your fill. Now, sir, you may be ashamed to
burden honest men with a matter of truth.

Vintner. Well, t'one of you hath this goblet about you.

Robin. You lie, drawer, 'tis afore me! Sirrah, you, I'll teach ye to impeach
honest men. Stand by, I'll scour you for a goblet. Stand aside, you had
best. I charge you in the name of Belzebub. Look to the goblet, Rafe.

Vintner. What mean you, sirrah?   20

Robin. I'll tell you what I mean. (*He reads.*) *Sanctobolorum Periphrasticon*—
nay, I'll tickle you, vintner—look to the goblet, Rafe. *Polypragmos
Belseborams framanto pacostiphos tostu Mephostophilis, etc.*

Enter Mephostophilis; *sets squibs at their backs; they run about.*

Vintner. O *nomine Domine*, what mean'st thou, Robin? Thou hast no goblet.

Rafe. Peccatum peccatorum, here's thy goblet, good vintner.

Robin. Misericordia pro nobis, what shall I do? Good devil, forgive me now
and I'll never rob thy library more.

Enter to them Mephostophilis.

Mephostophilis. Vanish villains, th'one like an ape, another like a bear, the
third an ass, for doing this enterprise.

   Monarch of hell, under whose black survey   30
   Great potentates do kneel with awful fear,
   Upon whose altars thousand souls do lie,
   How am I vexed with these villains' charms!

2 *Ecce signum*] 'Behold the proof'   9 but a etc] Presumably the actor was to fill in any
comic terms of abuse.   30–43 [This appears to be an alternate ending for the scene.

From Constantinople am I hither come,
Only for pleasure of these damned slaves.

Robin. How, from Constantinople? You have had a great journey. Will you take sixpence in your purse to pay for your supper, and be gone?

Mephostophilis. Well, villains, for your presumption I transform thee into an ape and thee into a dog, and so be gone.   *Exit.*

Robin. How, into an ape? That's brave! I'll have fine sport with the boys. I'll get nuts and apples enow.   41

Rafe. And I must be a dog!

Robin. I'faith thy head will never be out of the potage pot.   *Exeunt.*

[Act IV   Scene i]

Enter Emperor, Faustus, [Mephostophilis] *and a* Knight,
with Attendants

Emperor. Master Doctor Faustus, I have heard strange report of thy knowledge in the black art, how that none in my empire nor in the whole world can compare with thee for the rare effects of magic. They say thou hast a familiar spirit, by whom thou canst accomplish what thou list. This, therefore, is my request: that thou let me see some proof of thy skill, that mine eyes may be witnesses to confirm what mine ears have heard reported. And here I swear to thee, by the honour of mine imperial crown, that whatever thou dost, thou shalt be no ways prejudiced or endamaged.

Knight (aside). I'faith, he looks much like a conjurer.   10

Faustus. My gracious sovereign, though I must confess myself far inferior to the report men have published, and nothing answerable to the honour of your imperial majesty, yet for that love and duty binds me thereunto, I am content to do whatsoever your majesty shall command me.

Emperor. Then, Doctor Faustus, mark what I shall say.
As I was sometime solitary set
Within my closet, sundry thoughts arose
About the honour of mine ancestors:
How they had won by prowess such exploits,
Got such riches, subdu'd so many kingdoms,   20
As we that do succeed, or they that shall
Hereafter possess our throne, shall,
I fear me, never attain to that degree
Of high renown and great authority:
Amongst which kings is Alexander the Great,

12 nothing answerable to] in no way worthy of

> Chief spectacle of the world's pre-eminence,
> The bright shining of whose glorious acts
> Lightens the world with his reflecting beams;
> As when I hear but motion made of him,
> It grieves my soul I never saw the man.   30
> If, therefore, thou, by cunning of thine art,
> Canst raise this man from hollow vaults below,
> Where lies entomb'd this famous conqueror,
> And bring with him his beauteous paramour,
> Both in their right shapes, gesture and attire
> They us'd to wear during their time of life,
> Thou shalt both satisfy my just desire,
> And give me cause to praise thee whilst I live.

Faustus. My gracious lord, I am ready to accomplish your request, so far forth as by art and power of my spirit I am able to perform.   40

Knight (aside). I'faith, that's just nothing at all.

Faustus. But, if it like your Grace, it is not in my ability to present before your eyes the true substantial bodies of those two deceased princes, which long since are consumed to dust.

Knight (aside). Ay, marry, master doctor, now there's a sign of grace in you, when you will confess the truth.

Faustus. But such spirits as can lively resemble Alexander and his paramour shall appear before your grace, in that manner that they best lived in, in their most flourishing estate; which I doubt not shall sufficiently content your imperial majesty.   50

Emperor. Go to, master doctor; let me see them presently.

Knight. Do you hear, master doctor? You bring Alexander and his paramour before the Emperor.

Faustus. How then, sir?

Knight. I'faith, that's as true as Diana turned me to a stag.

Faustus. No sir, but when Actaeon died, he left the horns for you. Mephostophilis, be gone.   *Exit* Mephostophilis.

Knight. Nay, and you go to conjuring, I'll be gone.   *Exit* Knight.

Faustus. I'll meet with you anon for interrupting me so. Here they are, my gracious lord.   60

> *Enter* Mephostophilis *with* Alexander *and his* Paramour.

Emperor. Master doctor, I heard this lady while she lived had a wart or mole in her neck; how shall I know whether it be so or no?

Faustus. Your highness may boldly go and see.

Emperor. Sure, these are no spirits, but the true substantial bodies of those two deceased princes.

> *Exit* Alexander [*and his* Paramour].

Faustus. Will't please your highness now to send for the knight that was so
pleasant with me here of late?

Emperor. One of you call him forth.

Enter the Knight *with a pair of horns on his head.*

Emperor. How now, sir knight? Why, I had thought thou hadst been a
bachelor, but now I see thou hast a wife that not only gives thee horns,
but makes thee wear them. Feel on thy head. 71

Knight. Thou damned wretch and execrable dog,
    Bred in the concave of some monstrous rock,
    How dar'st thou thus abuse a gentleman?
    Villain, I say, undo what thou hast done.

Faustus. O not so fast, sir; there's no haste but good. Are you remembered
how you crossed me in my conference with the Emperor? I think I have
met with you for it.

Emperor. Good master doctor, at my entreaty release him; he hath done
penance sufficient. 80

Faustus. My gracious lord, not so much for the injury he offered me here in
your presence, as to delight you with some mirth, hath Faustus worthily
requited this injurious knight; which being all I desire, I am content to
release him of his horns: and, sir knight, hereafter speak well of scholars.
Mephostophilis, transform him straight. Now my good lord, having done
my duty, I humbly take my leave.

Emperor. Farewell, master doctor; yet, ere you go, expect from me a bounte-
ous reward. *Exit* Emperor [Knight *and* Attendants].

[Act IV Scene iv]

Faustus. Now Mephostophilis, the restless course
    That time doth run with calm and silent foot,
    Short'ning my days and thread of vital life,
    Calls for the payment of my latest years;
    Therefore, sweet Mephostophilis, let us
    Make haste to Wittenberg.

Mephostophilis.   What, will you go
    On horseback or on foot?

Faustus.   Nay, till I am past
    This fair and pleasant green, I'll walk on foot.

Enter a Horse-courser.

[Act IV Scene iv] In the A Text this scene is continuous with the conjuring of Alexander.

Horse-courser. I have been all this day seeking one master Fustian. Mass,
see where he is! God save you, master doctor.   10

Faustus. What, horse-courser! You are well met.

Horse-courser. Do you hear, sir? I have brought you forty dollars for your
horse.

Faustus. I cannot sell him so. If thou likest him for fifty, take him.

Horse-courser. Alas, sir, I have no more. I pray you, speak for me.

Mephostophilis. I pray you, let him have him. He is an honest fellow, and
he has a great charge, neither wife nor child.

Faustus. Well, come, give me your money. My boy will deliver him to you.
But I must tell you one thing before you have him: ride him not into the
water at any hand.   20

Horse-courser. Why, sir, will he not drink of all waters?

Faustus. Oh yes, he will drink of all waters; but ride him not into the water.
Ride him over hedge or ditch or where thou wilt, but not into the water.

Horse-courser. Well, sir. Now am I made man for ever. I'll not leave my
horse for forty. If he had but the quality of hey-ding-ding, hey-ding-ding,
I'd make a brave living on him; he has a buttock as slick as an eel. Well,
God b' wi' ye, sir; your boy will deliver him me. But hark ye sir: if my
horse be sick or ill at ease, if I bring his water to you, you'll tell me what
it is?

Faustus. Away, you villain! What, dost think I am a horse-doctor?   30

Exit Horse-courser.

What art thou, Faustus, but a man condemn'd to die?
Thy fatal time doth draw to final end:
Despair doth drive distrust into my thoughts.
Confound these passions with a quiet sleep.
Tush, Christ did call the thief upon the cross;
Then rest thee, Faustus, quiet in conceit.   *Sleep in his chair*.

Enter Horse-courser *all wet, crying*.

Horse-courser. Alas, alas, Doctor Fustian, quotha! Mass, Doctor Lopus was
never such a doctor. H'as given me a purgation, h'as purged me of forty
dollars: I shall never see them more. But yet like an ass as I was, I would
not be ruled by him, for he bade me I should ride him into no water.
Now I, thinking my horse had had some rare quality that he would not
have had me known of, I, like a venturous youth, rid him into the deep
pond at the town's end. I was no sooner in the middle of the pond but my
horse vanished away, and I sat upon a bottle of hay, never so near drowning
in my life. But I'll seek out my doctor and have my forty dollars again,

25 for forty] for anything   25 the quality of hey-ding-ding] 'I suspect he means a
complete horse and not a gelding' (Greg)   37 Doctor Lopus] Dr. Lopez, personal
physician to Queen Elizabeth, was executed in 1594 on a charge of attempting to poison
her. This is the most obvious instance of an actor's addition to Marlowe's text.

or I'll make it the dearest horse. Oh, yonder is his snipper-snapper. Do you hear? You, hey-pass, where's your master?

Mephostophilis. Why, sir, what would you? You cannot speak with him.

Horse-courser. But I will speak with him.

Mephostophilis. Why, he's fast asleep. Come some other time.　　　50

Horse-courser. I'll speak with him now, or I'll break his glass-windows about his ears.

Mephostophilis. I tell thee he has not slept this eight nights.

Horse-courser. And he have not slept this eight weeks I'll speak with him.

Mephostophilis. See where he is fast asleep.

Horse-courser. Ay, this is he. God save ye, master doctor. Master doctor! Master Doctor Fustian! Forty dollars, forty dollars for a bottle of hay!

Mephostophilis. Why, thou seest he hears thee not.

Horse-courser. So, ho, ho! So, ho, ho!　　　*Holloa in his ear.*

No, will you not wake? I'll make you wake e'er I go.　　　60

Pull him by the leg, and pull it away.

Alas, I am undone! What shall I do?

Faustus. Oh, my leg, my leg! Help, Mephostophilis. Call the officers. My leg, my leg!

Mephostophilis. Come, villain, to the constable.

Horse-courser. Oh lord, sir, let me go and I'll give you forty dollars more.

Mephostophilis. Where be they?

Horse-courser. I have none about me. Come to my hostry and I'll give them you.

Mephostophilis. Be gone, quickly!　　　69

Horse-courser runs away.

Faustus. What, is he gone? Farewell he! Faustus has his leg again, and the horse-courser, I take it, a bottle of hay for his labour. Well, this trick shall cost him forty dollars more.

Enter Wagner.

Faustus. How now, Wagner, what's the news with thee?

Wagner. Sir, the Duke of Vanholt doth earnestly entreat your company.

Faustus. The Duke of Vanholt! An honourable gentleman to whom I must be no niggard of my cunning. Come, Mephostophilis, let's away to him.

Exeunt.

51 glass-windows] spectacles

[Act V   Scene i lines 36–52]

[The Old Man's speech]

Old Man. Ah Doctor Faustus, that I might prevail
　　To guide thy steps unto the way of life,
　　By which sweet path thou may'st attain the goal
　　That shall conduct thee to celestial rest.
　　Break heart, drop blood, and mingle it with tears,
　　Tears falling from repentant heaviness
　　Of thy most vile and loathsome filthiness,
　　The stench whereof corrupts the inward soul
　　With such flagitious crimes of heinous sins
　　As no commiseration may expel,
　　But mercy, Faustus, of thy saviour sweet,
　　Whose blood alone must wash away thy guilt.

The Massacre at Paris

Unhappily, this play survives only in a brutally mangled form. The undated Octavo, perhaps printed in the early years of the seventeenth century, bears all the signs of having been set up from a theatrical prompt-book which, in turn, was a reconstruction of the play from memory by one or more of the actors. There is, however, a single manuscript page, written on both sides, which gives a version of Scene xix and which may well be in Marlowe's own handwriting. The soldier's speech here (ll. 1–12) is tauter than that of the printed text, and the Guise is given an additional nine lines (21–9). The present edition departs from usual practice and incorporates this MS. version of the scene into the text, printing O's version as an Appendix. Short though it is, the scene gives some indication of how much has been lost.

The swift action of the play is easily divided into snapshot episodes or scenes; Act division is impossible.

No single source has been traced for *The Massacre at Paris*, but a major contributary was Varamund's *A true and plaine report of the Furious outrages of Fraunce*. Marlowe dealt freely with his material, omitting, rearranging, and compressing events to suit his dramatic purposes; the technique here seems much like that in *Edward II*, but the tone is closer to that of *The Jew of Malta*.

THE
MASSACRE
AT PARIS;

With the Death of the Duke
of Guise.

As it was plaide by the right honourable the
Lord high *Admirall* his Seruants.

Written by *Christopher Marlow*.

AT LONDON

Printed by *E. A.* for *Edward White*, dwelling neere
the little North doore of S. Paules
Church, at the signe of
the Gun.

[DRAMATIS PERSONAE

Charles IX, King of France
Duke of Anjou, his brother; later *King Henry III*
Duke of Guise
Cardinal of Lorraine } brothers to the Duke of Guise
Duke Dumaine
Son to the Duke of Guise
Gonzago } followers of the Duke of Guise
Retes
Mountsorell
Epernoun
Joyeux } minions of Anjou
Mugeroun
King of Navarre, later *King Henry IV*
Prince of Condé
Lord High Admiral
The Admiral's Man
Pleshé } friends of Navarre
Bartus
Cossin, Captain of the Guard
Loreine
Seroune } victims in the Massacre
Ramus
Taleus, friend to Ramus

Catherine, Queen-Mother of France
Joan, Old Queen of Navarre, mother to Navarre
Margaret, Queen of Navarre, daughter to Catherine, wife to Navarre
Duchess of Guise
Wife to Seroune
Maid to the Duchess of Guise

Apothecary
Two Lords of Poland
Cutpurse
Friar
Surgeon
The English Agent
Three Murderers

Protestants, Schoolmasters,
Soldiers, Attendants, Messengers]

[Scene i]

Enter Charles *the French King,* [Catherine] *the Queen-Mother, the
King of* Navarre, *the Prince of* Condé, *the* Lord High Admiral,
and [Margaret] *the Queen of Navarre, with others.*

Charles. Prince of Navarre, my honourable brother,
    Prince Condé, and my good Lord Admiral,
    I wish this union and religious league,
    Knit in these hands, thus join'd in nuptial rites,
    May not dissolve till death dissolve our lives,
    And that the native sparks of princely love,
    That kindled first this motion in our hearts,
    May still be fuell'd in our progeny.
Navarre. The many favours which your grace hath shown,
    From time to time, but specially in this,   10
    Shall bind me ever to your highness' will,
    In what Queen-Mother or your grace commands.
Catherine. Thanks, son Navarre; you see we love you well,
    That link you in marriage with our daughter here;
    And, as you know, our difference in religion
    Might be a means to cross you in your love.
Charles. Well, Madam, let that rest.
    And now, my lords, the marriage-rites perform'd,
    We think it good to go and consummate
    The rest with hearing of a holy mass.   20
    Sister, I think yourself will bear us company.
Margaret. I will, my good lord.
Charles. The rest that will not go, my lords, may stay.
    Come, mother,
    Let us go to honour this solemnity.
Catherine. Which I'll dissolve with blood and cruelty.

               Exeunt [Charles] *the King,* [Catherine] *Queen-Mother and*
      [Margaret] *the Queen of Navarre* [*with others*]. *And manent* Navarre,
              the Prince of Condé, *and the* Lord High Admiral.

Navarre. Prince Condé and my good Lord Admiral,
    Now Guise may storm—but do us little hurt,
    Having the King, Queen-Mother on our sides
    To stop the malice of his envious heart,   30

3 union . . . league] The marriage between Margaret (Charles's sister) and Navarre was an
attempt to reconcile Catholics and Protestants.   7 motion] suggestion.   23 that will
not go] Being a Protestant, Navarre cannot hear the nuptial mass with his bride.

That seeks to murder all the Protestants.
Have you not heard of late how he decreed,
If that the King had given consent thereto,
That all the Protestants that are in Paris
Should have been murdered the other night?
Admiral. My lord, I marvel that th' aspiring Guise
    Dares once adventure, without the King's consent,
    To meddle or attempt such dangerous things.
Condé. My lord, you need not marvel at the Guise,
    For what he doth the Pope will ratify—   40
    In murder, mischief, or in tyranny.
Navarre. But He that sits and rules above the clouds
    Doth hear and see the prayers of the just,
    And will revenge the blood of innocents
    That Guise hath slain by treason of his heart,
    And brought by murder to their timeless ends.
Admiral. My lord, but did you mark the Cardinal,
    The Guise's brother, and the Duke Dumaine,
    How they did storm at these your nuptial rites,
    Because the house of Bourbon now comes in,
    And joins your linnage to the crown of France?   50
Navarre. And that's the cause that Guise so frowns at us,
    And beats his brains to catch us in his trap,
    Which he hath pitch'd within his deadly toil.
    Come, my lords, let's go to the church, and pray
    That God may still defend the right of France,
    And make his gospel flourish in this land.   *Exeunt.*

[Scene ii]

Enter the Duke of Guise.

Guise. If ever Hymen lour'd at marriage-rites,
    And had his altars deck'd with dusky lights;
    If ever sun stain'd heaven with bloody clouds,
    And made it look with terror on the world;
    If ever day were turn'd to ugly night,
    And night made semblance of the hue of hell;
    This day, this hour, this fatal night,
    Shall fully show the fury of them all.
    Apothecary!

46 timeless] untimely   51 linnage] the form of 'lineage' used until the late 17th century
54 toil] net

Enter the Apothecary.

Apothecary. My lord?   10
Guise. Now shall I prove and guerdon to the full
    The love thou bear'st unto the house of Guise:
    Where are those perfum'd gloves which I sent
    To be poison'd? Hast thou done them? Speak;
    Will every savour breed a pang of death?
Apothecary. See where they be, my good lord,
    And he that smells but to them, dies.
Guise. Then thou remainest resolute?
Apothecary. I am, my lord, in what your grace commands,
    Till death.   20
Guise. Thanks, my good friend, I will requite thy love.
    Go then, present them to the Queen Navarre:
    For she is that huge blemish in our eye,
    That makes these upstart heresies in France.
    Be gone my friend, present them to her straight.   *Exit* Apothecary.
    Soldier!

Enter a Soldier.

Soldier. My lord?
Guise. Now come thou forth, and play thy tragic part.
    Stand in some window opening near the street,
    And when thou see'st the Admiral ride by,   30
    Discharge thy musket and perform his death,
    And then I'll guerdon thee with store of crowns.
Soldier. I will, my lord.   *Exit.*
Guise. Now, Guise, begins those deep-engender'd thoughts
    To burst abroad those never-dying flames
    Which cannot be extinguish'd but by blood.
    Oft have I levell'd, and at last have learn'd
    That peril is the chiefest way to happiness,
    And resolution honour's fairest aim.
    What glory is there in a common good,   40
    That hangs for every peasant to achieve?
    That like I best that flies beyond my reach.
    Set me to scale the high Pyramides,
    And thereon set the diadem of France,
    I'll either rend it with my nails to naught,
    Or mount the top with my aspiring wings,
    Although my downfall be the deepest hell.
    For this I wake, when others think I sleep;

11 guerdon] reward   37 levell'd] guessed at   45 it] i.e. the Pyramides

For this I wait, that scorns attendance else;
For this, my quenchless thirst whereon I build,   50
Hath often pleaded kindred to the King;
For this, this head, this heart, this hand and sword,
Contrives, imagines, and fully executes,
Matters of import aim'd at by many,
Yet understood by none.
For this, hath heaven engender'd me of earth;
For this, this earth sustains my body's weight,
And with this weight I'll counterpoise a crown,
Or with seditions weary all the world.
For this, from Spain the stately Catholics   60
Sends Indian gold to coin me French ecues;
For this, have I a largess from the Pope,
A pension and dispensation too;
And by that privilege to work upon,
My policy hath fram'd religion.
Religion! *O Diabole!*
Fie, I am asham'd, however that I seem,
To think a word of such a simple sound,
Of so great matter should be made the ground.
The gentle King, whose pleasure uncontroll'd   70
Weak'neth his body and will waste his realm,
If I repair not what he ruinates,
Him as a child I daily win with words,
So that for proof he barely bears the name;
I execute, and he sustains the blame.
The Mother Queen works wonders for my sake,
And in my love entombs the hope of France,
Rifling the bowels of her treasury,
To supply my wants and necessity.
Paris hath full five hundred colleges,   80
As monasteries, priories, abbeys, and halls,
Wherein are thirty thousand able men,
Besides a thousand sturdy student Catholics;
And more—of my knowledge, in one cloister keeps
Five hundred fat Franciscan friars and priests.
All this and more, if more may be compris'd,
To bring the will of our desires to end.
Then, Guise,
Since thou hast all the cards within thy hands,
To shuffle or cut, take this as surest thing,   90

86 compris'd] conceived

That, right or wrong, thou deal thyself a king.
Ay, but Navarre, Navarre—'tis but a nook of France,
Sufficient yet for such a petty king,
That with a rabblement of his heretics
Blinds Europe's eyes, and troubleth our estate.
Him will we—(*Pointing to his sword.*)
But first let's follow those in France
That hinder our possession to the crown.
As Caesar to his soldiers, so say I:
Those that hate me will I learn to loathe.   100
Give me a look that when I bend the brows,
Pale death may walk in furrows of my face;
A hand that with a grasp may gripe the world;
An ear to hear what my detractors say;
A royal seat, a sceptre, and a crown,
That those which do behold, they may become
As men that stand and gaze against the sun.
The plot is laid, and things shall come to pass
Where resolution strives for victory.   *Exit.*

[Scene iii]

Enter the King of Navarre *and Queen* [Margaret] *and his Mother
Queen* [Joan], *the Prince of* Condé, *the* Admiral, *and the*
Apothecary *with the gloves; and* [he] *gives them to the
Old Queen.*

Apothecary. Madam,
    I beseech your grace to accept this simple gift.
Joan. Thanks, my good friend. Hold, take thou this reward.
Apothecary. I humbly thank your majesty.   *Exit.*
Joan. Methinks the gloves have a very strong perfume,
    The scent whereof doth make my head to ache.
Navarre. Doth not your grace know the man that gave them you?
Joan. Not well, but do remember such a man.
Admiral. Your grace was ill-advis'd to take them, then,
    Considering of these dangerous times.   10
Joan. Help, son Navarre! I am poison'd!
Margaret. The heavens forbid your highness such mishap.
Navarre. The late suspicion of the Duke of Guise
    Might well have mov'd your highness to beware
    How you did meddle with such dangerous gifts.
Margaret. Too late it is, my lord, if that be true,

        To blame her highness; but I hope it be
        Only some natural passion makes her sick.
Joan. O, no, sweet Margaret, the fatal poison
        Works within my head; my brain-pan breaks,   20
        My heart doth faint; I die!   *She dies.*
Navarre. My mother poison'd here before my face!
        O gracious God, what times are these?
        O grant, sweet God, my days may end with hers,
        That I with her may die and live again.
Margaret. Let not this heavy chance, my dearest lord
        (For whose effects my soul is massacred)
        Infect thy gracious breast with fresh supply
        To aggravate our sudden misery.
Admiral. Come, my lords, let us bear her body hence,   30
        And see it honoured with just solemnity.

                    As they are going, the Soldier *dischargeth his*
                                musket at the Lord Admiral.

Condé. What, are you hurt, my Lord High Admiral?
Admiral. Ay, my good lord, shot through the arm.
Navarre. We are betray'd! Come, my lords, and let us go tell the King of
        this.
Admiral. These are the cursed Guisians, that do seek our death.
        O, fatal was this marriage to us all.

                            They bear away the Queen and go out.

                        [Scene iv]

Enter the King [Charles], [Catherine *the*] Queen-Mother, *Duke of*
        Guise, *Duke* Anjou, *Duke* Dumaine [,Cossin, *and* Attendants].

Catherine. My noble son, and princely Duke of Guise,
        Now have we got the fatal, straggling deer
        Within the compass of a deadly toil,
        And as we late decreed, we may perform.
Charles. Madam, it will be noted through the world
        An action bloody and tyrannical—
        Chiefly since under safety of our word
        They justly challenge their protection.
        Besides, my heart relents that noble men,
        Only corrupted in religion,   10
        Ladies of honour, knights, and gentlemen,
        Should for their conscience taste such ruthless ends.

18 passion] suffering   iv, 2 fatal] doomed

Anjou. Though gentle minds should pity others' pains,
Yet will the wisest note their proper griefs,
And rather seek to scourge their enemies
Than be themselves base subjects to the whip.
Guise. Methinks, my lord, Anjou hath well advis'd
Your highness to consider of the thing,
And rather choose to seek your country's good
Than pity or relieve these upstart heretics.   20
Catherine. I hope these reasons may serve my princely son
To have some care for fear of enemies.
Charles. Well, Madam, I refer it to your majesty,
And to my nephew here, the Duke of Guise:
What you determine, I will ratify.
Catherine. Thanks to my princely son. Then tell me, Guise,
What order will you set down for the massacre?
Guise. Thus, Madam.
They that shall be actors in this massacre
Shall wear white crosses on their burgonets,   30
And tie white linen scarfs about their arms;
He that wants these, and is suspected of heresy,
Shall die, be he king or emperor. Then I'll have
A peal of ordinance shot from the tower, at which
They all shall issue out, and set the streets;
And then, the watchword being given, a bell shall ring,
Which when they hear, they shall begin to kill,
And never cease until that bell shall cease;
Then breathe a while.

Enter the Admiral's Man.

Charles. How now, fellow, what news?   40
Man. And it please your grace, the Lord High Admiral,
Riding the streets, was traitorously shot;
And most humbly entreats your majesty
To visit him, sick in his bed.
Charles. Messenger, tell him I will see him straight.   *Exit Admiral's* Man
What shall we do now with the Admiral?
Catherine. Your majesty were best go visit him,
And make a show as if all were well.
Charles. Content; I will go visit the Admiral.
Guise. And I will go take order for his death.   50

Exit Guise.

24 nephew] kinsman (no precise relationship is implied)   35 set] beset

[Scene v]

Enter the Admiral *in his bed.*

Charles. How fares it with my Lord High Admiral?
　　　Hath he been hurt with villains in the street?
　　　I vow and swear, as I am King of France,
　　　To find and to repay the man with death,
　　　With death delay'd and torments never us'd,
　　　That durst presume, for hope of any gain,
　　　To hurt the noble man their sovereign loves.
Admiral. Ah, my good lord, these are the Guisians,
　　　That seek to massacre our guiltless lives.
Charles. Assure yourself, my good Lord Admiral,　　　　　　　10
　　　I deeply sorrow for your treacherous wrong,
　　　And that I am not more secure myself
　　　Than I am careful you should be preserv'd.
　　　Cossin, take twenty of our strongest guard,
　　　And under your direction see they keep
　　　All treacherous violence from our noble friend,
　　　Repaying all attempts with present death
　　　Upon the cursed breakers of our peace.
　　　And so be patient, good Lord Admiral,
　　　And every hour I will visit you.　　　　　　　　　　　　20
Admiral. I humbly thank your royal majesty.　　　　*Exeunt omnes.*

[Scene vi]

Enter Guise, Anjou, Dumaine, Gonzago, Retes, Mountsorrell,
and Soldiers *to the massacre.*

Guise. Anjou, Dumaine, Gonzago, Retes, swear
　　　By the argent crosses in your burgonets,
　　　To kill all that you suspect of heresy.
Dumaine. I swear by this to be unmerciful.
Anjou. I am disguis'd, and none knows who I am,
　　　And therefore mean to murder all I meet.
Gonzago. And so will I.

Scene v] Clearly a new episode starts here, although the characters (except Guise) remain
on stage. Perhaps the Admiral's bedroom was located on the inner stage and revealed at this
point by drawing the curtain.　　　12 I am . . . myself] I am not more concerned about
my own safety　　　14 Cossin] Subsequent events suggest that O's 'Cosin' should be taken
as referring to Cossin, mentioned in Varamund by name as Captain of the Guard, and not
modernized as 'Cousin'.

Retes. And I.

Guise. Away, then, break into the Admiral's house.

Retes. Ay, let the Admiral be first dispatch'd.   10

Guise. The Admiral,
    Chief standard-bearer to the Lutherans,
    Shall in the entrance of this massacre
    Be murder'd in his bed.
    Gonzago, conduct them thither, and then
    Beset his house, that not a man may live.

Anjou. That charge is mine. Switzers, keep you the streets;
    And at each corner shall the King's guard stand.

Gonzago. Come, sirs, follow me.   *Exit* Gonzago *and others with him.*

Anjou. Cossin, the captain of the Admiral's guard,   20
    Plac'd by my brother, will betray his lord.
    Now, Guise, shall Catholics flourish once again;
    The head being off, the members cannot stand.

Retes. But look, my lord, there's some in the Admiral's house.

    Enter [Gonzago *and others*] *into the* Admiral's *house; and he in his bed.*

Anjou. In lucky time: come, let us keep this lane,
    And slay his servants that shall issue out.

Gonzago. Where is the Admiral?

Admiral. O, let me pray before I die!

Gonzago. Then pray unto our Lady; kiss this cross.   *Stab him.*

Admiral. O God, forgive my sins!   30
                                [Dies.]

Guise. Gonzago, what, is he dead?

Gonzago. Ay, my lord.

Guise. Then throw him down.   *[The body of the* Admiral *is thrown down.]*

Anjou. Now, cousin, view him well;
    It may be it is some other, and he escap'd.

Guise. Cousin, 'tis he, I know him by his look.
    See where my soldier shot him through the arm;
    He miss'd him near, but we have struck him now.
    Ah, base Shatillian and degenerate,
    Chief standard-bearer to the Lutherans,   40
    Thus in despite of thy religion,
    The Duke of Guise stamps on thy lifeless bulk!

Anjou. Away with him! Cut off his head and hands,
    And send them for a present to the Pope;

17 Switzers] Swiss mercenaries   24 Admiral's house] As in Scene v, the 'house' must
be located on a different part of the stage—perhaps the balcony this time, since the body
is thrown down at l. 33.   29 this cross] i.e. the hilt of the sword   39 Shatillian]
Chatillon, the home (or the family) of the Admiral   41 despite] scorn

And, when this just revenge is finished,
Unto Mount Faucon will we drag his corse,
And he that living hated so the Cross,
Shall, being dead, be hang'd thereon in chains.
Guise. Anjou, Gonzago, Retes, if that you three
    Will be as resolute as I and Dumaine,   50
    There shall not a Huguenot breathe in France.
Anjou. I swear by this cross, we'll not be partial,
    But slay as many as we can come near.
Guise. Mountsorrell, go shoot the ordinance off,
    That they which have already set the street
    May know their watchword; then toll the bell,
    And so let's forward to the massacre.
Mountsorrell. I will, my lord.   *Exit.*
Guise. And now, my lords, let us closely to our business.
Anjou. Anjou will follow thee.   60
Dumaine. And so will Dumaine.

                The ordinance being shot off, the bell tolls.
Guise. Come, then, let's away.   *Exeunt.*

[Scene vii]

The Guise *enters again, with all the rest, with their swords drawn,*
                chasing the Protestants.

Guise. Tue, tue, tue!
    Let none escape! Murder the Huguenots!
Anjou. Kill them! Kill them!   *Exeunt.*
      Enter Loreine, *running;* Guise *and the rest pursuing him.*
Guise. Loreine, Loreine! Follow Loreine!—Sirrah,
    Are you a preacher of these heresies?
Loreine. I am a preacher of the word of God;
    And thou a traitor to thy soul and him.
Guise. 'Dearly beloved brother'—thus 'tis written.   *He stabs him.*
Anjou. Stay, my lord, let me begin the psalm.
Guise. Come, drag him away, and throw him in a ditch.   10
                               Exeunt.

46 Mount Faucon] where bodies rotted on their gibbets   vii, 1 *Tue, tue, tue*] 'Kill, kill, kill'

[Scene viii]

Enter Mountsorrell, *and knocks at* Seroune's *door*.

Seroune's Wife (within). Who is that which knocks there?

Mountsorrell. Mountsorrell, from the Duke of Guise.

Seroune's Wife. Husband, come down; there's one would speak with you,
   from the Duke of Guise.

Enter Seroune.

Seroune. To speak with me, from such a man as he?

Mountsorrell. Ay, ay, for this, Seroune; and thou shalt ha't.

Showing his dagger.

Seroune. O, let me pray, before I take my death!

Mountsorrell. Dispatch then, quickly.

Seroune. O Christ my Saviour!

Mountsorrell. Christ, villain!   10
   Why, darest thou to presume to call on Christ,
   Without the intercession of some saint?
   Sanctus Jacobus, he's my saint; pray to him.

Seroune. O, let me pray unto my God!

Mountsorrell. Then take this with you.   *Stab him.*

Exit.

[Scene ix]

Enter Ramus *in his study*.

Ramus. What fearful cries comes from the river Seine,
   That frights poor Ramus sitting at his book?
   I fear the Guisians have pass'd the bridge,
   And mean once more to menace me.

Enter Taleus.

Taleus. Fly, Ramus, fly, if thou wilt save thy life!

Ramus. Tell me, Taleus, wherefore should I fly?

Taleus. The Guisians are
   Hard at thy door, and mean to murder us.
   Hark, hark, they come! I'll leap out at the window.

Ramus. Sweet Taleus, stay.   10

Enter Gonzago *and* Retes.

Gonzago. Who goes there?

Retes. 'Tis Taleus, Ramus's bedfellow.

ix, s.d. Ramus] Professor of Eloquence and Philosophy in the Collège de France
4 s.d. Taleus] Professor of Rhetoric

Gonzago. What art thou?

Taleus. I am as Ramus is, a Christian.

Retes. O let him go; he is a Catholic.   *Exit* Taleus.

Gonzago. Come, Ramus, more gold, or thou shalt have the stab.

Ramus. Alas, I am a scholar, how should I have gold?
>   All that I have is but my stipend from the King,
>   Which is no sooner receiv'd but it is spent.

>   *Enter the* Guise *and* Anjou [*with* Dumaine, Mountsorrell, *and*
>   Soldiers].

Anjou. Who have you there?   20

Retes. 'Tis Ramus, the King's Professor of Logic.

Guise. Stab him.

Ramus. O good my lord,
>   Wherein hath Ramus been so offensious?

Guise. Marry, sir, in having a smack in all,
>   And yet didst never sound anything to the depth.
>   Was it not thou that scoff'dst the *Organon*,
>   And said it was a heap of vanities?
>   He that will be a flat dichotomist,
>   And seen in nothing but epitomes,   30
>   Is in your judgement thought a learned man;
>   And he, forsooth, must go and preach in Germany,
>   Excepting against doctors' axioms,
>   And *ipse dixi* with this quiddity,
>   *Argumentum testimonii est inartificiale.*
>   To contradict which, I say; Ramus shall die.
>   How answer you that? Your *nego argumentum*
>   Cannot serve, sirrah.—Kill him.

Ramus. O, good my lord, let me but speak a word!

Anjou. Well, say on.   40

Ramus. Not for my life do I desire this pause,
>   But in my latter hour to purge myself,
>   In that I know the things that I have wrote,
>   Which, as I hear, one Scheckius takes it ill,
>   Because my places, being but three, contains all his.
>   I knew the *Organon* to be confus'd,

27 *Organon*] the collective title of Aristotle's six treatises on logic   29 flat dichotomist] one who divides all things absolutely into two mutually exclusive classes (dividing *day*, for example, into A.M. and P.M.)   30 seen in] learned in   30 epitomes] summaries   34 *ipse dixi*] 'I have said it'; the argument that a statement is true because the speaker has made it   35 *Argumentum . . . inartificiale*] 'An assertion based on the speaker's authority is incapable of proof'. Guise makes such an assertion—'Ramus shall die'—and proves it by killing him.   37 *nego argumentum*] 'I deny your assertion'   44 Scheckius] Ramus's opponent in a famous dispute   45 places] topics

And I reduc'd it into better form:
And this for Aristotle will I say,
That he that despiseth him can ne'er
Be good in logic or philosophy;   50
And that's because the blockish Sorbonnists
Attribute as much unto their works
As to the service of the eternal God.

Guise. Why suffer you that peasant to declaim?
    Stab him, I say, and send him to his friends in hell.

Anjou. Ne'er was there collier's son so full of pride.   *Kill him.*

Guise. My lord of Anjou, there are a hundred Protestants,
    Which we have chas'd into the river Seine,
    That swim about and so preserve their lives.
    How may we do? I fear me they will live.   60

Dumaine. Go place some men upon the bridge
    With bows and darts to shoot at them they see,
    And sink them in the river as they swim.

Guise. 'Tis well advis'd, Dumaine; go see it straight be done.
                                                       [*Exit* Dumaine.]

    And in the meantime, my lord, could we devise
    To get those pedants from the King Navarre,
    That are tutors to him and the Prince of Condé—

Anjou. For that, let me alone; cousin, stay you here
    And when you see me in, then follow hard.

    He [Anjou] *knocketh, and enter the King of* Navarre *and Prince of*
                    Condé, *with their* Schoolmasters.

    How now, my lords! How fare you?   70

Navarre. My lord, they say
    That all the Protestants are massacred.

Anjou. Ay, so they are; but yet, what remedy?
    I have done what I could to stay this broil.

Navarre. But yet, my lord, the report doth run,
    That you were one that made this massacre.

Anjou. Who I? You are deceiv'd; I rose but now.

        Guise [*with* Gonzago, Retes, Mountsorrell, *and* Soldiers]
                            comes forward.

Guise. Murder the Huguenots, take those pedants hence!

Navarre. Thou traitor, Guise, lay off thy bloody hands!

Condé. Come, let us go tell the King.   80
                                        Exeunt [Condé *and* Navarre].

51 Sorbonnists] scholars of the Sorbonne   56 collier's son] Gossip had it that Ramus's
father, though nobly born, was impoverished and forced to sell charcoal.

Guise. Come sirs,

    I'll whip you to death with my poniard's point.   *He kills them.*

Anjou. Away with them both!

                Exit Anjou [*with* Soldiers *carrying the bodies*].

Guise. And now, sirs, for this night let our fury stay.

    Yet will we not that the massacre shall end.

    Gonzago, post you to Orleans,

    Retes to Dieppe, Mountsorrell unto Rouen,

    And spare not one that you suspect of heresy.

    And now stay that bell, that to the devil's matins rings.

    Now every man put off his burgonet,   90

    And so convey him closely to his bed.   *Exeunt.*

[Scene x]

Enter Anjou, *with two* Lords *of Poland.*

Anjou. My lords of Poland, I must needs confess

    The offer of your Prince Electors far

    Beyond the reach of my deserts;

    For Poland is, as I have been inform'd,

    A martial people, worthy such a king

    As hath sufficient counsel in himself

    To lighten doubts and frustrate subtle foes;

    And such a king whom practice long hath taught

    To please himself with manage of the wars,

    The greatest wars within our Christian bounds,   10

    I mean our wars against the Muscovites,

    And, on the other side, against the Turk,

    Rich princes both, and mighty emperors.

    Yet, by my brother Charles, our King of France,

    And by his grace's council, it is thought

    That if I undertake to wear the crown

    Of Poland, it may prejudice their hope

    Of my inheritance to the crown of France;

    For if th' Almighty take my brother hence,

    By due descent the regal seat is mine.   20

    With Poland, therefore, must I covenant thus:

    That if, by death of Charles, the diadem

    Of France be cast on me, then, with your leaves

    I may retire me to my native home.

    If your commission serve to warrant this,

    I thankfully shall undertake the charge

Of you and yours, and carefully maintain
The wealth and safety of your kingdom's right.
1 Lord. All this and more your highness shall command,
For Poland's crown and kingly diadem.   30
Anjou. Then come, my lords, let's go.   *Exeunt.*

[Scene xi]

Enter two, with the Admiral's *body.*

1. Now, sirrah, what shall we do with the Admiral?
2. Why, let us burn him for an heretic.
1. O no, his body will infect the fire, and the fire the air, and so we shall be poisoned with him.
2. What shall we do, then?
1. Let's throw him into the river.
2. O, 'twill corrupt the water, and the water the fish, and by the fish ourselves, when we eat them.
1. Then throw him into the ditch.
2. No, no, to decide all doubts, be ruled by me: let's hang him here upon this tree.   11
1. Agreed.   *They hang him [and exeunt].*

Enter the Duke of Guise, [Catherine *the*] *Queen-Mother and the*
Cardinal [*of Lorraine*] [*with* Attendants].

Guise. Now Madam, how like you our lusty Admiral?
Catherine. Believe me, Guise, he becomes the place so well
As I could long ere this have wish'd him there.
But come, let's walk aside; the air's not very sweet.
Guise. No, by my faith, Madam.
Sirs, take him away, and throw him in some ditch.
              [Attendants] *carry away the dead body.*
And now, Madam, as I understand,
There are a hundred Huguenots and more,   20
Which in the woods do hold their synagogue,
And daily meet about this time of day;
And thither will I, to put them to the sword.
Catherine. Do so, sweet Guise, let us delay no time;
For if these stragglers gather head again,
And disperse themselves throughout the realm of France,
It will be hard for us to work their deaths.
Be gone, delay no time, sweet Guise.
Guise. Madam,   29
I go as whirlwinds rage before a storm.   *Exit.*

Catherine. My lord of Lorraine, have you mark'd of late
    How Charles our son begins for to lament
    For the late night's work which my lord of Guise
    Did make in Paris amongst the Huguenots?
Cardinal. Madam, I have heard him solemnly vow,
    With the rebellious King of Navarre,
    For to revenge their deaths upon us all.
Catherine. Ay, but my lord, let me alone for that,
    For Catherine must have her will in France.
    As I do live, so surely shall he die,
    And Henry then shall wear the diadem;   40
    And if he grudge or cross his mother's will,
    I'll disinherit him and all the rest;
    For I'll rule France, but they shall wear the crown,
    And if they storm, I then may pull them down.
    Come, my lord, let us go.   *Exeunt.*

[Scene xii]

Enter five or six Protestants, *with books, and kneel together. Enter
also the* Guise [*and others*].

Guise. Down with the Huguenots! Murder them!
1 Protestant. O Monsieur de Guise, hear me but speak!
Guise. No, villain, that tongue of thine,
    That hath blasphem'd the holy Church of Rome,
    Shall drive no plaints into the Guise's ears,
    To make the justice of my heart relent.
    Tue, tue, tue! Let none escape.   *Kill them.*
    So, drag them away.   *Exeunt.*

[Scene xiii]

Enter the King of France [Charles], Navarre *and* Epernoun *staying
him; enter* [Catherine *the*] Queen-Mother, *and the* Cardinal
[*with* Pleshé *and* Attendants].

Charles. O let me stay and rest me here a while!
    A griping pain hath seiz'd upon my heart;
    A sudden pang, the messenger of death.
Catherine. O say not so! Thou kill'st thy mother's heart.
Charles. I must say so; pain forceth me complain.

xiii, s.d. *staying*] supporting   2 griping pain] There was a rumour that Charles, like the
Queen-Mother in Scene iii, had been poisoned.

Navarre. Comfort yourself, my lord, and have no doubt
    But God will sure restore you to your health.
Charles. O no, my loving brother of Navarre!
    I have deserv'd a scourge, I must confess;
    Yet is there patience of another sort   10
    Than to misdo the welfare of their king:
    God grant my nearest friends may prove no worse!
    O, hold me up! my sight begins to fail,
    My sinews shrink, my brains turn upside down;
    My heart doth break, I faint and die.   *He dies.*
Catherine. What, art thou dead? Sweet son, speak to thy mother!
    O no, his soul is fled from out his breast,
    And he nor hears nor sees us what we do!
    My lords, what resteth there now for to be done,
    But that we presently dispatch ambassadors   20
    To Poland, to call Henry back again,
    To wear his brother's crown and dignity?
    Epernoun, go see it presently be done,
    And bid him come without delay to us.
Epernoun. Madam, I will.   *Exit* Epernoun.
Catherine. And now, my lords, after these funerals done,
    We will, with all the speed we can, provide
    For Henry's coronation from Polony.
    Come, let us take his body hence.
                All go out but Navarre *and* Pleshé.
Navarre. And now, Navarre, whilst that these broils do last,   30
    My opportunity may serve me fit
    To steal from France, and hie me to my home,
    For here's no safety in the realm for me;
    And now that Henry is call'd from Poland,
    It is my due, by just succession;
    And therefore, as speedily as I can perform,
    I'll muster up an army secretly,
    For fear that Guise, join'd with the King of Spain,
    Might seem to cross me in mine enterprise.
    But God, that always doth defend the right,   40
    Will show his mercy and preserve us still.
Pleshé. The virtues of our true religion
    Cannot but march with many graces more,
    Whose army shall discomfort all your foes,
    And, at the length, in Pampelonia crown

28 Polony] Poland   39 seem] think fit   45 Pampelonia] Pamplona, capital of Navarre
but held at this time by Spain

(In spite of Spain, and all the popish power,
That holds it from your highness wrongfully)
Your majesty her rightful lord and sovereign.
Navarre. Truth, Pleshé; and God so prosper me in all,
As I intend to labour for the truth,   50
And true profession of his holy word.
Come, Pleshé, let's away whilst time doth serve.   *Exeunt.*

[Scene xiv]

Sound trumpets within, and then all cry 'vive le roi'
two or three times.

Enter Henry [Anjou] *crowned*, [Catherine *the*] *Queen*[-*Mother*],
Cardinal, *Duke of* Guise, Epernoun, *the King's Minions* [Joyeux
and Mugeroun], *with others, and the* Cutpurse.

All. Vive le roi, Vive le roi!   *Sound trumpets.*
Catherine. Welcome from Poland, Henry, once again,
    Welcome to France, thy father's royal seat!
    Here hast thou a country void of fears,
    A warlike people to maintain thy right,
    A watchful senate for ordaining laws,
    A loving mother to preserve thy state,
    And all things that a king may wish besides;
    All this and more hath Henry with his crown.
Cardinal. And long may Henry enjoy all this, and more!   10
All. Vive le roi, Vive le roi!   *Sound trumpets.*
Henry. Thanks to you all. The guider of all crowns
    Grant that our deeds may well deserve your loves!
    And so they shall, if fortune speed my will,
    And yield your thoughts to height of my deserts.
    What says our minions? Think they Henry's heart
    Will not both harbour love and majesty?
    Put off that fear, they are already join'd:
    No person, place, or time, or circumstance,
    Shall slack my love's affection from his bent.   20
    As now you are, so shall you still persist,
    Removeless from the favours of your king.
Mugeroun. We know that noble minds change not their thoughts
    For wearing of a crown, in that your grace
    Hath worn the Poland diadem before
    You were invested in the crown of France.

Henry. I tell thee, Mugeroun, we will be friends,
　And fellows too, whatever storms arise.
Mugeroun. Then may it please your majesty to give me leave
　To punish those that do profane this holy feast.　　　　　30
　　　　　　He cuts off the Cutpurse's *ear, for cutting of the gold*
　　　　　　　　　　　　　　　buttons off his cloak.

Henry. How mean'st thou that?
Cutpurse. O Lord, mine ear!
Mugeroun. Come sir, give me my buttons, and here's your ear.
Guise. Sirrah, take him away.
Henry. Hands off, good fellow; I will be his bail
　For this offence. Go, sirrah, work no more
　Till this our coronation-day be past.
　And now,
　Our solemn rites of coronation done,
　What now remains but for a while to feast,　　　　　　40
　And spend some days in barriers, tourney, tilt,
　And like disports, such as do fit the court?
　Let's go, my lords; our dinner stays for us.
　　　　　Go out all but [Catherine] *the Queen*[*-Mother*] *and the* Cardinal.
Catherine. My Lord Cardinal of Lorraine, tell me,
　How likes your grace my son's pleasantness?
　His mind, you see, runs on his minions,
　And all his heaven is to delight himself;
　And whilst he sleeps securely thus in ease,
　Thy brother Guise and we may now provide
　To plant ourselves with such authority　　　　　　　　50
　As not a man may live without our leaves.
　Then shall the Catholic faith of Rome
　Flourish in France, and none deny the same.
Cardinal. Madam, as in secrecy I was told,
　My brother Guise hath gather'd a power of men,
　Which, as he saith, to kill the Puritans;
　But 'tis the house of Bourbon that he means.
　Now, Madam, must you insinuate with the King,
　And tell him that 'tis for his country's good,
　And common profit of religion.　　　　　　　　　　　60
Catherine. Tush, man, let me alone with him,
　To work the way to bring this thing to pass;
　And if he do deny what I do say,
　I'll dispatch him with his brother presently,
　And then shall Monsieur wear the diadem.

65 Monsieur] Henry III's younger brother, Alençon

Tush, all shall die unless I have my will,
For while she lives Catherine will be Queen.
Come my lord, let us go seek the Guise,
And then determine of this enterprise.   *Exeunt.*

[Scene xv]

Enter the Duchess *of Guise and her* Maid.

Duchess. Go fetch me pen and ink—
Maid. I will, madam.   *Exit* Maid.
Duchess. That I may write unto my dearest lord.
　　Sweet Mugeroun, 'tis he that hath my heart,
　　And Guise usurps it 'cause I am his wife.
　　Fain would I find some means to speak with him,
　　But cannot, and therefore am enforc'd to write,
　　That he may come and meet me in some place,
　　Where we may one enjoy the other's sight.

Enter the Maid, *with* [*pen,*] *ink, and paper.*

　　So, set it down, and leave me to myself.   10

[*Exit* Maid.] *The* Duchess *writes.*

　　O would to God this quill that here doth write
　　Had late been pluck'd from out fair Cupid's wing,
　　That it might print these lines within his heart!

Enter the Guise.

Guise. What, all alone, my love? And writing too?
　　I prithee, say to whom thou writes.
Duchess. To such a one, my lord, as when she reads my lines
　　Will laugh, I fear me, at their good array.
Guise. I pray thee, let me see.
Duchess. O no, my lord; a woman only must
　　Partake the secrets of my heart.   20
Guise. But, madam, I must see.   *He takes it.*
　　Are these your secrets that no man must know?
Duchess. O pardon me, my lord!
Guise. Thou trothless and unjust, what lines are these?
　　Am I grown old, or is thy lust grown young,
　　Or hath my love been so obscur'd in thee,
　　That others needs to comment on my text?
　　Is all my love forgot which held thee dear,
　　Ay, dearer than the apple of mine eye?

17 good array] tidiness (with assumed light-hearted irony)

Is Guise's glory but a cloudy mist,   30
In sight and judgement of thy lustful eye?
Mort Dieu! Were't not the fruit within thy womb,
Of whose increase I set some longing hope,
This wrathful hand should strike thee to the heart.
Hence, strumpet! Hide thy head for shame,
And fly my presence, if thou look to live!   *Exit* [Duchess].
O wicked sex, perjured and unjust!
Now do I see that from the very first
Her eyes and looks sow'd seeds of perjury.
But villain he to whom these lines should go   40
Shall buy her love even with his dearest blood.   *Exit.*

[Scene xvi]

Enter the King of Navarre, Pleshé *and* Bartus, *and their train, with
drums and trumpets.*

Navarre. My lords, sith in a quarrel just and right
    We undertake to manage these our wars
    Against the proud disturbers of the faith,
    I mean the Guise, the Pope, and King of Spain,
    Who set themselves to tread us under foot,
    And rent our true religion from this land;
    But for you know our quarrel is no more
    But to defend their strange inventions,
    Which they will put us to with sword and fire,
    We must with resolute minds resolve to fight,   10
    In honour of our God and country's good.
    Spain is the council-chamber of the Pope,
    Spain is the place where he makes peace and war;
    And Guise for Spain hath now incens'd the King
    To send his power to meet us in the field.
Bartus. Then in this bloody brunt they may behold
    The sole endeavour of your princely care,
    To plant the true succession of the faith
    In spite of Spain and all his heresies.
Navarre. The power of vengeance now encamps itself   20
    Upon the haughty mountains of my breast;
    Plays with her gory colours of revenge,
    Whom I respect as leaves of boasting green
    That change their colour when the winter comes,

6 rent] rend

When I shall vaunt as victor in revenge.

Enter a Messenger.

How now, sirrah, what news?

Messenger. My lord, as by our scouts we understand,
A mighty army comes from France with speed,
Which are already muster'd in the land,
And means to meet your highness in the field.   30

Navarre. In God's name, let them come!
This is the Guise that hath incens'd the King
To levy arms and make these civil broils.
But canst thou tell who is their general?

Messenger. Not yet, my lord, for thereon do they stay;
But, as report doth go, the Duke of Joyeux
Hath made great suit unto the King therefore.

Navarre. It will not countervail his pains, I hope.
I would the Guise in his stead might have come!
But he doth lurk within his drowsy couch,   40
And makes his footstool on security:
So he be safe, he cares not what becomes
Of king or country; no, not for them both.
But come, my lords, let us away with speed,
And place ourselves in order for the fight.   *Exeunt.*

[Scene xvii]

Enter the King of France [Henry III], *Duke of* Guise, Epernoun
and Duke Joyeux.

Henry. My sweet Joyeux, I make thee general
Of all my army, now in readiness
To march against the rebellious King Navarre.
At thy request I am content thou go,
Although my love to thee can hardly suffer,
Regarding still the danger of thy life.

Joyeux. Thanks to your majesty; and so I take my leave.
Farewell to my lord of Guise, and Epernoun.

Guise. Health and hearty farewell to my lord Joyeux.   *Exit* Joyeux.

Henry. So kindly, cousin of Guise, you and your wife   10
Do both salute our lovely minion.   *He makes horns at the* Guise.
Remember you the letter, gentle sir,
Which your wife writ to my dear minion

38 It . . . pains] The king's decision will not go against his pleas

And her chosen friend?
Guise. How now my lord! Faith, this is more than need.
Am I thus to be jested at and scorned?
'Tis more than kingly or imperious;
And sure, if all the proudest kings
In Christendom should bear me such derision,
They should know how I scorn'd them and their mocks.   20
I love your minions? Dote on them yourself;
I know none else but holds them in disgrace;
And here by all the saints in heaven I swear,
That villain for whom I bear this deep disgrace,
Even for your words that have incens'd me so,
Shall buy that strumpet's favour with his blood,
Whether he have dishonour'd me or no.
Par la mort Dieu, il mourra!   *Exit.*
Henry. Believe me, this jest bites sore.
Epernoun. My lord, 'twere good to make them friends,   30
For his oaths are seldom spent in vain.

Enter Mugeroun.

Henry. How now, Mugeroun, met'st thou not the Guise at the door?
Mugeroun. Not I, my lord. What if I had?
Henry. Marry, if thou hadst, thou mightst have had the stab.
For he hath solemnly sworn thy death.
Mugeroun. I may be stabb'd, and live till he be dead.
But wherefore bears he me such deadly hate?
Henry. Because his wife bears thee such kindly love.
Mugeroun. If that be all, the next time that I meet her
I'll make her shake off love with her heels.   40
But which way is he gone? I'll go make a walk
On purpose from the court to meet with him.   *Exit.*
Henry. I like not this. Come Epernoun,
Let's go seek the Duke and make them friends.   *Exeunt.*

[Scene xviii]

Alarms within. The Duke Joyeux *slain. Enter the King of* Navarre
[*with* Bartus] *and his train.*

Navarre. The Duke is slain and all his power dispers'd,
And we are grac'd with wreaths of victory.
Thus God, we see, doth ever guide the right,

17 imperious] becoming for an emperor   28 *Par . . . mourra*] 'By God's death, he shall
die'   xviii, s.d. Joyeux *slain*] This would be indicated by a cry within.

          To make his glory great upon the earth.
Bartus. The terror of this happy victory,
          I hope will make the King surcease his hate,
          And either never manage army more,
          Or else employ them in some better cause.
Navarre. How many noble men have lost their lives
          In prosecution of these cruel arms,   10
          Is ruth and almost death to call to mind.
          But God, we know, will always put them down
          That lift themselves against the perfect truth;
          Which I'll maintain so long as life doth last,
          And with the Queen of England join my force
          To beat the papal monarch from our lands,
          And keep those relics from our countries' coasts.
          Come my lords, now that this storm is overpast,
          Let us away with triumph to our tents.   *Exeunt.*

[Scene xix]

Enter a Soldier *with a musket.*

Soldier. Now sir, to you that dares make a duke a cuckold, and use a counter-
    feit key to his privy chamber—though you take out none but your own
    treasure, yet you put in that displeases him, and fill up his room that he
    should occupy; herein sir, you forestall the market, and set up your stand-
    ing where you should not. But you will say, you leave him room enough
    besides: that's no answer; he's to have the choice of his own freeland—if
    it be not too free, there's the question. Now sir, where he is your landlord,
    you take upon you to be his, and will needs enter by default. What though
    you were once in possession, yet coming upon you once unawares he fray'd
    you out again; therefore your entry is mere intrusion. This is against the
    law, sir. And though I come not to keep possession (as I would I might),
    yet I come to keep you out, sir. You are welcome, sir. Have at you!   12

Enter Minion [Mugeroun]. *He kills him.*

Mugeroun. Traitorous Guise! Ah, thou hast murder'd me.   [*Dies.*]

Enter Guise.

Guise. Hold thee, tall soldier, take thee this and fly.   *Exit* [Soldier].
          Thus fall, imperfect exhalation,
          Which our great sun of France could not effect,
          A fiery meteor in the firmament.
          Lie there, the King's delight and Guise's scorn!

Scene xix] See p. 402, and Appendix, p. 442.   9 fray'd] frightened

Revenge it Henry, if thou list or dar'st;
I did it only in despite of thee.   20
Fondly hast thou incens'd the Guise's soul
That of itself was hot enough to work
Thy just digestion with extremest shame.
The army I have gather'd now shall aim
More at thy end than extirpation.
And when thou think'st I have forgotten this,
And that thou most reposest on my faith,
Then will I wake thee from thy foolish dream
And let thee see thyself my prisoner.   *Exit.*

[Scene xx]

Enter the King [Henry] *and* Epernoun [*and the Duke of* Guise].

Henry. My lord of Guise, we understand
    That you have gathered a power of men:
    What your intent is yet we cannot learn,
    But we presume it is not for our good.
Guise. Why, I am no traitor to the crown of France;
    What I have done, 'tis for the Gospel sake.
Epernoun. Nay, for the Pope's sake, and thine own benefit.
    What peer in France but thou, aspiring Guise,
    Durst be in arms without the King's consent?
    I challenge thee for treason in the cause.   10
Guise. Ah, base Epernoun, were not his highness here,
    Thou shouldst perceive the Duke of Guise is mov'd.
Henry. Be patient, Guise, and threat not Epernoun,
    Lest thou perceive the King of France be mov'd.
Guise. Why, I am a prince of the Valois's line,
    Therefore an enemy to the Bourbonites;
    I am a juror in the Holy League,
    And therefore hated of the Protestants:
    What should I do but stand upon my guard?
    And, being able, I'll keep an host in pay.   20
Epernoun. Thou able to maintain an host in pay
    That liv'st by foreign exhibition!
    The Pope and King of Spain are thy good friends,

23 digestion] consuming   25 extirpation] i.e. of the Protestants   xx, 15 I . . . line] Guise
in fact came from Lorraine, not from the royal family of Valois.   16 Bourbonites] the
family of Navarre   17 Holy League] the Holy Christian League, formed in 1576 to
pursue the interests of Catholicism   22 exhibition] pension

Else all France knows how poor a duke thou art.
Henry. Ay, those are they that feed him with their gold,
To countermand our will and check our friends.
Guise. My lord, to speak more plainly, thus it is:
Being animated by religious zeal,
I mean to muster all the power I can,
To overthrow those sectious Puritans.   30
And know, my lord, the Pope will sell his triple crown,
Ay, and the Catholic Philip, King of Spain,
Ere I shall want, will cause his Indians
To rip the golden bowels of America.
Navarre, that cloaks them underneath his wings,
Shall feel the house of Lorraine is his foe.
Your highness needs not fear mine army's force;
'Tis for your safety, and your enemies' wrack.
Henry. Guise, wear our crown, and be thou King of France,
And as dictator make or war or peace,   40
Whilst I cry *placet* like a senator!
I cannot brook thy haughty insolence.
Dismiss thy camp, or else by our edict
Be thou proclaim'd a traitor throughout France.
Guise. The choice is hard; I must dissemble.
My lord, in token of my true humility,
And simple meaning to your majesty,
I kiss your grace's hand, and take my leave,
Intending to dislodge my camp with speed.
Henry. Then farewell, Guise; the King and thou are friends.   50

Exit Guise.

Epernoun. But trust him not, my lord; for had your highness
Seen with what a pomp he enter'd Paris,
And how the citizens with gifts and shows
Did entertain him,
And promised to be at his command—
Nay, they fear'd not to speak in the streets,
That the Guise durst stand in arms against the King,
For not effecting of his holiness' will.
Henry. Did they of Paris entertain him so?
Then means he present treason to our state.   60
Well, let me alone. Who's within there?

Enter one with a pen and ink.

Make a discharge of all my council straight,

30 sectious] sectarian   41 *placet*] 'it pleases me'

And I'll subscribe my name, and seal it straight.
My head shall be my council, they are false;
And, Epernoun, I will be rul'd by thee.

Epernoun. My lord,
I think for safety of your royal person,
It would be good the Guise were made away,
And so to quite your grace of all suspect.

Henry. First let us set our hand and seal to this,   70
And then I'll tell thee what I mean to do.   *He writes.*
So, convey this to the council presently.   *Exit one.*
And Epernoun, though I seem mild and calm,
Think not but I am tragical within.
I'll secretly convey me unto Blois;
For now that Paris takes the Guise's part,
Here is no staying for the King of France,
Unless he mean to be betray'd and die.
But as I live, so sure the Guise shall die.   *Exeunt.*

[Scene xxi]

Enter the King of Navarre, *reading of a letter, and* Bartus.

Navarre. My lord, I am advertised from France
That the Guise hath taken arms against the King,
And that Paris is revolted from his grace.

Bartus. Then hath your grace fit opportunity
To show your love unto the King of France,
Offering him aid against his enemies,
Which cannot but be thankfully receiv'd.

Navarre. Bartus, it shall be so. Post then to France,
And there salute his highness in our name;
Assure him all the aid we can provide   10
Against the Guisians and their complices.
Bartus, be gone: commend me to his grace,
And tell him, ere it be long, I'll visit him.

Bartus. I will, my lord.   *Exit.*

Navarre. Pleshé!

Enter Pleshé.

Pleshé. My lord!

Nabarre. Pleshé, go muster up our men with speed,
And let them march away to France amain,

69 And . . . suspect] And in such a way as to free you from all suspicion

    For we must aid the King against the Guise.

    Be gone, I say; 'tis time that we were there.   20

Pleshé. I go, my lord.   *[Exit.]*

Navarre. That wicked Guise, I fear me much, will be

    The ruin of that famous realm of France,

    For his aspiring thoughts aim at the crown,

    And takes his vantage on religion,

    To plant the Pope and popelings in the realm,

    And bind it wholly to the See of Rome.

    But, if that God do prosper mine attempts,

    And send us safely to arrive in France,

    We'll beat him back, and drive him to his death   30

    That basely seeks the ruin of his realm.   *Exit.*

[Scene xxii]

Enter the Captain of the Guard [Cossin], *and three* Murderers.

Cossin. Come on, sirs. What, are you resolutely bent,

    Hating the life and honour of the Guise?

    What, will you not fear, when you see him come?

1 Murderer. Fear him, said you? Tush, were he here, we would kill him
    presently.

2 Murderer. O that his heart were leaping in my hand!

3 Murderer. But when will he come, that we may murder him?

Cossin. Well, then I see you are resolute.

1 Murderer. Let us alone, I warrant you.

Cossin. Then, sirs, take your standings within this chamber, for anon the
    Guise will come.   11

All 3 Murderers. You will give us our money?

Cossin. Ay, ay, fear not. Stand close: so, be resolute.

                         [The Murderers *conceal themselves.]*

    Now falls the star whose influence governs France,

    Whose light was deadly to the Protestants:

    Now must he fall, and perish in his height.

            Enter the King [Henry] *and* Epernoun.

Henry. Now, captain of my guard, are these murderers ready?

Cossin. They be, my good lord.

Henry. But are they resolute, and arm'd to kill,

    Hating the life and honour of the Guise?   20

Cossin. I warrant ye, my lord.

Henry. Then come, proud Guise, and here disgorge thy breast,

Surcharg'd with surfeit of ambitious thoughts;
Breathe out that life wherein my death was hid,
And end thy endless treasons with thy death.

Enter the Guise *and knocketh.*

Guise. Holà, varlet, *hé!* Epernoun! Where is the King?
Epernoun. Mounted his royal cabinet.
Guise. I prithee tell him that the Guise is here.
Epernoun. And please your grace, the Duke of Guise doth crave
Access unto your highness.   30
Henry. Let him come in.
Come, Guise, and see thy traitorous guile outreach'd,
And perish in the pit thou mad'st for me.

The Guise *comes to the King.*

Guise. Good morrow to your majesty.
Henry. Good morrow to my loving cousin of Guise.
How fares it this morning with your excellence?
Guise. I heard your majesty was scarcely pleas'd,
That in the court I bare so great a train.
Henry. They were to blame that said I was displeas'd;
And you, good cousin, to imagine it.   40
'Twere hard with me if I should doubt my kin,
Or be suspicious of my dearest friends.
Cousin, assure you I am resolute,
Whatsoever any whisper in mine ears,
Not to suspect disloyalty in thee:
And so, sweet coz, farewell.

Exit King [*with* Epernoun *and Captain*].

Guise. So;
Now sues the King for favour to the Guise,
And all his minions stoop when I command.
Why, this 'tis to have an army in the field.   50
Now by the holy sacrament I swear,
As ancient Romans over their captive lords,
So will I triumph over this wanton king,
And he shall follow my proud chariot's wheels.
Now do I but begin to look about,
And all my former time was spent in vain.
Hold, sword,
For in thee is the Duke of Guise's hope.

Enter [*Third*] *Murderer.*

Villain, why dost thou look so ghastly? Speak.

27 cabinet] study

3 Murderer. O pardon me, my lord of Guise!   60
Guise. Pardon thee! Why, what hast thou done?
3 Murderer. O my lord, I am one of them that is set to murder you!
Guise. To murder me, villain?
3 Murderer. Ay, my lord: the rest have ta'en their standings in the next
    room; therefore, good my lord, go not forth.
Guise. Yet Caesar shall go forth.
       Let mean conceits and baser men fear death:
       Tut, they are peasants. I am Duke of Guise;
       And princes with their looks engender fear.
1 Murderer [*within*]. Stand close, he is coming; I know him by his voice.
Guise. As pale as ashes! Nay, then, 'tis time to look about.   71

          Enter First and Second Murderers.

1 and 2 Murderers. Down with him, down with him!   *They stab him.*
Guise. O, I have my death's wound! Give me leave to speak.
2 Murderer. Then pray to God, and ask forgiveness of the King.
Guise. Trouble me not. I ne'er offended Him,
       Nor will I ask forgiveness of the King.
       O that I have not power to stay my life,
       Nor immortality to be reveng'd!
       To die by peasants, what a grief is this!
       Ah Sixtus, be reveng'd upon the King!   80
       Philip and Parma, I am slain for you!
       Pope, excommunicate, Philip, depose,
       The wicked branch of curs'd Valois his line!
       Vive la messe! Perish Huguenots!
       Thus Caesar did go forth, and thus he died.   *He dies.*

          Enter Captain of the Guard [Cossin].

Cossin. What, have you done?
       Then stay a while, and I'll go call the King.
       But see where he comes.

        [*Enter King* Henry, Epernoun, *and* Attendants.]

       My lord, see where the Guise is slain.
Henry. Ah, this sweet sight is physic to my soul!   90
       Go fetch his son for to behold his death.   [*Exit an* Attendant.]
       Surcharg'd with guilt of thousand massacres,
       Monsieur of Lorraine, sink away to hell!
       And in remembrance of those bloody broils,
       To which thou didst allure me, being alive,
       And here in presence of you all, I swear

67 conceits] imaginations   80 Sixtus] Pope Sixtus V   81 Philip and Parma] Philip II
of Spain and his general, the Duke of Parma

I ne'er was King of France until this hour.
This is the traitor that hath spent my gold
In making foreign wars and civil broils.
Did he not draw a sort of English priests   100
From Douai to the seminary at Rheims,
To hatch forth treason 'gainst their natural queen?
Did he not cause the King of Spain's huge fleet
To threaten England, and to menace me?
Did he not injure Monsieur that's deceas'd?
Hath he not made me in the Pope's defence
To spend the treasure, that should strength my land,
In civil broils between Navarre and me?
Tush, to be short, he meant to make me monk,
Or else to murder me, and so be king.   110
Let Christian princes, that shall hear of this,
(As all the world shall know our Guise is dead),
Rest satisfied with this: that here I swear,
Ne'er was there King of France so yok'd as I.

Epernoun. My lord, here is his son.

Enter the Guise's Son.

Henry. Boy, look where your father lies.
Guise's Son. My father slain! Who hath done this deed?
Henry. Sirrah, 'twas I that slew him; and will slay
    Thee too, and thou prove such a traitor.
Guise's Son. Art thou king, and hast done this bloody deed?   120
    I'll be reveng'd.   *He offereth to throw his dagger.*
Henry. Away to prison with him! I'll clip his wings
    Or e'er he pass my hands. Away with him.   *Exit Boy [guarded].*
    But what availeth that this traitor's dead,
    When Duke Dumaine, his brother, is alive,
    And that young Cardinal that is grown so proud?
    [*To the Captain.*] Go to the governor of Orleans,
    And will him, in my name, to kill the Duke.
    [*To the* Murderers.] Get you away, and strangle the Cardinal.
                    [*Exeunt Captain of the Guard and*
                                    Murderers.]

    These two will make one entire Duke of Guise,   130
    Especially with our old mother's help.
Epernoun. My lord, see where she comes, as if she droop'd
    To hear these news.

103 huge fleet] the Armada   105 Monsieur that's deceased] Alençon, who died in 1584,
was said to have been poisoned.

Henry. And let her droop; my heart is light enough.

                  Enter [Catherine *the*] *Queen-Mother.*

    Mother, how like you this device of mine?
    I slew the Guise, because I would be king.
Catherine. King! Why, so thou wert before:
    Pray God thou be a king now this is done.
Henry. Nay, he was king, and countermanded me:
    But now I will be king, and rule myself,
    And make the Guisians stoop that are alive.   140
Catherine. I cannot speak for grief. When thou wast born,
    I would that I had murder'd thee, my son!
    My son? Thou art a changeling, not my son.
    I curse thee, and exclaim thee miscreant,
    Traitor to God and to the realm of France!
Henry. Cry out, exclaim, howl till thy throat be hoarse!
    The Guise is slain, and I rejoice therefore.
    And now will I to arms; come, Epernoun,
    And let her grieve her heart out, if she will.   150

                    Exit the King and Epernoun.
Catherine. Away! Leave me alone to meditate.   [*Exeunt* Attendants.]
    Sweet Guise, would he had died, so thou wert here!
    To whom shall I bewray my secrets now,
    Or who will help to build religion?
    The Protestants will glory and insult;
    Wicked Navarre will get the crown of France;
    The Popedom cannot stand; all goes to wrack;
    And all for thee, my Guise! What may I do?
    But sorrow seize upon my toiling soul,
    For since the Guise is dead, I will not live.   160

                                        Exit.

                      [Scene xxiii]

      Enter two [Murderers] *dragging in the* Cardinal.

Cardinal. Murder me not, I am a cardinal.
1 Murderer. Wert thou the Pope, thou mightst not 'scape from us.
Cardinal. What, will you file your hands with churchmen's blood?
2 Murderer. Shed your blood! O Lord, no! For we intend to strangle you.
Cardinal. Then there is no remedy, but I must die?
1 Murderer. No remedy; therefore prepare yourself.
Cardinal. Yet lives my brother Duke Dumaine, and many moe,

158 for thee] for lack of thee   xxiii, 3 file] defile

    To revenge our deaths upon that cursed King,
    Upon whose heart may all the Furies gripe,
    And with their paws drench his black soul in hell!   10
1 Murderer. Yours, my Lord Cardinal, you should have said.

                                Now they strangle him.

    So, pluck amain.
    He is hard-hearted, therefore pull with violence.
    Come, take him away.   *Exeunt.*

[Scene xxiv]

Enter Duke Dumaine *reading of a letter, with others.*

Dumaine. My noble brother murder'd by the King!
    O, what may I do for to revenge thy death?
    The King's alone, it cannot satisfy.
    Sweet Duke of Guise, our prop to lean upon,
    Now thou art dead, here is no stay for us.
    I am thy brother, and I'll revenge thy death,
    And root Valois his line from forth of France,
    And beat proud Bourbon to his native home,
    That basely seeks to join with such a king,
    Whose murderous thoughts will be his overthrow.   10
    He will'd the governor of Orleans, in his name,
    That I with speed should have been put to death;
    But that's prevented, for to end his life,
    And all those traitors to the Church of Rome
    That durst attempt to murder noble Guise.

                    Enter the Friar.

Friar. My lord, I come to bring you news that your brother the Cardinal
    of Lorraine, by the King's consent, is lately strangled unto death.
Dumaine. My brother Cardinal slain, and I alive?
    O words of power to kill a thousand men!
    Come, let us away and levy men;   20
    'Tis war that must assuage this tyrant's pride.
Friar. My lord, hear me but speak.
    I am a friar of the order of the Jacobins,
    That for my conscience' sake will kill the King.
Dumaine. But what doth move thee above the rest to do the deed?
Friar. O my lord, I have been a great sinner in my days, and the deed is
    meritorious.

3 The King's . . . satisfy] The King's death is not by itself enough   26 is meritorious] will
be a form of penance

Dumaine. But how wilt thou get opportunity?

Friar. Tush, my lord, let me alone for that.

Dumaine. Friar, come with me;

    We will go talk more of this within.   30

                                                        Exeunt.

[Scene xxv]

Sound drum and trumpets; and enter the King of France, and Navarre,
Epernoun, Bartus, Pleshé, *and* Soldiers [*and* Attendants].

Henry. Brother of Navarre, I sorrow much

    That ever I was prov'd your enemy,

    And that the sweet and princely mind you bear

    Was ever troubled with injurious wars.

    I vow, as I am lawful King of France,

    To recompense your reconciled love

    With all the honours and affections

    That ever I vouchsaf'd my dearest friends.

Navarre. It is enough if that Navarre may be

    Esteemed faithful to the King of France,   10

    Whose service he may still command till death.

Henry. Thanks to my kingly brother of Navarre.

    Then here we'll lie before Lutetia walls,

    Girting this strumpet city with our siege,

    Till, surfeiting with our afflicting arms,

    She cast her hateful stomach to the earth.

                      Enter a Messenger.

Messenger. And it please your majesty, here is a friar of the order of the Jacobins, sent from the President of Paris, that craves access unto your grace.

Henry. Let him come in.   [*Exit* Messenger.]

                      Enter Friar, *with a letter.*

Epernoun. I like not this friar's look: 21

    'Twere not amiss, my lord, if he were search'd.

Henry. Sweet Epernoun, our friars are holy men,

    And will not offer violence to their king

    For all the wealth and treasure of the world.

    Friar, thou dost acknowledge me thy king?

Friar. Ay, my good lord, and will die therein.

Henry. Then come thou near, and tell what news thou bring'st.

Friar. My lord,

13 Lutetia] the old name for Paris

    The President of Paris greets your grace,   30
    And sends his duty by these speedy lines,
    Humbly craving your gracious reply.   [*Gives letter.*]
Henry. I'll read them, friar, and then I'll answer thee.
Friar. Sancte Jacobe, now have mercy upon me!
               He stabs the King with a knife as he readeth the letter, and
                       then the King getteth the knife and kills him.
Epernoun. O my lord, let him live a while!
Henry. No let the villain die, and feel in hell
    Just torments for his treachery.
Navarre. What, is your highness hurt?
Henry. Yes, Navarre; but not to death, I hope.
Navarre. God shield your grace from such a sudden death!   40
    Go call a surgeon hither straight.   [*Exit an* Attendant.]
Henry. What irreligious pagans' parts be these,
    Of such as hold them of the holy church!
    Take hence that damned villain from my sight.
               [Attendants *carry out the* Friar's *body.*]
Epernoun. Ah, had your highness let him live,
    We might have punish'd him to his deserts!
Henry. Sweet Epernoun, all rebels under heaven
    Shall take example by his punishment
    How they bear arms against their sovereign.
    Go call the English agent hither straight: [*Exit an* Attendant.]
    I'll send my sister England news of this,   51
    And give her warning of her treacherous foes.
              [*Enter a* Surgeon.]
Navarre. Pleaseth your grace to let the surgeon search your wound?
Henry. The wound, I warrant ye, is deep, my lord.
    Search surgeon, and resolve me what thou see'st.
               The Surgeon *searcheth* [*the wound*].
           Enter the English Agent.
    Agent for England, send thy mistress word
    What this detested Jacobin hath done.
    Tell her, for all this, that I hope to live;
    Which if I do, the papal monarch goes
    To wrack, and antichristian kingdom falls.   60
    These bloody hands shall tear his triple crown,
    And fire accursed Rome about his ears;
    I'll fire his crazed buildings, and incense
    The papal towers to kiss the holy earth.

42 parts] traits   53 search] examine   63 crazed] rotten

Navarre, give me thy hand: I here do swear
To ruinate that wicked Church of Rome,
That hatcheth up such bloody practices;
And here protest eternal love to thee,
And to the Queen of England specially,
Whom God hath bless'd for hating papistry.   70

Navarre. These words revive my thoughts, and comforts me.
To see your highness in this virtuous mind.

Henry. Tell me, surgeon, shall I live?

Surgeon. Alas, my lord, the wound is dangerous,
For you are stricken with a poison'd knife!

Henry. A poison'd knife! What, shall the French king die
Wounded and poison'd both at once?

Epernoun. O, that that damned villain were alive again,
That we might torture him with some new-found death!

Bartus. He died a death too good: 80
The devil of hell torture his wicked soul!

Henry. Ah curse him not, sith he is dead!
O, the fatal poison works within my breast!
Tell me, surgeon, and flatter not—may I live?

Surgeon. Alas, my lord, your highness cannot live!

Navarre. Surgeon, why say'st thou so? The King may live.

Henry. O, no, Navarre! Thou must be King of France!

Navarre. Long may you live, and still be King of France.

Epernoun. Or else die Epernoun!

Henry. Sweet Epernoun, thy king must die. My lords,   90
Fight in the quarrel of this valiant prince,
For he is your lawful king, and my next heir;
Valois's line ends in my tragedy.
Now let the house of Bourbon wear the crown;
And may it never end in blood, as mine hath done!
Weep not, sweet Navarre, but revenge my death.
Ah, Epernoun, is this thy love to me?
Henry thy king wipes off these childish tears,
And bids thee whet thy sword on Sixtus' bones,
That it may keenly slice the Catholics.   100
He loves me not that sheds most tears,
But he that makes most lavish of his blood.
Fire Paris, where these treacherous rebels lurk.
I die, Navarre; come bear me to my sepulchre.
Salute the Queen of England in my name,
And tell her, Henry dies her faithful friend.   *He dies.*

Navarre. Come, lords, take up the body of the King,

That we may see it honourably interr'd:
And then I vow for to revenge his death
As Rome, and all those popish prelates there,   110
Shall curse the time that e'er Navarre was king,
And rul'd in France by Henry's fatal death.

They march out with the body of the King lying on four men's
shoulders, with a dead march, drawing weapons on the ground.

FINIS.

Appendix

The Octavo version of Scene xix

Enter a Soldier.

Soldier. Sir, to you sir, that dares make the Duke a cuckold, and use a counterfeit key to his privy-chamber door; and although you take out nothing but your own, yet you put in that which displeaseth him and so forestall his market, and set up your standing where you should not; and whereas he is your landlord, you will take upon you to be his, and till the ground that he himself should occupy, which is his own free land— if it be not too free, there's the question. And though I come not to take possession (as I would I might), yet I mean to keep you out—which I will, if this gear hold. What, are ye come so soon? Have at ye, sir.

Enter Mugeroun. *He shoots at him and kills him.*

Enter the Guise.

Guise. Hold thee, tall soldier; take thee this and fly.   *Exit* Soldier.
Lie there, the King's delight and Guise's scorn.
Revenge it, Henry, as thou list or dare;
I did it only in despite of thee.   *Take him away.*